Techniques of Problem Solving

Steven G. Krantz

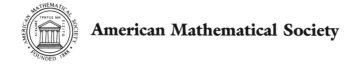

American Mathematical Society

1991 *Mathematics Subject Classification.* Primary 00A05, 00A06, 00A08, 00A35, 00A71; Secondary 00A69, 00A73.

Library of Congress Cataloging-in-Publication Data
Krantz, Steven G. (Steven George), 1951–
    Techniques of problem solving / Steven G. Krantz.
        p. cm.
    Includes bibliographical references (p.   –   ) and index.
    ISBN 0-8218-0619-X (acid-free paper)
    1. Problem solving.   I. Title.
QA63.K73   1996
510′.76—dc20

96-23878
CIP

This one is for little Josephine, who is no problem at all.

TABLE OF CONTENTS

CHAPTER 4: Problems of Logic

CHAPTER 5: Recreational Math

CHAPTER 6: Algebra and Analysis

CHAPTER 7: A Miscellany

CHAPTER 8: Real Life

PREFACE

OVERVIEW

A large component of everyday activity involves problem solving: What is the best method to finance that new car? How should one choose a spouse? What is the optimal method to schedule one's classes? How can one best budget money?

Analytical thinking is not a panacea. It is not the right approach for all contingencies and all problems. However it *is* a powerful method for dealing with many situations. Most high school and college courses that we take teach the *consequences* of analytical thinking; they do not, in fact, teach the *methodology* of analytical thinking.

There already exist a great many books on problem solving, some dating back to the last century. However the subject of problem solving, as viewed by this author, is more than just a disconnected list of brain teasers and recreations. It is a way of life. Scientists of every stripe— chemists, physicists, psychologists, social engineers, and many others— ply their trade by considering a set of data, deciding what techniques are relevant to these data, and then *solving a problem*. It is this view of problem solving that will be promulgated in the present book.

The purpose of this book is to teach the basic principles of problem solving. This will include both mathematical problems and non-mathematical problems. A major component of the book consists of learning to translate verbal discussions into analytical data. Another major component consists of learning problem solving methods for attacking collections of analytical questions or data. A third component involves building a personal arsenal of solved problems and internalized problem solving techniques; thus the student who has mastered the material in this book is an "armed problem solver," ready to do battle with a variety of puzzles in different parts of life.

TECHNIQUE AND TEXTURE

Among the problem solving techniques considered in this book are these: induction, contradiction, exhaustion, dissection, analogy, generalization, specialization, reformulation, decomposition, recombination, auxiliary analysis, counting, graphical methods, and diagraming. Of course this list is by no means exhaustive; also the solving of a typical problem might involve ideas from several of these methods.

While many of the illustrative problems provided in this book are mathematical in nature, it is also the case that many of them are not. We wish to provide the reader with a variety of analytical techniques that may be used in many situations. Since the author of this book is a mathematician, and since mathematics lends itself naturally to problem formulation and solution, it is natural that mathematics will come up frequently. But it is not the only point of this particular book.

Continuing the theme of the last paragraph, we will use this book as an opportunity to teach the reader some important mathematical or analytical ideas in context. These will include counting arguments, induction, the concept of "general position," proof by contradiction, graphing and visual analysis techniques, the pigeonhole principle, recursion relations, generating functions, ideas from probability and statistics, and so forth. These ideas should serve the student well in other courses and other contexts.

We also use this book, in a gentle fashion, as a device for introducing the student to the world of modern technology. By this we mean that, on occasion, in the course of solving a problem, we may say "at this stage we could use calculus, but instead get out your graphing calculator and do the following ...." Alternatively we might say "We have reduced the problem to solving a transcendental equation; this is virtually impossible to do by hand. Instead boot up your computer algebra software ...." These technological junctures occur only very occasionally in the book. They are a device for teaching the student to use the computer as a tool, just like a book or a slide rule or a calculator.

COMPARISON WITH EXISTING BOOKS

There already exist a number of books that philosophize at length about the *nature* of problem solving. Most notable among these are books by Lakatos, Polya, Shoenfeld, and others (see the Bibliography). We encourage the reader to become familiar with those works. The present work takes a more direct and practical approach to the subject matter. We feel that you learn to solve problems by *solving* problems (note that not all experts on problem solving agree with this point of view). This is very much in the vein that you learn to play the piano by *playing* the piano. Most piano studies contain a graded list of pieces to work on. They do not engage in extensive palaver about what it feels like to touch the keys. Just so, we will make didactic points in the context of solving problems, but will not provide discursive diatribes about the ontology of problem solving.

One of the features that sets this problem solving book apart from many others is that it incorporates exercises. These have two forms. After many a solved problem in the text there appears a "Challenge" problem for the reader to solve. This challenge usually involves techniques related to the problem that the reader has just seen. It might ask for an extension, or a variant, or for the solution of another problem with a similar flavor. The student should endeavor to do the challenge problems immediately upon encountering them—at least to give them a first try. Some challenge problems are tricky (intentionally so) and will require several attacks. Also, at the end of each chapter, there are many additional problems for the reader to tackle. All of these are related, at least to some extent, to material in the text. There are more than 350 of these in all. Solutions to most of the end-of-chapter exercises are available in the Solutions Manual.

PREREQUISITES

This book has minimal prerequisites. Certainly no calculus is required. (However an occasional optional problem will use calculus; these problems are *labeled* as such. The reader who is willing to suspend his/her disbelief will have no trouble with the handful of passages

Chapter 1

Basic Concepts

1.1 Introductory Remarks

Writing a book on problem solving is a bit foolish; it is also foolish to write a book on swimming or piano playing. For you cannot learn any of these skills by reading about them. You must *do* them. In fact you must *immerse yourself* in them. Just as developing your torso would entail pumping iron in a rigorous and planned fashion, so developing your problem solving skills will involve a regimen of practice and hard work.

Nevertheless, learning to solve problems can be fun and rewarding. It is a process of developing and extending your mental powers, and it will equip you with a body of techniques that will be useful in other parts of your studies and of your life.

This book is organized around certain types of problem solving techniques, and around certain mental processes that are involved in problem solving. Each concept is illustrated with a number of sample problems; these examples will help to train you in the techniques of problem solving. You should work through each example with care, for the specific examples are much more important than the philosophical remarks that precede them.

Some examples may take a fair amount of time for you to master; but it is important to do so. If you are using this book in a class, then be sure to talk to your instructor, and to your classmates, about the problems you are studying and the techniques you are learning. *Learn to ask questions.* Part of the learning process is to learn to formulate precise statements and precise questions. Another related part is to learn to *communicate* processes of reasoning and analysis. This is strenuous mental exercise. Do it alone, but also do it in a group. Throw the ball back and forth and run around the track (mentally).

Another critical part of this book, this course, and your education in general, is to *learn to read.* By this we do not mean the attainment of literacy. If you are reading these words then you have that problem solved. Instead we mean to read a problem, or an analytical passage, or a solution, and to get to the bottom of it, to completely understand it, and finally to internalize it.

Those ideas and techniques that you internalize are those that finally belong to you, that you can use in practice in your life, that are at your finger tips and have become your own personal tools. This book is designed to familiarize you with the process of internalization and to make it part of your working mental regimen.

Like most books, this one is written in linear order. That is to say, the ideas on any page may utilize, or at least make reference to, the ideas on the preceding pages. But it is no crime to flip ahead in the book, to look at problems that are coming up, or to dip into the book as your interest dictates.

In the next section we will begin to solve problems. At first, our main interest will be to learn to defeat "mental inertia." Even for an experienced and talented problem solver, a tempting way to react to a tough, meaty problem is to look off into space, scratch the old head, and say "Oh, gosh, I don't know. What's for lunch?" Your goal should instead be to train to become a problem fighting machine. You see a new problem and you say "I've seen something like that before. Let's try this ... Let's draw a figure ... Let's reformulate it as follows ... Let's try an example ..." Study this book and you will learn to think in this fashion, not just in math class but in any situation.

1.2   A First Problem

We begin with the analysis of a simple problem. It stands alone, in that one cannot imagine relating it to another problem, or another technique. Its solution requires no specialized knowledge or experience.

PROBLEM 1.2.1 *Determine how many zeros end the number 100!*

Solution: Recall that

$$100! = 100 \cdot 99 \cdot 98 \cdots 3 \cdot 2 \cdot 1.$$

Adding a zero to the end of a product occurs precisely when we multiply by 10. Thus multiplication by any number ending in 1,3,7,9 cannot possibly add a zero to the product (since none of these numbers divides 10). In fact the prime factorization of 10 is $10 = 5 \cdot 2$. We endeavor to solve this problem by counting the factors of 5 in 100!

In the numbers 1–10, only the numbers 5 and 10 have factors of 5. The number 5 may be paired with 2 to yield 10 and the number 10 does not need to be paired. The two resulting factors of 10 contribute two zeros to the full product that forms the factorial.

In the numbers 11–20, only the numbers 15 and 20 have factors of 5. Reasoning as in the last paragraph, we count two additional zeros.

The numbers between 21 and 30 are a bit different. As before, 25 and 30 are the only numbers having a factor of 5, but 25 has *two* factors of 5. Thus

$$22 \times 24 \times 25 = 11 \times 12 \times (2 \times 5) \times (2 \times 5)$$

and this will contribute $10 \times 10 = 100$, or two zeros. Thus the range 21–30 contributes a total of three zeros.

The ranges 31–40 is a simple one, like the first two ranges we considered. It contributes two zeros.

The range 41–50 is special because 45 contributes one factor of 5 but 50 contributes two factors. Thus this range of numbers contributes three zeros (as did the range 21–30).

The range 51–60 and the range 61–70 are like the first two. There are no multiple factors of 5, and each range contributes two zeros.

The range 71–80 is special because 75 contributes two factors of 5 and 80 contributes one factor of 5. The total contribution is three zeros.

The range 81–90 contributes two factors of 5 in the usual fashion, and thus adds two zeros.

The range 91–100 contains 95 and 100. The first of these contributes one factor of five and the second contributes two. Thus three zeros are added.

Taking all of our analyses into account, we have six ranges of numbers that each contribute two zeros and four ranges that each contribute three zeros. This gives a total of 24 zeros that will appear at the end of 100!   □

This example already exhibits several important features of successful problem solving:

- We identified the essential feature on which the problem hinges (that a trailing zero comes from multiplication by 10).

- We began by analyzing a special case (i.e., the product $10 \cdot 9 \cdot 8 \cdots 3 \cdot 2 \cdot 1$).

- We determined how to pass from the special case to the full problem.

It is not always true that examining a special case, or a smaller case, will lead to a solution of the problem at hand. But it will get you started. This will be one of our many devices for attacking a problem.

Looking back at our solution of the first problem, we see that we could have been more clever. The numbers from 1 to 100 contain $100 \div 5 = 20$ multiples of 5. Four of these multiples of 5 are in fact multiples of 25, hence contribute two 5's. That gives a total of 24 factors of 5 in 100! Pairing each of these with an even number gives a factor of ten, and hence a zero. We conclude that there are 24 zeros at the end of 100!

Here is another example of specialization:

PROBLEM 1.2.2 *A math class has 12 students. At the beginning of each class hour, each student shakes hands with each of the other students. How many handshakes take place?*

Solution: We begin with a special case and build up to the case of 12 students.

Suppose that there are just 2 students. Then only one handshake is possible.

Now suppose that a new student walks in the door. He/she must shake hands with each of the students that is already in the room. So that makes two more handshakes. The total number of handshakes is $1 + 2 = 3$.

If a fourth student walks in the door, then he/she must shake hands with each of the students already in the room. The total number of handshakes is then $1 + 2 + 3 = 6$.

The pattern is now clear: the addition of a fifth student would result in $1 + 2 + 3 + 4$ handshakes. When we get up to twelve students, we will have required

$$1 + 2 + 3 + \cdots + 9 + 10 + 11 = 66$$

handshakes.

That solves the problem.   □

Many times the solution or analysis of one problem will suggest others. Here is another problem that Problem 1.2.2 suggests:

PROBLEM 1.2.3 *Assume that k is a positive integer. What is the sum of the integers*

$$S = 1 + 2 + 3 + \cdots + (k - 1) + k \ ?$$

Before we present a solution, we conduct some preliminary discussion of this problem.

We think of S as function: set

$$S(k) = 1 + 2 + 3 + \cdots + (k - 1) + k.$$

What sort of function might this be? If a function $f(k)$ increases by a fixed amount, say 3, each time that k is increased by 1, then f must be a linear function. Indeed, f must have the form $f(k) = 3k + b$.

Likewise, if the function g increases by a linear function of k each time that k is increased by 1, then we might suspect that g is quadratic. (For those who know calculus, think of the concept of derivative: the derivative of a quadratic function is linear.) For instance, if $g(k) = k^2$ then $g(k+1) - g(k) = 2k + 1$, and that difference is linear.

These considerations motivate our attack on the present problem:

Solution: A useful method for analyzing a sum is to rewrite each term so that some cancellations are introduced. Notice that

$$
\begin{aligned}
2^2 - 1^2 &= 3 = 2 \cdot 1 + 1 \\
3^2 - 2^2 &= 5 = 2 \cdot 2 + 1 \\
4^2 - 3^2 &= 7 = 2 \cdot 3 + 1
\end{aligned}
$$

$$\cdots$$

$$
\begin{aligned}
k^2 - (k-1)^2 &= 2 \cdot (k-1) + 1 \\
(k+1)^2 - k^2 &= 2 \cdot k + 1
\end{aligned}
$$

Now we add the columns:

$$
\begin{aligned}
&[2^2 - 1^2] + [3^2 - 2^2] + [4^2 - 3^2] + \cdots + [(k+1)^2 - k^2] \\
&= [2 \cdot 1 + 1] + [2 \cdot 2 + 1] + [2 \cdot 3 + 1] + \cdots + [2 \cdot k + 1].
\end{aligned}
$$

The left hand side "telescopes" (that is, all but the first and last terms cancel) and the right side may be factored. The result is

$$(k+1)^2 - 1^2 = 2[1 + 2 + 3 + \cdots + k] + \underbrace{[1 + 1 + 1 + \cdots + 1]}_{k \text{ times}}$$

or

$$k^2 + 2k = 2 \cdot S + k.$$

Recall here that S is that sum that we wish to calculate.

Solving for S, we find that

$$S = \frac{k^2 + k}{2}. \qquad \square$$

The formula derived in the last problem is often attributed to Carl Friedrich Gauss (1777–1855), although there is evidence that it was known much earlier.

CHALLENGE PROBLEM 1.2.4 *Imitate the method used in the last problem to find a formula for the sum*

$$1^2 + 2^2 + 3^2 + \cdots + k^2$$

when k is a positive integer.

The solution of our last problem sheds some light on the preceding "handshake" problem. For if a class contains k students and the class period begins with everyone shaking everyone else's hand, then our solution of Problem 1.2.2 shows that the total number of handshakes that occurs is $1 + 2 + 3 + \cdots + (k - 1)$. Now Problem 1.2.3 teaches us that this last sum equals $[(k - 1)^2 + (k - 1)]/2 = [k^2 - k]/2$.

Here is another question that one might ask about the handshake problem:

PROBLEM 1.2.5 *Refer again to the situation in Problem 1.2.2, but suppose now that there are k students in the class. If k is even then will the number of handshakes that takes place be even or odd? If k is odd then will the number of handshakes that takes place be even or odd?*

Solution: If there are 2 students (an even value for k) then the total number of handshakes is 1, an odd number. If we add one student, that adds two handshakes: the number of students is 3 (odd) and the number of handshakes is 3 (odd). If we add yet another student then there are 3 additional handshakes. Thus the total number of handshakes is 6 (even) while the total number of students is 4 (even).

In fact if we draw up a chart then a pattern begins to emerge:

# students	# handshakes	parity of handshakes
0	0	even
1	0	even
2	1	odd
3	3	odd
4	6	even
5	10	even
6	15	odd
7	21	odd
8	28	even
9	36	even
10	45	odd
11	55	odd
12	66	even
13	78	even

As is sometimes done in mathematics, we include the somewhat silly cases of 0 students and 1 student for completeness, and to simplify the discussion that follows.

We see that the first two numbers for handshakes are even, then there are two odd, then there are two even, and so forth.

The pattern repeats itself in increments of *four*. Now notice that the number in the "# handshakes" column in the row for $(k + 1)$ students is obtained by adding the two numbers in the row for k students. We know that the number of handshakes for k students is $(k^2 - k)/2$. Verify this formula for yourself by plugging the numbers $1, 2, 3, 4, 5, 6, 7, 8$ into the expression. What you are in fact checking is that (for ℓ a nonnegative integer)

(i) In rows $4\ell, 4\ell + 1$, the number of handshakes is even;

(ii) In rows $4\ell + 2, 4\ell + 3$, the number of handshakes is odd.

That completes our analysis of the parity of the number of handshakes of k students. $\square$

Notice that our analysis of Problem 1.2.5 did not conform to the theme of this section: it was not solved by first considering a simple

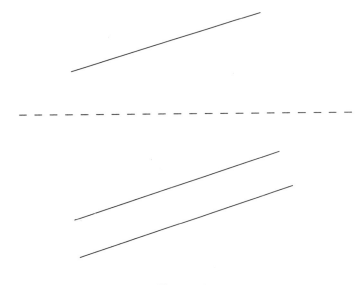

Figure 1

case. Instead, we explored Problem 1.2.5 as something of a side-track—because it was suggested by the result of Problem 1.2.2.

We now turn to a final example of the technique of specialization:

PROBLEM 1.2.6 *What is the greatest number of regions into which three straight lines (of infinite extent) can divide the plane?*

Solution: We begin with the simpler question: "What is the greatest number of regions into which one line can divide the plane?" Of course there is nothing to discuss, for one line will always separate the plane into two regions.

Next we look at two lines. Refer to Figure 1 (top). If the two lines coincide, then the plane is still divided into just two regions. If, instead, the two lines are distinct but parallel (Figure 1, bottom) then the plane is separated into three separate regions.

We think of the two cases just described as degenerate or atypical for the following reason: if you drop two straws onto a floor, then the probability that they will land on top of each other, or land in a configuration so that they are parallel, is zero. Rather, with probability one, the straws will land so that they are skew (or non-parallel). We refer to this last situation as "general position" for the two straws.

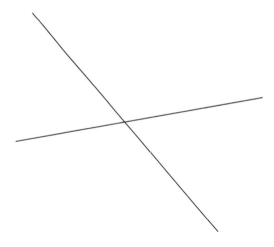

Figure 2

Now suppose that our two lines are in general position. This situation is illustrated in Figure 2. Then the plane is separated into four regions.

Finally we pass to three lines. If all three lines coincide, then we are in the situation for one line. If two of the lines coincide, then we are in the situation for two lines. So suppose that the three lines are distinct.

If the three lines are parallel, then the plane is separated into four regions (Figure 3). If two are parallel, and the third is skew to them, then the plane is separated into six regions (Figure 4). Now suppose that no two of the three lines are parallel.

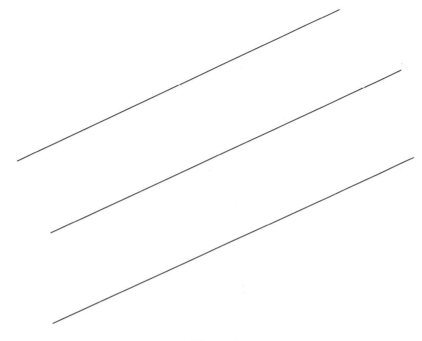

Figure 3

If the three lines pass through a single point, then (Figure 5) the plane is separated into six regions. If the three lines do not pass through a single point, and no two of them are parallel (this is the general position situation, that is, the one that occurs with probability one—see Figure 6) then the plane is separated into seven regions. Thus seven is the maximal number of regions into which three lines can divide the plane. $\square$

In the last problem we certainly used the method of specializing to simple cases to begin to get a grasp of how the problem works. But we also used the *method of exhaustion*. We used the notions of parallelism and intersection—what we ended up calling "general position"—to lay out all the possible configurations for the lines. You may find it an instructive exercise to generalize the last problem to four lines or five lines.

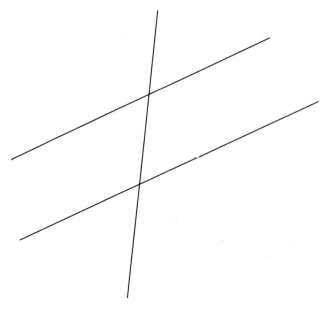

Figure 4

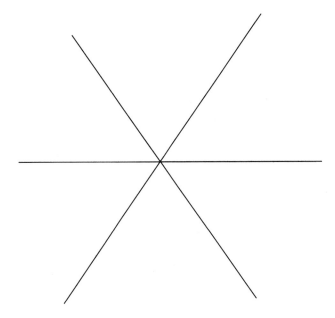

Figure 5

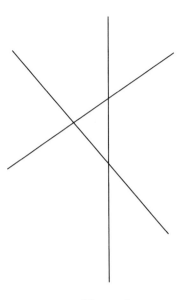

Figure 6

We wrap up the section with the second of several CHALLENGE PROBLEMS. These are problems—for you to do—that are closely related to those in the text. You should attempt to do them right away, right after you have read the cognate problems and solutions that have been presented in the text. Sometimes the CHALLENGE PROBLEMS will be routine, involving no essentially new ideas. Other times they will exceed the usual level of difficulty, or trickiness, of the typical examples in the text or the exercises. They are included to encourage you to stretch your abilities and imagination. Particularly, you should use them as an excuse to talk to others in an effort to generate ideas.

CHALLENGE PROBLEM 1.2.7 *What is the greatest number of regions into which five planes can divide three dimensional space?*

In fact the answer is 26 regions, and this is rather difficult to visualize. The remarkable fact is that the actual solution is not very difficult; what is difficult is harnessing your three dimensional geometric powers of visualization so that you can come upon the solution. John Sununu, a member of President George Bush's White House Staff, was able to solve this problem as a young man. We shall discuss its complete solution later in the book.

1.3 How to Count

Already in Problem 1.2.1 we got a taste of a "counting problem." Counting problems come up in many guises: How many different five card poker hands are there? How many different ways can you roll 8 with two dice? How many different ways can you make up $1 with nickels, dimes, and quarters?

The essence of counting technique is to have an organizational strategy. We begin with the most elementary counting question.

PROBLEM 1.3.1 *We are given k objects $\{a_1, \ldots, a_k\}$. How many different ordered pairs may be made up from those k objects?*

Solution: There are k possible choices (namely $a_1, a_2, \ldots, a_k$) for the first element of the ordered pair. Having chosen an object for the first element, how many choices remain for the second element? The answer is that there are $(k-1)$ of the original $\{a_1, \ldots, a_k\}$ remaining.

So if we chose a_1 for the first element then we may choose any of $a_2, a_3, \ldots, a_k$ for the second element—that's $(k-1)$ choices. If we chose a_2 for the first element then we may choose any of $a_1, a_3, a_4, \ldots, a_k$ for the second element—that's $(k-1)$ choices. And so forth.

In summary, there are k choices for the first element of the ordered pair. For each of those choices, there are $(k-1)$ choices for the second element of the ordered pair. The total number of possible ordered pairs, chosen from among $\{a_1, a_2, \ldots, a_k\}$, is then $k \cdot (k-1)$. $\qquad \square$

We can use the counting strategy from this last problem to come up with a basic fact about "permutations," or orderings, of finite sets:

PROBLEM 1.3.2 *We are given k objects $\{a_1, \ldots, a_k\}$. In how many different orders can we arrange these objects?*

Solution: Suppose that we have k positions into which to put the objects (Figure 7). There are k different objects (namely $a_1, a_2, \ldots, a_k$) that we may put in the first position.

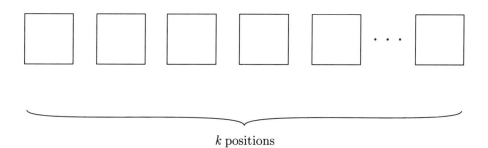

k positions

Figure 7

Having placed an object into the first position, there remain $(k-1)$ different objects to put into the second position. Thus, reasoning as in the last problem, there are $k \cdot (k-1)$ choices of pairs of objects to put into the first two positions.

Having chosen two objects to put into the first two positions, we see that there remain $(k-2)$ objects to put into the third position. Thus there are $k \cdot (k-1) \cdot (k-2)$ choices of objects to put into the first three positions.

We may continue to reason in this fashion. We find that there are $k \cdot (k-1) \cdot (k-2) \cdot (k-3)$ choices for the first four positions, $k \cdot (k-1) \cdot (k-2) \cdot (k-3) \cdot (k-4)$ choices for the first five positions, and so forth.

In the end, there are

$$k \cdot (k-1) \cdot (k-2) \cdots 3 \cdot 2 \cdot 1 = k!$$

possible different orderings of the k objects $\{a_1, a_2, \ldots, a_k\}$. $\square$

A successful attack on many counting problem relies on knowledge of the "choose function." We now turn to that notion:

PROBLEM 1.3.3 *We are given k objects $\{a_1, a_2, \ldots, a_k\}$. Suppose that m is a positive integer that is less than or equal to k. In how many ways can we choose m objects from among the original k?*

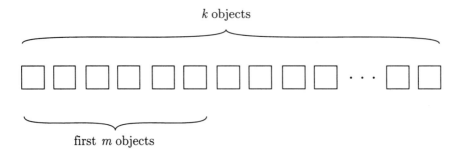

Figure 8

An example of this last type of problem is to ask how many different 5 card poker hands may be chosen from a deck of 52. Or how many different 11 person football teams may be chosen from a group of 25 people. What is interesting about the question, and differentiates it from the preceding problems, is that *we are not interested in ordering.* That is, the poker hand

$$A\spadesuit \ , \ K\heartsuit \ , \ J\spadesuit \ , \ 9\clubsuit \ , \ 7\diamondsuit$$

is just the same as the poker hand

$$K\heartsuit \ , \ 7\diamondsuit \ , \ 9\clubsuit \ , \ A\spadesuit \ , \ J\spadesuit.$$

Now we turn to the solution of our problem:

Solution: We need a system for selecting m objects from among the original k. Suppose we proceed as follows: We select an ordering for the entire set of k objects and choose as our subcollection of m objects the first m in the ordering. See Figure 8. Since there are $k!$ different ways to order the k objects (see the last problem), this suggests that there are $k!$ different subcollections of m objects.

Of course there must be something wrong with this reasoning, since the answer $k!$ does not seem to depend on m. What is wrong is this: We are counting different orderings of those first m objects as different (see Figure 9). We do not wish to do this, so we divide out by the

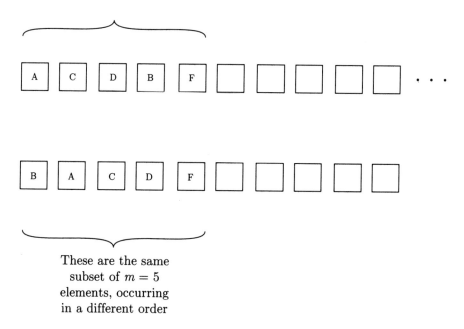

These are the same
subset of $m = 5$
elements, occurring
in a different order

Figure 9

number of possible orderings of these m objects—namely we divide out
by m! Likewise, we are counting different orderings of the last $k - m$
objects as different. So we must divide out by the number of possible
orderings of those objects—namely we divide out by $(k-m)$!. Now our
counting scheme is accurate, and enumerates different subcollections of
m objects chosen from among a total of k objects.

We have discovered that the number of different subcollections of
m objects chosen from among a total of k objects is

$$\frac{k!}{m! \cdot (k - m)!}.$$

Note once again that our strategy in deriving the formula was this:
we took the number of possible orderings of the totality of k objects,
and we thought in terms of selecting the first m from among any such
ordering. But we must divide out by the different possible orderings of
those first m objects. And we must divide out by the different possible
orderings of the remaining $k - m$ objects.   □

The quantity

$$\frac{k!}{m! \cdot (k-m)!}$$

is used universally in counting arguments, and is commonly referred to as "k choose m." It is written $\binom{k}{m}$. Thus we have

$$\binom{k}{m} = \frac{k!}{m! \cdot (k-m)!}.$$

PROBLEM 1.3.4 *How many different 5 card poker hands may be had from a deck of 52 cards?*

Solution: With the ideas that we have developed, this is an easy problem. For the number of such poker hands is just "52 choose 5:"

$$\# \text{ of poker hands} = \binom{52}{5} = \frac{52!}{5!47!} = 2,598,960. \qquad \square$$

PROBLEM 1.3.5 *How many pairs of bridge hands may be dealt from a deck of 52 cards?*

Solution: Recall that bridge is played by two teams of two people. Each person is dealt 13 cards. Consider one of the teams.

The first team member is dealt 13 cards from among the total of 52. The number of possible hands that this person could be dealt is

$$C_1 = \binom{52}{13} = \frac{52!}{13! \cdot 39!}.$$

The second team member is also dealt 13 cards, chosen from among the remaining 39 cards. [Notice here that in an actual game we do not first give 13 cards to the first team member and then give 13 cards to the second team member. But the order in which the cards are distributed is irrelevant here. The only point is that the first team member is given 13 cards at random and the second team member is given 13 *other* cards at random.] Thus the number of possibilities for the second team member are

$$C_2 = \binom{39}{13} = \frac{39!}{13! \cdot 26!}.$$

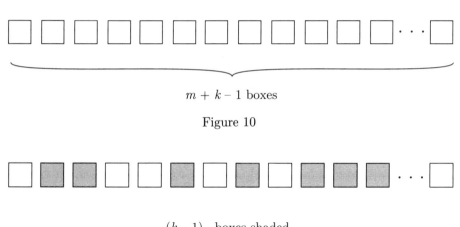

$m + k - 1$ boxes

Figure 10

$(k - 1)$ boxes shaded

m boxes unshaded

Figure 11

The total number of *pairs of hands* for the two team members is

$$C_1 \cdot C_2 = \binom{52}{13} \cdot \binom{39}{13} = \frac{52!}{13!\,39!} \cdot \frac{39!}{13!\,26!} \approx 5.1578 \times 10^{21}. \qquad \square$$

PROBLEM 1.3.6 *Assume that k and m are positive integers. How many different monomials of degree m are there in $\mathbb{R}^k$?*

First we clarify what we are asking here. The space $\mathbb{R}^k$ consists of elements of the form $(x_1, x_2, \ldots, x_k)$, where $x_1, x_2, \ldots, x_k$ are real numbers. A *monomial* is an expression like $(x_1)^2 \cdot (x_3)^3 \cdot (x_5)^6$. In other words, it consists of *some* powers of *some* of the variables multiplied together. We say that this particular monomial has *degree* 11 because the sum total of all the powers that occur is $2 + 3 + 6 = 11$. The problem asks for the number of all possible monomials of a given degree m in $\mathbb{R}^k$.

Solution: We now learn a new counting device. Consider $m + k - 1$ boxes, as shown in Figure 10. We will shade any $(k-1)$ of them. What remains is some clusters of unshaded boxes—the total number of these remaining boxes is m. Refer to Figure 11.

Between the leftmost edge of all the boxes and the first shaded box is a group of unshaded boxes. Say that there are m_1 of them. Note

Figure 12

that $0 \leq m_1 \leq m$. Next, to the right of the first shaded box and to the left of the second shaded box there is a group of unshaded boxes, say m_2 of them. Continue in this fashion.

We see that the shading of $k-1$ boxes gives rise to non-negative integers $m_1, m_2, \ldots, m_k$ such that $m_1 + m_2 + \cdots + m_k = m$. In turn, this k-tuple of numbers corresponds to the monomial $(x_1)^{m_1} \cdot (x_2)^{m_2} \cdots (x_k)^{m_k}$.

The process runs in reverse. Any monomial $(x_1)^{m_1} \cdot (x_2)^{m_2} \cdots (x_k)^{m_k}$ has a corresponding k-tuple $(m_1, m_2, \ldots, m_k)$, and this k-tuple in turn corresponds to a shading of $k-1$ boxes from among $m + k - 1$ boxes. In fact Figure 12 illustrates the shading of boxes that corresponds to $(x_1)^2 \cdot (x_3)^3 \cdot (x_5)^6$ in $\mathbb{R}^6$.

Thus counting the monomials of degree m in $\mathbb{R}^k$ corresponds exactly to counting the different ways to shade (or to choose) $k-1$ boxes chosen from among $m + k - 1$ boxes. *Note that there are no redundancies or ambiguities.* Thus the number of monomials that we wish to count is

$$\binom{m + k - 1}{k - 1} = \frac{(m + k - 1)!}{(k - 1)! \cdot m!} \qquad \square$$

1.4   The Use of Induction

Mathematical Induction is one of the most powerful techniques in all of mathematics. Before we begin to study it, we should draw a distinction between the use of "induction" in other fields of human endeavor and the use of "Mathematical Induction" in mathematics.

Most scientific subjects rely heavily on induction. A chemist or physicist or biologist examines a certain number of cases of some phenomenon and then attempts to *induct* from this data some general rule or dictum. The process of passing from the data to the rule can take many forms. It is not defined in advance. And the main test of whether the process has been valid is further experimentation and gathering of data.

"Mathematical Induction" is limited in scope, and proceeds in a more rigid fashion. Here is the scheme for mathematical induction. Suppose that we have a statement $P(k)$ for each positive integer k. For example, the statement could be "$k^2 - 2k + 1 \geq 0$." Or it could be "The number $2k + 4$ can be written as the sum of two odd primes." The method of Mathematical Induction is used to proved $P(k)$ for all k in the following fashion:

(i) First verify $P(1)$.
(ii) Verify that $P(j) \Rightarrow P(j + 1)$ for every $j \in \{1, 2, 3, \ldots\}$.

Assuming that these two statements have been verified, we notice the following. Using (i) and the special instance $j = 1$ of (ii) gives us $P(1)$ and $P(1) \Rightarrow P(2)$. From this we may conclude $P(2)$. Now the special instance $j = 2$ of (ii) gives us $P(2) \Rightarrow P(3)$. From this, and the statement $P(2)$ obtained in the preceding step, we may conclude $P(3)$. Continuing in this fashion, we see that $P(k)$ is true for every positive integer k.

The discussion that we have just presented to explain why the method of Mathematical Induction is a valid method of reasoning should be taken as intuitive. A rigorous treatment of the method is intimately bound up with set theory and the construction of the natural numbers; we cannot go into the details here. We refer the reader to [KRA1] and [SUP] for more detailed discussions.

Now we turn to some examples where induction is useful.

PROBLEM 1.4.1 *Verify the formula*

$$1 + 2 + 3 + \cdots + (k - 1) + k = \frac{k + k^2}{2}.$$

Solution: We solved this problem by a different method in Section 1.2. The technique that we used at the time may have seemed like an unmotivated trick. Once you get used to induction, by studying examples like the one we are doing now, it will seem like a standard device for problems like this one.

When using the method of induction (we now use this language, instead of the more formalistic Mathematical Induction), it is important to proceed systematically.

First, what is the statement $P(k)$ that is to be verified? It is

$$1 + 2 + 3 + \cdots + (k - 1) + k = \frac{k + k^2}{2}.$$

To verify $P(1)$, we note that

$$1 = \frac{1 + 1^2}{2}.$$

The most interesting, and subtle, part of the method of induction is part (ii). We *assume* that $P(j)$ is known to hold. Thus, in the present problem, we are assuming that

$$1 + 2 + 3 + \cdots + j = \frac{j + j^2}{2}. \qquad (*)$$

From this we wish to derive the corresponding statement for $(j + 1)$.

To this end, we add $(j + 1)$ to both sides of $(*)$. We obtain

$$1 + 2 + 3 + \cdots + j + (j + 1) = \frac{j + j^2}{2} + (j + 1).$$

Simplifying, we have

$$1 + 2 + 3 + \cdots + (j + 1) = \frac{j + j^2 + 2(j + 1)}{2}$$

or

$$1 + 2 + 3 + \cdots + (j + 1) = \frac{(j + 1) + (j + 1)^2}{2}.$$

This last is precisely the statement $P(j + 1)$.

Notice that, assuming the validity of $P(j)$, we have derived $P(j+1)$. That is precisely part (ii) of the method of induction.

The verification is complete. According to the method of induction, once we have verified Steps (i) and (ii), then we can be sure that $P(k)$ holds for all k. Thus we have solved the problem. $\qquad \square$

Sometimes it is convenient to begin an induction at a point other than $j = 1$. In the next problem we begin at $j = 0$.

PROBLEM 1.4.2 *Suppose that S is a set with k elements. Show that S has precisely 2^k subsets.*

Solution: We will use the method of induction. First recall that a set A is said to be a subset of a set B if each element of A is also an element of B. In particular, $\emptyset \subset A$, where $\emptyset$ is the "empty set" (or the set with no elements). Also $A \subset A$.

Now our inductive statement $P(k)$ is this: "If a set S has k elements then S has 2^k subsets."

As already noted, we begin our induction at 0, rather than 1. For step (i), notice that if $S = \{\} = \emptyset$ has no elements then the only subset of S is S itself. Thus S has $1 = 2^0$ subsets. Thus we have verified $P(0)$.

For step (ii), we assume that $P(j)$ is valid. This means that any set with j elements has 2^j subsets. Now let $S = \{s_1, s_2, \ldots, s_j, s_{j+1}\}$ be a set with $(j + 1)$ elements. Set $S' = \{s_1, s_2, \ldots, s_j\}$. Notice that the set S' has j elements. By hypothesis, S' has a total of 2^j subsets. Now we count the subsets of S itself.

Certainly any subset of S' is also a subset of S. That accounts for 2^j subsets of S. Also, if A is any subset of S' then $A \cup \{s_{j+1}\}$ is a subset of S. That accounts for another 2^j subsets of S. We thus have identified a total of $2^j + 2^j = 2^{j+1}$ subsets of the set S. Notice that we have in fact accounted for *all* the subsets of S, since any subset of S either contains s_{j+1} or it does not. Therefore we have derived $P(j + 1)$ from $P(j)$. That is part (ii) of the method of induction.

The verification is complete. $\qquad\square$

PROBLEM 1.4.3 *Suppose that we have an admissible graph on the unit sphere in three dimensional space. Here, by "admissible graph" we mean a connected configuration of arcs. Two arcs may be joined only at their endpoints. The endpoints of the arcs in the graph are called vertices. The arcs are called edges. An edge is that portion of an arc that lies between two vertices. A face is any two dimensional region, without holes, that is bordered by edges and vertices. Figure 13 illustrates an admissible graph and a non-admissible graph.*

This problem asks you to verify Euler's formula for an admissible graph. We let V be the number of vertices, E the number of edges,

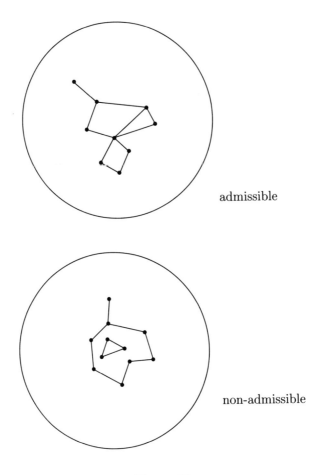

Figure 13

and F the number of faces. Then Euler's formula is

$$V - E + F = 2.$$

Solution: We begin with some special cases, just to be sure that we understand what is going on.

The simplest graph that is admissible, according to our definitions, consists of a single vertex and nothing else (Figure 14). The complement of that single vertex, in the sphere, is a valid face. Thus $V = 1$, $E = 0$, and $F = 1$. Then

$$V - E + F = 1 - 0 + 1 = 2$$

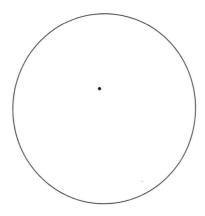

Figure 14

and we see that Euler's formula is valid.

The next most complex graph has one edge, with a vertex on each end, and nothing else. The complement (in the sphere) of this edge with its endpoints is a single valid face. See Figure 15. Thus, in this case, $V = 2$, $E = 1$, and $F = 1$. We see that

$$V - E + F = 2 - 1 + 1 = 2.$$

Thus Euler's formula is valid in this case as well.

Now we let $P(k)$ be the statement "Euler's formula is valid for any admissible graph with k edges." We shall use induction to prove this statement for every k.

The statement $P(1)$ has already been verified. That is part (i) of the method of induction.

For part (ii), we assume that Euler's formula is valid for any admissible graph having j edges. Now let $\mathcal{G}$ be a graph having $(j+1)$ edges. There is some edge that can be removed from $\mathcal{G}$ so that the remaining graph $\mathcal{G}'$ is still admissible (exercise—for example, an edge that separates two different faces will do). Say that V', E', and F' denote the numbers of vertices, edges, and faces for the graph $\mathcal{G}'$. Now consider what the corresponding numbers V, E, F for the graph $\mathcal{G}$ might be.

The graph $\mathcal{G}$ is obtained from $\mathcal{G}'$ (we are reversing the construction that produced $\mathcal{G}'$) by adding an edge. If the edge is added by attaching

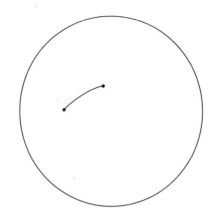

Figure 15

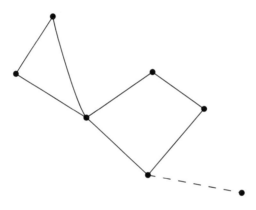

Figure 16

one end, and leaving the other free (the added edge is dotted in Figure 16), then the number of faces does not change, the number of edges is increased by one, and the number of vertices is increased by one. See Figure 16. Thus $V = V' + 1$, $E = D' + 1$, and $F = F'$. Since, by hypothesis, $V' - E' + F' = 2$, it follows that $V - E + F = 2$ as desired. If instead the edge is added by attaching *both ends* (again the added edge is dotted in Figure 17—there are two possibilities, as shown), then the number of faces is increased by one, the number of edges is increased by one, and the number of vertices does not change. Therefore $V = V'$, $E = E' + 1$, and $F = F' + 1$. Since, by hypothesis, $V' - E' + F' = 2$,

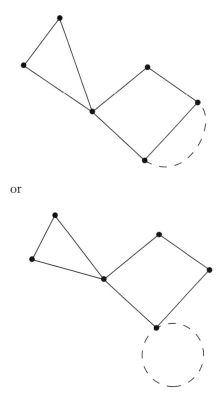

Figure 17

it follows that $V - E + F = 2$.

Since these are the only two ways that a new edge can be attached, we have established step (ii) of the inductive procedure. Our argument is complete. ☐

PROBLEM 1.4.4 *Assume that k is a positive integer. If $(k + 1)$ letters are delivered to k mailboxes, then show that one mailbox must contain at least two letters.*

Solution: Although many solutions are possible, we will use induction just to illustrate the method.

The statement $P(k)$ is "If $(k+1)$ letters are delivered to k mailboxes then some mailbox must receive at least two letters."

For the case $k = 1$, notice that if $k + 1 = 2$ letters are delivered to $k = 1$ mailboxes then some mailbox (namely the *only* mailbox) will receive two letters (indeed, all the letters).

Now assume that $P(j)$ has been proved. Assume that $(j + 1) + 1$ letters have been delivered to $(j + 1)$ mailboxes.

- If the last mailbox is empty, then all the letters have been delivered to the first j mailboxes. In particular, at least $(j + 1)$ (indeed, $(j + 2)$) letters have been delivered to these first j mailboxes. So the inductive hypothesis applies and one of these first j mailboxes contains at least two letters.

- If the last mailbox contains precisely one letter, then the remaining $(j + 1)$ letters have been delivered to the first j mailboxes. Once again, the inductive hypothesis applies to the first j mailboxes. So one of them will contain at least two letters.

- If the last mailbox contains two or more letters, then we are done because some mailbox (namely the last one) contains at least two letters.

That completes the verification of our statement.   □

The principle embodied in the statement of the last problem is of pre-eminent importance in mathematics. It is commonly called the "pigeonhole principle." It was originally called the *Dirichletscher Schubfachschluss* (Dirichlet's drawer-shutting principle) because it was formulated by the German mathematician Peter Gustav Lejeune Dirichlet (1805-1859). In the next section, you will learn about arguing by contradiction. As an exercise, you can check then that the pigeonhole principle can easily be verified using the method of contradiction.

CHALLENGE PROBLEM 1.4.5 *A group of people gathers for a party. A lot of handshaking goes on. Show that the number of people who shake hands an odd number of times is even.*

PROBLEM 1.4.6 *Suppose that six people are in a room. Explain why either three of these people all know each other or else there are three of the people none of whom knows each other.*

Solution: Of course we are supposing that if A knows B then B knows A and vice versa. Call one of the people Joe. Of the other five people, either Joe knows three of them or he does not know three of them. Say that the first case obtains. In fact, say that he knows Harry, Mary, and Larry. Now if two of those people know each other (for instance, Harry knows Larry), then the triple {Joe, Harry, Larry} is a mutually acquainted triple. If, instead, it is not the case that two of these three people know each other, then {Harry, Mary, Larry} is a triple of people no two of whom know each other. □

CHALLENGE PROBLEM 1.4.7 *We can reinterpret the last problem as follows.*

> *You have six points on a piece of paper. Each of the fifteen possible pairs of these points will be joined either by a red line segment or by a blue line segment. Show that there will either be a triangle that is all blue or a triangle that is all red.*

Explain why this formulation is equivalent to the original one.

CHALLENGE PROBLEM 1.4.8 *Refer to the last problem and the last challenge problem. Suppose now that you have three colors in which you can render the line segments: red, blue, and yellow. Then, with six points, it will not be the case that there must be a triangle that is all of one color. Explain why.*

In fact how many points do you need, with every pair connected by either a red, a blue, or a yellow line segment, so that you are guaranteed to have a triangle of just one color?

CHALLENGE PROBLEM 1.4.9 *Formulate a generalization of the last challenge problem. Suppose that you have k colors. How many points are required to guarantee that the process of joining all possible pairs of points with line segment segments of one of these colors will guarantee that there is a triangle of just one color?*

1.5   Problems of Logic

Logic plays a role in every problem that we solve. But some problems are primarily geometrical in nature, others are counting problems, and still others are analytical. In the present section we use logic itself as the chief tool both for formulating and for solving problems. We begin with a classic from the genre of "Liar and Truth Teller" problems.

PROBLEM 1.5.1 *You are on an island that is populated by two types of people: truth tellers and liars. When asked a* YES–NO *question, a truth teller always tells the truth and a liar always lies. There is no visual method for telling a truth teller from a liar. What single question could you ask anyone that you meet on the island to determine whether that person is a truth teller or a liar?*

Solution: If you ask a direct question such as "Are you a truth teller?" then a truth teller will answer "Yes" and a liar (who must lie) will also answer "Yes". You will get a similar result if you ask "Are you a liar?" Thus an elementary, direct question provides no basis for differentiation.

Therefore a compound question, such as a conditional, or an "or" question, or an "and" question is called for. One of the things that we learn in a basic logic course is that any question that is of one of these three types can be reformulated as a question of any one of the other three types (see [KRA1]). We concentrate on formulating an "if-then" question that will do the job.

The question that we formulate could be of the form "If it is raining then what would you say to …" or "If you are a Doctor of Letters then what would be your answer to …." However it is clear that these conditions have nothing to do with the matter at hand.

Probably more relevant would be a question of the form "If you were a truth teller then what would you say to …." Likewise the concluding part of the question ought to have something to do with the problem that we are trying to solve. We now try the question

> **If you are a truth teller then how would you answer**
> **the question, 'Are you a liar?'**

Now we analyze how the two different types of island inhabitants would answer this question.

Obviously a truth teller would answer the question "Are you a liar?" by saying "No". If you pose the displayed question to a truth teller, then he will report truthfully on the answer just given, so he/she will say "No".

A liar can think just as clearly as a truth teller. He/she also knows that a truth teller, if asked whether he/she is a liar, will say "No". But the liar must lie. So he/she will say "Yes".

Thus we have found a question to which a truth teller will always answer "No" and a liar will always answer "Yes". This certainly gives a means for differentiating truth tellers from liars, and answers our problem.   □

You might have some fun modifying the question that we formulated in the last problem and seeing what the results would be. Try the question "If you are a liar then how would you answer the question 'Are you a truth teller?' " There are other variations that you might try as well. What would happen if you used the question "Are you a duck?"

Here is a problem of the same sort that you can try as a challenge:

CHALLENGE PROBLEM 1.5.2 *You are on the island of truth tellers and liars. Two people walk up to you. Call them A and B. What single yes/no question can you ask A that will enable you to determine whether B is a liar or a truth teller?*

CHALLENGE PROBLEM 1.5.3 *An island is inhabited by Liars, Truth Tellers, and people who lie part of time and tell the truth part of the time. These people cannot be differentiated by studying their external appearance. If you meet an island inhabitant, what single question can you ask him/her to determine which of the three types of people you have encountered?*

The next problem has received a considerable amount of publicity in the last few years. It was inspired by the television game show LET'S MAKE A DEAL. The nature of the game show (a bit over-simplified)

is as follows. The contestant is faced with three doors. He/she knows
that behind one door is a very desirable prize—say a fancy car. Behind
the other two doors are rather pesky and undesirable items—say that
a goat is behind each. The contestant is to pick a door (blind), and is
awarded the prize that is behind the door. But the game show host,
Monty Hall, teases and cajoles and bribes the contestant, encouraging
the contestant to change his/her mind and forcing the contestant to
become confused over which is the most desirable door.

What has become known as the "Monty Hall" problem is this: The
contestant picks a door. For the sake of argument, we say that he/she
has picked Door Three. Before the door is opened, revealing what is
behind it, Monty Hall says "I will now reveal to you what is behind one
of the other doors." A door is opened and there stands a goat. Then
Monty Hall says "Would you like to change *your* door selection?" Very
interesting.

Clearly the contestant will not pick the door that Monty Hall has
already opened, since that has a goat behind it. So the issue is whether
the contestant will switch from the currently selected door to the remaining door (the one that the contestant has not chosen and Monty
Hall did not open). A naive approach would be to say there is an equal
probability for there to be a goat behind the remaining door and behind the door that the contestant has already selected—after all, one
door has a goat and one has a car. What is the point of switching?
However this naive approach does not take into account the fact that
there are two distinct goats. A more careful analysis of cases occurs in
our solution to the problem, and reveals a surprising answer.

PROBLEM 1.5.4 *Use a case-by-case analysis to solve the Monty Hall*
problem.

Solution: We denote the goats by G_1 and G_2 (for goat one and goat
two) and the car by C. For simplicity, we assume that the contestant
will always select Door Three. We may not, however, assume that
Monty Hall always reveals a goat behind Door One; for there may not
be a goat behind Door One (it could be behind Door Two). Thus there
are several cases to consider:

Door 1	Door 2	Door 3
G_1	G_2	C
G_2	G_1	C
G_1	C	G_2
G_2	C	G_1
C	G_1	G_2
C	G_2	G_1

As we know from Section 1.4, there are $6 = 3!$ possible permutations of three objects. That is why there are six rows in the array.

1. In the first case, Monty Hall will reveal a goat behind either Door 1 or Door 2. It is *not* to the contestant's advantage to switch, so we record **N**.

2. The second case is similar to the first, it is not to the contestant's advantage to switch, and we record **N**.

3. In the third case, Monty Hall will reveal a goat behind Door 1, and it *is* to the contestant's advantage to switch. We record **Y**.

4. The fourth case is like the third, and it is to the contestant's advantage to switch. We record **Y**.

5. In the fifth case, Monty Hall will reveal a goat behind Door 2. It *is* to the contestant's advantage to switch, so we record **Y**.

6. The sixth case is like the fifth, it is to the contestant's advantage to switch, and we record **Y**.

Observe that the tally of our case-by-case analysis is four **Y**'s and just two **N**'s. Thus the odds are two against one in favor of switching after Monty Hall reveals the goat. □

This last problem was in the nature of a probability problem. Many elementary probability problems are amenable to careful case-by-case, or counting, arguments. Chapters 3 and 8 will give you more experience with probability problems.

PROBLEM 1.5.5 *There are more adults than boys, more boys than girls, more girls than families. If no family has fewer than 3 children, then what is the least number of families that there could be?*

Solution: If there were just one family then there would be at least two girls, at least three boys, and at least four adults. But four adults make two families, and that is a contradiction.

If there were just two families, then there would be at least three girls, at least four boys, and at least five adults. But five adults means that there cannot be just two families; there are at least three. That is a contradiction.

If there were just three families, then there would be at least four girls, at least five boys, and at least six adults. That is not a contradiction. Thus three families *might* satisfy the conditions.

In fact suppose that there are three married couples. The first couple has two girls and a boy, the second has two girls and a boy, and the third has three boys. Then there are six adults, five boys, four girls and three families. All conditions of the problem are met.

The answer is that three families is the smallest number that there could be. □

The method of solution in the last problem is one of "exhaustion." It would not be a very satisfactory method to use if the answer to the problem were 357, for it would take a great deal of work to reach that answer. Nevertheless, exhaustion is an important and systematic tool to have in our arsenal.

PROBLEM 1.5.6 *Explain why there are infinitely many prime numbers.*

Solution: Recall that a prime number is a positive integer, not 1, that has no divisors other than 1 and itself. The first several primes are 2,3,5,7,11,13,17,19,23,.... Every positive integer is divisible by a prime number—indeed can be factored in a unique manner into prime factors. That is the content of the Fundamental Theorem of Arithmetic.

We solve the present problem by using the method of proof by contradiction. Suppose that there were in fact only finitely many primes in the world. Call these primes $p_1, p_2, \ldots, p_k$. Consider the number $N = (p_1 \cdot p_2 \cdots p_k) + 1$—the product of all these primes, with 1 added to it. Now N must be divisible by *some* prime number—as noted in the last paragraph. However it is not divisible by p_1, since division by p_1 results in a remainder of 1. Likewise, N is not divisible by p_2, because division by p_2 results in a remainder of 1. In fact we see that N is not divisible by any of $p_1, p_2, \ldots, p_k$. But these were all the primes in the universe. Yet N must be divisible by some prime! That is a contradiction.

We conclude that there cannot be just finitely many primes. There must be infinitely many. ☐

"Proof by contradiction" is a simple but powerful device in mathematical and analytical reasoning. The scheme is as follows: We wish to prove a proposition P. Now P is either true or it is false. There is no "wait and see" or "in-between" status; it must be one or the other (see [KRA1] for further discussion of this concept). The strategy in "proof by contradiction" is to eliminate the possibility that P is false. So we *assume* that P is false and argue that that assumption is untenable (it leads to a contradiction). The only possible conclusion is that P is true. Problem 1.5.6 illustrates this method of reasoning.

The proof that there are infinitely many primes is usually attributed to Euclid; it is more than 2000 years old. It was one of the first proofs by contradiction. Interestingly, proof by contradiction did not become a standard mathematical tool until the twentieth century.

1.6 Issues of Parity

The most elementary example of parity is "oddness vs. evenness", but there are many others. We shall explore various aspects of parity in this section.

PROBLEM 1.6.1 *An $8' \times 8'$ bathroom is to have its floor tiled. Each tile is $2' \times 1'$. In one corner of the bathroom is a sink, and its plumbing occupies a $1' \times 1'$ square in the floor. In the opposite corner is a toilet, and its plumbing occupies a $1' \times 1'$ square in the floor. The situation*

Figure 18

is shown in Figure 18. [Figure 19 exhibits a way to envision the floor broken up into one foot squares.]

How is it possible to achieve the required tiling of the floor?

Solution: The area to be tiled is $8' \times 8'$ less two square feet—in other words, we must tile an area of 62 square feet. Thus we will use 31 tiles.

Figure 20 shows one possible arrangement of tiles; notice that it fails to cover the entire floor. There are two squares remaining (on the lower right), and they cannot be covered by a single tile. Other attempts fail similarly. (Try this with your checkerboard; put coins on two of the opposite corners to signal that the tiles may not cover those squares).

We start to smell a rat. Perhaps the floor cannot be tiled. But how can we produce a cogent argument that explains why no tiling can work? There are many hundreds of ways to attempt to tile this floor, and it is distasteful to consider *all possible tilings.* The idea that we now introduce—one inspired by the concept of parity—is to color the bare floor of the bathroom like a checkerboard. Look at Figure 21. Notice that when we place a $2' \times 1'$ tile on the floor then it will cover two adjacent squares. One of these will be black and one will be white. Thus if we place two tiles on the floor, they will cover a total of two black squares and two white squares. In general, k tiles placed on the floor will cover k black squares and k white squares. Yet the bathroom floor that we are dealing with has 32 black squares and 30

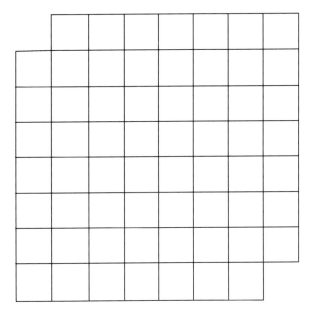

Figure 19

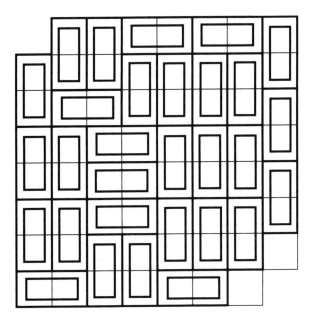

Figure 20

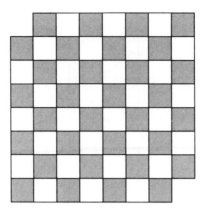

Figure 21

white squares. Since the number of black squares covered will always equal the number of white squares covered, we have an insurmountable problem. This bathroom floor can never be tiled!   □

The use of parity that came into the last problem was the device of coloring the floor. It would have required intricate combinatorial reasoning to solve this problem without the intervention of the coloring.

PROBLEM 1.6.2 *We have a container that contains 6 quarts and another that contains 4 quarts. We fill these containers by immersing them in the river. How can we use them to fill one of the containers with 3 quarts of water?*

Solution: What is implicit in the problem, and what we make explicit now, is that the only moves we are allowed are (i) to fill a container, (ii) to empty a container, or (iii) to pour one container into the other. This being the case, our various pouring operations correspond to adding and subtracting multiples of 4 and 6. Now addition and subtraction of even numbers always results in an even number answer. Thus there is no way to obtain the number 3.

The problem cannot be solved.   □

CHALLENGE PROBLEM 1.6.3 *Now suppose that you have a 9 quart container and a 4 quart container. How can you put exactly 6 quarts of water into the large container?*

We have given two examples in which the notion of parity taught us that a certain problem cannot be solved. Now we give one in which parity leads to a positive solution.

PROBLEM 1.6.4 (Maşek) *Imagine a polyhedron with 1981 vertices. [This is not as difficult as it sounds. Just place 1981 points on the unit sphere in three dimensional space. Now connect them with line segments in an obvious way to obtain a polyhedron.]*

Imagine that each edge is assigned an electrical charge of +1 or −1. Explain why there must be a vertex such that the product of the charges of all the edges that meet at that vertex must be +1.

Solution: Suppose that we multiply together all the products corresponding to all the vertices. Then every edge is counted twice (since each edge has *two* vertices on its ends) so every +1 is counted twice and every −1 is counted twice. Thus the product is +1.

But there are an odd number of vertices. Thus it cannot be the case that the product coming from each vertex is −1 (since the product of an odd number of −1's is equal to −1). Therefore at least one vertex has product equaling +1. □

PROBLEM 1.6.5 *A herd of cattle invades a barn dance. Suddenly the barn is running amok with both cattle and people. A quick count reveals 120 heads and 300 feet. How many cattle are there, and how many people?*

Solution: We write p for the number of people and c for the number of cattle. Then the total number of cattle plus people is $c + p$ while the total number of feet is $4c + 2p$ (since a head of cattle has four feet while a person has two). Thus

$$c + p = 120$$
$$4c + 2p = 200.$$

We solve this system to find that $c = 30$ and $p = 90$.   □

CHALLENGE PROBLEM 1.6.6 *Suppose you are told in advance that 10 of the cattle present are lame, and only have three feet. But the count yields 120 heads and 300 feet. How many cattle and how many people are there?*

PROBLEM 1.6.7 (Halmos) *A party is held at the house of the Schlobodkins. There were four other couples present (besides Mr. and Mrs. Schlobodkin), and many, but not all, pairs of people shook hands. Nobody shook hands with anyone twice, and nobody shook hands with his/her spouse. Both the host and hostess shook some hands.*

At the end of the party, Mr. Schlobodkin polls each person present to see how many hands each person (other than himself) shook. Each person gives a different answer. Determine how many hands Mrs. Schlobodkin must have shaken.

Solution: We write S for the two Schlobodkins and we denote each of the other four couples by A, B, C, and D.

Nobody shook 9 hands, since nobody shook the hand of his/her spouse. Therefore the numbers 0 through 8 are used in describing the different numbers of handshakes performed by each of the nine people (other than Mr. Schlobodkin).

Someone shook 8 hands. Say that it is Mr. A. Then how many hands did Mrs. A shake? Everyone in couples B, C, D, S must have shaken Mr. A's hand, in order to account for 8 shakes. So each of the people in couples B, C, D, S shook hands at least once. But somebody shook hands zero times. It must be Mrs. A.

Now we eliminate Mr. and Mrs. A from our consideration. Someone shook exactly 7 hands. Say that it is Mrs. B. We know already that Mrs. B shook the hand of Mr. A. She did *not* shake the hand of Mrs. A, since nobody did. To obtain a total of 7 shakes, she must also have shaken the hands of all the people in couples C, D, S. But someone had to shake only one hand (the people in C, D, S have now each shaken at least two hands, since they each shook Mr. A's hand, as well as Mrs. B's hand). It must be Mr. B who shook only one hand.

Continuing in this fashion, we see that the person who shook 6 hands is betrothed to the person who shook 2. And the person who shook 5 hands is betrothed to the person who shook 3. That leaves only Mrs. Schlobodkin, who must have shaken 4 hands—four being the only remaining number (and note also that 4 is the only number that cannot be paired).

The answer to our problem is that Mrs. Schlobodkin shook four hands. □

CHALLENGE PROBLEM 1.6.8 *Go back to the beginning of the solution of the last problem. How can we be sure that it was not Mrs. Schlobodkin who shook 8 hands?*

PROBLEM 1.6.9 *A sheep can clear a certain field, eating the grass, in one day. A cow can clear the same field in half a day. How long does it take the sheep and the cow, working together, to clear the field?*

Solution: According to the information in the problem, a cow is like two sheep (when it comes to clearing the field, that is). So the cow and the sheep together is like three sheep. Thus they will clear the field in a third of a day. □

CHALLENGE PROBLEM 1.6.10 *A wildebeest can clear a certain field in two days. A llama can clear it in three days. And a goat can clear it in four days. How long does it take the three animals together to clear the field?*

PROBLEM 1.6.11 *What is the last digit of* 3^{4798}*?*

Solution: Clearly the last thing we want to do is to calculate this number. Even using a system like MATHEMATICA we are liable to encounter memory or storage problems. Instead let us think.

Notice that $3^1 = 3, 3^2 = 9, 3^3 = 27, 3^4 = 81, 3^5 = 243$, etc. The only possible last digits are 3,9,7, and 1; then the pattern repeats. In this list, 1 is special because $1 \cdot 1 = 1$. And the digit 1 occurs when we raise 3 to the *fourth* power. This suggest that we write

$$3^{4796} = [3^4]^{1199} \cdot 3^2.$$

Here we simply divided the exponent 4798 by 4, obtaining a quotient of 1199 and a remainder of 2. Then we used elementary laws of exponents.

Now, by what we have already observed, the expression in brackets will terminate with a 1. If we raise it to the 1199 power, it will still terminate with a 1. On the other hand, 3^2 is 9. We conclude that 3^{4796} terminates with a 9.   □

CHALLENGE PROBLEM 1.6.12 *What is the last digit of* 7^{65432}?

CHALLENGE PROBLEM 1.6.13 (THIS IS TRICKY.) *What are the last three digits of* 3^{4798}?

EXERCISES for Chapter 1

1. Show that any positive integral power of $(\sqrt{2} - 1)$ can be written in the form $\sqrt{N} - \sqrt{N-1}$ for N a positive integer. [*Hint:* Use induction. Consider separately the cases of even powers of $(\sqrt{2}-1)$ and odd powers of $(\sqrt{2} - 1)$.]

2. Calculate the sum of the first k odd integers.

3. Calculate the sum of the first k cubes of integers.

4. Demonstrate that, in any collection of 52 distinct positive integers, there are two distinct numbers whose sum or whose difference is divisible by 100.

5. Find all pairs of integers m, n such that $m \cdot n = m + n$.

6. How many zeros end the number $(200!)$?

7. How many zeros end the number $2^{300} \cdot 5^{600} \cdot 4^{400}$?

8. A bunch of people are in a room. Some of them shake hands. Some do not. What can you say about the number of people who shake hands an even number of times?

9. How many digits are used to number the pages of a book having 100 pages—numbered from 1 to 100?

10. How many positive integers k are there with the property that $k!$ does *not* end in a zero?

11. A certain number k is a multiple of 9. Add the digits together. If the result has more than one digit, add those together. Continue adding digits together until you have a one digit answer. It will be a 9. Can you explain why this is so?

12. Refer to Exercise 11. Give the following instructions to a friend: "Pick an integer from 1 to 10. Multiply it by 9. Add the digits together. Subtract 5. Now you have a single digit. Think of the letter of the alphabet that corresponds to that digit—1 is A, 2 is B, and so forth. Think of a country whose name begins with that letter. Now take the second letter of that country name. Think of an animal whose name begins with that letter." Let the friend think about this for a moment. Then say "But there are no elephants in Denmark!"

What is the joke? Why does it work?

13. Fix a positive prime integer p. Suppose that n is any positive integer. Find a formula for the number of factors of p that occur in $n!$

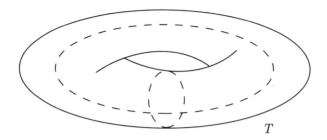

Figure 22

14. [Halmos] A watermelon weighs 500 pounds. It turns out that 99% of the weight of the watermelon is due to water in the watermelon. After the watermelon has sat in a drying room for a while, it turns out that it is only 98% water by weight. How much does it weigh now?

15. Fifteen teams play in a tournament. Each team plays every other team exactly once. A team receives 3 points for a win, 2 points for a draw, and 1 point for a loss. Every team ends up with a different total score. The team with the lowest total scored 21 points. Explain why the best team had at least one loss.

16. Suppose that T is a torus, as illustrated in Figure 22.

Determine the correct number γ so that the formula $V - E + F = \gamma$ will hold for any admissible graph on the surface of the torus T (recall that, for a sphere, the number γ was 2, but for the torus it will be a different number). The number γ is called the *Euler characteristic* of the torus. We learned in the text that the Euler characteristic of the sphere is 2.

Devise a proof that this number γ will work for any admissible graph in T.

17. Suppose that S is a sphere with k handles (see Figure 23). [In a certain sense, a torus is a sphere with one handle. Can you explain this assertion?] What is the correct number γ so that the formula $V - E + F = \gamma$ will be true for any admissible graph on the surface S? Once you find γ, can you explain why this formula is valid?

18. Each point of the cartesian plane is colored either red or blue or yellow. Explain why we can conclude that some unit segment in the plane has both ends the same color.

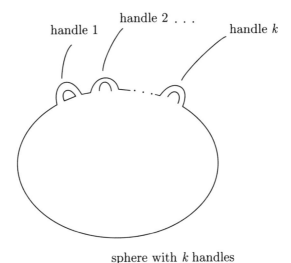

handle 1 handle 2 . . . handle *k*

sphere with *k* handles

Figure 23

19. Show that if each point in the plane is colored one of seven colors—red, blue, yellow, green, purple, orange, magenta—then it is possible that no segment of unit length has both ends the same color.

20. A certain primitive village has the following social rules: Whenever a husband is unfaithful to his wife, every other wife knows immediately, but not the wife who has been cheated on. The wives never talk to anyone about these matters, and neither do the husbands. As soon as a wife can determine irrefutably that her husband has cheated, she tatoos the letter "*A*" on his forehead before sundown of that same day.

On a given day the mayor announces that there is at least one unfaithful husband in the village (he does *not*, however, say how many unfaithful husbands there are). If in fact there are 37 unfaithful husbands in the village, what will transpire? [*Hint:* First think about the situation where the mayor makes his announcement but there is in fact just one unfaithful husband in the village. Then try the case where there are just two unfaithful husbands in the village. Now use induction.] This problem comes from [HAL].

21. How does the last problem change if the mayor actually announces the number of unfaithful husbands?

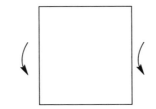

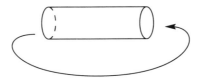

Figure 24

22. Say that you have a square piece of paper. Imagine pasting the upper edge to the lower edge (Figure 24) and the left edge to the right edge. Do this in such a way that the orientations of these edges are preserved. What geometric figure results?

Now imagine that, when the left and right edges are glued we first give the left edge a twist (Figure 25 suggests what is meant by this). The result is an object called the Klein bottle; the Klein bottle cannot actually be realized as a surface in space, but we may think about it mathematically from the description just given.

What is the correct number γ so that the formula $V - E + F = \gamma$ will hold for any admissible graph on the surface of the Klein bottle? Can you prove that your choice of γ is correct?

23. Calculate the sum in closed form:

$$\frac{1}{2!} + \frac{2}{3!} + \frac{3}{4!} + \cdots + \frac{n}{(n+1)!}.$$

24. Assume that S is a set with k elements. We know that S has 2^k subsets. What does this statement have to do with the binomial coefficients? [Hint: Look at $(1 + x)^k$.]

match the orientation of the arrows

Figure 25

25. An urn contains a white balls and b black balls; we know that $a + b \geq 3$. Players A and B play a game with the urn and the balls. Consider two strategies:

1. Player A draws a ball at random. If it is white he wins, otherwise he loses.

2. Player A draws a ball and throws it away without looking at it. Player B then draws a black ball. Next, A draws another ball. If this second ball for A is white then he wins. Otherwise he loses.

Show that, with the first strategy, player A wins with probability $a/(a + b)$. But with the second strategy he wins with probability $a/(a + b) + a/[(a + b)(a + b - 2)]$. Clearly the second strategy is preferable.

What does this problem have to do with the Monte Hall problem?

26. You have a wooden cube that is $3'' \times 3'' \times 3''$. By drawing a 3×3 grid on each face of the cube, you can indicate how the cube subdivides into 27 sub-cubes of equal size. Refer to Figure 26.

Is it possible for a termite to eat his way through each of the outside cubes just once, and then finish his journey in the middle cube?

27. Examine the example from the text about tiling the bathroom floor. What happens if the two omitted squares are in adjacent corners of the bathroom instead of opposite corners? What happens if the two omitted squares are adjacent to each other (in this last case, does it

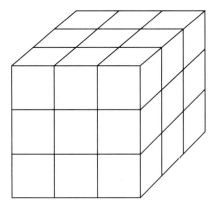

Figure 26

matter *where* the two omitted squares are—in a corner, in the middle
of a side, or in the middle of the floor?). Do some experimenting!

28. Find at least two methods for calculating the sum $101 + 102 + 103 +$
$\cdots + 200$. [*Note:* Just adding them up does not count as a "method."]

29. An auditorium has 500 seats. The decorator has three different
colors of fabric—red, blue, and yellow, and will randomly upholster each
seat with one of the three colors. So some will end up red, some blue,
and some yellow, with no particular pattern. In how many different
ways can this be done?

30. Five people play "seven card stud" poker. In seven card stud, you
are dealt five cards face down and two face up. Joe is showing two aces
for his face up cards. No other aces show on the table. What are the
odds that he has another ace among his five face down cards?

Chapter 2

A Deeper Look at Geometry

2.1   Classical Planar Geometry

The problems in the present section will be based on the classical Euclidean conception of geometry. We shall be concerned with triangles and circles, with ruler and compass constructions, with right angles, adjacent angles, and opposite angles. Later, we shall also consider some questions of solid geometry. Everything that we do in the present section will be in the plane.

PROBLEM 2.1.1 *We let ℓ and m be two lines in the plane that are skew to each other (that is, they intersect at a single point X). Let P be a point (other than X) that is on the line ℓ. Using a ruler and compass, construct a circle that is tangent to both lines and passes through P.*

Solution: If we can construct the center C of the circle, then we can construct the circle. For the radius is the distance of C to P, and we can measure that distance with the compass (Figure 27).

Since P is a point of tangency, we note that the radial segment that terminates at P will be perpendicular to ℓ. Thus it will be useful to construct the perpendicular line to ℓ at P (Figure 28). We can measure the distance from X to P. Thus we can locate a point P' on m that has the same distance from X. By the symmetry of the situation, the circle that we seek will be tangent to m at P'.

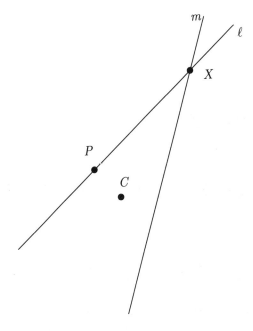

Figure 27

If we can construct the perpendicular to ℓ at P and the perpendicular to m at P' then the intersection of these two perpendiculars must be the center of the circle that we seek. See Figure 28. We have reduced our problem to constructing the perpendicular line to a give line at a give point on that line.

Refer to Figure 29. The point Q lies on the line n. Use the compass to locate points A and B, lying on n on either side of Q and equidistant from Q. The perpendicular line that we seek will be the set of all points equidistant from A and B. We already know one point on the line— namely Q. We just need one more, for two points determine a line.

Set the compass at a length to equaling the distance from A to B. Strike an arc, centered at A, with that radius. See Figure 30. Strike another arc, centered at B, with that radius. Clearly the two points C, D of intersection of these two arcs are equidistant from A and B. Thus C, D, Q all lie on the line we seek. The unique line that they determine passes through Q and is perpendicular to the line n.

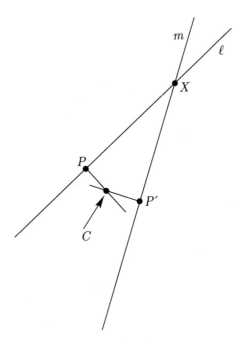

Figure 28

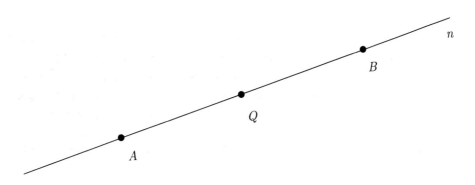

Figure 29

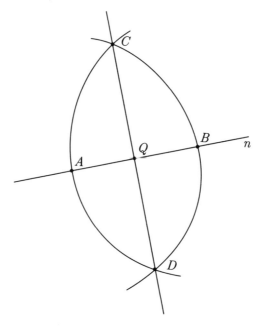

Figure 30

We have learned how to construct the perpendicular to a given line at a given point. Combining this information with the earlier analysis of our problem of constructing a tangent circle to two lines completes the solution of the problem.   □

An interesting feature of our solution to the last problem is that it involved *reduction*: constructing the desired circle reduced to finding its center; finding the center reduced to constructing certain perpendiculars, and so forth. *A good problem solver is adept at reducing the given problem to simpler problems, perhaps a sequence of simpler problems.*

PROBLEM 2.1.2 *Of all parallelograms with a given perimeter, which has the greatest area?*

Solution: Denote the perimeter by p. Consider a parallelogram with that perimeter (Figure 31). Notice that if we cut off a triangle as shown in Figure 32, and rearrange as in Figure 33, then the area remains the same but the perimeter decreases (because the *width* is unchanged but

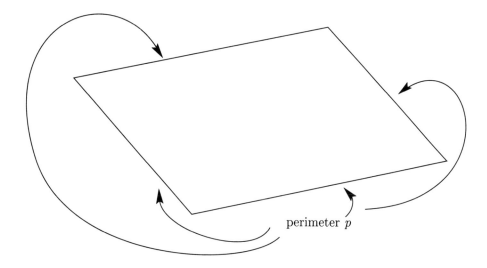

perimeter p

Figure 31

the other two sides have become vertical, hence shorter). It follows that the optimal area will be obtained if we concentrate our attention on *rectangles* rather than general parallelograms.

Now consider a rectangle, not necessarily a square, as shown in Figure 34. Assume, as before, that the perimeter is p. We may represent the length of the rectangle as $(p/4) + \epsilon$ and the width as $(p/4) - \epsilon$ for some $\epsilon \geq 0$. Notice that the perimeter sums to p, just as it should (Figure 35). The *area* of this rectangle is

$$\left[\frac{p}{4} + \epsilon\right] \cdot \left[\frac{p}{4} - \epsilon\right] = \frac{p^2}{16} - \epsilon^2.$$

This area is maximized when $\epsilon \geq 0$ is made as small as possible. Indeed, the maximum is clearly achieved when $\epsilon = 0$. But this just says that the optimal area occurs when the rectangle is a square. □

There are several points to the last example. One is that one can do quite a lot without calculus. Exploiting symmetry, and geometric reasoning, are decisive techniques. One could do this problem with calculus, or one could do it using analytic geometry. But ingenuity serves as a powerful substitute for those more sophisticated tools.

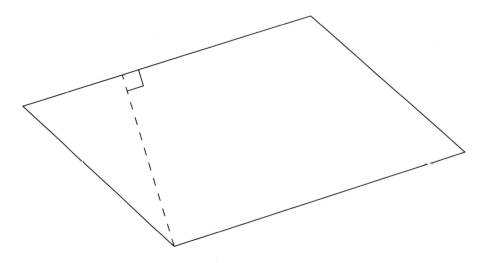

Figure 32

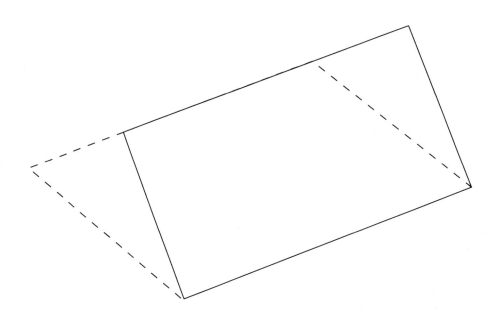

Figure 33

perimeter p

Figure 34

$p/4 + \varepsilon$

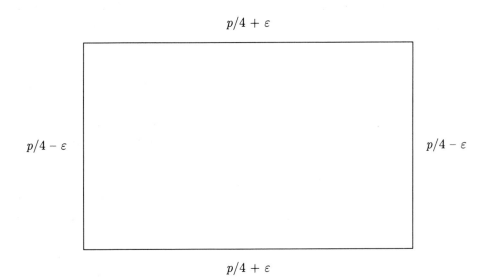

$p/4 - \varepsilon$ $p/4 - \varepsilon$

$p/4 + \varepsilon$

Figure 35

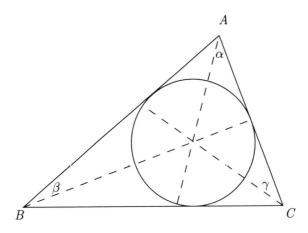

Figure 36

PROBLEM 2.1.3 *Using a ruler and compass, find the center of the inscribed circle of a given triangle.*

Solution: We assume here no particular knowledge of inscribed circles—just what the concept means geometrically. We take it for granted, at least for the moment, that the inscribed circle exists; that is, given a triangle, we assume that there is a circle that is internally tangent to the interiors of each of the three sides of the triangle. We will worry about the existence issue later.

Refer to Figure 36. The circle that we seek is tangent to the sides AB and AC. Thus the center of the circle is equidistant from the two sides of the angle at A, so it lies on the angle bisector of the angle α at A. This analysis applies to the other two pairs of sides as well. In sum, if we can construct the three angle bisectors, and if we assume in advance that the inscribed circle exists, then those three angle bisectors intersect at a point and that point is the center of the inscribed circle.

The problem has been reduced to finding the angle bisector of a given angle. Refer to Figure 37. We need to find a point that is, in some sense, equidistant from the two rays that bound the angle. We cannot do so by measuring from the vertex. So we open the compass to a fixed amount d and mark off two points X and Y, on each side of the angle, having distance d from the vertex. See Figure 38.

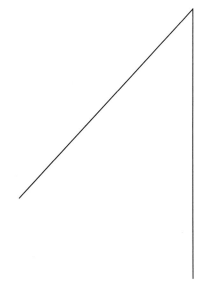

Figure 37

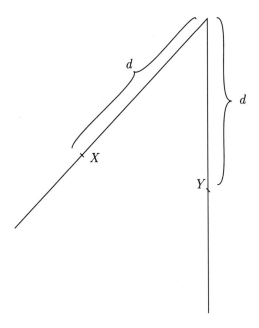

Figure 38

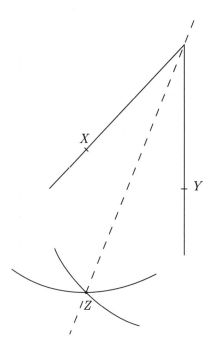

Figure 39

Now put the compass point at X and strike an arc of radius d as shown in Figure 39. Put the compass point at Y and strike an arc of radius d. The point Z of intersection will be equidistant from X and Y. The line through Z and the vertex will of course pass through the vertex of the angle and will be the angle bisector that we seek.

Having determined a method for constructing angle bisectors, the preceding argument shows how to find the center of an inscribed circle to a given triangle. That solves our problem. □

It remains to say a few words about the existence of the inscribed circle. Notice that the angle bisector emanating from vertex A is equidistant from sides AB and AC. Also the angle bisector emanating from vertex B is equidistant from sides AB and BC. It follows that the point of intersection of these two bisectors is equidistant from AB, AC, and BC as well. Thus the point of intersection of the bisectors emanating from A and from B will also lie on the bisector emanating from C. This

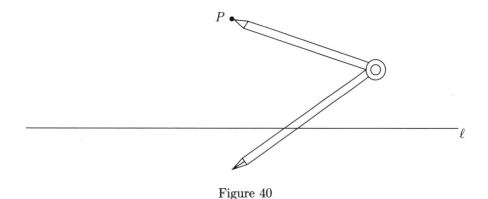

Figure 40

demonstrates that there is indeed a single common point of intersection of the three angle bisectors. Since this point is equidistant from all three sides of the triangle, it is the center of the inscribed circle. The radius of that circle will be the common distance of this point from any of the sides. The next problem makes it clear how to find this radius.

PROBLEM 2.1.4 *Let ℓ be a line and P a point that does not lie on that line. Use a ruler and compass to construct the line through P that is perpendicular to ℓ.*

Solution: Place the point of the compass at P and open the compass so that it spans a distance greater than the distance from P to ℓ (Figure 40).

Strike an arc, noting the two points of intersection with the line ℓ. Call these points A and B (Figure 41).

Now place the point of the compass at A, and open the compass so that the writing end touches B. Strike an arc as shown in Figure 42.

Repeat this process with the point of the compass at B and the writing end reaching to A. The result is shown in Figure 43.

The points of intersection of the arcs are equidistant from A and B. They determine the line m of *all* points equidistant from A and B. It will be perpendicular to ℓ. And it will pass through P, since P is certainly equidistant from A and B. $\qquad\qquad\square$

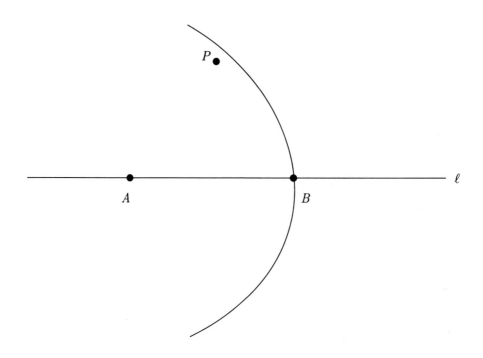

Figure 41

Figure 42

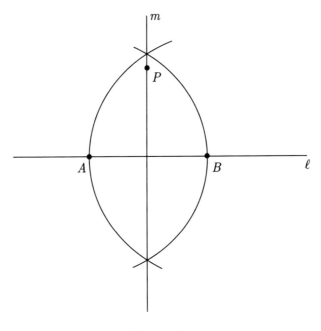

Figure 43

Note that the circle with center P that is tangent to ℓ has radius that can now be measured as the distance of P to the point of intersection of ℓ and m.

PROBLEM 2.1.5 *Suppose we are given a triangle T with base $\overline{AB}$. Give a constructive method for drawing a segment parallel to $\overline{AB}$, terminating on the sides $\overline{CA}$ and $\overline{CB}$ of the triangle, that divides the triangle into two equal areas.*

Solution: Look at Figure 44. Suppose that the height of the triangle is h and that the distance of the vertex C to the segment we seek to construct is k. [Note that in the preceding problem we already learned how to construct a height or perpendicular.]

The portion P of the triangle T that lies above the segment we are constructing is also a triangle, and it is *similar* to T itself. This is clear because their respective sides are parallel. If the ratio of the height k of the smaller triangle to the height h of the larger triangle is α then this is also the ratio of their bases as well. Thus the ratio of their areas

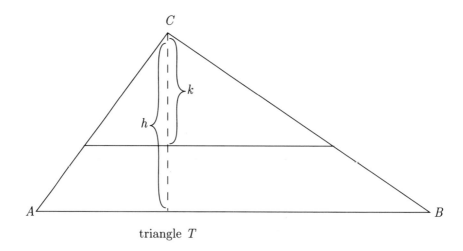

triangle T

Figure 44

is α^2 (since area is half of base times height). Thus we seek to choose the horizontal segment in such a way that $\alpha^2 = 1/2$ or $\alpha = 1/\sqrt{2}$. In other words, we want $k = (1/\sqrt{2})h$.

The problem has been reduced to producing a segment that has length $1/\sqrt{2}$ times the length of a given segment. If ℓ is a given segment, as in Figure 45, then we may use ideas from the preceding problems, together with a ruler and compass, to construct an isosceles right triangle with hypotenuse equal to ℓ. (In detail: construct a square with side ℓ; draw the diagonals of this square.) Then each leg of this right triangle will have length $\ell/\sqrt{2}$. That is the desired construction.   □

Once again, we see the method of reduction at play. We exploited the power of similar triangles to reduce a sophisticated geometry problem to an elementary geometry problem.

PROBLEM 2.1.6 *Assume that P is a regular polygon with k sides. What is the measure of any of the k angles formed by P?*

Solution: What do we already know about angles in a polygon? The basic fact with which we are all familiar is that the sum of the angles in

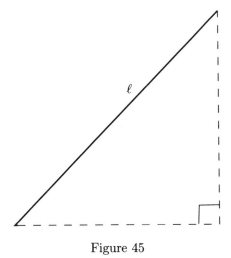

Figure 45

a *triangle* is 180° (or π in radian measure). Can we relate the problem at hand to this fact?

We attempt to break the polygon P up into triangles. Figure 46 suggests one way to do it, and Figure 47 suggests another. We will analyze each of these separately.

Notice that Figure 46 exhibits P as the union of k isosceles triangles. Each of those triangles has angles summing to 180°. The sum of all the angles in *all* the triangles is thus $(180 \cdot k)°$. However *the sum of all the angles in all the triangles is not equal to the sum of the angles in the polygon.* In fact there is an overage consisting of the sum of the angles in the center. As a result of this reasoning, we see that

$$\text{(sum of angles in } P) + 360°$$
$$= \text{ sum of angles in all the triangles}$$
$$= (180 \cdot k)°.$$

In other words,

$$\text{sum of angles in } P = (180 \cdot (k - 2))°.$$

Presumably an analysis of the triangles in Figure 47 will give us the same answer. Let us see. Since P has k sides, we determine that we

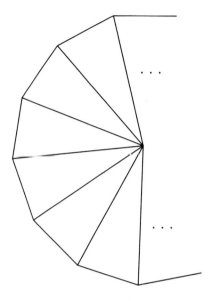

Figure 46

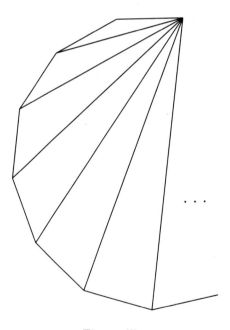

Figure 47

have, in Figure 47, broken up the polygon into $(k - 2)$ triangles. This time the sum of all the angles in all the triangles precisely equals the sum of the angles in the polygon, with no overage. Therefore

$$\text{sum of angles in } P = (180 \cdot (k - 2))^\circ.$$

This is the same answer that we derived in studying Figure 46.

According to either analysis, the measure of a single angle in the polygon P is

$$\alpha = \frac{\text{sum of the angles in } P}{k} = \frac{(180 \cdot (k - 2))}{k}.$$

$\square$

CHALLENGE PROBLEM 2.1.7 *Explain why the sum of the three angles in any triangle equals* 180°. *[NOTE: We used this fact in our analysis of Problem 2.1.6. So we may not now invoke our solution of 2.1.6 to solve this challenge problem.]*

Our solution of the last problem illustrated an important principle: when solving a new problem, ask yourself what you already know that might be related. Try to find something to get you started. The next problem gives another instance of this philosophy at work:

PROBLEM 2.1.8 *A lattice point is a point in the plane whose cartesian coordinates are both integers. Figure 48 exhibits a number of lattice points. We let C_R be the circle with center the origin and radius $R > 0$. Write $M(R)$ for the number of lattice points lying inside (not on) the circle C_R. Develop an asymptotic formula for $M(R)$ as $R \to +\infty$.*

Solution: It is virtually impossible to obtain an *exact* formula for $M(R)$. What we seek instead is a calculable quantity $\mu(R)$ such that $\mu(R)/M(R) \to 1$ as $R \to +\infty$. Read on.

A powerful tool in counting problems of this kind is the use of area. Notice that any closed square with sides parallel to the coordinate axes, having length 1, will contain at least one lattice point. For convenience,

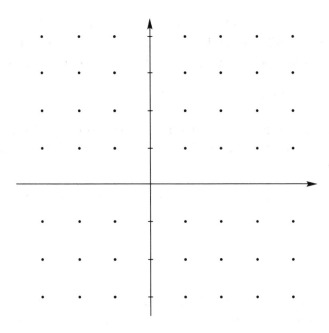

Figure 48

we restrict attention to squares of this sort having *centers* at points of the form (m, n) with m, n integers. Call these "good squares." Each such square has a lattice point at its center and contains no other.

Now inside the circle C_R of center 0 and radius R we place the circle D_R of center 0 and radius $(R - \sqrt{2})$—see Figure 49. Any good square that intersects D_R will lie strictly inside C_R. Likewise let E_R be the circle of center 0 and radius $R + \sqrt{2}$. Any good square that intersects C_R will lie inside E_R. Refer to Figure 50.

Now we may do our analysis:

$$\pi \cdot (R - \sqrt{2})^2 \quad = \quad \text{area inside } D_R$$
$$\leq \quad \text{sum of areas of good squares inside } C_R$$
$$\leq \quad \text{sum of areas of good squares containing}$$
$$\text{lattice points that are inside } C_R$$
$$= \quad \text{number of lattice points inside } C_R$$
$$\leq \quad \text{number of good square that are either}$$

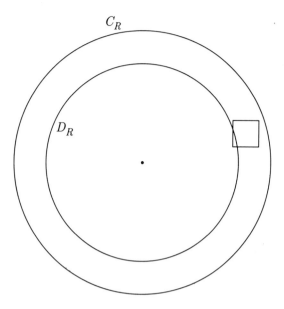

Figure 49

$$\text{inside } C_R \text{ or intersect } C_R$$
$$\leq \quad \text{sum of areas of all squares inside } E_R$$
$$\leq \quad \text{area inside } E_R$$
$$= \quad \pi \cdot (R + \sqrt{2})^2.$$

Thus we see that

$$\pi \cdot (R - \sqrt{2})^2 \leq \text{number of lattice points inside } C_R \leq \pi \cdot (R + \sqrt{2})^2.$$

We may draw the following conclusions: First, divide these inequalities through by πR^2. We see that

$$\frac{\pi \cdot (R - \sqrt{2})^2}{\pi R^2} \leq \frac{\text{number of lattice points inside } C_R}{\pi R^2} \leq \frac{\pi \cdot (R + \sqrt{2})^2}{\pi R^2}.$$

Letting $R \to +\infty$, we conclude that

$$\frac{\text{number of lattice points inside } C_R}{\pi R^2} \to 1.$$

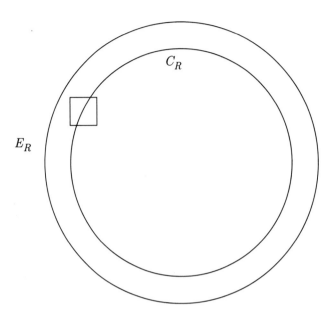

Figure 50

This answers the original question, namely that the asymptotic number of lattice points inside the circle of center zero and radius R is πR^2. But we may refine this answer in an interesting way. For

$$\pi \cdot (R - \sqrt{2})^2 = \pi[R^2 - 2\sqrt{2}R + 2] = \pi R^2 \left[1 - \frac{2\sqrt{2}}{R} + \frac{2}{R^2}\right]$$

and

$$\pi \cdot (R + \sqrt{2})^2 = \pi[R^2 + 2\sqrt{2}R + 2] = \pi R^2 \left[1 + \frac{2\sqrt{2}}{R} + \frac{2}{R^2}\right]$$

Thus

number of lattice points inside $C_R = \pi R^2[1 + \mathcal{E}(R)]$,

where the error term $\mathcal{E}(R)$ is of size not exceeding C/R.   □

PROBLEM 2.1.9 *Prove the Pythagorean theorem.*

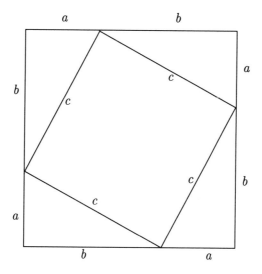

Figure 51

Solution: It is worth noting that this is the theorem in mathematics that has the greatest number of proofs (in excess of 300—see [GUI]). One of the proofs is due to President James A. Garfield! We shall give two proofs of the Pythagorean theorem.

Denote the legs of the right triangle by a and b and let the hypotenuse be c. Refer to Figure 51. Notice that the large outer square has side $a + b$. So it has area $(a + b)^2$.

On the other hand, the large square is made up of four triangles and a smaller square of side c. Each triangle has area $ab/2$ and the smaller square has area c^2. Thus, equating areas, we find that

$$(a + b)^2 = 4 \cdot (ab/2) + c^2.$$

Simplifying gives $a^2 + b^2 = c^2$, which is the Pythagorean theorem.

For a second proof, look at Figure 52. [For convenience, we are assuming in this figure that $b > a$.] Now the large outer square has side c. Thus it has area c^2.

On the other hand, the large square is made up of four triangles and a smaller square. Each triangle has area $ab/2$; the little square has

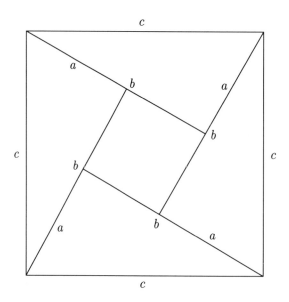

Figure 52

side $(b-a)$ (assuming that $b > a$) hence area $(b-a)^2$. Equating areas, we find that

$$c^2 = 4 \cdot (ab/2) + (b-a)^2.$$

Simplifying gives $c^2 = b^2 + a^2$, which is the Pythagorean theorem. □

CHALLENGE PROBLEM 2.1.10 *Prove the law of sines: if $\triangle ABC$ is a triangle and α, β, γ are the angles at the vertices A, B, C respectively then*

$$\frac{\sin \alpha}{BC} = \frac{\sin \beta}{AC} = \frac{\sin \gamma}{AB}.$$

[*Hint:* Write the height of the triangle in two different ways.]

CHALLENGE PROBLEM 2.1.11 *Prove the law of cosines: given a triangle $\triangle ABC$, if α is the angle determined by sides AB and AC, then*

$$|BC|^2 = |AB|^2 + |AC|^2 - 2|AB|\,|AC|\,\cos \alpha.$$

2.2 Analytic Geometry

In the last section we were concerned primarily with what is called
synthetic geometry, as practiced by Euclid and the ancient Greeks.
In the present section we concentrate on the coordinate geometry of
Descartes. Many problems can be solved using either one of these
methodologies, and you should take it as a challenge to find solutions
in the one geometry when the text presents a solution in the other.

PROBLEM 2.2.1 *Suppose that T is a triangle in the plane. We let
P, Q, R be the midpoints of each of the three sides. Prove that the
triangle determined by P, Q, R is similar to the original triangle T.*

Solution: Two triangles are similar if they have either the same angles
or, equivalently, if their side lengths are proportional. In either case,
one triangle is a magnification of the other.

We concentrate on the angles. If we could show that the triangle
determined by P, Q, R has sides parallel to the sides of T then of course
the angles will be the same (Figure 53 is labeled in such a way as to help
you see this). We have already reduced our problem to the following
simpler assertion

> If $T = \triangle ABC$ is a triangle and M is the midpoint of side
> $\overline{AB}$ and N is the midpoint of side $\overline{AC}$, then the segment
> $\overline{MN}$ is parallel to the side BC (Figure 54).

We use Cartesian geometry to verify this last assertion. It is important when using coordinates to *choose* the coordinates so that they suit
the problem, and so that they help us rather than hinder us. By applying a rotation and a vertical translation to our triangle, we may assume
that the vertices B and C are horizontally situated on the x-axis and
the vertex A above the x-axis. By applying a horizontal translation,
we may then assume that the vertex A is on the positive y-axis. Refer
to Figure 55. We write $A = (0, a)$, $B = (b, 0)$, and $C = (c, 0)$.

The midpoint of side $\overline{AB}$ is now easily calculated to be $M = (b/2, a/2)$. The midpoint of side $\overline{AC}$ is $N = (c/2, a/2)$. Notice that
the slope of $\overline{MN}$ is

$$\frac{a/2 - a/2}{c/2 - b/2} = 0.$$

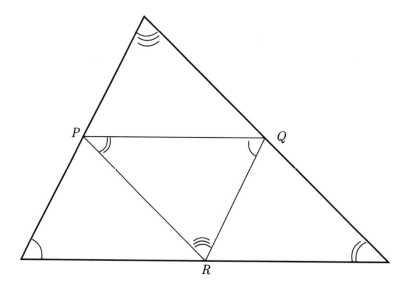

Figure 53

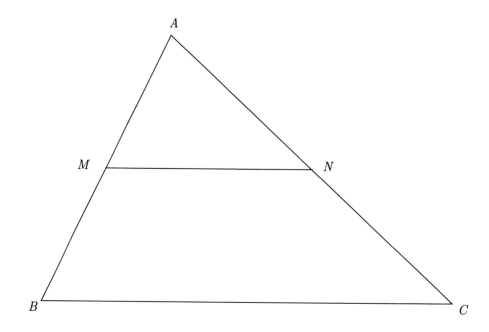

Figure 54

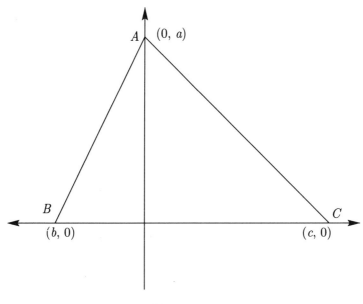

Figure 55

In other words, $\overline{MN}$ is horizontal. But the base BC of the triangle is also horizontal. We conclude that MN is parallel to BC. That is the desired conclusion. □

Note once again that, in the last solution, we have used the methodology of *reduction*: we successively reduced the original problem to more and more basic questions.

PROBLEM 2.2.2 *Prove that any angle subtended by a semi-circle is a right angle.*

Solution: Refer to Figure 56. It serves to remind you what it means for an arc of a circle to subtend an angle. We will also use the figure in our solution to the problem.

We need to introduce some coordinates. We assume that the center of the semi-circle is the origin, the radius is r, and the vertex of the angle in question is $X = (a, b)$ (Figure 57).

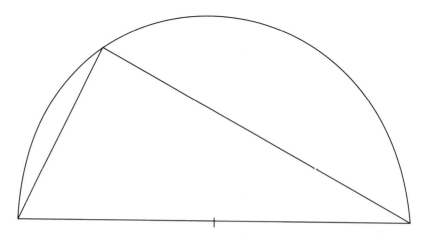

Figure 56

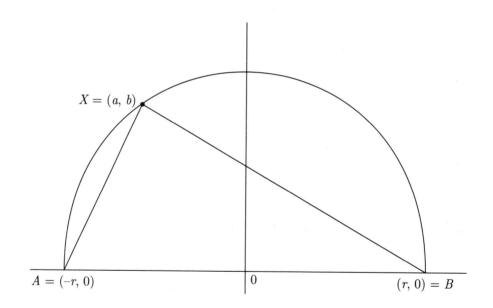

Figure 57

The slope of the segment AX is $(b - 0)/(a - (-r))$. The slope of the segment XB is $(b - 0)/(a - r)$. The product of these two slopes is

$$\frac{b^2}{a^2 - r^2}. \tag{$*$}$$

But, since the point (a, b) lies on the circle, we know that $a^2 + b^2 = r^2$ or $b^2 = r^2 - a^2$. Substituting this identity into $(*)$ yields that the product of the two slopes is -1. We conclude that the two sides of the angle are perpendicular. In other words, the angle is a right angle. $\qquad\square$

CHALLENGE PROBLEM 2.2.3 *Assume that B and C are fixed distinct points in the plane. The letter α denotes an angle between $0°$ and $90°$. Consider the locus of all points P such that the angle $\angle BPC$ has measure α. Show that this locus consists of two circular arcs.*

PROBLEM 2.2.4 TRUE or **FALSE**: *If the diagonals of a parallelogram are perpendicular then the parallelogram is a rectangle.*

Let us be careful about what is being asserted. Figure 58 shows a rectangle whose diagonals are plainly *not* perpendicular to each other. But the assertion is not that every rectangle has perpendicular diagonals. Instead, it is that if a parallelogram has perpendicular diagonals then it is a rectangle.

Solution: We set up coordinates as in Figure 59. Notice that two of the vertices of the parallelogram are $(a, 0)$ and (b, c). The fact that we are dealing with a parallelogram then forces the ordinate of the upper right vertex to be c and the abscissa of the that vertex to be $a + b$. (Of course the lower left vertex is $(0, 0)$.)

The slope of the main diagonal is $c/(a + b)$. The slope of the minor diagonal is $c/(b - a)$. The hypothesis that the diagonals are perpendicular means that the product of these two slopes is -1. Thus

$$\frac{c}{b - a} \cdot \frac{c}{b + a} = -1$$

or

$$c^2 = -(b^2 - a^2).$$

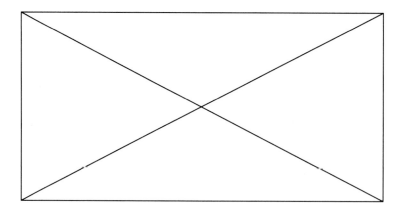

Figure 58

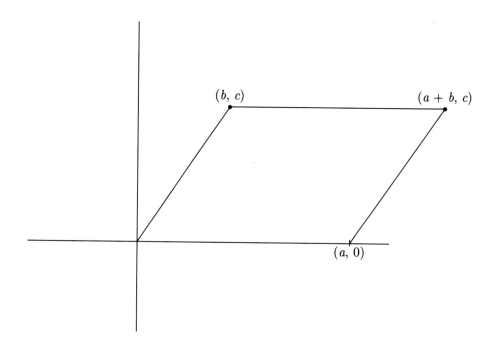

Figure 59

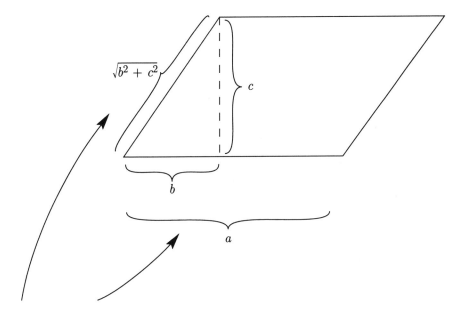

These lengths are equal

Figure 60

This may be rearranged to read

$$b^2 + c^2 = a^2. \tag{$**$}$$

The identity that we have thus derived looks extremely promising, for it has the form of the Pythagorean theorem. This means that the side of the parallelogram with endpoints $(0,0)$ and $(a,0)$ has the same length as the side with endpoints $(0,0)$ and (b,c). See Figure 60. Thus the parallelogram is certainly a rhombus.

However we seem to have used all the information in the problem. Such an eventuality makes us wonder whether we are pursuing the wrong goal. We now draw a few parallelograms by way of experimenting with the assertion of the problem.

The parallelogram in Figure 61 has the property that its diagonals are perpendicular. However it is plainly *not* a rectangle (it is, however, a rhombus). The answer to the problem is **FALSE**. $\square$

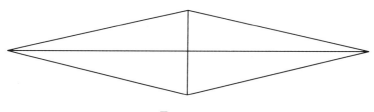

Figure 61

The last problem contains a simple but important lesson: just because a problem has a nice ring to it does not mean that it is correct, or correctly formulated. The problems that we encounter in real life have this property; we never know whether we are asking the correct question, nor whether the question has an affirmative answer (or, often, any answer at all). While these may sound like platitudes, they describe a reality which is virtually impossible to convey with a textbook or a classroom environment.

PROBLEM 2.2.5 *Express the area of a triangle with a formula using only the lengths of the triangle's three sides.*

Solution: We write the side lengths as α, β, γ as shown in Figure 62. We place the triangle on a coordinate system, as shown in Figure 63. Thus $\alpha = \sqrt{a^2 + c^2}$, $\beta = \sqrt{b^2 + c^2}$, and $\gamma = b - a$. Our plan is to express the area in terms of a, b, c, and then translate that to an expression involving only α, β, γ.

Obviously the area of the triangle is

$$A = \text{Area} \; = \; \frac{1}{2} \cdot \text{base} \cdot \text{height}$$

$$= \; \frac{1}{2} \cdot (b - a) \cdot c.$$

Now we know that $b - a = \gamma$ so that our formula for area becomes

$$A = \frac{1}{2} \cdot \gamma \cdot c.$$

Our problem will be solved if we can express c in terms of α, β, γ.

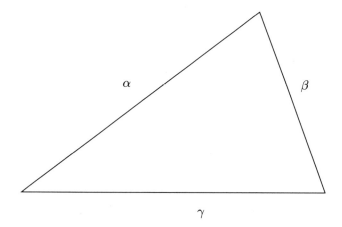

Figure 62

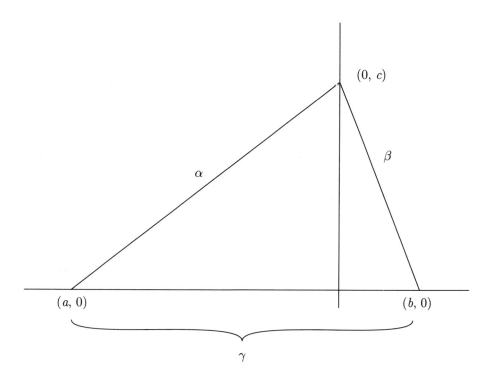

Figure 63

In effect, we are simultaneously solving the equations

$$\begin{aligned}
\alpha^2 &= a^2 + c^2 \\
\beta^2 &= b^2 + c^2 \\
\gamma &= b - a
\end{aligned}$$

for the variable c in terms of α, β, γ. Of course these are not linear equations, so the problem does not bow to any standard technique. We will resort to fiddling (a technique that is *not* to be underestimated).

Looking at the figure, we see that the roles of α and β in the problem are symmetric. Thus we would expect our final expression for c to be symmetric in α and β. Thus it is natural to consider the expression $\alpha^2 + \beta^2$. We subtract γ^2 from it in order to cancel some terms. Thus

$$\alpha^2 + \beta^2 - \gamma^2 = 2c^2 + 2ab. \qquad (*)$$

Another symmetric expression in α and β is $\alpha \cdot \beta$. However this will involve some nasty square roots so instead we consider $\alpha^2 \cdot \beta^2$. Thus

$$\alpha^2 \cdot \beta^2 = (a^2 + c^2) \cdot (b^2 + c^2) = a^2b^2 + a^2c^2 + c^2b^2 + c^4. \qquad (**)$$

Now if we expect to combine $(*)$ and $(**)$ then we have a mismatch. For the terms in $(*)$ are of second order and those in $(**)$ are of fourth order. Thus we consider

$$(\alpha^2 + \beta^2 - \gamma^2)^2 = (2c^2 + 2ab)^2 = 4c^4 + 4a^2b^2 + 8abc^2. \qquad (***)$$

Certainly there are a number of terms in $(***)$ that also appear in $(**)$. In order to obtain useful cancellations, we thus finally calculate

$$\begin{aligned}
4[\alpha^2 \cdot \beta^2] - (\alpha^2 + \beta^2 - \gamma^2)^2 & \\
&= 4[a^2b^2 + a^2c^2 + c^2b^2 + c^4] \\
&\quad -[4c^4 + 4a^2b^2 + 8abc^2] \\
&= 4a^2c^2 + 4b^2c^2 - 8abc^2 \\
&= 4c^2[b - a]^2 \\
&= 4c^2\gamma^2.
\end{aligned}$$

In summary,

$$c = \frac{\sqrt{4[\alpha^2 \cdot \beta^2] - (\alpha^2 + \beta^2 - \gamma^2)^2}}{2\gamma}.$$

Notice that we have succeeded in expressing c in terms of α, β, γ and nothing else.

Finally, the area of the triangle is

$$A = \frac{1}{2}\gamma \cdot c = \frac{1}{4}\sqrt{2\alpha^2\gamma^2 + 2\beta^2\gamma^2 + 2\alpha^2\beta^2 - \alpha^4 - \beta^4 - \gamma^4}. \qquad \square$$

Notice that the formula that we have derived is symmetric in α, β, and γ. That is to say, if we permute the roles of α, β, γ then the formula is unchanged. Think carefully about why this must be the case. Some books of tables (see [CRC]) give the area of the triangle in its more classical form:

$$A = \sqrt{s(s - \alpha)(s - \beta)(s - \gamma)},$$

where $s = (\alpha + \beta + \gamma)/2$, or half the perimeter of the triangle. $\qquad \square$

Take it as a (small) challenge problem to see that the formula that we have derived for A and that taken from [CRC] are really equivalent.

2.3 Miscellaneous and Exotic Geometry Problems

This section will contain a variety of geometry problems—mostly planar geometry—that do not fit into any standard category. They are presented in part with the lesson in mind that human knowledge, and in particular problem solving technique, does not know any seams or boundaries. Even though this book is organized by topics, you should not think of problem solving as being compartmentalized. It is self-defeating to look at a problem and hope to be able to say "Oh, this is a geometry problem and therefore I ought to use these methods." You just never know what methods might be relevant, and your mind should be open to all possibilities.

So, yes, the problems in this section are geometrical. But the techniques for solving them are varied.

PROBLEM 2.3.1 *Say that T is a triangle in the plane. Show that there is a triangle that is similar to T and such that its area equals its perimeter.*

Solution: Let P be the perimeter of the triangle T and let A be its area. For $a > 0$ let aT denote the triangle T with its sides magnified (or shrunk) by a factor of a. For instance, if $a = 2$ then $2T$ has sides that are twice as long as the corresponding sides of the original T; if $a = 1/2$ then $(1/2)T$ has sides that are half the length of the corresponding sides of T; if $a = 1$ then $1T$ is just the triangle T itself.

Consider the graphs, plotted on the same set of axes, of the perimeter $P(a)$ and the area $A(a)$ of the triangle aT. The horizontal axis should be the a-axis and the vertical axis should be either $y = P(a)$ or $y = A(a)$.

Now the perimeter is a *linear* function of a: when the triangle is dilated by a factor of a then each side is dilated by a and therefore the perimeter is multiplies by a. Thus the graph of $P(a)$ is a line passing through the origin and having positive slope; in fact $P(a) = P \cdot a$. By contrast, the area is a *quadratic* function of a: when the triangle is dilated by a factor of a then the base is dilated by a and the height is dilated by a so that the area is dilated by a^2. Thus the graph of $A(a)$ is an upward opening parabola with vertex at the origin; in fact $A(a) = A \cdot a^2$.

One sees immediately from Figure 64 that the graph of $y = P(a)$ and the graph of $y = A(a)$ intersect at two points in the (closed) first quadrant. First, they intersect at the origin; this fact is of no interest. The other point of intersection, namely $a = P/A$, is more significant for our problem. For that is a non-trivial value of a for which the perimeter and the area of aT are equal. And since aT is similar to T, we have solved our problem.   □

PROBLEM 2.3.2 (Advanced) *We write $\gamma : [0, 1] \to \mathbb{R}^2$ for a closed curve that does not cross itself. This notation means that γ is a function, its domain is the interval $[0, 1] \equiv \{x \in \mathbb{R} : 0 \le x \le 1\}$, and its range is the set of ordered pairs of real numbers. We are assuming that $\gamma(0) = \gamma(1)$ but $\gamma(s) \ne \gamma(t)$ otherwise. See Figure 65. Prove that there*

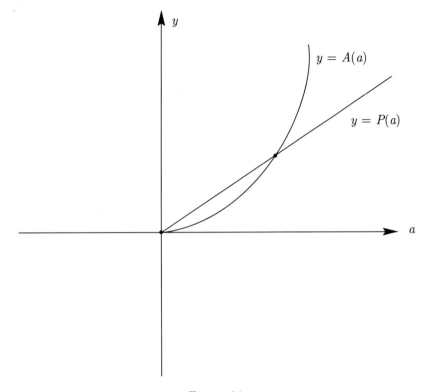

Figure 64

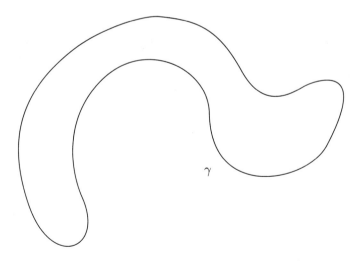

Figure 65

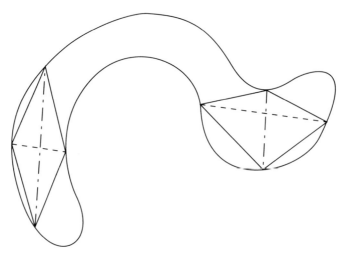

Figure 66

are four points A, B, C, D lying on the curve such that these four points are the vertices of a rectangle.

Solution: Look at Figure 66. At the left is a quadrilateral with vertices on the given curve. At the right there is also a quadrilateral with vertices on the given curve. In each quadrilateral the diagonals are distinguished: one diagonal is dotted and the other is dashed.

Now imagine that the leftmost quadrilateral is continuously deformed to the rightmost quadrilateral by moving the vertices along the curve. The leftmost quadrilateral has dashed diagonal longer than the dotted diagonal. The rightmost quadrilateral has dashed diagonal shorter than the dotted diagonal. It is plausible therefore that at some intermediate position the dotted and the dashed diagonal have equal length (Figure 67). If we could also arrange for these two equal diagonals to meet at their midpoints, then the quadrilateral would have to be a rectangle.

What we have just described is a very simple form of what is called the "continuity method." In fact this argument alone is not sufficient to locate the desired rectangle. We need a more sophisticated continuity method that will keep track both of the lengths of the diagonals and of their centers at the same time. We caution the reader that a couple of

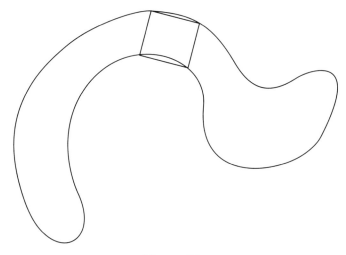

Figure 67

sophisticated ideas are used along the way. Do not expect to completely understand the reasoning the first time through. But take it as an invitation to some new geometrical ideas.

Consider pairs of elements of the curve γ, but identify the pair (P, Q) with the pair (Q, P). In other words, consider *unordered* pairs of elements of γ (we will come back to this idea momentarily, and clarify what geometrical object this actually is). Denote the set of these unordered pairs with the letter S. Denote an element of S, that is an unordered pair of points on γ, by $[P, Q]$.

Now think of the curve γ as lying in the x-y plane in 3 dimensional space. For each $[P, Q] \in S$ we find the midpoint of the segment $\overline{PQ}$ and then let $f([P, Q])$ be the point in space that lies a distance $|P - Q|$ above that midpoint. See Figure 68. This f is a continuous function from S into three dimensional Euclidean space.

Now what geometrical object is S? The set of ordered pairs of elements of γ corresponds in a natural way to a torus—see Figure 69. However we are making the situation more complex by identifying (P, Q) with (Q, P). The markings in Figure 70 (a) suggest how this is done. The resulting geometric object is what is called a "non-orientable" surface—in fact it is a Möbius strip (see Figure 70 (b)).

But the function f is a continuous function of S into three dimen-

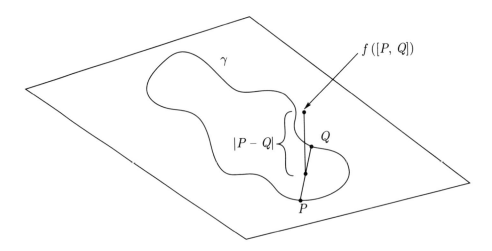

Figure 68

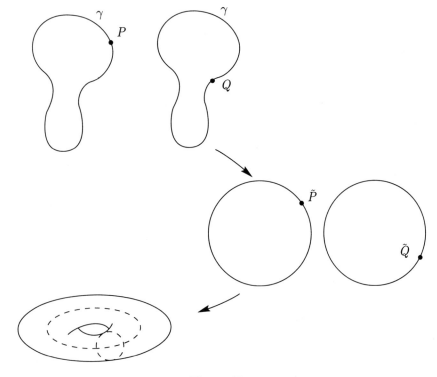

Figure 69

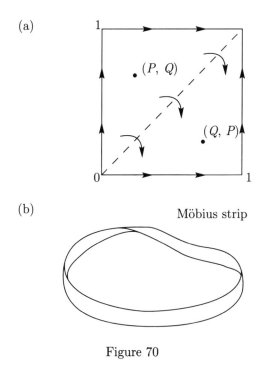

(a)

(b)   Möbius strip

Figure 70

sional space. If f were one-to-one then its image would be a realization of S as a subset of three dimensional space. This is not yet a contradiction, because the torus with the additional identifications that we have specified is equivalent to the Möbius strip. But we now obtain a contradiction as follows. The bounding edge of the embedded surface is a simple closed curve. Paste a topological "disc" to it to make the surface closed. The result is a "cross cap"—in other words it is a realization of the projective plane as an embedded surface in three dimensional space. This is known to be impossible. [You may wish to get some help with this idea.] Therefore f cannot be one-to-one. What does this mean?

It means that there are two (unordered) pairs $[P, Q]$ and $[P', Q']$ that have the same image under f. This means that the segment $\overline{PQ}$ and the segment $\overline{P'Q'}$ have the same midpoint; moreover, it means that $\overline{PQ}$ and $\overline{P'Q'}$ have the same *length*, for the heights of the points $f([P, Q])$ and $f([P', Q'])$ above the x-y plane are the same.

But now look at Figure 71. The segments $\overline{PQ}$ and $\overline{P'Q'}$ having the

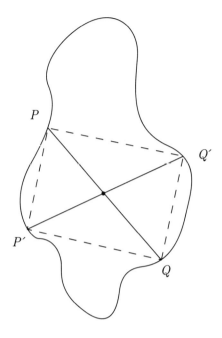

Figure 71

same length and the same midpoint implies that they are the diagonals of a rectangle. In other words, the points P, Q, P', Q' are four points on the curve γ that are the corners of a rectangle.   □

At this writing, it is an open problem to determine whether any curve γ as in Problem 2.3.2 has on it four points that are the corners of a square.

PROBLEM 2.3.3 *Let $P_1, P_2, P_3, \ldots, P_k$ be points in the plane—just finitely many of them—that are not all collinear. Show that there is a line in the plane that passes through just two of these points.*

Solution: Just to illustrate the ideas, look at Figure 72. The first part exhibits three points, not all collinear. It also shows a line that passes through just two of them. The second part of Figure 72 shows

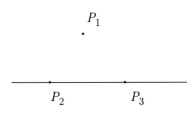

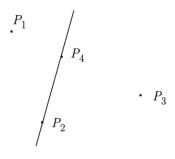

Figure 72

four points, not all collinear. It also show a line that passes through just two of them.

If we are given a large, but finite, collection of points—configured in a fairly arbitrary manner—then how might we find two of them through which a line passes that contains none of the other points P_j? We solve this problem by using one of the most powerful techniques in all of mathematics: that is, we solve an extremal problem.

Consider the set T of all ordered pairs (ℓ, P_m) consisting of a line that passes through *at least* two of the P_j's and a point P_m *not on that line* (such a point P_m must exist since the points are assumed to not all be collinear). Define a function

$$f : T \to \mathbb{R}$$

by

$$f((\ell, P_m)) = \text{distance of } \ell \text{ to } P_m.$$

Notice that f always takes positive values. Also the domain of f is a finite set (since there are only finitely many lines ℓ and finitely many

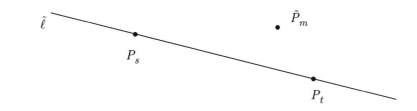

Figure 73

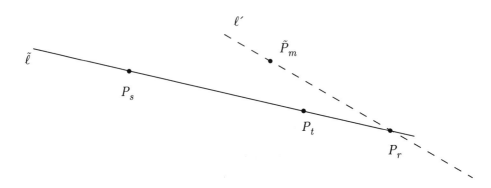

Figure 74

points P_m). Therefore there will be a pair $(\widetilde{\ell}, \widetilde{P_m})$ at which f takes a minimum value. We claim that this line $\widetilde{\ell}$ is the one we seek.

Examine Figure 73. It shows one possible configuration of the line $\widetilde{\ell}$ and the point $\widetilde{P}_m$. Recall that, by definition, $\widetilde{\ell}$ is a line that contains (at least) two of the points P_j. One possible configuration of two of those points is shown in Figure 73. We claim that $\widetilde{\ell}$ could not contain a third point P_r.

If P_r were situated as in Figure 74 then the line ℓ' through $\widetilde{P}_m$ and P_r would be closer to P_t than $\widetilde{P}_m$ is to $\widetilde{\ell}$. That would contradict the minimality of the function f on the pair $(\widetilde{\ell}, \widetilde{P}_m)$. If instead P_r were situated as in Figure 75 then the line ℓ'' through $\widetilde{P}_m$ and P_s would be closer to P_r than $\widetilde{P}_m$ is to $\widetilde{\ell}$. That would contradict the minimality of the function f on the pair $(\widetilde{\ell}, \widetilde{P}_m)$. If instead P_r were situated as in Figure 76 then the line ℓ''' through $\widetilde{P}_m$ and P_r would be closer to P_s than $\widetilde{P}_m$ is to $\widetilde{\ell}$. That would contradict the minimality of the function

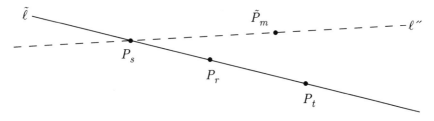

Figure 75

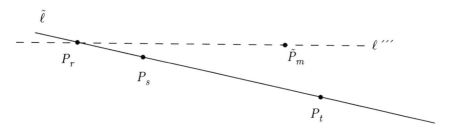

Figure 76

f on the pair $(\widetilde{\ell}, \widetilde{P}_m)$.

We have just argued, in detail, that if the minimal pair $(\widetilde{\ell}, \widetilde{P}_m)$ is configured as in Figure 73, then $\widetilde{\ell}$ can have only two of the P_j's on it. We invite you to consider other possible configurations of $(\widetilde{\ell}, \widetilde{P}_m)$ and argue that no third point P_r could be on the line $\widetilde{\ell}$—otherwise there would be a contradiction to the minimality of the function f on the pair $(\widetilde{\ell}, \widetilde{P}_m)$.

In conclusion, the line $\widetilde{\ell}$ taken from the pair $(\widetilde{\ell}, \widetilde{P}_m)$ that minimizes f is a line passing through just two of the points $P_1, P_2, P_3, \ldots, P_k$. $\square$

CHALLENGE PROBLEM 2.3.4 *Show that the assertion of the last problem can be false if the given collection of points has infinitely many elements.*

Hint: Think about the integer lattice.

CHALLENGE PROBLEM 2.3.5 *Find a solution of the last problem that*

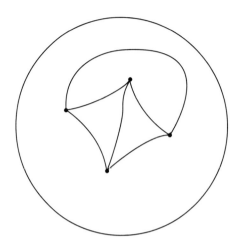

Figure 77

does not rely on an extremal problem, but instead breaks the issue up into cases.

Refer to Section 1.4, Problem 1.4.3, for a discussion of graphs in the sphere and Euler's formula. The *complete graph* on k vertices $P_1, P_2, \ldots, P_k$ is defined to be the graph consisting of all arcs connecting all possible pairs of these points. *No crossings of these arcs are allowed, since crossings would necessitate additional vertices.*

Figure 77 shows the complete graph on four vertices. Notice that we can realize it, as a subset of the sphere, without any additional crossings. Verify for yourself that each of the six possible pairs is connected by an arc, or edge.

PROBLEM 2.3.6 *Verify that it is impossible to realize the complete graph on five vertices as a subset of the sphere.*

Solution: To do this, we will use Euler's formula. Suppose to the contrary that we *could* realize the complete graph as a subset of the sphere. Obviously there would be five vertices, since we are considering the complete graph on five vertices. So $V = 5$. Also there would be ten edges, since the number of possible edges corresponds to the number of possible pairs of vertices and is therefore equal to $\binom{5}{2} = 10$. Thus

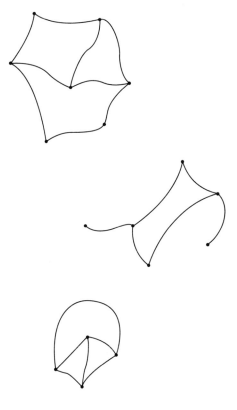

Figure 78

$E = 10$. How many countries would there be? Look at Figure 78. It exhibits several graphs. Notice that it is possible to have a face that has more than three edges only when some pair of vertices is not connected. If all pairs of vertices are connected (and only once for each pair), then all faces are triangles.

Clearly we are in the latter situation. How many triangles are there? Obviously $\binom{5}{3}$ or 10. Thus $F = 10$. By Euler's formula, we have

$$2 = V - E + F = 5 - 10 + 10 = 5.$$

This is plainly absurd. The only possible conclusion is that the complete graph on five vertices *cannot* be realized as a subset of the sphere (the technical terminology is that the complete graph on five vertices

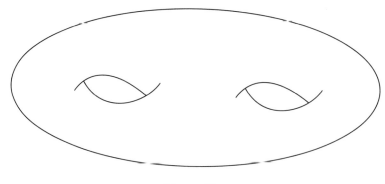

Figure 79

cannot be *imbedded* in the sphere). That solves our problem.   □

CHALLENGE PROBLEM 2.3.7 *Show that the complete graph on five vertices can be imbedded in the torus.*

CHALLENGE PROBLEM 2.3.8 *What is the greatest k such that the complete graph on k vertices can be imbedded in the torus?*

CHALLENGE PROBLEM 2.3.9 *What is the greatest k such that the complete graph on k vertices can be imbedded in the two-holed torus (Figure 79)?*

A segment $\overline{AB}$ is said to be a *chord* of a planar region U if A and B are boundary points of U. In the following discussion we shall only consider closed, convex regions. [A convex region U is one with the property that if points P, Q lie inside U then the segment $\overline{PQ}$ connecting P to Q lies inside U.] Thus the chord will always lie in the region. A point P in the interior of the region is said to be an *equichordal point* if all chords passing through P have the same length.

PROBLEM 2.3.10 *Does every closed, convex region have an equichordal point? Does any closed, convex region have an equichordal point?*

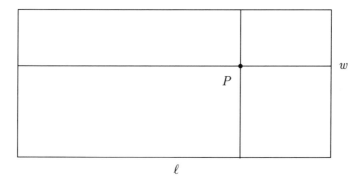

Figure 80

Solution: The rectangle shown in Figure 80 has no equichordal point. To see this, notice that no matter what point P we choose in the interior, there will be a horizontal chord through it of length ℓ and there will also be a vertical chord through it of length w. Since $\ell \neq w$, P will not be an equichordal point.

The disc shown in Figure 81 does have its center P as an equichordal point. Any chord through P will be a diameter of the bounding circle, and all diameters have the same length. □

PROBLEM 2.3.11 *Is there any closed, convex planar figure—other than a disc—that has an equichordal point?*

Solution: Before you read the "official solution," do some experimenting with your pencil and paper (or use your computer graphics know-how, if suitable hardware and software are available to you). Do you have a conjecture as to what the answer is?

In fact there are infinitely many different closed, convex planar figures that have equichordal points. We shall now describe a technique for creating such regions. We begin with the one region that we know that has an equichordal point: the disc in Figure 81. We think of this region as composed of the union of its chords through the origin; this is almost a disjoint union, for the chords only intersect at the origin. Now we will perturb some of those chords.

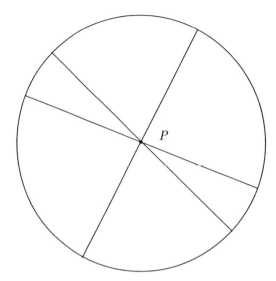

Figure 81

Look at Figure 82. A fairly flat curve has been drawn across the top part of the disc. Now we will take each chord through the origin that intersects that curve and translate it, along itself, in a downward direction until its upper endpoint meets the flattened curve. Figure 83 shows the operation performed on a selection of chords. The result of translating all these (infinitely many) segments is the new region in Figure 84. Notice that it is still closed and convex, and still equichordal. It has just the same chords as before, except that some of them have been translated downward. Note that the resulting region is *not* a disc. We have succeeded in creating a new region with an equichordal point.   □

CHALLENGE PROBLEM 2.3.12 *Create a new closed, convex region that has an equichordal point by taking a chord of fixed length (say a needle dipped in ink) and moving it through 360° while keeping the needle passing through a fixed point. One region that you should be able to generate in this fashion is a "rounded triangle."*

"It has recently been proved by Marek R. Rychlik[1] that there does

---

[1]Marek R. Rychlik, A complete solution to the equichodal point problem of Fujiwara, Blaschke, Rothe and Weizenböck, *Inventiones Math.* 129 (1997), 141–212.

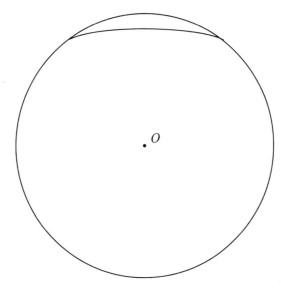

Figure 82

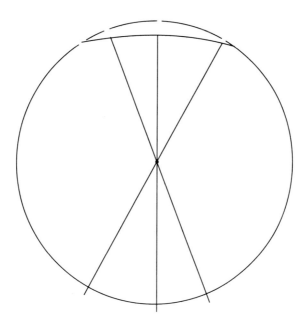

Figure 83

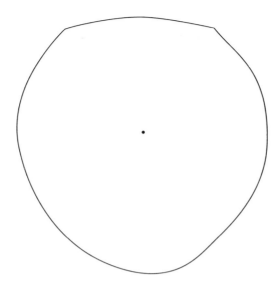

Figure 84

not exist a closed, convex planar region with two equichordal points.

PROBLEM 2.3.13 (Bertrand's Paradox) *Fix a circle of radius 1. Draw the inscribed equilateral triangle as shown in Figure 85. We let ℓ denote the length of a side of this triangle. Suppose that a chord d (with length m) of the circle is chosen "at random." What is the probability that the length m of d exceeds the length ℓ of a side of the inscribed triangle?*

Solution: The "paradox" is that this problem has three equally valid solutions. We now present these apparently contradictory solutions in sequence. At the end we shall explain why it is possible for a problem like this to have three distinct solutions.

Solution 1: Examine Figure 86. It shows a shaded, open disc whose boundary circle is internally tangent to the inscribed equilateral triangle. If the center of the random chord d lies *inside* that shaded disc, then $m > \ell$. If the center of the random chord d lies *outside* that shaded disc, then $m \leq \ell$. Thus the probability that the length d is greater than

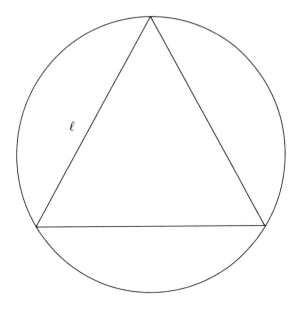

Figure 85

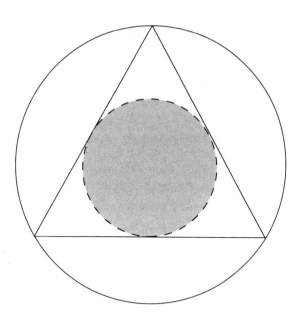

Figure 86

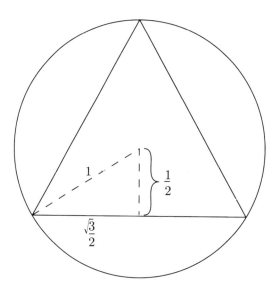

Figure 87

the length ℓ is

$$\frac{\text{area of shaded disc}}{\text{area of unit disc}}.$$

But an analysis of the equilateral triangle (Figure 87) shows that the shaded disc has radius $1/2$ hence area $\pi/4$. The larger unit disc has area π. The ratio of these areas is $1/4$. We conclude that the probability that the length of the randomly chosen chord exceeds ℓ is $1/4$.

Solution 2: Examine Figure 88. We may as well assume that our randomly chosen chord is horizontal (other positions of the chord may be analyzed in a similar fashion). Notice that if the height, from the base of the triangle, of the chord d is less than or equal to $1/2$ then $m \leq \ell$ while if the height is greater than $1/2$ (and not more than 1) then $m > \ell$. We thus see that there is probability $1/2$ that the length m of d exceeds the length ℓ of a side of the equilateral triangle.

Solution 3: Examine Figure 89. We may as well assume that one vertex of our randomly chosen chord occurs at the lower left vertex A of the inscribed triangle. Now look at the angle θ that the chord subtends with the tangent line to the circle at the vertex A (shown in

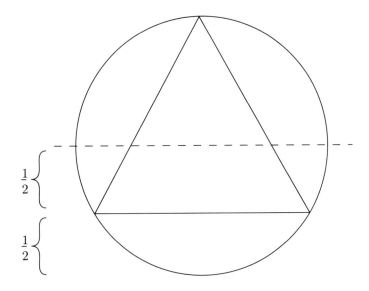

$\frac{1}{2}$

$\frac{1}{2}$

Figure 88

the Figure 90). If that angle is between 0° and 60° inclusive then the chord is shorter than or equal to ℓ. If the angle is strictly between 60° and 120° then the chord is longer than ℓ. Finally, if the angle is between 120° and 180° inclusive then the chord is shorter than ℓ. In sum we see that the probability is $60/180 = 1/3$ that the randomly chosen chord has length exceeding ℓ.

How can a perfectly reasonable problem have three distinct solutions: probabilities $1/4, 1/3, 1/2$? And be assured that each of these solutions is correct! The answer is that, when one is dealing with a probability space having infinitely many elements (that is to say, a problem in which there are infinitely many outcomes—in this case there are infinitely many positions for the random chord) then there are infinitely many different ways to fairly assign probabilities to those different outcomes.

For many years, because of paradoxes such as these, the subject of probability theory was in ill repute. It was not until the invention of a branch of mathematics called "measure theory" (Henri Lebesgue, 1906) that the tools became available to put probability theory on a

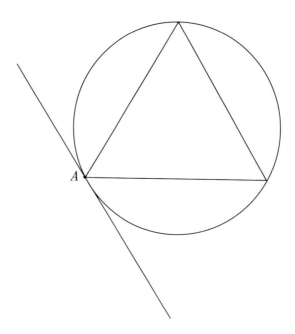

Figure 89

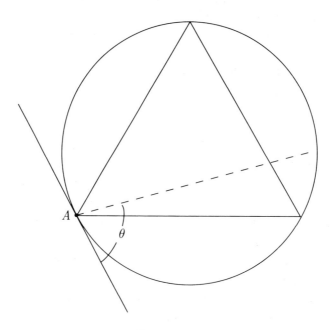

Figure 90

rigorous footing. Problems like these are treated in an advanced course on probability.

2.4 Solid Geometry

It is no longer the case that solid geometry is a basic part of the high school or the college mathematics curriculum. Spherical trigonometry is another venerable subject that has fallen by the wayside. Nevertheless, we all have some exposure to solid geometry through our calculus course and our real variable course. The problems in this section presuppose no particular special knowledge of solid geometry. Some of their solutions will require ideas that we have introduced earlier in this book. Others will just require determination and insight.

PROBLEM 2.4.1 *A polyhedron is a solid whose boundary surface consists of the union of finitely many planar polygons. Examples are the Platonic solids such as the cube or the tetrahedron or the dodecahedron. We will restrict our attention to polyhedra that are "topologically trivial"—this just means that they have no holes. For example, we would not consider a polyhedron that was shaped like a donut, or like a cylinder.*

Show that a polyhedron with three triangular faces meeting at each vertex must in fact have a total of four faces.

Solution: We reason using the formula of Euler that we discovered in Section 1.4: $V - E + F = 2$. We proved this formula for a graph on a sphere, but it is not difficult to see that any polyhedron may be continuously deformed so that its boundary lies on a sphere. So the formula applies to the polyhedron being considered in the present problem.

We let V denote the number of vertices. We observe that there are three triangular faces meeting at each vertex. So there are three edges meeting at each vertex. Does it follow that $E = 3V$? Not quite, because this would mean that we counted each edge twice, once for the vertex on either end. What is true, then, is that $E = 3V/2$.

Likewise, since three triangular faces meet at each vertex, we may be tempted to say that $F = 3V$. But this would count every face three

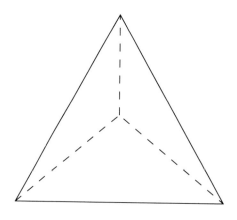

Figure 91

times: once for each vertex. So what is true is that $F = 3V/3 = V$. Euler's formula now becomes

$$2 = V - E + F = V - 3V/2 + V$$

or

$$V = 4.$$

We conclude that our polyhedron has 4 vertices. Thus it has $E = 3V/2 = 6$ edges and $F = V = 4$ faces. It is a classical tetrahedron (see Figure 91).   □

CHALLENGE PROBLEM 2.4.2 *Show that if a polyhedron has all square faces, three meeting at each vertex, then the polyhedron must be a cube.*

CHALLENGE PROBLEM 2.4.3 *Consider a polyhedron with three pentagonal faces meeting at each vertex. What can you conclude about the number of faces?*

CHALLENGE PROBLEM 2.4.4 *Explain why it is impossible to have a polyhedron with 6 triangular faces meeting at each vertex.*

CHALLENGE PROBLEM 2.4.5 *Consider a polyhedron with 5 triangular faces meeting at each vertex. How many faces will it have?*

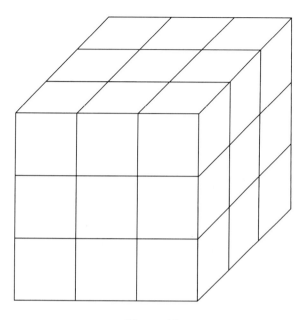

Figure 92

PROBLEM 2.4.6 *Imagine a wooden cube, of side 3″, with four parallel lines on each face as shown in Figure 92.*

How many straight cuts with a saw are needed to cut apart all 27 cubes delineated by the lines? What is the minimal number of cuts required?

Solution: Notice that we may actually cut along two parallel lines of one face, cutting the cube into three slices that are each one cube thick. See Figure 93.

Keeping the slices stacked, we may then cut through two parallel lines on the top slice, thus cutting the wood into nine strips of three (Figure 94). Finally, keeping the strips stacked together, we may make two more cuts (as indicated in Figure 95) to cut apart all the cubes. We have used a total of *six* cuts to separate all 27 subcubes from each other. The question is whether we can accomplish the job with *fewer* than six cuts.

The answer is "no." Notice that the *center* cube has six faces. Separating each of those faces from its surrounding wood will require

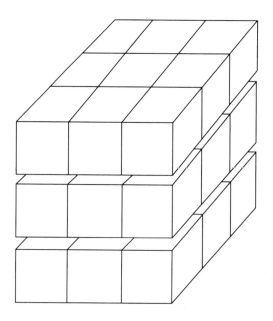

Figure 93

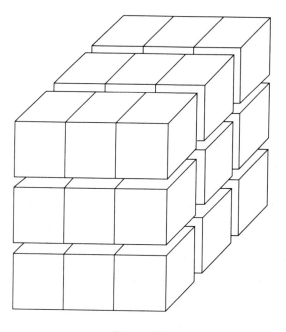

Figure 94

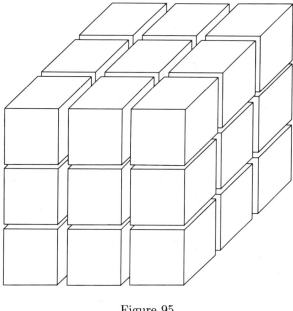

Figure 95

a separate cut. Thus we cannot get away with fewer than six cuts, no matter how clever we are at stacking the cut wood. □

PROBLEM 2.4.7 *Consider a unit cube with four of its eight vertices joined to form a regular tetrahedron with vertices A, B, C, D (Figure 96). What is the ratio of the surface area of the cube to the surface area of the tetrahedron?*

Solution: Plainly the cube has six faces, each with area 1. So the cube has surface area 6.

The tetrahedron has four faces each of which is an equilateral triangle. The side of each of those triangles, using the Pythagorean theorem, is $\sqrt{2}$. Now an equilateral triangle with side length a has height $\sqrt{3}a/2$ (see Figure 97). Thus it has area $\sqrt{3}a^2/4$. In our case, $a = \sqrt{2}$. Thus each face of the tetrahedron has area $\sqrt{3}/2$. [Alternatively, at this point, we could use the formula derived in Problem 2.2.5 for the area of a triangle in terms of the lengths of its sides.] Since there are four such faces on the tetrahedron, it has surface area $2\sqrt{3}$.

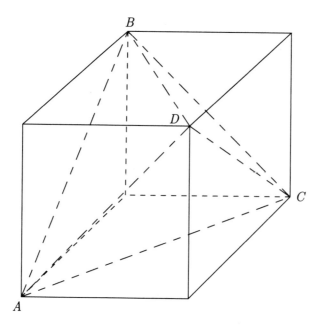

Figure 96

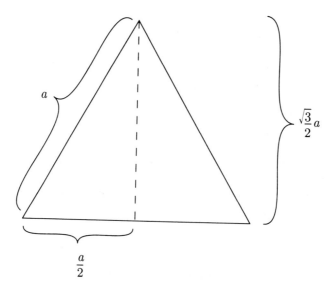

Figure 97

Finally, the ratio of the surface area of the cube to the surface area of the tetrahedron is

$$\text{Ratio} = \frac{6}{2\sqrt{3}} = \frac{3}{\sqrt{3}} = \sqrt{3}. \qquad \Box$$

CHALLENGE PROBLEM 2.4.8 *In the last problem, find the ratio of the volume of the box to the volume of the tetrahedron. [Hint: Do not calculate!]*

PROBLEM 2.4.9 *A right circular cone, as shown in Figure 98, has a cube inscribed in it. If the radius of the cone is 1, and its height is 3, then what is the volume of the cube?*

Solution: It is natural to try to find the side length of the cube. Examine Figure 99, in which certain triangles are emphasized. The triangles are similar, because their sides are parallel. Notice that α denotes half the length of the diagonal of the base of the cube (the distance from a corner of the base to the center of the base).

Now look at the smaller triangle. There are a number of useful relationships. Certainly $\alpha + \beta = 1$. Also $\alpha^2 + \alpha^2 = h^2$. And $h = 3\beta$ by the similarity of the triangles.

We have three equations in three unknowns, and we may attempt to solve them.

Substituting the last equation into the second gives

$$2\alpha^2 = 9\beta^2$$

or

$$\alpha = \frac{3}{\sqrt{2}}\beta.$$

Substituting this result into the first of our equations yields

$$\frac{3}{\sqrt{2}}\beta + \beta = 1.$$

Thus $\beta = \frac{\sqrt{2}}{3+\sqrt{2}}$. It follows immediately that

$$h = 3\beta = \frac{3\sqrt{2}}{3 + \sqrt{2}} = \frac{6}{3\sqrt{2} + 2}.$$

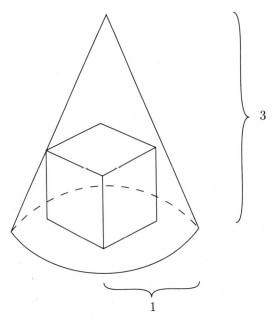

Figure 98

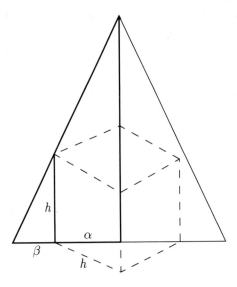

Figure 99

But then the volume of the inscribed cube is

$$V = h^3 = \left[\frac{6}{3\sqrt{2}+2}\right]^3 = \frac{108}{45\sqrt{2}+58}.$$

This is the desired result.   □

PROBLEM 2.4.10 *A subset U of three dimensional space is called convex if, whenever A and B are points of U then the segment connecting A to B lies in U. A convex set is called closed if it contains all its boundary points.*

A point P in a closed convex set U is called extreme if no non-trivial line segment lying in U contains P in its interior.

As an example, consider the set V consisting of the unit sphere together with its interior. This is a closed, solid ball. Intuitively, this is a closed convex set. No point of the interior is extreme since any interior point lies in a short segment that still lies in the interior. Any boundary point is extreme, because the boundary has positive curvature: if P is a boundary point and if ℓ were a segment in V containing P then ℓ would have to lie in the boundary of V. But then ℓ would have to have zero length.

Explain why every closed, bounded, convex set W must have at least one extreme point.

Solution: This problem is a good exercise in non-constructive reasoning. Since you do not know what W looks like, how could you possibly identify the extreme point (assuming that it exists)? Well, you cannot.

So we must reason differently. Consider the collection of all closed balls (spheres with their interiors) that are centered at the origin and which contain W. Such closed balls must exist, since W is bounded. In fact if $P \in W$ and if d is the diameter of W then the closed ball with center at the origin and radius $\|P\| + d$ will certainly contain W. Now let E be the intersection of all these closed balls.

First, E will still contain W since each of the balls that was intersected to make E contains W. Second, E is still a closed ball centered at 0. There must be a point Q that is both in the boundary of E and in

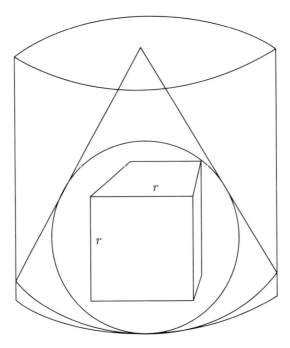

Figure 100

the boundary of W (otherwise we could make E smaller, which would be a contradiction). That point Q is certainly an extreme point for E, as the earlier discussion shows. Therefore it must be an extreme point for W.   □

PROBLEM 2.4.11 *A cube of side r is inscribed in a sphere. The sphere is inscribed in a cone with side length equal to the diameter of its base. The cone is inscribed in a right circular cylinder. What is the surface area of the cylinder (including top and bottom)?*

Solution: Refer to Figure 100. The sphere has diameter $\sqrt{3}r$—just the major diagonal of the cube—hence it has radius $[\sqrt{3}/2]r$. A simple diagram (Figure 101) shows that the cone must have base of diameter $3r$—hence side length $3r$. Thus the right circular cylinder has radius $[3/2]r$ and height $[3\sqrt{3}/2]r$.

In conclusion, the surface area of the cylinder is

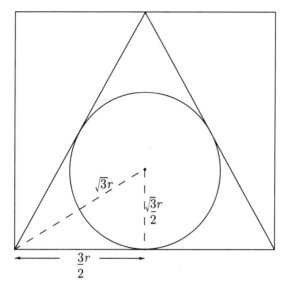

Figure 101

$$2\pi(\text{radius})^2 + \pi(\text{radius})(\text{height}) = 2\pi\left(\frac{3r}{2}\right)^2 + 2\pi\frac{3r}{2}\cdot\frac{3\sqrt{3}r}{2}$$
$$= \frac{9}{2}\pi r^2 \cdot \left[1 + \sqrt{3}\right].$$

That concludes the solution of this problem. □

PROBLEM 2.4.12 (The Platonic Solids)   *The classical term "Platonic Solid" is used to denote a polyhedron in three dimensional space with the property that (i) all faces are regular polygons and are congruent, (ii) the same number of faces meet at each vertex. An example is the cube. The cube has six faces that are squares. Three faces meet at each vertex.*

Find all the Platonic solids.

Solution: What is amazing is that there are a total of just five Platonic solids, and we can find them all. To do so, we exploit the formula of

Euler that we studied in Section 1.4:

$$V - E + F = 2.$$

Recall that V is the number of vertices, E the number of edges, and F the number of faces. We think of the edges and vertices of the Platonic solid as forming an admissible graph on the surface of the Platonic solid (which, topologically, is the same as a sphere).

Because we are describing a *regular polyhedron*, there are certain relationships among V, E, and F. We let m be the number of edges to a face, and let k be the number of edges that meet at any vertex.

First of all, since each face has m edges, we might think that $m \cdot F$ describes the total number of edges. However this is not quite right because each edge bounds two faces (one on each side of the edge) so we have counted each edge twice. Thus

$$E = \frac{m \cdot F}{2}. \tag{$*$}$$

Second, each face has m vertices (since it has m edges). But the quantity $m \cdot F$ counts each vertex k times, since each vertex is the meeting place of k edges, hence of k faces. Thus

$$V = \frac{m \cdot F}{k}. \tag{$**$}$$

Substituting ($*$) and ($**$) into Euler's formula yields

$$\frac{m \cdot F}{k} - \frac{m \cdot F}{2} + F = 2.$$

Multiplying through by $2k$ and factoring on the left side gives

$$F \cdot (2m + 2k - mk) = 4k. \tag{$\dagger$}$$

It turns out that ($\dagger$) is a very rich formula that tells us everything that we want to know. Now we proceed by numbered steps:

(1) It cannot be that both $m \geq 4$ and $k \geq 4$. If both inequalities held and if $m \geq k$ then

$$mk \geq 4m$$

and
$$mk \geq 4k.$$

Multiplying each inequality by $1/2$ and adding gives

$$mk \geq 2m + 2k.$$

This makes the left side of (†) less than or equal to zero, which is impossible (since the right side is positive). A similar contradiction would result if $k \geq m$. Thus, in what follows, we may assume that *either* $m < 4$ or $k < 4$.

(2) We cannot have either $k > 5$ or $m > 5$. First consider the case $k > 5$. Then, by the preceding step, $m \leq 3$. But $m = 1$ or $m = 2$ make no sense (since a polygonal face cannot have just one side or two sides). Thus if $k > 5$ then $m = 3$. Putting this information into the left side of (†) gives

$$F \cdot (2 \cdot 3 + 2k - 3k) = 4k$$

or

$$F \cdot (6 - k) = 4k.$$

But $k > 5$ makes the left side less than or equal to zero, which is again impossible.

A similar argument, which we omit, shows that $m > 5$ cannot be allowed.

(3) We have learned so far that both m and k must be less than or equal to 5, and they cannot both be greater than or equal to 4. Thus there are only finitely many cases to consider:

$$
\begin{array}{ll}
m = 3 & k = 3, 4, 5 \\
m = 4 & k = 3 \\
m = 5 & k = 3
\end{array}
$$

Note that $m = 1, 2$ make no sense geometrically, and neither do $k = 1, 2$. This limits our choices.

(4) We see that there are just five cases to consider, and each gives rise to a platonic solid:

(a) If $m = 3, k = 3$ then equation (†) yields that $F = 4$. This data corresponds to a polyhedron with four faces, each a triangle. And three triangles meet at each vertex. This is the *tetrahedron* (Figure 102a).

(b) If $m = 3, k = 4$ then equation (†) yields that $F = 8$. This data corresponds to a polyhedron with eight faces, each a triangle. And four triangles meet at each vertex. This is the *octahedron* (Figure 102b).

(c) If $m = 3, k = 5$ then equation (†) yields that $F = 20$. This data corresponds to a polyhedron with twenty faces, each a triangle. And five triangles meet at each vertex. This is the *icosahedron* (Figure 102c).

(d) If $m = 4, k = 3$ then equation (†) yields that $F = 6$. This data corresponds to a polyhedron with six faces, each a square. And four squares meet at each vertex. This is the *cube* (Figure 102d).

(e) If $m = 5, k = 3$ then equation (†) yields that $F = 12$. This data corresponds to a polyhedron with twelve faces, each a pentagon. And three pentagons meet at each vertex. This is the *dodecahedron* (Figure 102e).

This completes our description of the five Platonic solids.   □

Now we shall enunciate and solve the problem that was described at the end of Section 1.2.

PROBLEM 2.4.13 *Imagine five planes in three dimensional space in "general position" (refer to Section 1.2 for a discussion of the concept of general position). Into how many regions will these planes divide space?*

Solution: We will use a form of induction. Our starting fact, as determined at the end of Section 1.2, is that three lines in general position in a plane will divide that plane into 7 regions (Figure 103).

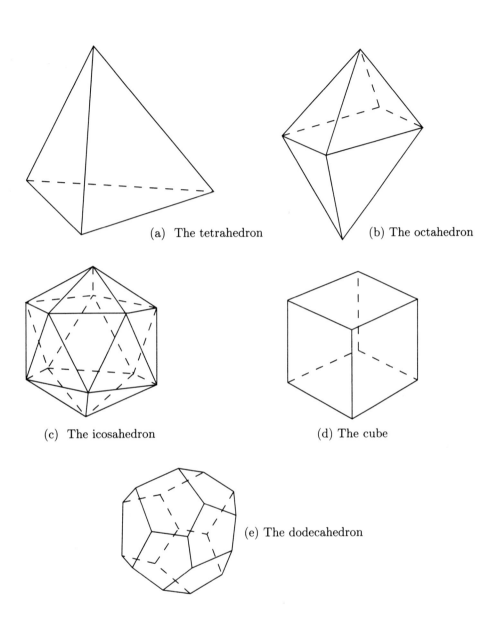

(a) The tetrahedron

(b) The octahedron

(c) The icosahedron

(d) The cube

(e) The dodecahedron

Figure 102

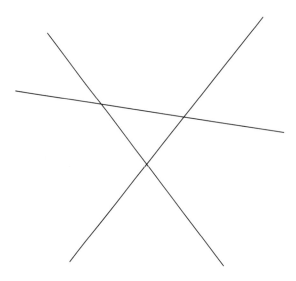

Figure 103

Now suppose that a fourth line in general position is added in this plane (Figure 104). Notice that this line intersects each of the original three lines just once. Thus there are three points of intersection on the new line. These three points separate the new line into four segments. Each of those four segments divides one of the existing planar regions in two. So there are now four new regions. This gives a total of $7 + 4 = 11$ regions. That is the number of regions into which four lines, in general position, divide the plane.

Now we apply what we learned in the last paragraph to the originally posed problem. Clearly two planes in general position (that is, not parallel to each other) divide space into four regions (Figure 105). Now add a plane. That plane will intersect each of the original two planes in a line. This will result in two lines in general position in the third, added plane. Two lines in general position in that plane divide the plane into four regions (refer to Section 1.2). Each of those four planar regions will divide one of the four spatial regions resulting from the first two planes into two. This creates four new regions. So we have a total of $4 + 4 = 8$ regions into which three planes in general position divide space. Examine Figure 106 to confirm our calculations. It will

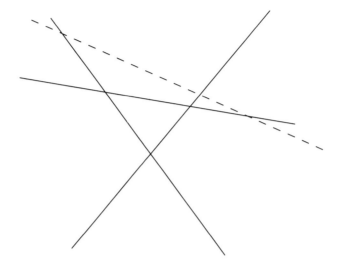

Figure 104

be the last figure you see, for now it becomes too difficult to draw good figures. We must rely on our reasoning instead.

Fix three planes in general position in space as in the last paragraph. This divides space, as we have learned, into eight spatial regions. Now add a fourth plane. This plane will intersect each of the original three planes in a line. This gives three lines, in general position, in the newly added plane. Three such lines divide the newly added plane into 7 planar regions. Each of these planar regions divides one of the eight spatial regions into two. Thus the total number of spatial regions is increased by seven. We have a total number of $8 + 7 = 15$ spatial regions.

The next step, almost impossible to visualize, is now easy. Now we add a fifth plane in general position. It intersects each of the four existing planes in a line. The result is four lines in general position in the new plane. Said lines will divide the new plane into 11 planar regions, as we learned in the first paragraph. Each of those planar regions will divide an existing spatial region into two. This creates 11 new spatial regions. Thus the total number of spatial regions that we have is $15 + 11 = 26$.

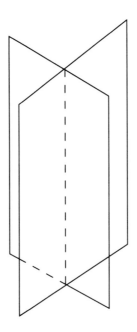

Figure 105

The answer to our problem is that 5 planes in general position in three dimensional space separate space into 26 regions.   □

CHALLENGE PROBLEM 2.4.14 *Devise a formula for the number of regions into which k planes in general position divides three dimensional space.*

CHALLENGE PROBLEM 2.4.15 *[You can think about this problem if you are accustomed to thinking about spaces of dimension four or higher. You may wish to seek guidance in thinking about this problem.] Devise a formula for the number of regions into which k subspaces of dimension $n - 1$ in general position divide n-dimensional space.*

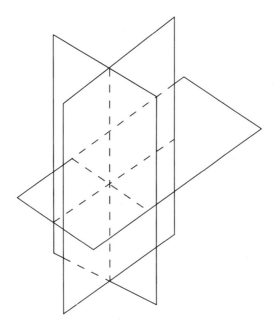

Figure 106

EXERCISES for Chapter 2

1. It is a theorem of Appel and Haken that any graph drawn on the sphere can be colored with at most four colors. Here one colors the *vertices* of the graph: the rule is that any two vertices joined by an edge must have different colors. The number 4 is called the *chromatic number* of the sphere because (i) no graph will require more than 4 colors and (ii) there is a graph that *does* require 4 colors.

   a) Exhibit a graph on the sphere that really does require 4 colors, and explain why four colors are necessary.

   b) Exhibit a graph on the torus that requires 7 colors.

   c) Make a conjecture for the chromatic number of a torus with two holes.

2. Suppose that the plane is divided into regions by drawing finitely many circles. The circles may intersect or not, and may have different radii and, of course, different centers. How many colors are needed to always be sure that such a collection of regions may always be colored— so that no two adjacent regions are the same color? [Remember that

for two regions to be adjacent they must share a portion of an edge, not just a vertex.]

3. A circle of radius 1 is inscribed in an equilateral triangle of suitable size. Then three more circles are inscribed between the first circle and the two sides of the triangle near each vertex. The process continues indefinitely, with progressively smaller circles. What is the sum of the radii of all the circles?

4. Take Q to be a closed unit square (i.e. each side has length 1), together with its interior. Take five distinct points, at random, in Q. Show that some two of the points are no more than $\sqrt{2}/2$ units apart.

5. Assume that n is a positive integer. How many triangles, with integral side lengths, are there such that the longest side has length n?

6. The perimeter of a certain right triangle is 60 inches. The height perpendicular to the hypotenuse is 12 inches. What are the lengths of the three sides of the triangle?

7. Imagine a huge rectangular table. There are two interesting ways to pack the table with pennies.

1. One is to configure the pennies in rows and columns. Each penny has four neighbors: two on the left and right and two above and below. The lines radiating out from the center of any given penny through the centers of its four neighbors form 90° angles with each other. This is the *rectilinear packing*.

2. One is to let each penny have six neighbors. The lines radiating out from the center of any given penny through the centers of its six neighbors form 60° angles with each other. This is the *hexagonal packing*.

Compare the merits of these two packings. Which is more efficient at covering the table (i.e. leaves the least percentage of uncovered space)? Compute, asymptotically, the percentage of the plane covered by each packing.

8. The plane can be tiled with regular hexagons that are $1''$ on a side. Here, by "tiled," we mean that the plane can be filled up with these hexagonal tiles in a non-overlapping fashion with no space remaining. Draw a figure to show how this tiling would be accomplished. Explain

why the plane *cannot* be tiled by regular pentagons that are $1''$ on a side.

9. Refer to Exercise 8 for terminology. We let T be any fixed triangle. Can the plane be tiled by tiles that are all congruent to T?

10. Refer to Exercise 8 for terminology. Suppose that R is a rectangle with rational side lengths. Demonstrate that the plane can be tiled with tiles congruent to R in *infinitely many different ways*.

11. Take U to be a closed, bounded set in the plane. The *diameter* of U is the greatest distance between any two points of U. **TRUE** or **FALSE**: If U has diameter d then there is a closed disc of diameter d that contains U.

12. Fix real numbers $\alpha < \beta$. Define $S = \{(x,y) \in \mathbb{R}^2 : \alpha \leq x \leq \beta\}$. We call the set S a *strip* of width $\beta - \alpha$. Any set that can be obtained by rotating S is also called a strip. We say that a closed set X has *width* d if it is contained in some strip of width d. What is the connection between the concept of width d and the concept of diameter d? Does a set of width d have diameter at most d? Or is the opposite true? Give examples.

13. We take X and Y to be planar sets. Define $X + Y = \{x + y : x \in X, y \in Y\}$. We call $X + Y$ the *sum* of X and Y. If X and Y are each convex sets then is their sum convex? If X and Y each have diameter at most d then what can you say about the diameter of $X + Y$? If X and Y each have width at most d, then what can you say about the width of $X + Y$? [Refer to Exercises 11 and 12 for terminology.]

14. Refer to Exercise 13 for terminology. How is the area of $X + Y$ related to the area of X and the area of Y?

15. Let S be a closed, bounded set in the plane. Define $2S$ to be the set of all $\{(2x, 2y) : (x,y) \in S\}$. How is the area of $2S$ related to the area of S? Does the original position of S have any bearing on your answer?

16. Assume that S is a closed, bounded set in the plane—not containing the origin. Define $S' = \{s/\|s\|^2 : s \in S\}$. What is the relationship between the area of S and the area of S'?

17. Answer Exercise 13 for subsets of the line.

18. Take a $1''$ long sewing needle. Dip it in ink. Place it on a piece of paper, and move it in the plane of the paper so that the ends switch position. How can you do this so that the ink blot that you leave is

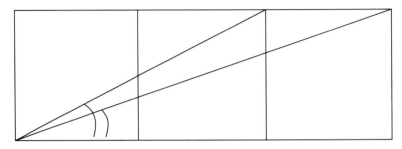

Figure 107

as small in area as possible? This is the classical formulation of the celebrated Kakeya Needle Problem. The surprising answer is that, if $\epsilon > 0$, then there is a way to move the needle through $180°$ so that the ink blot left behind has area smaller than ϵ. Do some experiments and see how small an inkblot you can create. See [CUN].

19. Look at the two angles depicted in Figure 107. Show that the sum of these two angles is $45°$. [*Hint:* One method is to use trigonometry; another is to use a reflection.]

20. Show that the diagonals of a quadrilateral are perpendicular if and only if the sum of the squares of one pair of opposite sides of the quadrilateral equal the sum of the squares of the other pair of opposite sides.

21. If triangle T lies inside a polygon P then explain why the perimeter of the triangle does not exceed the perimeter of P.

22. The lengths of the sides of a triangle form a sequence of positive integers: $n, (n+1), (n+2)$. The area of the triangle is 6. Find the sides and the angles of the triangle.

23. Suppose that $\triangle ABC$ is a right triangle. Explain why there must exist a point N inside the triangle such that the angles $\angle NBC$, $\angle NCA$, and $\angle NAB$ are equal.

24. Look at the triangular figures, subdivided into smaller triangles, in Figure 108. Notice that the first figure has one "row" of smaller triangles, and the total number of smaller triangles is 1. In the next figure, the (first) two rows together have a total of $2^2 = 4$ smaller triangles. In the next figure, the (first) three rows together have a total of $3^2 = 9$ smaller triangles. The pattern continues: the first n rows

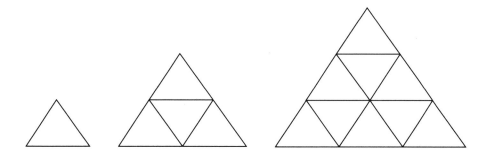

Figure 108

together have a total of n^2 smaller triangles. Explain why this is so.

25. Suppose that T is an equilateral triangle and let P be any point interior to T. We write a, b, c for the distances of P to each of the three sides of T. Then show that $a + b + c = h$, the altitude of T.

26. We let $T_{x,y}$ be a triangle with side lengths $x, y, 1$ and such that $x \leq y \leq 1$. Think of a correspondence between this triangle and the point (x, y) in the plane.

1. Sketch all those points (x, y) that correspond to valid triangles.

2. Sketch all those points (x, y) that correspond to isosceles triangles.

3. Sketch all those points (x, y) that correspond to equilateral triangles.

4. Sketch all those points (x, y) that correspond to right triangles.

27. A right triangle has sides of length $\ell, m, 10$. Note that 10 is *not* the hypotenuse, and that both ℓ and m are integers. Given this information, find ℓ and m.

28. Show that if two medians of a triangle are equal then the triangle is isosceles. [*Hint:* Let the two equal medians emanate from vertices A and B. Call them AP and BQ. Write X for the point of intersection of the two equal medians. Then $AX = (2/3)AP$ and $BX = (2/3)BQ$. Alternatively, use Cartesian geometry.]

29. Prove that if a plane figure has precisely two axes of symmetry then these axes are perpendicular.

30. Prove *Sylvester's theorem*: Given a finite number of points in the plane, if a line drawn through any two of these points always passes through a third, then all the points are collinear.

31. A hole is bored through the center of a solid round ball. The hole, measured at the edge, is six inches in length. What is the volume of that part of the ball that remains? [*Hint*: Note that we are asserting that the answer you obtain will be independent of the radius of the hole, and also independent of the radius of the ball.]

32. Consider a square of side 1. What is the triangle of greatest area that will fit inside it? What happens if "square of side 1" is replaced by "rectangle of area 1"? What happens if "square of side 1" is replaced by "circle of diameter 1"?

33. Pick a point P in the first quadrant. Use this point to determine a triangle in the first quadrant by drawing a line through P that crosses the positive x-axis and the positive y-axis. Which line, depending on the coordinates of P, will give the triangle of least area?

34. Show that there is a universal constant $C > 0$ with the following property:

If we are given a finite collection of complex numbers $\{a_j\}_{j=1}^{m}$, then there is a subcollection $a_{j_1}, \ldots, a_{j_k}$ such that

$$|a_{j_1} + a_{j_2} + \cdots a_{j_k}| \geq C[|a_1| + |a_2| + \cdots + |a_m|].$$

35. Suppose that S is a closed surface in three space—such as a sphere, a torus, a torus with two holes, etc. We say that S has *genus g* if it has g tunnels: the sphere has genus 0, the standard torus has genus 1, the torus with two holes has genus 2, and so forth. A formula of Heawood, later verified by Ringel and Youngs [RIN] when $g > 0$, says that the *chromatic number* of a closed surface S with genus g is

$$\chi(S) = \left[\frac{1}{2}\left(7 + \sqrt{1 + 48g}\right)\right].$$

Here [ ] denotes the "greatest integer" function. Also, the "chromatic number" of a surface is the least number of colors it will ever take to color any map on that surface. Notice that, for the torus, $g = 1$ and

Heawood's formula gives $\chi = 7$. What answer does it give for a torus with two holes? With three holes? Can you give examples of maps that show that this number is sharp? [*Hint:* Refer to Exercise 1 for suggestions on how to proceed.]

36. Suppose that $a_1, a_2, \ldots$ are infinitely many distinct points in the plane. Suppose that the distance between any two of them is some integer (different pairs will have different integer distances). Show that all of the a_j's must be collinear.

37. We let Q be a convex quadrilateral lying in the plane. Now imagine the plane sitting in space. Demonstrate that Q is the "perspective image" of some square in space. [Here is what "perspective image" means. Fix a point Z in space; this point is the focus of the perspective. Fix a set S. Finally, fix a plane so that S is between Z and the plane. One imagines an observer at Z focusing on each point of S and projecting it to the plane as follows. If $s \in S$ then draw the unique line determined by s and Z. The point of intersection of that line with the given plane is the perspective image of that point s. The image of the entire set S is the union of all such projected points.]

38. A pyramid is a polyhedron with five faces. The base is a square. The four sides are triangles which meet at a vertex at the top. The volume of a pyramid is one third of the base area times the height. Without using calculus, but instead using ideas of "similarity," explain why this fact about the volume is true.

39. Consider a solid donut (a "torus" with interior) in space. You are to give it three planar slices. What is the greatest number of pieces into which you can thereby cut the solid?

40. Consider a solid wooden cube with side length 4 inches. You are to drill a circular hole, one inch in diameter, along the main diagonal— from the top left rear corner to the front right bottom corner. What is the volume of the solid that remains? [*Hint:* You may find that mathematics fails you in thinking about this problem. If that is the case, devise another method for determining the volume. Be practical!]

41. Consider a square of side 1. Here is a scheme for measuring the length of its diagonal. We do so by a sequence of approximations. The first approximation is shown in Figure 109a. The second approximation is shown in Figure 109b. The third is shown in Figure 109c. You can see the pattern, and how to make the approximating, piecewise linear curve

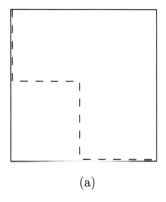

(a)

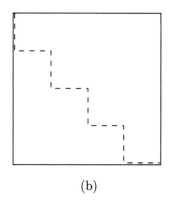

(b)

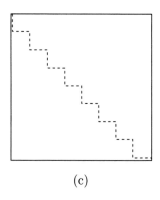

(c)

Figure 109

closer and closer to the diagonal that we wish to study. What is the
length of each of these approximations? What does this exercise suggest
that the length of the diagonal is? What does the Pythagorean theorem
tell us that the length of the diagonal is? What is the explanation for
this apparent contradiction?

42. Imitate the technique of Exercise 41 to obtain a fallacious answer
for the circumference of a circle of radius 1.

Chapter 3

Problems Involving Counting

3.1 Elementary Problems in Probability

The sort of counting techniques that we have covered earlier in this book will certainly be brought to bear in the present chapter. But probability problems have another dimension. In a probability problem it is vital to delineate the *sample space*. The world of probability is littered with puzzles and paradoxes that are connected with a misunderstanding of the sample space, or space of possibilities. We shall take special pains in this section to tutor the reader in this matter.

PROBLEM 3.1.1 *Eight slips of paper with the letters A, B, C, D, E F, G, H written on them are placed into a bin. The eight slips are drawn one by one from the bin. What is the probability that the first four to come out are A, C, E, H (in some order)?*

Solution: This problem is much less exciting than it sounds. After we choose the first four slips, it does not matter what we do. We could burn the others, or go drink coffee, or enroll in truck driving school. And the statement of the problem rules out the *order* in which the slips are drawn. Stripping away the language, we see that we are randomly selecting four objects from among eight. We want to know whether a particular four, in any order, will be the ones that we select.

The number of different ways to choose four objects from among eight is

$$\binom{8}{4} = \frac{8!}{4! \cdot 4!} = \frac{8 \cdot 7 \cdot 6 \cdot 5}{4 \cdot 3 \cdot 2 \cdot 1} = 70.$$

Of these different subsets of four, only one will be the set $\{A, C, E, H\}$. Thus the probability of the first four slips being the ones that we want will be $1/70$.   □

PROBLEM 3.1.2 *Suppose that you write 37 letters and then you address 37 envelopes to go with them. Closing your eyes, you randomly stuff one letter into each envelope. What is the probability that just one envelope contains the wrong letter?*

Solution: Say that the envelopes are numbered 1–37 and the letters are numbered 1–37. If letters 1 through 36 go into envelopes 1–36 then what remains are letter 37 and envelope 37. So that last letter is *forced* to go into the correct envelope.

Of course there is nothing special about the numbering used in the last paragraph. It just helped us to make a simple point: it is impossible to have just one letter in the wrong envelope. If one letter is in the wrong envelope then at least two letters are in the wrong envelope.

Thus the answer to our problem is that the probability is zero. □

The last problem illustrates a simple but important point: Namely, a problem is not always what it seems. A problem with a simple and elegant statement may be inconsistent or may not have any solution at all.

Somewhat more interesting is the next problem:

PROBLEM 3.1.3 *Suppose that you have 37 envelopes and you address 37 letters to go with them. Closing your eyes, you randomly stuff one letter into each envelope. What is the probability that precisely two letters are in the wrong envelopes and all others in the correct envelope?*

Solution: If just two letters are to be in the wrong envelope then they will have to be switched; for instance, letter 5 could go into envelope 19 and letter 19 into envelope 5. Thus the number of different ways that we can get just two letters in the wrong envelopes is just the same as the number of different ways that we can choose two letters from among 37. [All of the other 35 letters must go into their *correct* envelopes, so there is no choice involved for those 35.] This number is

$$N = \binom{37}{2} = \frac{37!}{2!35!} = \frac{37 \cdot 36}{2 \cdot 1} = 666.$$

Now if we imagine the envelopes, in their correct order (numbers 1 to 37), lying in a row on the table, then a random distribution of letters among the envelopes just corresponds to a random ordering of the letters. Thus the number of different possible ways to distribute 37 letters among 37 envelopes is 37! (a very large number). In conclusion, the probability that all letters but two will be in the correct envelopes is

$$P = \frac{666}{37!} \approx 4.86 \cdot 10^{-41}. \qquad \square$$

In the next section we shall treat a truly sophisticated problem that arises from stuffing letters into envelopes.

PROBLEM 3.1.4 *A woman goes to visit the house of some friends whom she has not seen in many years. She knows that, besides the two married adults in the household, there are two children of different ages. But she does not know their genders.*

On entering the house, she sees a football helmet. What is the probability that both children are boys?

Solution: This is an ideal example for illustrating the concept of sample space. An incorrect analysis would be: "At least one child is a boy. There is equal probability that the other is a boy or a girl. So the odds of a boy are .5.

What is wrong with this reasoning? The error is that we are given in advance that there are two children. The sample space consists of all possible *pairs of children.* If we consider all possible pairs of children, in the order (oldest, youngest), then the possibilities are

$$(B, B) \ , \ (B, G) \ , \ (G, B) \ , \ (G, G).$$

There are four possible pairs of children. We do not know whether the child who owns the helmet is the youngest or the oldest. So we have no idea whether this child is the first in a pair or the second. Thus any of the first three ordered pairs could be the one describing the children in this family.

Of these three ordered pairs, two reveal the second child to be a girl and one reveals the second child to be a boy. Thus there is a 1/3 probability in our problem that the second child is a boy.   □

CHALLENGE PROBLEM 3.1.5 *Suppose that we modify our analysis of the last problem as follows: Consider all possible pairs of children in the order (owns the helmet, other). The first child is the one who owns the helmet, the second is the other child. Then the possibilities are*

$$(B, B) \ , \ (B, G) \ , \ (G, B) \ , \ (G, G).$$

The fact that one (male) child owns the helmet eliminates the last two possibilities. The remaining pairs are (B, B) and (B, G). We conclude that there is .5 probability that the second child (the one who doesn't own the helmet) is a boy. What is wrong with this analysis? **ANSWER THIS QUESTION BEFORE YOU READ ON.**

CHALLENGE PROBLEM 3.1.6 *To confuse you further, we now alter the analysis in this way. Consider all possible pairs of children in the order (owns the helmet, other). The first child is the one who owns the helmet, the second is the other child. Then the possibilities are*

$$(B_1, B_2) \ , \ (B_2, B_1) \ , \ (B, G) \ , \ (G, B) \ , \ (G_1, G_2) \ , \ (G_2, G_1).$$

The change we have made is insightful: if there are two boys, then either could be the one owning the helmet. So we must distinguish these possibilities. The same reasoning applies if there are two girls.

As before, we note that since the child with the helmet is a boy, the last three ordered pairs must be eliminated from our analysis. Only the first three are relevant.

The remaining pairs are (B_1, B_2), (B_2, B_1), and (B, G). We conclude that there is 2/3 probability that the second child (the child who does not own the helmet) is a boy. What is wrong with this analysis?
ANSWER THIS QUESTION BEFORE YOU READ ON.

If you are skeptical of the outcome of these "answering the door" problems, then you are encouraged to perform an experiment. Replace "boy" and "girl" with "heads" and "tails." Now flip a coin twice and record the two results in a row. Flip the coin twice again and record the results in a row. Repeat the process 50 times so that you have 50 experimental pieces of data. This represents fifty families, each with two children. Two heads corresponds to two boys, two tails corresponds to two girls, and so forth.

Now, without thinking analytically, we examine our experimental data. Consider the question "Given that one member of the pair is a head, what is the probability that the other is a head?" As an illustration, this author has performed 50 pairs of flips as in the last paragraph. His results are recorded in the next table:

T	H		T	H		H	T		H	H		T	H
H	H		T	H		H	T		T	H		T	T
T	H		H	T		H	H		H	H		T	T
H	T		T	H		H	T		H	H		H	H
H	H		H	T		H	H		T	T		H	H
H	T		T	H		H	T		T	H		T	T
H	H		H	H		H	T		H	H		H	T
H	T		T	H		T	H		T	T		H	T
H	T		T	H		H	H		T	T		H	H
H	T		H	H		H	T		H	T		T	T

Notice that there are 43 pairs in which one member is a head. Of those, 15 consist of two heads. Based on this sample, we calculate that the probability of *both* flips being a head, *given that one is a head*, is $15/43 \approx .3488$. This is very close to 1/3, which is what our analysis predicted.

In order to put the first problem, and the experiment, in perspective, let's change the parameters a bit.

PROBLEM 3.1.7 *A woman goes to visit the house of some friends whom she has not seen in many years. She knows that, besides the two married adults in the household, there are two children of different ages. But she does not know their genders.*

When she knocks on the door of the house, a boy answers. He says "I am the oldest child in this family. My sibling is in the back room asleep."

What is the probability that the other child is a boy?

Solution: This is a different question! Recall that all possible pairs of children, in the order (oldest, youngest), are

$$(B, B)\ ,\ (B, G)\ ,\ (G, B)\ ,\ (G, G).$$

The only ones that apply to the hypothesis that the eldest is a boy are the first and second pairs. *Of those pairs*, one has a boy as the second child and one has a girl. Thus the probability that the sleeping child is a boy is equal to the probability that the sleeping child is a girl. The answer to the present question is .5.   □

It is again useful to look at our experimental data—the fifty pairs of flips. Recall that "heads" corresponds to boys and "tails" to girls. Notice that there are 31 pairs that have "heads" (boy) as the first, or eldest, entry. Of those, 15 have heads as the second entry and 16 have tails as the second entry. Thus the experimental data suggests (within a reasonable error) that there is a probability of .4839 that the second child is a boy and a probability of .5161 that the second child is a girl.

PROBLEM 3.1.8 *You draw four parallel lines on a piece of paper (Figure 110). You fold the paper along the dotted line indicated in Figure 111.*

You explain to a friend that you will, on one half of the paper, connect the lines in two pairs. [There are three different ways to do this; Figure 112 shows the three different things that you might do.] You do not show the friend what you have done. With your work face

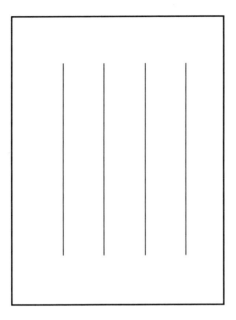

Figure 110

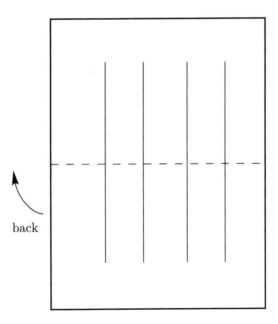

Figure 111

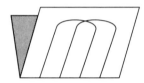

Figure 112

down on the table, you then invite the friend to do as you did: connect the four remaining loose ends in two pairs.

Then you place a bet with the friend: if the resulting figure, when the paper is unfolded, is a continuous loop then you win the bet; if the resulting figure is instead two disjoint loops, then the friend wins the bet.

The bet is even money. Is your friend wise to take this bet?

Solution: This is another one of those situations that, on the surface, sounds eminently fair. It is not.

Examine Figure 113. With the paper unfolded, it shows all the different things you might have done (your work is always on the top) plotted against all the things that your friend might have tried (her work is always on the bottom).

Notice that in six of the nine possible configurations the result is a single continuous loop whereas in only three of the nine configurations does the result consist of two disjoint loops. You have a 2/3 chance of winning the bet.

Your friend would be foolish to take this bet.   □

Figure 113

It is curious to note that you, as the perpetrator, do not even have to *know* anything to be the odds on favorite to win this bet. *No matter what configuration you choose for your end of the paper*, you have a two out of three chance of ending up with a single closed loop and thus winning the bet. Figure 113 illustrates this last point.

The next example also illustrates a "rigged bet" situation.

PROBLEM 3.1.9 *You hand a friend a standard deck of 52 playing cards face down. You ask him to divide the deck into three sub-decks, using simple cuts, and to place them face down on the table. Then you say "I'll bet you even money that one of those three top cards is a face card" (here a face card is a jack, queen, or king).*

Would your friend be wise to accept the bet?

Solution: Your friend may be thinking that there are only 12 face cards in a deck of 52. The chances of selecting a face card are therefore $12/52 \approx .2308$. Clearly the bet is in his favor and he should accept it.

Unfortunately, your friend (if he is indeed thinking this way) does not understand the concept of sample space, nor how to count accurately. Here is a correct analysis.

If you set aside all the hocus pocus, then what you and your friend are doing is selecting three cards at random from a deck of 52. The question is what is the probability that one of those three cards is a face card. Now there are $\binom{52}{3}$ ways to select three cards from among 52. It turns out—and this is true in many probability problems—to be convenient to now calculate how many ways there are of *not* choosing a face card. In other words, we shall calculate the probability of failing, rather than succeeding.

If we are going to select three cards, none of which is a face card, then we must select three cards from among the $40 = 52 - 12$ that are not face cards. The number of ways of doing this is $\binom{40}{3}$. Thus the probability of our *failing* to select a face card is

$$\frac{\binom{40}{3}}{\binom{52}{3}} = \frac{40!/(3! \cdot 37!)}{52!/(3! \cdot 49!)}$$

$$= \frac{49 \cdot 48 \cdot 47 \cdot 46 \cdot 45 \cdot 44 \cdot 43 \cdot 42 \cdot 41 \cdot 40 \cdot 39 \cdot 38}{52 \cdot 51 \cdot 50 \cdot 49 \cdot 48 \cdot 47 \cdot 46 \cdot 45 \cdot 44 \cdot 43 \cdot 42 \cdot 41}$$

$$= \frac{40 \cdot 39 \cdot 38}{52 \cdot 51 \cdot 50}$$

$$\approx .44706.$$

As a result of this calculation, the probability that we *did* get a face card among the three that we selected is

$$P = 1 - .44706 = .55294.$$

Notice that the odds are *better than even* that one of the three top cards is a face card. Therefore the situation described is a good bet for you and not a good bet for your friend.

This example is taken from [SIM1]; that source, however, has an error in its analysis.   □

Notice, in the last problem, that the sample space is not the set of 52 cards. If it were, then the odds of picking a face card would be

12/52, as already discussed. Instead, the sample space is the set of all triples of cards, and the question is what are the odds that one card in the triple is a face card. This considerably alters the odds.

3.2 More Sophisticated Problems in Probability

In this section we consider some more subtle questions related to probability, gambling, and counting.

We will find it convenient, both here and later in the book, to use mathematical summing notation. This is notation of the form

$$\sum_{j=1}^{k} a_j = a_1 + a_2 + \cdots + a_k,$$

where the expression on the left is shorthand for the written out sum on the right. Some examples are

$$\sum_{j=1}^{5} [j^2 + 1] = [1^2 + 1] + [2^2 + 1] + [3^2 + 1] + [4^2 + 1] + [5^2 + 1] = 60$$

and

$$\sum_{j=1}^{4} \frac{1}{j} = \frac{1}{1} + \frac{1}{2} + \frac{1}{3} + \frac{1}{4}.$$

The summation notation can be used to indicate a sum that begins at an index other than 1:

$$\sum_{k=3}^{7} [j - 2] = [3 - 2] + [4 - 2] + [5 - 2] + [6 - 2] + [7 - 2]$$

and

$$\sum_{\ell=-2}^{3} \ell^3 = (-2)^3 + (-1)^3 + (0)^3 + (1)^3 + (2)^3 + (3)^3.$$

As you read along in the book, you will find yourself becoming rapidly accustomed to the summation notation.

PROBLEM 3.2.1 *A bag of marbles contains some number of red marbles and some number of blue marbles. The number of each may be positive or zero. A marble is pulled blind from the bag and it turns out to be red. If a second marble is pulled, what is the probability that it, too, will be red?*

Solution: What is new here is that we do not know how many marbles are in the bag nor how many there are of each kind. We do know that, to begin, there is at least one red marble. But all the rest could be red, or none of them. How do we take this information (or lack of it) into account?

Say that the total number of marbles in the bag is N. We will perform N different analyses depending on how many of the marbles (call the number k) in the bag are red. We write S_k for the situation in which there are k red marbles in the bag, $1 \leq k \leq N$.

Imagine that set before us are N bags of marbles: B_1 is a bag representing situation S_1 (one red marble), B_2 is a bag representing situation S_2 (two red marbles), and so on. Taken altogether, there are $1+2+3+\cdots+(N-1)+N = N(N+1)/2$ red marbles in all the bags. Each has a likelihood of

$$\frac{1}{N(N+1)/2} = \frac{2}{N(N+1)}$$

of being selected. The probability that the first red marble selected is in B_1 is $1 \cdot 2/[N(N+1)]$—because B_1 has just one red marble; the probability that the first red marble selected is in B_2 is $2 \cdot 2/[N(N+1)]$—because B_2 has just two red marbles; the probability that the first red marble selected is in B_3 is $3 \cdot 2/[N(N+1)]$; and so forth. The probability that the first red marble selected is in B_k is $k \cdot 2/[N(N+1)]$

After the first red marble is selected from bag B_k, then there are $(k-1)$ red marbles remaining and $(N-1)$ marbles total left in the bag. So the probability that the second selected marble is red is $(k-1)/(N-1)$. The probability of the first event conjoined with the second event is the product of their probabilities:

$$P_k = \frac{k \cdot 2}{N(N+1)} \cdot \frac{k-1}{N-1}.$$

Since each of the k bags is equally likely to have been picked (i.e. each of the marble distributions is equally likely to have occurred), the overall probability of the second marble being red is

$$P = \sum_{k=1}^{N} P_k = \sum_{k=1}^{N} \frac{k \cdot 2}{N(N+1)} \cdot \frac{k-1}{N-1}.$$

This is a quantity that we can calculate. Now

$$P = \frac{2}{(N-1) \cdot N \cdot (N+1)} \sum_{k=1}^{N} k(k-1)$$

$$= \frac{2}{(N-1) \cdot N \cdot (N+1)} \cdot \left[\sum_{k=1}^{N} k^2 - \sum_{k=1}^{N} k \right].$$

We have previously calculated that $\sum_{k=1}^{N} k = N(N+1)/2$ and that $\sum_{k=1}^{N} k^2 = (2N^3 + 3N^2 + N)/6$ (see Section 1.2). As a result,

$$P = \frac{2}{(N-1) \cdot N \cdot (N+1)} \cdot \left[\frac{2N^3 + 3N^2 + N}{6} - \frac{N(N+1)}{2} \right] = \frac{2}{3}.$$

In conclusion, the probability that the second marble is red is $2/3$.

□

Although the reasoning in the last example is airtight, the result may be counterintuitive. The reader is encouraged to perform experiments to bear out the results.

PROBLEM 3.2.2 *A ten foot pole is dropped into a milling saw and randomly cut into three shorter poles. What is the probability that these three pieces will form a triangle?*

Solution: What is the characterizing property of three lengths, call them A, B, C, that form a triangle? It is that the triangle inequality will hold: the sum of any two of the lengths will be at least as great as the third. For instance, lengths $1, 2, 4$ could not form a triangle.

If any of the pieces has length 5 feet then the triangle will be flat and trivial; so we rule out this situation (the probability that any piece will have length five feet, or any particular pre-specified length, is zero). So we assume that each of the three pieces has length either greater than 5 feet or less than 5 feet.

But if any piece, say A, has length exceeding 5 feet then the triangle inequality $A \le B+C$ must fail. Thus, to form a triangle, all three pieces must have length less than 5 feet. But when this is the case, then all three triangle inequalities will hold (since the sum of any two lengths will exceed 5 feet) and hence a triangle can indeed be formed.

So the problem posed is equivalent to the question: "What is the probability that each piece will have length less than five feet?"

It is convenient, for the purposes of calculating our probabilities, to translate this last condition into a question about where the saw cuts will fall. First, the saw cuts must lie on opposite sides of the midpoint of the pole (otherwise the largest piece will have length exceeding 5 feet). Second, the distance between the two saw cuts must not be greater than or equal to 5 feet (otherwise the middle piece cut from the pole will have length greater than or equal to 5 feet). Refer to Figure 114. These two conditions taken together will guarantee that all three pieces have length less than 5 feet.

A moment's thought (there are four possibilities) reveals that the probability that the cuts lie on opposite sides of the midpoint is .5. Now the distance d between the two cuts (if we rule out distance exactly 5, as discussed above) is either $0 < d < 5$ or $5 < d < 10$. These eventualities are equally likely. Thus the probability that the distance between the cuts is less than 5 feet is .5.

The probability that the two eventualities—(i) cuts on opposite sides of the midpoint and (ii) cuts with distance less than 5 feet between them—will both occur is the *product* of the two probabilities. That is, it is $P = .5 \cdot .5 = .25$.

The probability is .25 that the three pieces will form a triangle. □

CHALLENGE PROBLEM 3.2.3 *A ten foot pole is accidentally dropped into a milling saw. It is cut, at random, into two pieces. The mill operator gets so upset that he takes one of the pieces and throws it into the mill saw. That one piece gets cut in two—with the location of*

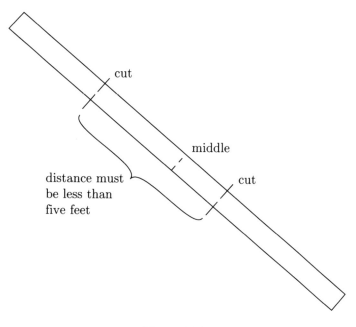

Figure 114

the cut being random. What is the probability that the three resulting pieces will form a triangle?

PROBLEM 3.2.4 *Find the least positive integer N so that, in a room containing N people, the odds are better than even that two of the people have the same birthday (not the year, just the day). [Hint: Forget about leap year. Assume that a year has 365 days.]*

Solution: As has been indicated previously, it is sometimes convenient to calculate the probability that something will *not* happen, and then subtract that result from 1.

With this in mind, we fix N and determine the probability that no two people, in a room of N people, have the same birthday. Say that the people are $P_1, P_2, \ldots, P_N$. Now person P_1 may have any of the 365 days of the year for his birthday without contradicting the condition that no two people in the room will have the same birthday. Once person P_1 has fixed a birthday (this is usually fixed on the day that he/she is born, but we are rewriting history for the sake of our analysis), then person P_2 is not allowed to have that birthday if we are to maintain distinct birthdays. Thus person P_2 has 364 choices for his/her birthday.

And so it goes. If we are to maintain distinct birthdays, then person P_3 has 363 choices for his/her birthday. In summary, the total number of birthday combinations for N people, with no two being the same, is

$$365 \cdot 364 \cdot 363 \cdots [365 - (N - 1)].$$

The total number of *all possible* birthday distributions among N people, without regard for duplication or lack of duplication, is

$$\underbrace{365 \cdot 365 \cdot 365 \cdots \cdot 365}_{N \text{ times}}.$$

In summary, the probability that N people in a room will all have distinct birthdays is

$$P = \frac{365 \cdot 364 \cdot 363 \cdots [365 - (N - 1)]}{365^N}.$$

For the purposes of calculation, so that we do not have to deal with huge numbers, we rewrite this formula as

$$P = \frac{365}{365} \cdot \frac{364}{365} \cdot \frac{363}{365} \cdots \frac{365 - (N - 1)}{365}.$$

And now we must bring out our computer or calculator and begin to calculate. Begin at the left, multiplying the fractions together. When your product falls below $1/2$ you are finished. The last fraction that you multiplied in will tell you what N should be (because the last fraction that you multiplied in was $\frac{365-(N-1)}{365}$).

The author has performed this calculation. He multiplied together 23 terms to obtain a probability of .4927027. Using only 22 terms yielded a probability of .5243046. Clearly the least N to yield a probability of less than half that each person in the room will have a distinct birthday is $N = 23$.

We conclude that if there are 23 people in a room then the odds are better than even (in fact the odds are $P = 1 - 0.4927027 = .5072973$) that two of them will have the same birthday.   □

CHALLENGE PROBLEM 3.2.5 *Modify the preceding problem in the following way. Assume that a year consists of 52 consecutive weeks, each containing seven days (of course we are not assuming that a week begins on Sunday, or on any particular day). What is the least N such that, if N people are in a room, two of them will have their birthday in the same week (not the same year or the same day, just the same week).*

How does your answer differ, if at all, from the answer in the last problem?

CHALLENGE PROBLEM 3.2.6 *How does the birthday problem change if you do take leap year into account?*

The next is a problem on envelope stuffing to which we alluded in the last section. After you study this problem, refer back to the more elementary envelope stuffing problems that we saw in Section 3.1. Why were those so easy and why is this one so tricky?

PROBLEM 3.2.7 *Suppose that you have 37 addressed envelopes and you write 37 letters. Closing your eyes, you randomly stuff one letter into each envelope. What is the probability that just one envelope contains the right letter, and the other 36 each contain the wrong letter?*

Solution: We will see that this problem is quite different from the earlier one, even though its form is similar.

Suppose, as in our last solution, that the letters are numbered from 1 to 37 and that so are the envelopes numbered from 1 to 37. Now just one of the letters is in the correct envelope.

Say that letter 1 goes into envelope 1. Then the number of possible configurations of the other 36 letters are that each of letters 2-37 goes to one of envelopes 2-37, but no letter goes to its identically numbered envelope. Therefore we must count the number of permutations of 36 items in which no item goes to its original position.

A similar analysis applies if only letter 2 goes to envelope 2. Once again, we must count the number of permutations of 36 items in which no item goes to its original position.

A similar analysis applies if only letter 3 goes to envelope 3 or if only letter 4 goes to envelope 4, and so on.

So the total number of possible distributions of the letters is this: 37 times the number of permutations of 36 objects in which every object is moved to a new position. Thus the problem has devolved upon computing this last quantity. At the end, we will have to divide by 37!, or the number of permutations of 37 objects.

As happens many times in analytical reasoning, our original problem has led to a new problem with interest of its own. We formulate and solve the new problem, and then return to the present problem.

Sub-Problem 3.2.8 (Bernoulli-Euler: Advanced) *Suppose that you have k distinct objects in positions 1 through k. In how many different ways can they be re-ordered so that no object is in its original position?*

Solution: We call the objects $a_1, a_2, \ldots, a_k$ and we call their positions $P_1, \ldots, P_k$. The number that we seek will be called $M(k)$—the number of rearrangements of $a_1, \ldots, a_k$ among the positions $P_1, \ldots, P_k$ so that no a_j lands on its corresponding P_j.

We consider two different cases separately: (i) when a_1 lands in P_2 and a_2 lands in P_1 and, further, $a_3, \ldots, a_k$ are distributed among $P_3, \ldots, P_k$; (ii) when a_1 lands in P_2 but a_2 does *not* land in P_1.

Case (i) The positions of a_1 and a_2 are mandated in advance. The remaining $k-2$ elements $a_3, \ldots, a_k$ are to be distributed among $P_3, \ldots, P_k$ so that no a_j lands on P_j. But the number of possible ways to do this is just $M(k-2)$.

Case (ii) It is convenient to view the second case in this way: we are distributing $a_2, a_3, a_4, \ldots, a_k$ among $P_1, P_3, P_4, \ldots, P_k$. But the first of these objects (namely a_2) is not allowed to land in the first of these positions (namely P_1), the second of these objects (namely a_3) is not allowed to land in the second of these positions (namely P_3), and so forth. In other words, we are describing $M(k-1)$.

Taken altogether, the number of allowable rearrangements in which a_1 lands in P_2 is $M(k-2) + M(k-1)$.

Now we could do a similar analysis to determine the number of allowable arrangements in which a_1 lands in P_3. Of course the answer will be the same: $M(k-2) + M(k-1)$. And if we repeat the analysis to determine the number of allowable arrangements in which a_1 lands in P_4, we will also obtain the answer $M(k-2) + M(k-1)$. And the same result will hold if we consider a_1 landing in P_5 or P_6, etc., all the way up to a_1 landing in P_k. In sum, counting the "lands in P_2" case all the way up to the "lands in P_k" case, we have $k-1$ repetitions of the same number of arrangements: $M(k-2) + M(k-1)$. Altogether then, we find that the number we seek—the total number of allowable rearrangements of $a_1, a_2, \ldots, a_k$—is

$$M(k) = (k-1)[M(k-2) + M(k-1)].$$

We rearrange the terms and rewrite this as

$$M(k) = k \cdot M(k-1) - M(k-1) + (k-1) \cdot M(k-2)$$

or

$$M(k) - k \cdot M(k-1) = (-1)[M(k-1) - (k-1) \cdot M(k-2)]. \quad (*)$$

This is what is called a *recursion relation* for the function $M(k)$. Recursion relations are an important device in finite mathematics.

Writing out the cases $3, 4, 5, \ldots, k$ of $(*)$ we have

$$
\begin{aligned}
M(3) - 3 \cdot M(2) &= (-1)[M(2) - 2 \cdot M(1)] \\
M(4) - 4 \cdot M(3) &= (-1)[M(3) - 3 \cdot M(2)] \\
M(5) - 5 \cdot M(4) &= (-1)[M(4) - 4 \cdot M(3)]
\end{aligned}
$$

$$\cdots$$

$$M(k) - k \cdot M(k-1) = (-1)[M(k-1) - (k-1) \cdot M(k-2)]$$

Plainly we may substitute the first of these equations into the second to obtain

$$M(4) - 4 \cdot M(3) = (-1)^2[M(2) - 2 \cdot M(1)].$$

We may then substitute this equation into the third one above, and so forth. The end result is

$$M(k) - k \cdot M(k-1) = (-1)^{k-2}[M(2) - 2 \cdot M(1)].$$

Now $(-1)^{k-2} = (-1)^k$. Also $M(1) = 0$ and $M(2) = 1$ (just stop and count). Putting this information into the last equation gives us

$$M(k) - k \cdot M(k-1) = (-1)^k.$$

Dividing through by $k!$ gives

$$\frac{M(k)}{k!} - \frac{M(k-1)}{(k-1)!} = \frac{(-1)^k}{k!}. \qquad (**)$$

Now we write out the formula $(**)$ for the cases $2, 3, 4, \ldots, k$. We obtain

$$\frac{M(2)}{2!} - \frac{M(1)}{1!} = \frac{(-1)^2}{2!}$$
$$\frac{M(3)}{3!} - \frac{M(2)}{2!} = \frac{(-1)^3}{3!}$$
$$\frac{M(4)}{4!} - \frac{M(3)}{3!} = \frac{(-1)^4}{4!}$$
$$\cdots$$
$$\frac{M(k)}{k!} - \frac{M(k-1)}{(k-1)!} = \frac{(-1)^k}{k!}$$

We add these equations together. Notice that virtually everything cancels out on the left side (we call this *telescoping*). The result is

$$\frac{M(k)}{k!} = \frac{(-1)^2}{2!} + \frac{(-1)^3}{3!} + \frac{(-1)^4}{4!} + \cdots + \frac{(-1)^k}{k!}.$$

Thus our final result is

$$M(k) = k! \left(\frac{1}{2!} - \frac{1}{3!} + \frac{1}{4!} - + \cdots + \frac{(-1)^k}{k!} \right).$$

This counts the admissible arrangements, or permutations. This completes our solution of the sub-problem.   □

Now we return to Problem 3.2.7, and complete the solution. We have already determined that the number of ways of getting one letter

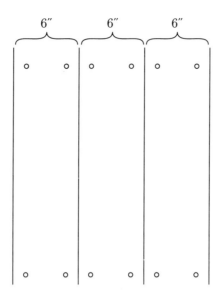

Figure 115

into the right envelope and the other 36 letters each into the wrong envelope is $37 \cdot M(36)$ (here we are using the notation from the sub-problem 3.2.8). The *probability* of getting such an arrangement is then

$$
\begin{aligned}
P &= \frac{37 \cdot M(36)}{37!} \\
&= \frac{37 \cdot 36!(1/2! - 1/3! + 1/4! - + \cdots + (-1)^{36}/(36)!)}{37!} \\
&= \frac{1}{2!} - \frac{1}{3!} + \frac{1}{4!} - + \cdots + \frac{1}{(36)!}.
\end{aligned}
$$

This is the final solution to Problem 3.2.7. □

PROBLEM 3.2.9 (Buffon; some calculus) *A floor is made of long planks that are six inches wide (Figure 115). A girl drops a thin stick that is four inches long onto the floor. She does so a great many times— say N times. Calculate the probability that the stick will land on a crack (between two planks) in the floor as a function of N. What is its asymptotic value as $N \to \infty$?*

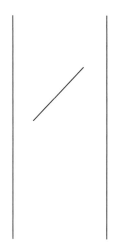

Figure 116

Solution: This is a classic problem that is known as "Buffon's Needle Problem." Clearly the probability that the stick will land on a crack depends on the angle at which the stick falls (Figure 116). For instance, if the stick falls parallel to the cracks, then it is highly unlikely that the stick will cross a crack. If, instead, the stick is perpendicular to the cracks, then it is fairly likely that it will hit a crack. Since the question of whether the stick will cross a crack depends on the angle at which the stick falls, you may not be surprised to learn that our answer will involve π. In fact it turns out that dropping a stick on the floor is one method for calculating π.

We set up a coordinate system as in Figure 117. The x-axis is perpendicular to the direction of the cracks. The y-axis is parallel to the cracks. We arrange for the origin to lie on a crack, so that the y-axis runs along a crack.

In order to make this problem tractable, we are now going to make some normalizing assumptions. First, we assume that the stick is infinitely thin—like a line segment. Next, we assume that one end of the stick is painted red. We measure the "angle of the stick" as follows: translate the stick, without rotating it, so that the unpainted end is at the origin. Now measure the directed angle beginning at the positive x-axis, in the counterclockwise direction to the stick (just as you do

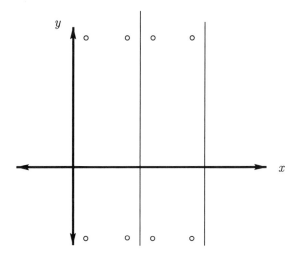

Figure 117

when learning about the sine and cosine functions). If that angle is θ radians, then we say that the stick subtends an angle of θ radians with the positive x-axis.

Now fix an angle $0 \leq \theta \leq \pi/2$. We restrict attention to a stick that will fall onto the floor in such a fashion that it subtends an angle of θ, but is otherwise random. What is the probability that it will cross a crack? Clearly the vertical position of the stick is of no interest, for it does not affect whether the stick crosses a crack. All that matters is the left-right position of the stick. And the problem is periodic: as the left end of the stick moves from 0 to 6, with the angle staying the same, then the following occurs. For a certain distance the stick will not touch a crack. Then it starts to cross a crack and the stick will move left-to-right across the crack. When the left end of the stick reaches 6, we are again at a situation that is identical to when the left end of the stick is at 0.

Now we use a little trigonometry. The stick has length 4 inches. When it subtends angle θ, then the left-to-right extent of the stick is $4\cos\theta$. Thus when the left end of the stick is between 0 and $6 - 4\cos\theta$ then the stick will not cross a crack. However when the left end of the stick is between $6 - 4\cos\theta$ and 6 then the stick *will* cross a crack. Thus the probability that a stick subtending an angle θ will cross a crack is

$$P_\theta = \frac{4\cos\theta}{6}.$$

A moment's thought reveals that the situation repeats itself when $\pi/2 \leq \theta \leq \pi$ or when $\pi \leq \theta \leq 3\pi/2$ or when $3\pi/2 \leq \theta \leq 2\pi$. So we may concentrate attention on $0 \leq \theta \leq \pi/2$.

The stick is just as likely to land so that it subtends any one angle as it is to land so that it subtends any other angle. Thus all the probabilities P_θ are equally likely to apply. We obtain our final answer by averaging P_θ over $0 \leq \theta \leq \pi/2$. Thus the ultimate probability that our stick will cross a crack is

$$\frac{1}{\pi/2}\int_0^{\pi/2}\frac{4\cos\theta}{6}\,d\theta = \frac{4}{3\pi}\int_0^{\pi/2}\cos\theta\,d\theta = \frac{4}{3\pi}. \qquad \square$$

[*Hint:* This is the only place in the solution of the present problem that we actually use calculus. And it could be avoided. Indeed, it is avoided by using the ideas that go into developing calculus. Instead of averaging P_θ using an integral—something which you may have never seen—instead do this. Divide the interval $[0, \pi/2]$ into one hundred tiny subintervals of equal length. Evaluate P_θ at one hundred values of θ, one chosen from among each of these subintervals. (Use a computer, of course.) Add together the one hundred values that you obtain and divide by 100. You will obtain an answer that is very close to $4/3\pi$.]

The author of this book performed an experiment dropping a stick of length 4 inches onto a floor with 6 inch wide planks. After 100 drops, the stick crossed a crack 46 times. Thus the calculated probability of hitting a crack is .46. Equating this with the expression $4/(3\pi)$ yields an approximate value for π of 2.9. This is not very accurate, and one would expect to have to perform perhaps a great many more drops to achieve any real accuracy.

In 1850, an experiment was performed by Wolf in Zurich. He used a needle of length 36 mm. and planking of width 45 mm. Of course he had to adjust the formula from the last problem accordingly. After dropping the needle 5000 times he arrived at the value 3.1596 for π.

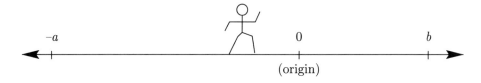

Figure 118

Analogous experiments conducted by Fox in England in 1864, using 1100 throws, gave a value of 3.1419 for π. Smith in England (1855) used 3200 throws and found the value 3.1553 for π.

CHALLENGE PROBLEM 3.2.10 *Do an analysis of Buffon's Needle Problem when the planks are distance d apart and the stick has length ℓ. What interesting new feature appears when $\ell > d$?*

Next we discuss an important part of probability theory called "random walks."

PROBLEM 3.2.11 *Imagine a person walking along the real line, in units of 1, beginning at the origin. The person moves one step, of unit length, at a time—either left or right. The direction of the move is determined by the flip of a coin: heads corresponds to one step to the (viewer's) left, tails corresponds to one step to the (viewer's) right. Thus if the first six flips of the coin are H, H, T, H, T, H then the walker goes two steps left, one right, one left, one right, and one left. The walker is then, after six steps, at the point -2.*

Now imagine that two "absorbing barriers" have been set up: at $-a$ and at b, where a and b are fixed positive integers. Refer to Figure 118. If the walker ever reaches $-a$ or b then she is 'absorbed' and the journey ends immediately. The question we wish to consider is this: What is the probability that the game will end with the walker exiting at $-a$?

Solution: It is at least intuitively clear that if $a = b$ then the walker, who begins at the origin (equidistant from the two absorbing barriers), is equally likely to exit at a or at b. If $a > b$ then the walker is more likely to exit at b than at $-a$ (because b is closer to the origin); if $a < b$

then the walker is more likely to exit at $-a$ than at b (because then $-a$ is closer to the origin). But we wish to obtain quantitative answers.

It is useful to introduce some notation. Suppose that the walker is currently standing at n. Use r_n to denote the probability that the walker is then absorbed at $-a$. We may relate r_n, r_{n-1}, and r_{n+1} as follows. When the walker is standing on n, then the next move will take her to either $n-1$ or to $n+1$ with equal likelihood. If that next moves takes the walker to $n-1$ then the likelihood of exiting at $-a$ becomes r_{n-1}; if instead the next move takes the walker to $n+1$ then the likelihood of exiting at $-a$ becomes r_{n+1}. Each of these probabilities is equally likely. In summary,

$$r_n = \frac{1}{2}[r_{n-1} + r_{n+1}].$$

But this last equation says that r_n is a linear function of n (draw a picture of $r_n = r(n)$ graphed against n). Thus

$$r_n = \alpha n + \beta;$$

this is the general form of a linear function. However we have two pieces of information about this line: if the walker is at $-a$ then the game ends, so $r_{-a} = 1$; also if the walker is at b then the game ends, so $r_b = 0$. Thus

$$1 = r_{-a} = \alpha \cdot (-a) + \beta$$

and

$$0 = r_b = \alpha \cdot b + \beta.$$

We may solve these two equations to find that

$$\alpha = \frac{-1}{a+b} \qquad \beta = \frac{b}{a+b}.$$

In conclusion,

$$r_n = \left(-\frac{1}{a+b}\right) n + \frac{b}{a+b} = \frac{b-n}{a+b}.$$

What does this last equation tell us about the original question? Recall that r_n denotes the probability that the game will end with the walker being absorbed at $-a$, given that the walker is presently standing at n. In particular, if the walker is presently standing at 0 then

$$r_0 = \frac{b}{a+b}.$$

Reversing the roles of a, and b, we may also see that, if the walker is presently standing at 0, then the probability s_0 of exiting at b is

$$s_0 = \frac{a}{a+b}.$$

Thus we see explicitly that, when a and b are equal, then the probabilities are equal. We also see quantitative realizations of the other statements at the beginning of this solution. $\qquad\square$

CHALLENGE PROBLEM 3.2.12 *The expected value of a probability is the average of all possible outcomes. What is the expected number of steps before the game in the last problem ends? [Hint: We let M_n denote the number of steps until the walker is absorbed, given that the walker is currently standing at n. The symbol $E(M_n)$ denotes be the expected value of M_n. In analogy with the solution of the last problem, relate $E(M_n)$ with $E(M_{n-1})$ and $E(M_{n+1})$. Note that the relationship will not be exactly as in the last problem, since now we are counting the number of steps rather than the probability!]*

As a final remark, we comment on the famous "ruin problem." This is a game with two players A and B. Player A begins with a dollars and player B begins with b dollars. At each play, a coin is flipped. If it comes up heads, then A pays B one dollar. If it comes up tails, then B pays A one dollar. Interpret the last problem, and the last challenge problem, in terms of this new game.

3.3   More on Counting

PROBLEM 3.3.1 *Draw a planar grid that is 31 squares wide and 17 squares high. How many different non-trivial rectangles can be drawn,*

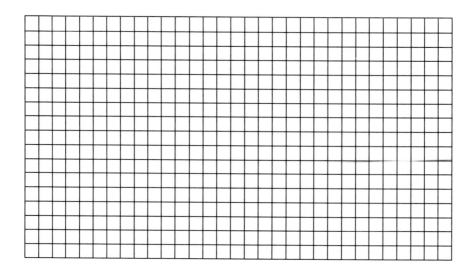

Figure 119

using the lines of the grid to determine the boundaries? See Figure
119. [Here "non-trivial" means that the rectangle has positive width
and positive height.]

Solution: We need a cogent method for counting the rectangles. Note
that any rectangle is uniquely specified by the location of its lower left-
hand corner, its length, and its width.

We think of the lower left point of the grid in Figure 119 as the
origin and locate points in the usual cartesian fashion (with the side of
a square in the grid being a unit).

How many rectangles can have their lower left corner at the origin?
Well, there are 31 possible widths, from 1 to 31, and 17 possible heights,
from 1 to 17. That is a total of $31 \times 17 = 527$ possible rectangles with
lower left corner at 0.

This is a good start, but will constitute an awfully tedious manner
of enumerating *all* the possible rectangles. We will now be a bit more
analytical. Suppose that we consider rectangles with lower left corner
at (j, k), with $0 \leq j \leq 30$ and $0 \leq k \leq 16$. There are $(31 - j)$
possible widths for such rectangles and $(17 - k)$ possible heights. Thus,
altogether, there are $(31 - j) \times (17 - k)$ rectangles with lower left corner

at (j, k). Given the range of j and k, the total number of all possible non-trivial rectangles is

$$S = \sum_{j=0}^{30} \sum_{k=0}^{16} (31 - j) \times (17 - k).$$

It is useful to expand the summands using the distributive law and then to regroup. We have

$$S = \sum_{j=0}^{30} \sum_{k=0}^{16} [527 - 17j - 31k + jk].$$

This, in turn, equals

$$\sum_{j=0}^{30} \sum_{k=0}^{16} 527 - \sum_{j=0}^{30} \sum_{k=0}^{16} 17j - \sum_{j=0}^{30} \sum_{k=0}^{16} 31k + \sum_{j=0}^{30} \sum_{k=0}^{16} jk$$

$$= [527 \cdot 31 \cdot 17] - 17 \cdot 17 \cdot \sum_{j=0}^{30} j$$

$$-31 \cdot 31 \cdot \sum_{k=0}^{16} k + \left[\sum_{j=0}^{30} j \right] \cdot \left[\sum_{k=0}^{16} k \right].$$

Now we may use Gauss's formula from Section 1.2 to evaluate each of the sums in the last formula. We obtain

$$
\begin{aligned}
S &= 277729 - 289 \cdot 465 - 961 \cdot 136 + 465 \cdot 136 \\
&= 277729 - 134385 - 130696 + 63240 \\
&= 75888.
\end{aligned}
$$

$\square$

In Chapter 1 we saw how to use the method of induction to calculate certain finite sums, such as $1 + 2 + 3 + \cdots k$, in closed form. Now we look at another type of sum, known as a *geometric sum*.

PROBLEM 3.3.2 *Let λ be a real number and k a positive integer. Calculate*

$$S = 1 + \lambda + \lambda^2 + \cdots + \lambda^k.$$

Solution: The key is to note that multiplying S by λ does not change it very much. Indeed

$$\lambda S = \lambda + \lambda^2 + \lambda^3 + \cdots + \lambda^{k+1}.$$

The sums S and λS differ only in the presence of 1 in the first of these and the presence of λ^{k+1} in the second. In other words

$$S - 1 = \lambda S - \lambda^{k+1}.$$

That is,

$$(\lambda - 1)S = \lambda^{k+1} - 1.$$

We finally write this as

$$S = \frac{\lambda^{k+1} - 1}{\lambda - 1}.$$

$\square$

An example of what the solution of the last problem tells us is as follows: Suppose that we want to know explicitly the value of the sum $S = 1 + (1/3) + (1/3)^2 + \cdots (1/3)^{100}$. It would be quite tedious to add all these numbers up by hand. But this question fits the paradigm of the geometric series, with $\lambda = 1/3$ and $k = 100$. Thus

$$S = \frac{(1/3)^{101} - 1}{(1/3) - 1} = \frac{3}{2} \cdot \left(1 - \left[\frac{1}{3}\right]^{101}\right).$$

Now a calculator may be used to see that the value of this last expression is about $1.5 - 9.702 \cdot 10^{-49}$.

Sometimes it is convenient, when $-1 < \lambda < 1$, to reason as follows: For $k \in \{1, 2, 3, \ldots\}$ we set

$$S_k = 1 + \lambda + \lambda^2 + \cdots \lambda^k.$$

We know, from the last problem, that

$$S_k = \frac{1 - \lambda^{k+1}}{1 - \lambda}. \tag{$*$}$$

Now we could ask what happens if, instead of adding just finitely many powers of λ, we add *all* powers of λ. This would correspond (in a sense that you will learn about more precisely when you take calculus) to letting k tend to infinity in equation $(*)$.

The result is that the sum $S = 1 + \lambda + \lambda^2 + \cdots$ of *all* non-negative powers of λ is obtained by asking what happens to the right hand side of $(*)$ when k becomes large without bound. Since $|\lambda| < 1$, it is plausible that λ^{k+1} becomes smaller and smaller, in fact tends to 0, as k increases without bound. In other words, $S_k \to 1/(1 - \lambda)$. We write

$$\sum_{j=0}^{\infty} \lambda^j = \frac{1}{1 - \lambda}. \qquad (**)$$

This is a variant of the standard mathematical notation for summation (see the beginning of Section 3.2). The symbol $\sum$ is called a "capital sigma," and denotes the summation process. The lower limit means that we begin our summing with the exponent j equaling 0 and the upper limit having no bound (in other words, we sum *all powers* of λ.

Here is an illustrative example: What is the sum

$$1 + \frac{1}{2} + \left(\frac{1}{2}\right)^2 + \left(\frac{1}{2}\right)^3 + \cdots$$

equal to? Draw a picture of the interval $[0, 2]$ on your scratch pad. The sum of the first two terms is $3/2$. Add one additional term and you cover half the remaining distance to 2. Add the fourth term and you again cover half the remaining distance to 2. In fact each additional term repeats this key property. It is plausible to suppose that the *entire sum* equals 2.

In fact our new formula makes this supposition concrete:

$$\sum_{j=0}^{\infty} \left(\frac{1}{2}\right)^j = \frac{1}{1 - (1/2)} = 2.$$

We will use these new ideas about geometric series, in a very simple form, in the next problem.

PROBLEM 3.3.3 *The Fibonacci sequence is famous in mathematics, indeed in all of science. It is formed in the following way: The first two* terms are each equal to 1. The next term is obtained by adding the preceding two: thus the third term equals 2. The next term (the fourth) is obtained by adding the preceding two: $1 + 2 = 3$. The next term is obtained by adding the preceding two: $2 + 3 = 5$. In fact the first ten terms of the Fibonacci sequence are

$$1, 1, 2, 3, 5, 8, 13, 21, 34, 55.$$

We denote the jth term of the Fibonacci sequence by a_j. Thus

$$a_0 = 1, a_1 = 1, a_2 = 2, a_3 = 3, a_4 = 5,$$

and so forth.

Show that the following formula for the Fibonacci sequence is valid:

$$a_j = \frac{\left(\frac{1+\sqrt{5}}{2}\right)^j - \left(\frac{1-\sqrt{5}}{2}\right)^j}{\sqrt{5}}.$$

Solution: We shall use the method of *generating functions*, a powerful technique that is used throughout the mathematical sciences.

We write $F(x) = a_0 + a_1 x + a_2 x^2 + \cdots$. Here the a_j's are the terms of the Fibonacci sequence and the letter x denotes an unspecified variable. What is curious here is that we do not care about what x is. We intend to manipulate the function F in such a fashion that we will be able to solve for the coefficients a_j. Just think of $F(x)$ as a polynomial with a *lot* of coefficients.

Notice that

$$xF(x) = a_0 x + a_1 x^2 + a_2 x^3 + a_3 x^4 + \cdots$$

and

$$x^2 F(x) = a_0 x^2 + a_1 x^3 + a_2 x^4 + a_3 x^5 + \cdots.$$

Thus, grouping like powers of x, we see that

$$\begin{aligned}
F(x) &- xF(x) - x^2 F(x) \\
&= a_0 + (a_1 - a_0)x + (a_2 - a_1 - a_0)x^2 \\
&\quad + (a_3 - a_2 - a_1)x^3 + (a_4 - a_3 - a_2)x^4 + \cdots.
\end{aligned}$$

But the basic property that defines the Fibonacci sequence is that $a_2 - a_1 - a_0 = 0$, $a_3 - a_2 - a_1 = 0$, etc. Thus our equation simplifies drastically to

$$F(x) - xF(x) - x^2 F(x) = a_0 + (a_1 - a_0)x.$$

We also know that $a_0 = a_1 = 1$. Thus the equation becomes

$$(1 - x - x^2)F(x) = 1$$

or

$$F(x) = \frac{1}{1 - x - x^2}. \qquad (***)$$

It is convenient to factor the denominator as follows:

$$F(x) = \frac{1}{\left[1 - \frac{-2}{1-\sqrt{5}}x\right] \cdot \left[1 - \frac{-2}{1+\sqrt{5}}x\right]}$$

(just simplify the right hand side to see that it equals $(***)$).

A little more algebraic manipulation yields that

$$F(x) = \frac{5 + \sqrt{5}}{10}\left[\frac{1}{1 + \frac{2}{1-\sqrt{5}}x}\right] + \frac{5 - \sqrt{5}}{10}\left[\frac{1}{1 + \frac{2}{1+\sqrt{5}}x}\right].$$

Now we want to apply the formula $(**)$ to each of the fractions in brackets ([ ]). For the first fraction, we think of $-\frac{2}{1-\sqrt{5}}x$ as λ. Thus the first expression in brackets equals

$$\sum_{j=0}^{\infty}\left(-\frac{2}{1-\sqrt{5}}x\right)^j.$$

Likewise the second sum equals

$$\sum_{j=0}^{\infty}\left(-\frac{2}{1+\sqrt{5}}x\right)^j.$$

All told, we find that

$$F(x) = \frac{5 + \sqrt{5}}{10}\sum_{j=0}^{\infty}\left(-\frac{2}{1-\sqrt{5}}x\right)^j + \frac{5 - \sqrt{5}}{10}\sum_{j=0}^{\infty}\left(-\frac{2}{1+\sqrt{5}}x\right)^j.$$

Grouping terms with like powers of x, we finally conclude that

$$F(x) = \sum_{j=0}^{\infty} \left[\frac{5 + \sqrt{5}}{10} \left(-\frac{2}{1 - \sqrt{5}}x \right)^j + \frac{5 - \sqrt{5}}{10} \left(-\frac{2}{1 + \sqrt{5}}x \right)^j \right] x^j.$$

But we began our solution of this problem with the formula

$$F(x) = a_0 + a_1 x + a_2 x^2 + \cdots.$$

The two different formulas for $F(x)$ must agree. In particular, the coefficients of the different powers of x must match up. We conclude that

$$a_j = \frac{5 + \sqrt{5}}{10} \left(-\frac{2}{1 - \sqrt{5}} \right)^j + \frac{5 - \sqrt{5}}{10} \left(-\frac{2}{1 + \sqrt{5}} \right)^j.$$

We rewrite

$$\frac{5 + \sqrt{5}}{10} = \frac{1}{\sqrt{5}} \cdot \frac{1 + \sqrt{5}}{2} \qquad\qquad \frac{5 - \sqrt{5}}{10} = -\frac{1}{\sqrt{5}} \cdot \frac{1 - \sqrt{5}}{2}$$

and

$$-\frac{2}{1 - \sqrt{5}} = \frac{1 + \sqrt{5}}{2} \qquad\qquad -\frac{2}{1 + \sqrt{5}} = \frac{1 - \sqrt{5}}{2}.$$

Making these four substitutions into our formula for a_j, and doing a few algebraic simplifications, yields

$$a_j = \frac{\left(\frac{1 + \sqrt{5}}{2} \right)^j - \left(\frac{1 - \sqrt{5}}{2} \right)^j}{\sqrt{5}}$$

as desired. $\square$

The exercises at the end of the chapter will give you some opportunities to become adept at the method of generating functions. Before trying your hand at those, you should first review the technique that we used in analyzing the Fibonacci sequence. Notice how we combined F, xF, and $x^2 F$ so that important cancellations would take place. That is how we used the special properties of the Fibonacci sequence. In other problems, such as those at the end of the chapter, you will need to use different combinations, with possibly different coefficients, that are tailored to each specific problem.

3.4 The Classical Marriage Problem and Related Ideas

In order to describe and motivate this problem, let us be a bit old fashioned and simple minded. And not politically correct, perhaps. We describe a social situation which coincides with the way that many people remember American life to have been sixty years ago.

A young man comes of age. His aim is to get married. In seeking a wife, he decides to date at most 100 women. After he dates a woman for a while, he must either marry her, or reject her and move on to another. Once a woman is rejected, he may not return to her later. Ultimately he must choose just one woman and marry her.

The interesting feature of the problem is that the young man may look back, but he may not look ahead. At any point he may say "my current lady friend is more appealing, and we are more compatible together, than any woman that I've dated previously." On that basis he may decide to marry her. Or he may think "this woman is terrific but I am going to gamble that someone better will come along soon."

The "marriage problem" is to determine the best strategy for the young man just described. In order to remove the emotional claptrap from the problem, we reformulate it as follows:

PROBLEM 3.4.1 *A hat is filled with 100 slips of paper. On each slip of paper is written some positive integer (note that any positive integer may appear on the slips—not just the integers from 1 to 100). The integers do not necessarily appear in any sequence or pattern. Each of the slips has a different integer on it, so there is just one slip with the greatest integer.*

A person, who has no prior knowledge of which numbers appear on the slips—but who does know that there are 100 slips—is to blindly pull slips from the hat one by one. The person looks at each slip, then either agrees to accept that number of dollars and quit the game or decides to go on and choose another slip.

Note that the contestant looks at each slip as he/she proceeds, and then decides whether to quit or to go on. He/she can go forward, but cannot go back. If no choice is made by the time the 100th *slip is* reached, then the contestant must accept the number of dollars on the 100th slip.

What is the best strategy for the contestant? [Here "best strategy" means that the contestant will garner the greatest number of dollars.]

This author is embarrassed to admit that, when he was first told this problem, he thought a minute and said "Well, there is no strategy. It's hopeless." In part, the difficulty was that he didn't understand what a strategy was. The main problem was that he wasn't thinking.

We suppose in advance that a 'strategy' will take the following form: the contestant will draw out a certain number of slips—say k of them—and make careful note of the numbers recorded. After the k slips have been drawn, the contestant will determine to select the next slip that satisfies 'Property P', where Property P is to be determined. We shall discuss later why it is reasonable to concentrate on this type of strategy.

Solution: We call the first slip that is drawn "slip 1," the next one drawn "slip 2," and so forth.

Our goal is to optimize the number of dollars received. Any strategy that would result in choosing the $(\ell+1)^{\text{st}}$ slip, $\ell \geq k$, can be improved by remembering the largest recorded number M on the slips $1, 2, \ldots, \ell$ and then selecting the next slip that comes up that has a number greater than M (if no such slip ever comes up then the contestant is stuck with the last slip). Applying this observation over and over again, we find that the best strategy, given the parameters set in the paragraph before this solution began, is to take note of the largest number M on any of the slips $1, 2, \ldots, k$ and then select the next slip that has a number exceeding M.

This scheme having been established, our job is then to choose the best possible k. Suppose that the largest overall number Q (of all 100 slips) appears on slip $r + 1$. The contestant will not be successful in selecting that slip unless two conditions are fulfilled:

1) $r \geq k$ (because we are going to reject the first k slips, so if $r < k$ then the $(r + 1)^{\text{st}}$ slip, bearing the highest number, gets rejected).

2) the highest number on slips number 1 through r is also the highest number on slips 1 through k (for if the highest number P on slips

1 through r is *greater* than the highest number M on slips 1 through k then $P < Q$ and P will get chosen before the $(r+1)^{\text{st}}$ slip is ever reached).

The probability that the overall largest number Q is on slip $r+1$ (or on *any particular slip*, for that matter) is $1/100$. The probability of finding the slip with number Q on it, assuming that that is slip number $r+1$, is k/r (think, for example, of what can go wrong if $r = k+1$). In sum, the probability of winning the game with the slip having largest number Q, given that that slip is the $(r+1)^{\text{st}}$ and that we will reject the first r and choose the $(r+1)^{\text{st}}$, is

$$p_r = \frac{1}{100} \cdot \frac{k}{r}.$$

The allowable values for r are $r = k, k+1, \ldots, 99$. Thus the probability of winning the game, using the designated strategy, is

$$P = \sum_{r=k}^{99} p_r = \frac{k}{100} \sum_{r=k}^{99} \frac{1}{r}. \qquad (*)$$

But now here is an important lesson about the sum on the right hand side of the last formula:

If x is small and positive then we may write

$$\ln(1+x) = x \cdot \left\{ \ln[(1+x)^{1/x}] \right\}$$

and the expression inside the logarithm on the right is the expression that we use to define Euler's number $e \approx 2.718\ldots$ as $x \to 0$. Thus we have that

$$\ln(1+x) \approx x \cdot \ln e = x.$$

We apply this observation to our sum as follows:

$$
\begin{aligned}
\ln N &= \ln\left[\frac{N}{N-1} \cdot \frac{N-1}{N-2} \cdots \frac{3}{2} \cdot \frac{2}{1} \right] \\
&= \ln\left(\frac{N}{N-1} \right) + \ln\left(\frac{N-1}{N-2} \right) + \cdots + \ln\left(\frac{3}{2} \right) + \ln\left(\frac{2}{1} \right) \\
&= \ln\left(1 + \frac{1}{N-1} \right) + \ln\left(1 + \frac{1}{N-2} \right) \\
&\quad + \cdots + \ln\left(1 + \frac{1}{2} \right) + \ln\left(1 + \frac{1}{1} \right).
\end{aligned}
$$

Now we may apply our observation that $\ln(1 + x) \approx x$ to each of these summands, with the role of $x > 0$ being played by $1/(N - 1)$, $1/(N - 2), \ldots$ The result is that

$$\ln N \approx \frac{1}{N - 1} + \frac{1}{N - 2} + \cdots + \frac{1}{2} + \frac{1}{1}.$$

[Check this approximation formula on your calculator or computer to see how accurate it is!] Thus we see that

$$\sum_{r=k}^{99} \frac{1}{r} = \sum_{r=1}^{99} \frac{1}{r} - \sum_{r=1}^{k-1} \frac{1}{r} \approx \ln 99 - \ln(k - 1) = \ln\left(\frac{99}{k - 1}\right).$$

But, with this approximation, the formula $(*)$ for the probability of getting the slip with the biggest number by passing up k slips and then picking the succeeding slip with the next largest number that we see is

$$P \approx \frac{k}{100} \cdot \ln\left(\frac{99}{k - 1}\right).$$

We wish to select k so that this probability is as large as possible.

Of course calculus is custom made for maximizing a function of this sort. But this book does not presuppose that the reader knows any calculus. Instead, take out your graphing calculator or computer algebra software and, by inspecting the graph of the function

$$P(x) = \frac{x}{100} \cdot \ln\left(\frac{99}{x - 1}\right),$$

determine where P takes its largest value. You will find that the answer is approximately at $x = 100/e$, where e (as previously noted) is Euler's number $e \approx 2.718\ldots$.

We conclude from this analysis that the player should examine the first $100/e$ slips (rounded off to the nearest whole number, which is 37) that he/she draws, remembering the largest number observed on these slips. The next slip that comes up that has a number larger than that observed maximum is the one to choose. This is the optimal strategy.
□

EXERCISES for Chapter 3

1. Show that the number of different ways to deal n distinct playing cards to two players is $2(2^{n-1} - 1)$. [*Hint:* You must allow for the possibility of giving different numbers of cards to each of the players. Each player gets at least one card.]

2. There are five women in a hotel room with a cache of stolen diamonds. They are to divide the loot evenly. When the others are diverted, one woman decides to divide up the diamonds and take her share. She divides them evenly with one left over, which she gives to the maid. She then hides her 'share,' and puts the other four shares together into a single pile.

Later on, a second woman divides the remaining diamonds into five equal shares, with one diamond left over. She gives the odd diamond to the maid, takes her "share," and puts the remaining diamonds into a pile.

Each of the other three women, when the opportunity arises, secretly takes a turn at dividing up what diamonds remain, taking her share, and recombining the others into a single pile. In each instance there is an odd diamond, which the woman gives to the maid.

Finally all five women get together and divide up the (remaining) diamonds equally. One diamond is left over, and it is given to the maid.

What is the fewest number of diamonds that there could have been in the first place?

3. Consider the array in Figure 120. Note that, after the first two rows, each successive row is formed as follows: (i) a 1 goes on each end; (ii) the term one in from the end is obtained by adding the two terms above it; (iii) the terms that are two or more in from the ends are obtained by adding the three terms above it. Explain why each row, beginning with the third, will have at least one even number in it.

4. A little boy has his dollar changed into six coins. Running down the street with the coins in his hand, he loses one down a sewer grate. What is the probability that it was a dime?

5. What is the expected number of children that a married couple must have so that the odds favor their having (at least) two boys and a girl?

6. A spider must eat three flies a day to survive. After he has eaten his three, he quits for the day. For any fly that passes in his path, he has

$$1$$

$$1 \quad 1 \quad 1$$

$$1 \quad 2 \quad 3 \quad 2 \quad 1$$

$$1 \quad 3 \quad 6 \quad 7 \quad 6 \quad 3 \quad 1$$

$$1 \quad 4 \quad 10 \quad 16 \quad 19 \quad 16 \quad 10 \quad 4 \quad 1$$

$$\bullet \quad \bullet \quad \bullet$$

Figure 120

an even chance of nabbing that fly. Given that five flies have sallied past the spider today (some surviving and some not), what is the next fly's chance of survival?

7. With each purchase of a pack of baseball cards, the purchaser receives (for free) one card from a standard deck of 52 playing cards. What is the expected number of packs of baseball cards that one must purchase in order to get a complete deck of 52 distinct playing cards?

8. Bluesky and Truesky are both excellent dart players. Each can hit any target with 50% probability. They stand twenty feet apart and commence to take turns throwing darts at each other. The first to hit the other wins. If Bluesky is the first dart thrower, then what are his odds of winning this battle?

9. Three dots of ink are flung at random onto a disc-shaped target. What is the probability that they are all in the same half disc?

10. Do Exercise 9 with "disc" replaced by "sphere" and "half disc" replaced by "hemisphere."

11. Do Exercise 9 with "disc replaced by "square" and "half disc" replace by "half square." Does it matter whether the square is divided in half horizontally, vertically, or diagonally?

12. A hat contains 1000 slips of paper, each with a different positive integer from 1 to 1000 written on it. Four slips of paper are drawn blind from the hat. What is the probability that the numbers on them occur in increasing order?

13. How does problem 12 change if there are still 1000 slips with 1000 distinct numbers, but we do not know in advance what those numbers are, or how they are sequenced? [Still assume, however, that the 1000 numbers are all distinct.]

14. Five red marbles and four blue marbles are placed in a bag. Five marbles are selected blind from the bag. What is the probability that they are all red?

15. We wish to bring from the river 1 quart of water, but we only have a 8 quart container and a 5 quart container and *no other containers*. How do we do it?

16. Begin writing out the positive integers, beginning with 1. What is the 50,000th digit that you will write?

17. A book with 750 pages is to have its pages numbered in the usual fashion. How many digits will this require?

18. Suppose that T is a triangle. We write s for one of its sides. What is the probability that the length of s is less than the arithmetic mean of the other two sides?

19. Forty one students took three exams each in Algebra, Biology, and Chemistry. We have the following data:

- Twelve students failed the Algebra exam.

- Five students failed the Biology exam.

- Eight students failed the Chemistry exam.

- Two students failed both Algebra and Biology.

- Six students failed both Algebra and Chemistry.

- Three students failed both Biology and Chemistry.

- One student failed all three exams.

[*Note:* Here is how to read this data: Five students failed Biology; of those, two failed both Algebra and Biology. And so forth.]

How many students passed in all three subjects?

20. You are rolling two fair dice, and you are blindfolded. After a certain roll, your friend tells you that you have rolled at least a 9.

What is the probability that you have actually rolled an 11? What is the probability that you have rolled *at least* 11?

21. In the literature of sociology one can find articles that make the following assertion: "The majority of convicted felons in the U.S.A. come from larger than average families." The articles go on to advocate that social engineering should be enacted to address this familial connection between crime and family size.

Consider whether this is an appropriate correlation. Could it be that *most people* come from larger than average families? Set up a statistical model and determine whether that could be true. Perform some experiments!

22. Five men and five women belong to a social club. At the end of the first year, each man ranks the women according to desirability for marriage. Also each woman ranks each man according to desirability for marriage. Given all this data, will there always be five marriages with the property that everyone is satisfied? [Here "satisfied" means that if man x is married to woman y then there is none of the four remaining women with the property than if x instead married her then both he would be married to someone more desirable and so would she, and so that the other resulting marital re-arrangements would be at least as desirable as they already are.]

23. Imagine k clear water glasses. These glasses correspond to the elements of a set S with k elements. Drop just one grape into one glass. Now drop a grape into another. Do this as many times as you like, and then stop. [When you are finished, no glass should contain more than one grape, and some glasses will perhaps have no grapes at all.] Then you have designated a subset of S. Use this as a scheme for counting the subsets of S, and give a new proof that the total number of subsets is 2^k.

24. I knock on the door of some old friends whom I have not seen in years. Their daughter Mary answers the door. Mary says "Oh, we are so glad to see you. I'll go into the back room and get my sibling." What is the probability that the sibling is a boy?

25. Three cards, identical in shape and texture, are produced. One is red on both sides. One is black on both sides. One is red on one side and black on the other. The cards are placed in a hat and you pull one out; *you look only at one side of the card that you have selected.* It is

red. What is the probability that the card that you hold is red on both sides?

26. A fair die is rolled six times. What is the probability of rolling at least a 5 at least five times?

27. What is the number of distinct positive whole number divisors of the integer $30^4 = 810000$?

28. Partition the set $S = \{1, 2, 3, 4, 5\}$ into two disjoint subsets whose union is all of S. Then one of those two subsets must contain two numbers and their difference. Why?

29. To number the pages of a large book, the printer uses 1890 digits. How many pages are in the book?

30. Examine the equations

$$
\begin{aligned}
1 &= 1 \\
2 + 3 + 4 &= 1 + 8 \\
5 + 6 + 7 + 8 + 9 &= 8 + 27 \\
10 + 11 + 12 + \cdots + 16 &= 27 + 64.
\end{aligned}
$$

Determine the pattern and prove the identity.

31. Examine the equations

$$
\begin{aligned}
1 &= 1 \\
1 - 4 &= -(1 + 2) \\
1 - 4 + 9 &= 1 + 2 + 3 \\
1 - 4 + 9 - 16 &= -(1 + 2 + 3 + 4).
\end{aligned}
$$

Determine the pattern and prove the identity.

32. George has 44 dimes and ten pockets in which to put them. Can he distribute them in such a way that he has put a different number of dimes in each pocket?

33. Examine the equations

$$
\begin{aligned}
1 &= 1 \\
3 + 5 &= 8 \\
7 + 9 + 11 &= 27 \\
13 + 15 + 17 + 19 &= 64 \\
21 + 23 + \cdots + 29 &= 125.
\end{aligned}
$$

Determine the pattern and prove the identity.

34. You can compose 50 cents in fifty different ways— using standard American currency consisting of pennies, nickels, dimes, quarters, and half dollars. Show this. In how many different ways can you produce 25 cents?

35. A sign at the entrance to a large American city reads

TOLEDO

OHIO

Each letter is printed on a separate board, and the boards are all of the same size. A great wind comes up and blows the ten boards to the ground. A helpful illiterate comes along and replaces the boards; but his efforts are random since he cannot read. What is the probability that he got 'OHIO' correct? [Assume here that an upside down or backwards **I, H, O** is still a valid **I, H, O**.] What is the probability that he got TOLEDO correct? What is the probability that he got both words correct?

36. Consider a rectangular grid of size $m \times n$. How many different paths, drawn along the grid, are there from the lower left corner to the upper right corner (where only motion up and to the right is allowed)?

37. Three teams play a round robin tournament. The team from New York sits out the first game. After that, the loser of any particular game sits out the following game. A total of eleven games are played. Each team won a different number of games, and New York lost the last game. What are the won-lost records for each of the three teams?

38. Five married couples are to be seated at a round table with ten chairs. How many distinct ways are there to do this so that no person sits next to his/her spouse? [*Hint:* First try this with two or three couples.]

39. It is said that the subject of probability was born when, in 1654, the Chevalier de Méré wrote to his friend Blaise Pascal (an eminent seventeenth century mathematician) and asked him why he lost so consistently when he gambled at dice. It turns out that he was betting even money that, in twenty-four consecutive rolls of a pair of dice, he would come up with a twelve. Emulate Pascal, analyze the situation, and explain what the good Chevalier was doing wrong.

40. Which is more likely: that you will get a 6 at least once when rolling just one die four times, or that you will get a 12 at least once when rolling two dice twenty-four times?

41. Imagine a game played by five people in which each flips a coin at the same time. If all but one of the coins comes up the same, then the odd person wins (for example, if there are four heads and a tail then the "tail" wins). If such a situation does not occur, then the players flip again. What is the probability that the game is settled on the first toss? On the second toss?

42. A hat contains one white ball, two red balls, three green balls, four blue balls, five black balls, six yellow balls, seven orange balls, and eight purple balls. Your friend draws a ball at random, and does not show it to you. You are allowed to ask the friend questions with yes/no answers in order to determine the color of the selected ball. What is your best strategy?

43. A sequence is defined by the rule $a_0 = 2, a_1 = 1$, and $a_j = 3a_{j-1} - a_{j-2}$. Use the method of generating functions to find a formula for a_j.

44. A sequence is defined by the rule $a_0 = 4, a_1 = -1$, and $a_j = -a_{j-1} + 2a_{j-2}$. Use the method of generating functions to find a formula for a_j.

45. A sequence is defined by the rule $a_0 = 0, a_1 = -1$, and $a_j = 3a_{j-1} - 2a_{j-2}$. Use the method of generating functions to find a formula for a_j.

46. Separate a standard deck of 52 playing cards into five piles. What is the probability that one of the top five cards is a face card (King, Queen, or Jack)?

47. How does your answer to Exercise 45 change if there are k piles of cards?

48. One hundred white balls and one hundred black balls are distributed among three hats. You close your eyes, pick a hat, and select a ball from it. Is the probability that you chose a white ball dependent on how you distributed the balls among the hats in the first place?

49. A certain veterinarian specializes in testing herds of cattle for hoof-and-mouth disease. It is convenient for him to treat the cattle in groups of 100. Typically, just one in 500 cattle has the disease (if he catches it early—otherwise the entire herd will have it). The test that he administers is a blood test.

In order to increase efficiency and save costs, the veterinarian comes up with the idea of taking a small portion of the blood sample from each of the cattle in a group of 100, mixing these portions together, and then testing the mixture. If the results are negative, then he can pronounce the entire group of 100 cattle clean, and he has only had to perform one test. If the results are positive, then he will have to go back and examine each of the blood samples from each of the 100 cattle. So in this circumstance he will have to perform 101 tests.

What is the expected number of tests that the veterinarian will have to perform on a total population of 5000 cattle if he uses the procedures outlined above?

50. A tank contains 5 gallons of pure water and one cup (a cup is 1/16 of a gallon) of red dye. The two liquids are thoroughly mixed. You then remove one cup of the *mixture* and replace it with one cup of pure water.

Next, stir up the solution again and remove one cup of the new mixture. Replace it with one cup of pure water.

Keep doing this procedure over and over again: remove one cup of the mixture, replace with pure water, and mix. Obviously the concentration of dye is getting lower and lower (why)? Does the concentration of dye tend to zero if you repeat this operation enough (but finitely many) times? Does the concentration ever become less than 1%? Does it ever become less than .1%? Is there a lower bound on how low the concentration of dye will go?

51. On the front of a 3″ × 5″ card, write the integers 1 through 4, equally spaced in a row. Make them all the same size and shape, so that none of them stands out from the rest. On the back of the card write "Why did you pick 3"?

Now show the front of the card to a friend and ask her to pick a number. You will surprised at how often people pick 3. In that instance, you can instantly turn the card over and create a real surprise.

Why does this work? You will also find that, if you instead use the numbers 1 through 10, people pick 3 and 7 a large part of the time (more often than abstract probability would suggest). Why do you suppose that is?

52. People's stomachs vary in size by a range of 15 to 1, from largest to smallest. Hearts vary in size by a range of 2 to 1; there is a variation

of 3 to 1 in pumping rate. Say that a person's attribute is "average" if it is in the middle third. If these attributes are randomly distributed among people, what percentage of the population will be average with respect to all three characteristics?

53. In poker, the weakest respectable hand is a "pair." A pair consists of two cards of the same denomination: two 7's or two Kings, for instance. Here the 7's could be the 7 of diamonds and the seven of clubs; the Kings could be the King of hearts and the King of spades. A hand in draw poker consists of five cards dealt to each player. For simplicity, suppose that there are only you and one other player in the game. If you are dealt a pair, then is it more likely, or less likely, that the other player will also have a pair (as compared to the situation where you had no pair)?

54. You have a pot of beads. The beads are all identical in size and shape, but come in two different colors. You wish to make a beaded necklace consisting of ten beads. How many different necklaces could you make? Note that two necklaces are *equivalent*, and count as just one necklace, if a rotation of one gives the other. [After you have solved this problem, try replacing "ten" with n and "two" with k and solve it again.]

55. In your drawer there is a pair of green gloves and a pair of brown gloves. You reach in with your eyes closed and pull out two gloves at random. What is the probability that you have a matched pair?

Chapter 4

Problems of Logic

4.1 Straight Logic

The problems in this section tend to involve no mathematics but just plain logic and/or reasoning.

PROBLEM 4.1.1 *Six people, named A, B, C, D, E, F, are in the dining car of a train. They are one each from New York City, Chicago, Tulsa, St. Louis, Milwaukee, and Atlanta. The following facts are known:*

1. *A and the man from New York City are physicians.*

2. *E and the woman from Chicago are teachers.*

3. *The person from Tulsa and C are engineers.*

4. *B and F are veterans of the Gulf war, but the person from Tulsa has never served in the military.*

5. *The person from Milwaukee is older than A.*

6. *The person from Atlanta is older than C.*

7. *At St. Louis, B and the man from New York get off.*

8. *At San Francisco, C and the man from Milwaukee gets off.*

177

Match the names of the people with their professions and their cities.

Solution: It is impossible to overestimate the importance of visual aids. They can help to organize data in a fashion that mere scribblings cannot. With this admonition in mind, we construct the following chart:

	A	B	C	D	E	F
New York	x	x	x		x	
Chicago	x		x		x	
Tulsa	x	x	x		x	x
St. Louis						
Milwaukee	x	x	x			
Atlanta			x			

We put an x in a box when that connection is impossible. For example, statement 1 guarantees that A is not the man from New York, so we put an x in the A column opposite New York. Likewise, statement 7 guarantees that B is not from New York. Statements 1 and 2 taken together imply that A, who is a physician, cannot be from Chicago (since the Chicagoan is a teacher). The other x's come from similar reasoning.

Having entered all these x's, we see that C can only be from St. Louis. But then the only possible city for A is Atlanta. Once St. Louis was fixed for C, it is of course eliminated for the other five people and we mark those with #. Likewise, we eliminate Atlanta for all but A. We put a * to indicate that a city has been matched with a person:

	A	B	C	D	E	F
New York	x	x	x		x	
Chicago	x		x		x	
Tulsa	x	x	x		x	x
St. Louis	#	#	*	#	#	#
Milwaukee	x	x	x			
Atlanta	*	#	x	#	#	#

Now we quickly see that B must be from Chicago, E from Milwaukee, F from New York, and finally D from Tulsa.

Finally, statements 1-3 connect six initials or cities to professions. We conclude that

- A is from Atlanta and is a physician

- B is from Chicago and is a teacher

- C is from St. Louis and is an engineer

- D is from Tulsa and is an engineer

- E is from Milwaukee and is a teacher

- F is from New York and is a physician

The problem is solved. □

CHALLENGE PROBLEM 4.1.2 *Are all eight of the statements in the last problem really needed in order to solve it?*

PROBLEM 4.1.3 *What is the greatest amount of American money that you could have, in pennies, nickels, dimes, and quarters, such that you still could not make up an even dollar?*

Solution: We use the method of elimination. Clearly we cannot have more than 3 quarters, nor more than 9 dimes, nor more than 19 nickels nor more than 99 pennies. Of course things are more complex when we mix the coins.

It is clear that we can make up 99 cents in any number of ways. The trick is to see whether we can make up more than a dollar without being able to make up an even dollar. This could only be possible if some subset of our coins made up an amount less than one dollar, but adding the last coin pushed us past a dollar. For instance, we could have nine dimes and one quarter. Then seven dimes and a quarter makes 95 cents, nine dimes makes 90 cents, eight dimes and a quarter make $1.05, and the lot makes $1.15.

Can we improve on the last example? Clearly the phenomenon we have uncovered hinges on having an odd number of quarters present and then using the fact that dimes cannot make up the difference with one dollar (pennies and nickels always *can* make up the difference). We plainly cannot allow one quarter and ten dimes, for ten dimes make an even dollar. Adding nickels makes things worse rather than better, for that evens out the odd five cents in 25 cents. We could add four pennies: nine dimes, one quarter, and four pennies gives $1.19, and it is not possible to make a dollar from these coins. [Note that we cannot have five pennies since then an even dollar could be composed.]

A second approach would be to have three quarters, four dimes (five dimes would allow an even dollar to be made up), and four pennies. This also makes $1.19. A moment's thought shows that no improvement over $1.19 is possible.   □

CHALLENGE PROBLEM 4.1.4 *Solve the preceding problem with "one dollar" replaced by "fifty cents". How about "seventy five cents"?*

PROBLEM 4.1.5 *Three people stand in a circle with their eyes closed. A hat is placed on each of their heads. Each hat is either red or black in color, and all three players know this. They all open their eyes simultaneously, and each player who sees a red hat is to raise a hand. The first player to then be able to correctly identify the color of his/her own hat will win a prize.*

With this setup, what will happen if two hats are red and one is black?

Solution: This is too easy. Suppose that the players are called A, B, and C. Say that C wears the black hat.

Since there are two red hats, all three players raise their hands. Player A sees that C is wearing a black hat. She reasons that *she* cannot be wearing a black hat; for if she were, then B would not have his hand raised. Thus A concludes that she must be wearing a red hat. Player B can reason similarly. Thus either A or B, whoever is quickest, will speak up and win.

Player C must lose. He sees that both A and B are wearing red hats and both have their hands raised. Player C realizes that he could have either a red hat or a black hat and that no further conclusion is possible.   □

PROBLEM 4.1.6 *Do an analysis of the last problem in which we assume that each player wears a red hat.*

Solution: Again call the players A, B, and C. Obviously all three players will raise their hands, because each will see a red hat (indeed, two red hats). Suppose, for the sake of argument, that A is the quickest of the three players. He knows that his hat cannot be black. For, if it were black then B would know that *his* hat cannot be black, otherwise C would not have his hand raised. So, if A's hat were black, then B would have figured this all out and would have concluded that his own hat was red and would have said so. Player C could have reasoned in the same way, if A's hat had been black, and would have spoken up. Since neither B nor C has spoken up, A concludes that his own hat is red, says so, and wins the prize.   □

CHALLENGE PROBLEM 4.1.7 *What happens in the preceding problem(s) if there are now four players, and each has a red hat? [Hint: How does this problem relate to Exercise 1.5.4?]*

PROBLEM 4.1.8 *Two vacationers travel to Hawaii. Each independently buys the same effigy of the war god Mauna Loa. Each puts her
purchase in checked baggage for the return flight home. The airline
loses both of these art treasures.*

*Each traveler applies for reimbursement (the travelers are unac-
quainted). Offering no proof, each traveler puts down a putative value
for the statue that she lost. The two claimants do not consult with
each other before making their claims.*

*The manager who is to evaluate the claims notifies the two travelers
beforehand that he is expecting two claims and will judge them as
follows: (i) All claims must be for a whole number of dollars between
$5 and $200, inclusive; (ii) The person submitting the lower claim must
be telling the truth and will be awarded the amount of her claim plus
three dollars reward for honesty; (ii) The person submitting the higher
claim must be lying and will therefore be awarded the amount of the
lower claim less three dollars for dishonesty. In case of a tie, both
claimants will be treated as in case (ii)*

*Both travelers are smart, and equally so. What is the best strategy
for each traveler to adopt?*

Solution: Clearly each traveler wants to maximize her return. Call
the travelers A and B.

If both travelers submit claims for $200 then each will garner $197.
Both travelers know this. Reasoning in this way, player A decides that
she had better claim only $199. But player B reasons in the same way,
and knows that A will have reasoned in this fashion also. Therefore
player B decides to claim $198.

Player A, however, can go through just the same reasoning that B
performed in the last paragraph, and knows that B can reason thus as
well, so A decides to bid $197.

Proceeding by backward induction, both players end up submitting
claims for $5 and receiving $2 for their pains. □

The analysis of the last problem is troubling. It is an example, of
the sort that often occurs in game theory, of both players using correct
reasoning but coming to a conclusion that seems preposterous. What
is operative here is *point of view*. If each player could know what was

going on in the other player's mind, and if they could communicate with each other, then a more desirable conclusion could be reached. Since both players are trying to out-fox each other, each player strategizes herself into what is, in effect, a losing position. For further insight into this type of problem, read [MON] to learn about the prisoner's dilemma (see also Exercise 18 at the end of Chapter 7).

CHALLENGE PROBLEM 4.1.9 *Try to find a different analysis of the last problem that leads to a more favorable conclusion for at least one of the players.*

CHALLENGE PROBLEM 4.1.10 *A game is played by two players. Sitting before them is a pile of fifty pennies. The players alternate turns. Each move consists of a player removing either one or two pennies from the pile.*

The game ends if either the supply of pennies is depleted or if some player opts to remove two pennies (in other words, if a player removes one penny then the game proceeds; otherwise it ends).

Given that each player wants to gather as many pennies as possible, what is an optimal strategy for the first player?

In the next section we shall give a more detailed treatment of the subject of "games".

4.2 Games

In this section we examine various games and game-like situations. Game theory has become a serious part of modern analytical thinking. One of the first works to help realize the importance of game theory was [MON] by von Neumann and Morgenstern. We shall not attempt to develop any applications of game theory, but shall instead concentrate on the games themselves.

PROBLEM 4.2.1 *A game is played by two players. They begin with a pile of 30 chips, all the same. For his or her move, a player may remove 1 to 6 chips. The player who removes the last chip wins. What strategy can the first player use so that he will always win?*

Solution: We call the first player A and the second player B. We wish to devise a strategy for A so that he/she can surely win.

Our idea is to work backwards. Clearly A would like to be left, on his last move, with a pile of 6 or fewer chips. Then he can pick up all the remaining chips, clear the table, and win the game. Thus, on the preceding move, B should be faced with a number of chips such that, after B selects his chips, A will be left with 6 or fewer.

If B is faced with, say, 8 chips, then he will pick just 1, leaving A with 7. That is not good for A, since then A cannot clear the table. The same is true if B is face with 9 chips, or even more. Best for A would be if B is faced with 7 chips. Note that B has to choose at least 1, but not more than 6. So that he will leave between 1 and 6 for A, and A will be able to clear the table. The upshot of our reasoning is that A wants B to be faced with 7 chips on the second-to-last move.

Reasoning backward from this result, and using the very same logic, we see that on the fourth-to-last move A would like B to be faced with 14 chips. Then, no matter how many B removes (from 1 to 6 chips), A can take the complementary number on the third-to-last move so that B is faced with 7 chips. We already know that that is a winning situation for A. [For example, if B is faced with 14 chips and B takes 3 then A will take 4.]

Repeating this strategy, we see that on the sixth-to-last move A would like B to be faced with 21 chips. And, on the eighth-to-last move A would like B to be faced with 28 chips.

The problems is solved: For his first move, A removes two chips, leaving B with 28. No matter how many B removes (from 1 to 6), A then takes the complementary number so that B is faced with 21 chips. Then, no matter how many B removes, A then takes the complementary number so that B is faced with 14 chips. Next, no matter how many chips B removes, A takes the complementary number so that B is faced with 7 chips. This is the final moment. No matter how many chips B removes on this, his last move, A can clear the table.

This completes our winning strategy for A. $\qquad\square$

CHALLENGE PROBLEM 4.2.2 *Consider the game in the last problem. Can you devise a winning strategy for the second player in this game?*

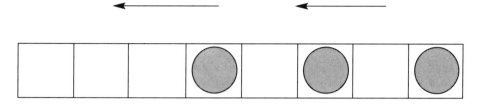

Figure 121

What if the first player is already implementing the strategy that we developed in our solution of the last problem?

PROBLEM 4.2.3 *A game is played on a board consisting of eight adjacent squares, as shown in Figure 121. The initial position for the three pieces is shown in the figure. A legal move is to move one piece to the left by one square. A piece can be moved on top of another piece or off of another piece. The goal is to move all three pieces to the square at the far left. The player who makes the last move wins. What is a winning strategy for the first player?*

Solution: Denote the first player by A and the second player by B. Draw a board, with $1'' \times 1''$ squares for this game. Use three nickels as pieces. Try playing several games. Either do it by yourself or with a friend. What do you notice? No matter what you do, A wins. How could this be?

Notice that the pieces move only forward (left) and never backward (right). Number the three pieces **1,2**, and **3** from left to right. In any game, piece **1** will be moved a total of three times on its journey to the far left. Piece **2** will be moved a total of five times on its journey to the far left. And piece **3** will be moved a total of seven times on its journey to the far left. So the total number of legal moves in any game is $3 + 5 + 7 = 15$. That is, any game will have the same odd number of moves.

Of those moves, A will make moves number 1, 3, 5, 7, 9, 11, 13, and 15. In other words, no matter what happens during the game, A will always make the last move. Therefore A will win.

The conclusion of our analysis is that *any strategy* is a winning strategy for A. □

PROBLEM 4.2.4 (Chinese Traditional) *This game is played beginning with two piles of chips. The piles may or may not have the
same number of chips. There are two players. A legal move is either
(i) to remove any number of chips from one pile, or (ii) to remove an
equal number of chips from each pile. The player who removes the last
chip from the table wins.*

*Give two examples of winning positions. Give two examples of losing
positions.*

Solution: The trick here is not to get too fancy. First, we decide what
a "winning position" is. It is a position such that the player facing it is
sure to win provided that he/she plays correctly. A "losing position" is
one such that the player facing it is sure to lose *no matter what he/she
does* (provided, of course, that the other player plays wisely).

A trivial example of a winning position in this game is $(1, 0)$. This
notation means that there is one chip in the first pile and no chips
in the second pile. It is a winning position because the player facing
it will invoke rule (i) and remove all the (one) chips from the first
pile. Likewise the position $(k, 0)$, for k a positive integer, is a winning
position. For the player facing it will simply remove all the chips from
the first pile.

Both of the examples in the last paragraph are deemed "trivial"
because the player facing the position wins instantly, on that move,
provided he/she does the right thing. A "non-trivial" winning position
would be one for which the player facing the position has to plan ahead
for at least one move by the other player.

Working backwards from what we learned in the last paragraph, we
see that any position $(j, j + 1)$ for $j \geq 2$ is a winning position. The
player facing it will invoke rule (ii) and remove $(j - 1)$ chips from each
pile. That will leave the position $(1, 2)$ for the other player to face.
Now that other player is cooked no matter what he/she does:

1) If the other player removes 1 chip from each pile then that leaves
$(0, 1)$ and the first player wins.

2) If the other player removes all chips from the first pile, then that
leaves $(0, 2)$ and the first player removes all chips from the second pile
and wins.

3) If the other player removes one chip from the second pile, then that leaves $(1, 1)$. The first player can then remove both piles at once, clearing the table.

4) If the other player removes all chips from the second pile, then that leaves $(1, 0)$ and the first player removes all (one) chips from the first pile and wins.

Building on what we have learned so far, we see that any position $(1, k)$ with $k > 2$ is a winning position. For the player facing it removes $(k - 2)$ chips from the second pile. This leaves the other player with $(1, 2)$, which we know to be a losing position from our earlier analysis.

We have seen several winning positions. Along the way, we have seen one losing position: namely $(1, 2)$ (and, for that matter, $(2, 1)$) is a losing position. No matter what a player faced with that position does, he/she will lose.

The position $(3, 5)$ is also a losing position. We analyze and discover why. If the player facing this position removes 1 chip from the second pile, then the other player has $(3, 4)$ and we have already noted that this is a win. If he/she instead removes 2 chips from the second pile, then the other player invokes rule (ii) and clears the table. If our player removes 3 chips from the second pile then the other player is left with a $(j + 1, j)$ situation and wins. If our player removes 4 chips from the second pile then $(3, 1)$ remains; the other player removes one chip from the first pile, leaving our player in the losing $(2, 1)$ position. If our player removes the entire second pile, then the other player wins by rule (i).

If our player removes 1 chip from the first pile then the other player removes 4 from the second, leaving us in a losing position. If our player removes 2 chips from the first pile then the other player removes 3 from the second pile and we are in a losing position. Once again, it is an immediate loss to clear the entire first pile in one move.

It remains to check the cases where our player removes an equal number of chips from each pile. These are similar to the ones already discussed, and the details are left for you. $\square$

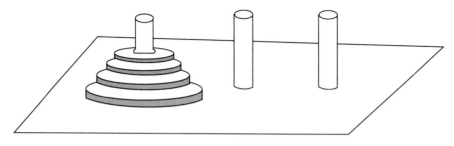

Figure 122

CHALLENGE PROBLEM 4.2.5 *Is it true that any position of the form* $(k, k + 2)$ *is a losing position?*

CHALLENGE PROBLEM 4.2.6 *A pile of fifteen chips sits on the table. Two players take turns removing chips. At each turn, a player may remove 1, 2, or 3 chips. That player wins who ends up with an odd number of chips in his possession.*

Devise a winning strategy for either player.

PROBLEM 4.2.7 (The Tower of Hanoi) *Figure 122 illustrates the setup for the famous "Tower of Hanoi" puzzle. [Hackers know that the strategy that we are going to develop in the study of this problem is used as a model for rotating tapes in backing up computer systems.] Notice that there are four discs, of increasing size, on the leftmost post. The goal is to move all the discs, in the same configuration, to the right most post. The rules are that any disc that is on top of any pile can be lifted and moved to any other post. However at no time are we allowed to place a larger disc atop a smaller disc.*

What is a strategy for moving all four discs to the rightmost post?

Solution: We begin with a simpler problem. Suppose that there are only two discs, with the small one on top and the large on the bottom, both on the far left post. As a first move we put the topmost small disc on the middle post. Then we put the larger disc on the right post. Then we move the small disc onto the right post, on top of the larger disc. That solves the problem for two discs.

Now we look at three discs. It is reasonable to suppose that the solution for three discs will make use of what we learned in thinking about two discs. Call the discs 1,2,3, with 1 being the smallest and 3 the largest. Call the posts A, B, C, where A is the leftmost and C is the rightmost.

Begin by putting 1 on C. Then put 2 on B. Now put 1 on B. Then put 3 on C. You can see that what we have accomplished is to transfer the larger disc to the rightmost post and to leave discs 1 and 2, in the proper order, on post B. This is precisely analogous to the situation in the first paragraph of this solution. So we may now repeat those moves to transfer 1 and 2 over to post C. That solves the case of three discs.

Now we consider four discs. Using what we learned in the last paragraph, our plan is to get the largest disc (call it 4) onto the rightmost post, while returning 1,2,3 (in their standard order) to the first or second post. This will reduce the situation to the problem solved in the last paragraph.

Begin by putting 1 on B. Now put 2 on C. Next put 1 on C. Then transfer 3 to B. Now 4 is freed up and we have to transfer it to C. Put 1 on A, 2 on B, and then 1 on B. Now post C is free, discs 1,2,3 are on B in their natural order, and 4 is alone on A. Transfer 4 to C. Finally, we transfer 1,2,3 to post C using our solution of the "three disc problem." That completes the solution of the four disc Tower of Hanoi problem. $\square$

Notice how, in our solution of the last problem, the solving of simpler cases was more than a formal exercise. Besides their use as "finger exercises," we also were able to use the simpler cases to organize our thoughts. Our solution of the two disc problem made the presentation of the solution of the three disc problem simple and elegant. Likewise, our solution of the three disc problem made it relatively straightforward to explain the solution of the four disc problem.

CHALLENGE PROBLEM 4.2.8 *Describe a solution of the five disc Tower of Hanoi problem.*

CHALLENGE PROBLEM 4.2.9 *Describe an algorithm for reducing the k disc Tower of Hanoi problem to the $(k-1)$ disc problem.*

CHALLENGE PROBLEM 4.2.10 *Demonstrate that the k disc Tower of Hanoi problem can be solved in not more than $2^k - 1$ moves. Indeed, find an algorithm that can be implemented by a computer (this algorithm will be closely related to our algorithm for solving certain magic squares—as presented in Section 5.1).*

PROBLEM 4.2.11 *Suppose that a pseudo-checkerboard is k squares by k squares, instead of 8×8. Is it possible to put k checkers on the board so that no two are in the same row, no two are in the same column, and none is on either of the diagonals?*

Solution: It is often useful to try a special case. A 2×2 checkerboard is too simple to be meaningful. We next try 3×3. The checker to go in the first column cannot go in the first row (for then it would be on a diagonal) and cannot go in the last row. So it must go in the second row. That means that the checker in the second column must go in either the first or third rows (it cannot go in the second row anyway, for then it would be on the diagonal). Since the two configurations are symmetric, say that it goes in the first row. Then the checker in the third column must go in the third row, so it is on the diagonal.

The situation in the last paragraph is inescapable. What the problem requests is impossible for a 3×3 pseudo-checkerboard. We might conjecture at this stage that the problem is impossible in general. We now try a 4×4 pseudo-checkerboard. After some fiddling, we find that we can place checkers in positions $(3, 1), (1, 2), (4, 3)$, and $(2, 4)$. [Here $(3, 1)$ means the position third from the top and one from the left; the position $(2, 4)$ means the position second from the top and fourth from the left; etc.] This arrangement will satisfy the conditions of the problem.

Now we modify our conjecture to this: if the pseudo-checkerboard has at least 4 squares on a side then it is possible to satisfy the conditions of the problem. We now verify this assertion using induction. But we use it in a (slightly) new fashion.

We have already verified that the checkers can be arranged, as requested, on a 4×4 board. You should verify by hand that you can do a 5×5 board, a 6×6 board, and a 7×7 board (or you may cheat by looking at Figure 123 on page 192).

Now we check the following assertion: if we can solve the problem for a $k \times k$ board then we can use that solution to solve the problem for a $(k + 4) \times (k + 4)$ board. To see this, examine Figure 124, which shows the $k \times k$ board sitting inside the $(k + 4) \times (k + 4)$ board in a convenient fashion. Place checkers in a winning position on the smaller $k \times k$ board. Now add checkers, as indicated in Figure 125, at positions $(1, 2), (2, 1), (k + 3, k + 4)$, and $(k + 4, k + 3)$ on the large board. Then the problem is solved for the $(k + 4) \times (k + 4)$ board.

Our solution is now completed in four steps. Begin by noting that the result of the last paragraph can now be applied beginning with the 4×4 board. This gives solutions for $k = 4, 8, 12, 16$, etc. Next we can apply the result of the last paragraph beginning with the 5×5 board. This gives solutions for $k = 5, 9, 13, 17$, etc. Next we can apply the result of the last paragraph beginning with the 6×6 board. This gives solutions for $k = 6, 10, 14, 18$, etc. Finally, we can apply the result of the last paragraph beginning with the 7×7 board. This gives solutions for $k = 7, 11, 15, 19$, etc.

A glance now shows that we have constructed solutions for all $k \geq 4$. □

CHALLENGE PROBLEM 4.2.12 *Can you place k checkers on a $k \times k$ pseudo-checkerboard so that each column has just one checker, each row has just one checker, and each diagonal has just one checker?*

4.3 Tracing Routes, and Learning from Parity

In this section we will consider some of the most famous elementary problems in all of mathematics. Some of these involve questions of tracing paths. For example:

PROBLEM 4.3.1 *Consider the geometric object in Figure 126. Notice that it has 16 segments delineated in its sides. Can we trace a continuous planar path that passes through each segment exactly once?*

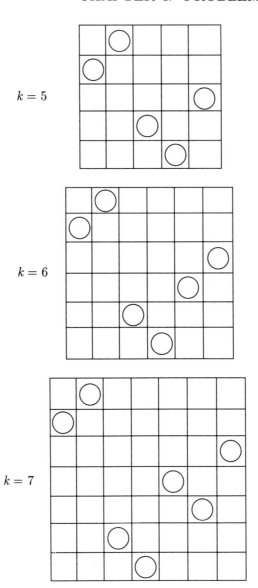

Figure 123

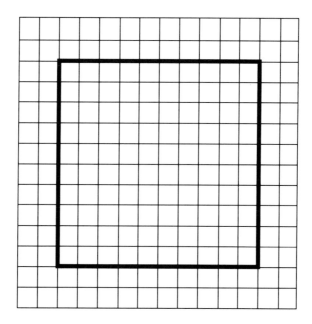

Figure 124

[Note: The path is not allowed to pass through a vertex; it can only pass into or out of a region by going through the interior of an edge.]

This problem has baffled people for ages. In fact it is impossible to produce such a path, and we will provide the correct logical argument for seeing this in a moment. The fact remains that there are those who refuse to believe these mathematical arguments, and who persist in seeking the elusive path. Always remember that a "solution" to a problem, like a mathematical proof, is a psychological device. Its purpose is to *convince* the reader that the problem is solved.

Solution: The large rectangle has been subdivided into five regions. Notice that three of those regions—the upper left, the upper right, and the lower middle—each has an odd number (five) of walls, or bounding edges. Now the critical fact about a region U with an odd number of bounding edges is this: if a path begins in U then it cannot terminate in U; if the path does *not* begin in U then it *must* terminate in U.

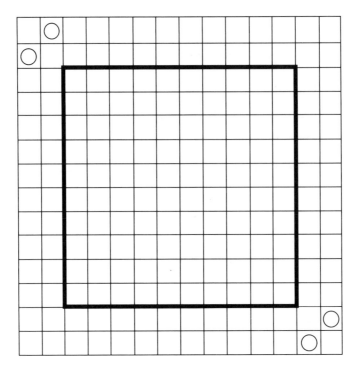

Figure 125

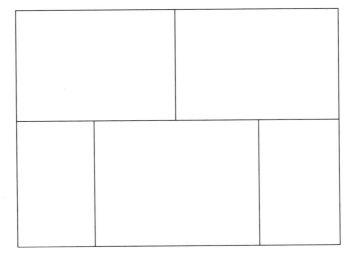

Figure 126

This point is so important that it bears some further thought. Suppose that a region V has two edges. We are only allowed to cross each edge once. If a path begins inside the region, then the first time it crosses an edge it will exit the region. Now one edge has been used up. There is just one edge remaining, for that region, to be crossed. The path may or may not cross that second edge immediately, but (according to the rules) it must do so eventually. When it does so, the path will cross from the outside of the region to the inside. Then the path is trapped, because it has already crossed (exactly once!) each edge that the region V possesses. It cannot leave, so the path must terminate there.

The same reasoning applies to a region that has 4 or 6 or any even number of edges: if the path begins inside that region then it must end there. If the path begins outside the region then it must terminate outside the region.

The reasoning for a region with an odd number of edges is just the opposite. Take a region W with three edges. Suppose that the path begins inside W. For a first move, the path can pass through one edge of W and then end up in the exterior of W. At some later time (perhaps not immediately), the path may cross another of the edges of W; this time it will be passing from the outside of W to the inside. Now there is just one edge of W left. The path is required to pass through every edge just once, so it will next pass through the remaining edge of W. Now all edges of W have been exhausted, and the path is outside W. It cannot get back into W because all edges of W have been used. The same reasoning would apply to a region having 5 or 7 or any odd number of edges.

Now we return to the problem at hand. There are three regions, already identified, each having an odd number of edges. Call these regions E_1, E_2, E_3. If the path begins at a point exterior to all three of these regions, then it must terminate inside *each one* of these regions. That is what our preceding reasoning demands. Since the interiors of the E_j are pairwise disjoint, this is plainly impossible. Thus the path must begin inside one (and only one) of these three regions. Say that it begins inside E_1. Then it is beginning at a point that is external to E_2 and external to E_3. Then our reasoning shows that the path must terminate at a point exterior to E_1 (no problem so far) but also *internal* to E_2 and E_3. However there are no points that are both internal to E_2 and internal to E_3.

Similar reasoning applies if the path begins at a point internal to E_2 or at a point internal to E_3.

We have eliminated all possible points where the path could begin. Thus we have an untenable situation, and there is no path that fits the description in the problem.   □

Notice the decisive use of "parity" in the solution of the first problem. The notion of parity we used is to distinguish between regions with an odd number of edges and regions with an even number of edges. If you attempt to construct a solution that sounds like "Well, we could start by crossing this edge, and then we could go up here. Well, now we have a choice of going to the left or going around the other side. Then the problem branches into four choices ... ," you will become most frustrated. It is nearly impossible to keep track of all the different possibilities and branchings. You will find that many times a parity argument (remember covering the bathroom floor with tiles in Chapter 1?) cuts through all the apparent complications and gives a crisp solution. Of course, a clever programmer could use a computer to actually *try* all the possibilities.

Here is a problem that is much like the first one. It is also historically significant: the celebrated mathematician Leonhard Euler (1707-1783) was instrumental in its solution. Some historians trace the foundations of the topology of the plane to this problem. So we include it for the sake of culture.

PROBLEM 4.3.2 (The Seven Bridges of Königsberg)   *In the town of Königsberg (now Kaliningrad, in Russia) there are seven bridges. [Well, actually, by some accounts it has eight. But the problem with eight bridges has a different solution—see below.] They are depicted in Figure 127. The problem is to draw a continuous path that crosses each bridge exactly once.*

Solution: The figure depicts the bodies of water as shaded, and the land masses and bridges as white. Notice that each of the four land masses gives way onto an odd number of bridges. Thus we have the

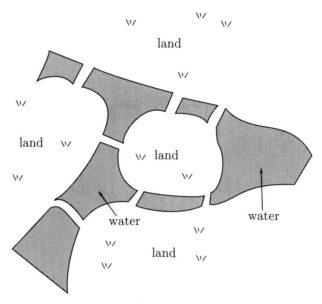

The seven bridges of Königsberg

Figure 127

same situation as in the last problem: if the path begins on a particular land mass, then it cannot terminate there.

As an exercise, complete the argument to see that no path, as demanded in the problem, is possible.   □

CHALLENGE PROBLEM 4.3.3 *Figure 128 shows the configuration of the town of Königsberg with an eighth bridge. Show that now it is possible to draw a continuous path that crosses each bridge exactly once.*

How many distinct ways are there to solve this problem?

CHALLENGE PROBLEM 4.3.4 *Can you find a subset of seven of the eight bridges in the last Challenge Problem so that a single continuous path may traverse all seven of those bridges?*

PROBLEM 4.3.5 (Sam Loyd) *Consider the diagram in Figure 129. It shows various letters which can be used to spell out the sentence*

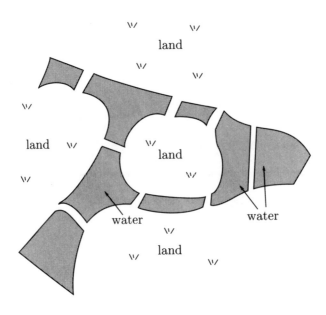

Figure 128

"WAS IT A CAT I SAW?" The question is this: in how many different ways, beginning on an edge, can you march along, from letter to letter, in the diagram and spell out this sentence?

Solution: If you attempt to actually count the various paths then you will quickly run out of patience. What we need is an idea.

A faulty attempt is as follows: Since the sentence ends with "SAW," and hence with a 'W', therefore it must terminate on an edge. Likewise, the sentence begins with "WAS," so begins with a 'W', and so must start on an edge. There are 24 distinct W's running around the edge. Each version of the sentence must begin at one of these W's and end at one of these W's. All different beginnings and endings are possible.

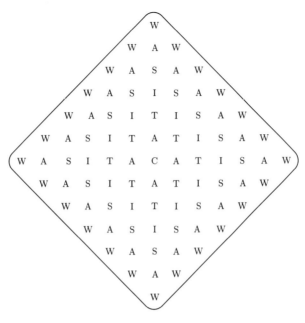

Figure 129

Therefore the number of different ways to trace out the sentence is 24 × 24 or 576 ways.

The count in the last paragraph falls far short. For we have overlooked the fact that the sentence is a *palindrome*: it reads the same forward as backwards. What one then notices is that one needs to (i) begin at a square on the edge, (ii) proceed to the center, spelling out 'WAS IT A C', and then proceed back out to the edge, spelling out 'AT I SAW'.

Counting all the branch routes, there are 252 different ways to begin at an edge square and proceed to the center (we leave this as an exercise for you). There are, of course, just as many ways to begin at the center and go back out to the edge. A *complete* path would consist of one of the first followed by one of the second. Thus the total number

Figure 130

of possibilities is $252^2 = 63504$. We see that our initial guess of 576 was off by several orders of magnitude.   □

The idea of a palindrome is one that has amused puzzle solvers for many years. The longest (sensible) palindrome known to this author is

GO HANG A SALAMI I'M A LASAGNA HOG.

The World Wide Web site

        http://www.cs.brown.edu/people/nfp/palindrome.html

contains myriad examples of palindromes, as well as information on how to create them.   □

CHALLENGE PROBLEM 4.3.6 *Three water glasses are arranged on a table as in Figure 130. Notice that the two on the ends are right side up and the middle one is upside down. You are allowed to turn glasses over two at a time. The goal is to end up with all glasses right side up.*

Show that this is impossible.

PROBLEM 4.3.7 *A lattice point in three dimensional space ($\mathbb{R}^3$) is one with all integer coordinates. Take any nine different lattice points in $\mathbb{R}^3$. Explain why one of the (thirty six) line segments connecting two of them must have midpoint that is a lattice point.*

Solution: First notice that it is not automatic for the midpoint of a segment connecting two lattice points to be a lattice point. For instance, $A = (0, 0, 0)$ and $B = (1, 1, 1)$ are lattice points, but their midpoint is $C = (1/2, 1/2, 1/2)$, which is *not* a lattice point.

As we see from this simple example, what can go *wrong* is the following: When we compute the midpoint of the segment determined by $A = (a, b, c)$ and $A' = (a', b', c')$ then the coordinates of that midpoint are $([a+a']/2, [b+b']/2, [c+c']/2)$. In order for each of these coordinates to be whole numbers, it must be that $a + a'$ is even, $b + b'$ is even, and $c + c'$ is even. Thus a, a' must either both be even or both be odd. Likewise for b, b' and c, c'. This is the determining feature.

We let e stand for "even" and o stand for "odd." Then the possible parities for a lattice point in space are

$$(e, e, e) \qquad (e, e, o) \qquad (e, o, o)$$
$$(e, o, e) \qquad (o, o, o) \qquad (o, o, e)$$
$$(o, e, e) \qquad (o, e, o)$$

In other words, there are a total of *eight* possibilities. But, in the problem, we are given *nine* lattice points. Thus two of them must have the same parity. By the preceding reasoning, the midpoint of those two points must also be a lattice point. □

4.4 Mysterious Arithmetic Problems

In this section we shall explore a class of problems that goes back to the English mathematician Berwick in the first part of this century, and probably predates even Berwick by several years.

PROBLEM 4.4.1 *Consider the letters in the display*

```
    L E T S
    W A V E
    ---------
    L A T E R
```

This represents an addition problem. Different letters stand for different digits (chosen from among $0, 1, 2, \ldots, 9$). Two occurrences of the same letter (such as A) stand for the same digit. The problem is to identify all the digits.

Solution: We begin with the leftmost L in **LATER**. This L arises from the carrying operation of arithmetic. Since the L and W that we added to get this leftmost L can each be no greater than 9, there is no way (even if we did some carrying from adding the E and the A) that the leftmost L could be anything other than a 1 (we could not allow this particular L to be zero, since a zero in that position would ordinarily never be written). Thus $L = 1$ in the leftmost and therefore in *both occurrences*.

Now W could only be an 8 or a 9, since we have to add it to $L = 1$ to force a carrying operation. However it cannot be 8, since then A must be zero and there will have to be carrying from the addition of E and A to bump $L + W = 1 + 8$ up to 10. With A being zero, that would force E to be equal to 9, and we would have to carry from the addition of T and V so that E would not equal T. But even that wouldn't help, because after the carrying the result would be that $T = 0$ and 0 is already taken. So W cannot equal 8; it must equal 9.

Our display now reads as follows:

$$
\begin{array}{c}
1\ E\ T\ S \\
9\ 0\ V\ E \\
\hline
1\ 0\ T\ E\ R
\end{array}
$$

Now, whatever E is, T will have to be one greater (from carrying) so that T will be unequal to E. But $T + V$ must yield E again. How could this be, unless V is 9? But V cannot be 9 because 9 is taken. So V must be equal to 8, and the addition of S and E will have to force a carry. Now we have

$$
\begin{array}{c}
1\ E\ T\ S \\
9\ 0\ 8\ E \\
\hline
1\ 0\ T\ E\ R
\end{array}
$$

Notice that T cannot be 2, because then E is 1 and 1 is taken. If $T = 3$ then E is 2 and we have

```
    1 2 3 S
    9 0 8 2
   ---------
  1 0 3 2 R
```

Since 9 and 8 are taken, then S cannot be greater than 7. But then the addition in the rightmost column does not result in a carry and nothing works.

If $T = 4$ then $E = 3$ and we have

```
    1 3 4 S
    9 0 8 3
   ---------
  1 0 4 3 R
```

We are stuck again because if $S = 7$ then $R = 0$ and 0 is taken; if $S = 6$ then there is no carry in the rightmost column. So we cannot allow $T = 4$.

The possibility of $T = 5$ is eliminated in the same fashion. You should work out this case as an exercise. Now we try $T = 6$. Then $E = 5$ and we have

```
    1 5 6 S
    9 0 8 5
   ---------
  1 0 6 5 R
```

What is different now is that $S = 7$, $R = 2$ is a viable choice, and everything works. We have solved our puzzle as

```
    1 5 6 7
    9 0 8 5
   ---------
  1 0 6 5 2
```

It is an exercise for you to check that $T = 7$ cannot work; $T = 8$ is not an option because 8 is taken. Thus we have found the unique solution to our problem.   □

CHALLENGE PROBLEM 4.4.2 *Solve the addition problem*

```
            S E N D
            M O R E
          ---------
          M O N E Y
```

Follow the rules given in the last problem.

Here is a slightly different problem, of intermediate difficulty:

PROBLEM 4.4.3 *Consider the division problem*

```
                    *  5  3
                 -------------
      *  *  9  |  6  *  8  *  *  *
                 *  *  *  2
                 -------
                    *  9  *  *
                    *  *  4  *
                    -------
                       *  *  4  *
                       *  *  *  *
                       -------
```

in which a number of the digits have been obliterated. It turns out that each of the missing digits is uniquely determined by the information provided. Solve for the missing digits.

Solution: First, we rename the *'s with letters so that we may refer to them easily:

```
                a 5 3
            ------------
b c 9 | 6 d 8 e f g              First   line
        h i j 2                  Second  line
        -------
          k 9 l m                Third   line
          n o 4 p                Fourth  line
          -------
            q r 4 s              Fifth   line
            t u v w              Sixth   line
            -------
```

Notice that $3 \cdot bc9$ gives the Sixth line. This forces w to be a 7, with 2 carried. But then c must be 4 so that the next step of the multiplication $3 \cdot bc9$ gives a 4 in the second-to-last place. Of course s must equal w, so must be 7. We get that $p = 5$ immediately because the Third line is $5 \cdot b49$. Now we have

```
                a 5 3
            ------------
b 4 9 | 6 d 8 e f g              First   line
        h i j 2                  Second  line
        -------
          k 9 l m                Third   line
          n o 4 5                Fourth  line
          -------
            q r 4 7              Fifth   line
            t u 4 7              Sixth   line
            -------
```

The visuals are helpful. Now we see that m must be 9 (because $9 - 5 = 4$), so that f is 9. Note also that a must be 8 so that the last digit of the Second line turns out to be a 2. This makes j a 9. So now we have

```
                  8 5 3
            -------------
  b 4 9 | 6 d 8 e 9 g                First  line
          h i 9 2                    Second line
          -------
            k 9 1 9                  Third  line
            n o 4 5                  Fourth line
            -------
              q r 4 7                Fifth  line
              t u 4 7                Sixth  line
              -------
```

Notice that g is a 7, and h must turn out to be a 6. Thus b is either a 7 or an 8. If b is an 8 then $hi92$ is 6792 and $no45$ is 4245. Our diagram becomes

```
                  8 5 3
            -------------
  8 4 9 | 6 d 8 e 9 7                First  line
          6 7 9 2                    Second line
          -------
            k 9 1 9                  Third  line
            4 2 4 5                  Fourth line
            -------
              q r 4 7                Fifth  line
              t u 4 7                Sixth  line
              -------
```

Now we have a problem because k must turn out to be a 4. This means that d is a 2, but then the subtraction of the Second line from the First does not work since the Second line is too small. So we cannot allow b to equal 8. It must equal 7. Our diagram is now

```
                    8 5 3
              -------------
  7 4 9 | 6 d 8 e 9 7          First  line
          5 9 9 2              Second line
          -------
            k 9 1 9            Third  line
            3 7 4 5            Fourth line
            -------
              q r 4 7          Fifth  line
              2 2 4 7          Sixth  line
              -------
```

But now we have the complete divisor and the complete quotient. We may multiply them to find that the dividend equals 638897. The rest of the digits may now be found using ordinary arithmetic. □

Next is Berwick's problem itself. It is, in essence, no more complicated than the one we have already examined. But it requires many more steps for its solution. It is perhaps the most famous problem of its kind.

PROBLEM 4.4.4 (Berwick) *Consider the long division problem*

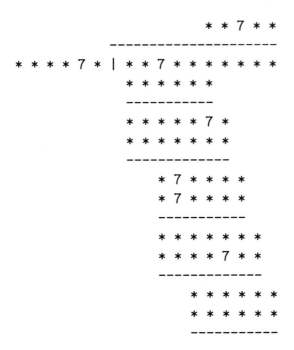

Apart from the 7's shown, all the digits in the problem have been suppressed. The challenge is to restore the missing digits.

Solution: Following the solution given in Dörrie [DOR], we shall label each of the missing digits so that we can refer to them by name. We shall also number several of the lines.

```
                      : ; 7 " &
            ---------------------
+ - ? | 7 % | A B 7 C D E F G H I
            J K L M N O
            -----------
            P Q R S T 7 U        Third  line
            W X Y Z ! @ #        Fourth line
            -------------
              a 7 b c d e        Fifth line
              f 7 g h i j        Sixth line = 7x(Divisor)
              -----------
              k l m n o p q      Seventh line
              r s t u 7 v w      Eighth  line
              -------------
                x y z $ ~ ^ Ninth line
                x y z $ ~ ^ Tenth line
                -----------
```

The reader will note that we ran out of alphanumeric characters
and had to resort to various ASCII symbols to stand for the unknowns.
These will disappear in due course.

We denote the divisor (the number by which we are dividing) by
$\mathcal{D}$. The first numeral + in $\mathcal{D}$ must be a 1. For if it were a 2 then
$7 \cdot \mathcal{D}$ would possess seven digits; as the Sixth line plainly shows, that
product only has six.

Now, since the remainder in the Third line is composed of the six
digits P Q R S T 7, it must be that P = 1; for otherwise the divisor
$\mathcal{D}$ would go into A B 7 C D E another time. The same reasoning then
shows that k must be 1. But then, examining the subtraction, we see
that W = 1 and r = 1.

Now the divisor $\mathcal{D}$ cannot be any greater than 199979. And " cannot be any greater than 9. Thus the Eighth line, which is the product
of these, cannot exceed 1799811. In particular, s < 8. Now l can only
be 9 or 0 (since it results from subtracting 7 from 7); but it cannot be
9 (since no digits appear in the Ninth line, below r and s). So l = 0.
But k = 1, hence s = 0. Note that k = 1, l = 0 also forces a = f +
1. We conclude that f ≤ 8. Thus the Sixth line cannot be any greater

than 87ghij.

If - were equal to 3 (or greater) then, no matter what the other
digits of the divisor, $\mathcal{D}$ would be at least 130000 so that the sixth line,
resulting from $7 \cdot \mathcal{D}$, would be greater than 900000. We have already
ruled this out. So - is either 0 or 1 or 2. We can rule out - equaling
0 because if it were then the Eighth line could not contain seven digits.

If - were equal to 1 then ? would have to be 0 or 1. This is
so because, if ? were at least 2, then $7 \cdot \mathcal{D}$ (the third digit of the
quotient time the divisor) would entail $7 \cdot ?$ which would be a two
digit number, forcing a carry. But then there is no way that the second
digit of the Sixth line could be a 7. So ? is either 0 or 1. But we can
rule out ? equaling 0, since that would make the divisor too small:
the Eight line could never have seven digits. Thus ? must be 1.

If we assume that ? is 1, then our divisor looks like 111|7%. Now
the Eighth line results from multiplying this number by " . Thus
 | and % and " must be chosen so that the Eighth line is a seven
digit number. This could only happen if " is 9. But then the third-
to-last figure of the Eighth line can be 7 only if | is 0 or | is 9. But
 | equaling 0 is impossible, since then the Eighth line would have just
six digits. And | equaling 9 is impossible, since then the Sixth line
would begin with 783. By elimination, we have shown that ? cannot
be 1.

We now recap our reasoning. We have been considering whether
 - could be equal to 1. If it is, then ? can only be 0 or 1. But
we have eliminated those two possibilities for ? . The conclusion is
that - cannot be 1. Since we have already eliminated - being 0, it
must be that - assumes the only remaining possible value, which is
2. Knowing this, we see immediately that f is 8 and therefore a is 9.

Now we consider the third digit ? of $\mathcal{D}$. It can only equal 4 or 5.
This is so because $7 \cdot 12600$ is greater than the Sixth line and $4 \cdot 12600$
is less than the Sixth line. Likewise, since $9 \cdot 124000$ is greater than the
Eighth line and $7 \cdot 126000$ is less than the Eighth line, then " must
equal 8.

Now we decide whether ? is equal to 4 or to 5. Now $8 \cdot 124979 <
1000000$ hence ? equaling 4 would contradict the Eighth line. Thus
 ? must be 5.

Now we summarize what we have learned by drawing a new diagram:

```
                    : ; 7 8 &
            ---------------------
1 2 5 | 7 % | A B 7 C D E F G H I
            J K L M N O
            ------------
            1 Q R S T 7 U        Third  line
            1 X Y Z ! @ #        Fourth line
            ------------
                9 7 b c d e      Fifth line
                8 7 g h i j      Sixth line = 7x(Divisor)
                ------------
                1 0 m n o p q    Seventh line
                1 0 t u 7 v w    Eighth  line
                ------------
                    x y z $ ˜ ˆ  Ninth line
                    x y z $ ˜ ˆ  Tenth line
                    ------------
```

Now we see that $7 \cdot 125|7\%$ is the Eighth line, and the third-to-the-last digit of that line is 7. It follows that $|$ can only be 4 or 9 (just try out the possibilities). It turns out that $|$ equaling 9 is impossible because that would make $7 \cdot 125970$ a lower bound for the Sixth line, and that is too big. Thus $|$ equals 4. But then $\%$ can only be a digit chosen from among $0, 1, 2, 3, 4$ (eliminate the others just by testing them against the fact that $8 \cdot 12547\%$ must have a 7 as the third to last digit). Whichever of these five possibilities is the correct one, we can conclude that g must be 8 just by considering $7 \cdot 12547\% = 878 * **$. Similarly, the Eighth line tells us that $8 \cdot 12547\% = 10037 * *$ and hence $t = 0$ and $u = 3$.

Because $(;) \cdot (\mathcal{D}) = (;) \cdot (12547\%)$ produces the seven digit of the Fourth line, and since only $8 \cdot \mathcal{D}$ and $9 \cdot \mathcal{D}$ have seven digits, it follows that either $;$ equals 8 or $;$ equals 9.

Now $t = 0$ and $x \geq 1$ (together with $k = r = 1$ and $l = s = 0$) imply that $m \geq 1$. But $g = 8$ and $b \leq 9$ then imply $m \leq 1$. It follows that $m = 1$. But then $b = 9$ and $x = 1$. But this last fact, together with $2 \cdot \mathcal{D} > 20000$ (Ninth line) implies that $\& = 1$. Furthermore, $y = 2$, $z = 5$, $\$ = 4$, $˜ = 7$, and $ˆ = \%$.

We once again record our results on the diagram:

```
                        :  ;  7  8  1
            ---------------------------
1 2 5 4 7 % | A B 7 C D E F G H %
              J K L M N O
              -----------
              1 Q R S T 7 U        Third  line
              1 X Y Z ! @ #        Fourth line
              -------------
                979 c d e          Fifth line
                878 h i j          Sixth line = 7x(Divisor)
                -----------
                1 0 1 n o p q      Seventh line
                1 0 0 3 7 v w      Eighth  line
                -------------
                    1 2 5 4 7 %    Ninth line
                    1 2 5 4 7 %    Tenth line
                    -----------
```

Recall that % is one of the digits $0, 1, 2, 3, 4$. These correspond, respectively, to the two digit sequences

$$v\,w \;=\; 60\,,\; 68\,,\; 76\,,\; 84\,,\; 92$$
$$o\,p\,q \;=\; 290\,,\; 297\,,\; 304\,,\; 311\,,\; 318.$$

Now, depending on whether ; is 8 or 9, either

$$@\,\# \;=\; 60\,,\; 68\,,\; 76\,,\; 84\,,\; 92$$

or

$$@\,\# \;=\; 30\,,\; 39\,,\; 48\,,\; 57\,,\; 66\,.$$

Thus we have ten possibilities to test. Working backwards, and performing the additions, from the Ninth line to the Third line, we find that only % equaling 3 and ; equaling 8 give the needed 7 in the next to last place in the Third line. Then we find that vw = 84, nopq = 6331, hij = 311, cde = 944, XYZ!@# = 003784, and QRST7U = 101778. In conclusion, our problem takes the following form:

```
                        : 8 7 8 1
            ------------------------
1 2 5 4 7 3 | A B 7 C D E 8 4 1 3
            J K L M N 0
            -----------
            1 1 0 1 7 7 8        Third  line
            1 0 0 3 7 8 4        Fourth line
            -------------
              9 7 9 9 4 4        Fifth line
              8 7 8 3 1 1        Sixth line = 7x(Divisor)
              -----------
              1 0 1 6 3 3 1      Seventh line
              1 0 0 3 7 8 4      Eighth  line
              -------------
                1 2 5 4 7 3 Ninth line
                1 2 5 4 7 3 Tenth line
                -----------
```

Notice that, of all the multiples of the divisor $\mathcal{D}$, only $5 \cdot \mathcal{D}$ (compare the third line) gives a number containing a 7 in the third to last place. Thus : $= 5$. It also follows that JKLMNO $= 627365$ and AB7CDE $= 737542$. This allows us to write our display as

```
                            5 8 7 8 1
                 ---------------------
1 2 5 4 7 3 | 7 3 7 5 4 2 8 4 1 3
                 6 2 7 3 6 5
                 -----------
                 1 1 0 1 7 7 8        Third line
                 1 0 0 3 7 8 4        Fourth line
                 -------------
                     9 7 9 9 4 4      Fifth line
                     8 7 8 3 1 1      Sixth line = 7x(Divisor)
                     -----------
                     1 0 1 6 3 3 1    Seventh line
                     1 0 0 3 7 8 4    Eighth  line
                     -------------
                         1 2 5 4 7 3 Ninth line
                         1 2 5 4 7 3 Tenth line
                         -----------
```

Check for yourself that all the steps of the division now work. A review of the derivation shows that every single digit is uniquely determined.   □

4.5   Surprises

There are certain problems with the property that many people, even those who are adept problems solvers, would just dismiss as ridiculous. We have had a taste of these in earlier sections. Problem 3.2.4 showed that if 23 people are in a room then it is better than even odds that two have the same birthday. Problem 3.1.8 showed that if a deck of fifty two cards is split into three sub-decks, then it is better than even odds that one of the three top cards will be a face card. In this section we shall explore some other problems and phenomena of this nature.

PROBLEM 4.5.1 (Calculus) *You have an unlimited supply of dominoes that measure 1″ × 2″. You are working in a room that is 10 feet*

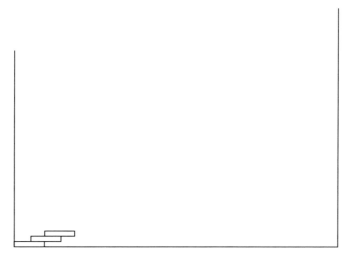

Figure 131

long and has no ceiling. You begin at one wall, place a domino on the floor, place another atop it (not necessarily squarely), and proceed to pile dominoes (Figure 131). Will your pile be able to reach the other wall, 10 feet away, without toppling?

Solution: The key physical observation is that if the jth domino protrudes a distance of λ_j inches beyond the end of the $(j-1)^{\text{th}}$ domino, then the moment of inertia of the jth domino is

$$\int_0^{\lambda_j} \rho t \, dt.$$

Here ρ is the linear density of the domino. For simplicity, we assume that ρ is 1. Then the moment of inertia of the jth domino is $(\lambda_j)^2/2$.

If we stack N dominoes in the manner indicated, then the total moment of inertia of the system is

$$M = \sum_{j=2}^{\infty} \frac{\lambda_j^{\,2}}{2}.$$

[Notice that we start the sum with $j=2$ since the first domino lies flat on the ground and has no moment that is relevant to this problem.]

Assume that c is a positive constant. Suppose that we take $\lambda_2 = c/2$, $\lambda_3 = c/3$, and, in general, $\lambda_j = c/j$. Then

$$M = \sum_{j=2}^{N} \frac{(c/j)^2}{2} = \frac{c^2}{2} \sum_{j=2}^{N} \frac{1}{j^2}.$$

We know that this sum converges to a finite number that depends on the parameter c but is independent of N. However the sum of the lengths of the protrusions is

$$L = \sum_{j=2}^{N} \lambda_j = \sum_{j=2}^{N} \frac{c}{j} = c \cdot \sum_{j=2}^{N} \frac{1}{j}.$$

This sum becomes large without bound as N becomes larger and larger.

If c is a very small positive number then we see that the moment of inertia is as small as we please; we can certainly choose c small enough that the stack will not tumble. But, since the sum defining L becomes large without bound, the stack of dominoes will reach arbitrarily far to the right.

The answer to the problem is "yes", the stack of dominoes can reach 10 feet to the far end of the room.   □

CHALLENGE PROBLEM 4.5.2 (THIS IS TRICKY) *Find an estimate for how many dominoes will be needed to reach across the room, as indicated in the problem. [Hint: The number required is enormous. You may wish to use your computer as an experimental tool.]*

The next problem does not have a surprising answer, but its solution offers something of a surprise.

PROBLEM 4.5.3 *Two train engines are aproaching each other as shown in Figure 132. They begin at a distance of 20 miles, and are each traveling at a rate of 10 miles per hour. At the instant they begin, a fly takes off from the front of one train at a rate of 15 miles per hour. When it meets the front of the other train, it immediately turns around and heads back towards the first train. It continues back and forth until it is crushed when the two trains meet.*

What is the total linear distance traveled by the fly on its zig-zag journey before it meets its end?

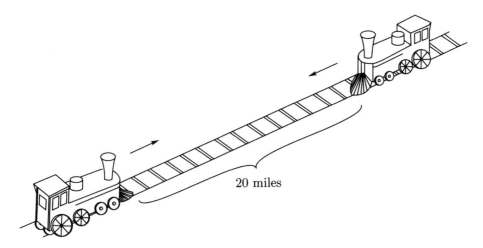

20 miles

Figure 132

This is a famous problem that has made the rounds of the puzzle circuit for at least fifty years. When it was posed to John von Neumann, one of the most brilliant and versatile scientists and problem solvers of this (or any) century, he gave the answer in a few seconds. He later revealed that he had actually calculated the infinitely many distances that the fly traveled—back and forth and back and forth—and summed them up. We shall offer a solution that is more in the spirit of this book: hard work is important and has its place, but sometimes an elegant idea can cut through a lot of drudgery.

Solution: How far does each train travel before the crash? That's easy, for they are separated by 20 miles and each travels at the constant speed of 10 miles per hour. We see that each travels 10 miles up to the point of impact, so each travels for one hour. But, during that one hour, the fly travels 15 miles. □

PROBLEM 4.5.4 *Imagine a steel band strapped tightly around the equator of the earth. Such a band would be about 25,000 miles long. Now suppose that we lengthen the band just enough so that it stands uniformly one foot off the surface of the earth (but still forms a continuous circular loop). How long will it be now? [Assume in solving this* *problem that the earth is spherical and that the band strapped tightly about the equator forms a circle.]*

Solution: The imagination runs rampant with visions of this huge band lifting off the surface of the earth, with miles of band being added just to achieve a half inch of lift off the surface. The solution that you are about to read points up the difference between intuition and analytical thought. Intuition has its place, but it is only a guidepost to the final solution.

We let R denote the radius of the earth at the equator, measured in *feet*. The corresponding circumference is designated by C. Then $C = 2\pi R$. Now our goal is to increase the radius by 1, that is to replace R by $R' = R + 1$. Call new circumference C'. Then $C' - C$ is the amount of steel band that must be added to make the band stand one foot off the surface of the earth.

We calculate that

$$C' = 2\pi \cdot R' = 2\pi(R+1) = 2\pi R + 2\pi.$$

Thus $C' - C = 2\pi$. The conclusion is that we must add 2π feet, or about 6.28318 feet, to the band to achieve our goal.   □

CHALLENGE PROBLEM 4.5.5 *Now imagine, for simplicity, that the surface of the earth is a sphere. Say that it is covered tightly by a spherical sheet of plastic. How many square feet of plastic would have to be added so that the spherical sheet stands one foot off the surface of the earth? [Hint: You may assume that the radius of the earth is 4,000 miles.]*

CHALLENGE PROBLEM 4.5.6 (THIS IS TRICKY.) *Denote by V_N the volume of the unit ball $\{x \in \mathbb{R}^N : \|x\| \leq 1\}$ in N-dimensional Euclidean space $\mathbb{R}^N$. Show that $V_N \to 0$ as $N \to \infty$.*

Can the same be said for the surface area of the unit sphere in $\mathbb{R}^N$?

CHALLENGE PROBLEM 4.5.7 (THIS IS EASIER.) *Let V_N be as in the last challenge problem. Explain why, as N gets large, the volume of the unit ball is concentrated more and more near the outer surface of the sphere.*

EXERCISES for Chapter 4

1. Solve the following crypto-arithmetic problems. In any given problem, different letters denote different integers; identical letters denote the same integer.

a)
```
        D O N A L D
      + G E R A L D
      ---------------
        R O B E R T
```

b)
```
          W R O N G
        + W R O N G
        ------------
          R I G H T
```

c)
```
          S E V E N
        + E I G H T
        ------------
          T W E L V E
```

d)
```
            O N E
          + O N E
          -------
            T W O
```

e)
```
            O N E
          + F O U R
          ---------
            F I V E
```

f)
```
            A B C
          + D E F
          ---------
            G H I
```

g)
```
          G D A
        + H E B
          -------
          I F C
```

```
                1/2
h)          (A T O M)      =  A + TO + M
```

i)   AB x CDE = FGHI

2. In each of the following crypto-arithmetic problems, different x's stand for different digits. In other words, no digit may be used (to substitute for x) twice in the same problem. You also need to determine what the arithmetic operation is in each problem.

a)
```
          x x x
            x x
        ---------
        x x x x 1
```

b)
```
          x x 2
            x x
        ---------
        x x x x x
```

c)
```
          x x x
            x x
        ---------
        x x x 8 x
```

d)
```
          2 x x
            x x
        -------
        x x x x
```

e)
```
      6 x x
      x x x
    -------
    x x x x
```

3. On which of Saturday or Sunday does New Years Day fall most frequently?

4. On which day of the week does the 30th of the month fall most frequently?

5. A game is played by two players at a flat, rectangular table. The players take turns placing round poker chips on the table. The chips are to be placed so that they are flat on the table, non-overlapping, and so they do not extend over the edge. The winner is the player who is last to place a chip on the table. Suggest a strategy so that the first player will always win.

6. On the New York to Washington train there are, among others, three passengers named Smith, Brown, and Pistilgaglioni. It happens that the engineer, the conductor, and the waiter in the dining car have the last names Smith, Brown, and Pistilgaglioni as well (though not necessarily in that order). We also know the following:

1. Passenger Smith lives in New York.

2. The conductor lives halfway between New York and Washington.

3. The passenger with the same last name as the conductor lives in Washington.

4. The passenger who lives nearest to the conductor earns three times as much as a conductor.

5. Passenger Brown earns $2000 per month.

6. Crew man Pistilgaglioni recently beat the waiter at racquetball.

What is the engineer's last name?

7. [This problem is from *Scripta Mathematica*.]

At school one day, a teacher's purse is stolen. Based on a variety of evidence, the search for the culprit was quickly narrowed to Lillian, Judy, David, Theodore, and Margaret. The children made these statements:

Lillian: I did not take the purse. I've never stolen anything. Theodore did it.

Judy: I did not take the purse. My father is plenty rich, and I have my own purse. Margaret knows the real culprit.

David: I did not take the purse. I was not acquainted with Margaret before the beginning of this school year. Theodore did it.

Theodore: I did not do it. Margaret did it. Lillian is lying when she says that I stole the purse.

Margaret: I did not take the purse. Judy took the purse. David can vouch for me because he has known me for many years.

Later, using fiendish inducements, the authorities got each student to admit that two of his/her statements was true but one was false. Who stole the purse?

8. In these crypto-arithmetic problems, identical letters stand for the same digit, different letters stand for different digits, and *'s stand for any digit.

a)

```
            A T O M
            A T O M
          ---------
          * * * * *
        * * * * *
      * * * * *
    * * * * *
    ---------------
    * * * * A T O M
```

b)
```
            A B C
            B A C
         ----------
         *  *  *  *
            *  *  A
      *  *  *  B
      --------------
      *  *  *  *  *  *
```

c)
$$D O + R E = M I ;$$
$$F A + S I = L A ;$$
$$R E + S I + L A = S O L .$$

9. Three Boy Scouts were swapping information about various acquaintances. The scoutmaster told them that Winken, Blinken, and Nod would arrive tomorrow. Their first names are Blotzky, Schmotzky, and Plotzky, but not necessarily in that order.

   One Boy Scout said that he thought Blotzky's last name was Winken. The scout leader declared that to be wrong, and offered some hints:

1. The father of Mrs. Nod is a brother of Schmotzky's mother.

2. Schmotzky began school in the first grade when he was 7 years old. This year I overheard him tell someone that he is now beginning sixth grade arithmetic.

3. The butcher, Mr. Blinken, is Blotzky's grandfather.

4. Blinken is one year older than Schmotzky. And Plotzky is one year older than Schmotzky.

   Match the first name of each boy with a last name, and give their ages.

10. When I am as old as my father is now, I will be five times as old as my son is now. But at that time my son will be eight years older than I am now. At present, the sum of the ages of my father and myself is 100. How old is my son?

11. Switch the minute and hour hands on a clock. How many different times can the clock then show as the day progresses?

12. On which days of the week can the first day of a century fall?

13. In the game of chess, a knight can move in an L-shape: either two squares sideways and one square up or down; or one square sideways and two squares up or down. If the knight begins in the lower left hand corner of the board, then in how many moves can the knight visit all 64 squares of the chessboard at least once?

14. A scrap of paper was found in an old desk. Obviously it was a poultry bill, for it read

$$72 \text{ turkeys} \qquad \$ * 67.9 * .$$

We see that the first and last digits of the price have been smudged, and are represented here by $*$'s. What are the two smudged digits and what is the price of one turkey (in whole numbers of dollars and cents)?

15. Using pennies, nickels, dimes, and quarters, how many different ways can you form fifty cents? How about a dollar? How about k dollars?

16. It is a hot day. Four couples, in the course of an afternoon, consume a great many sodas. Selma has 2, Hyacinth has 3, Lucinda has 4, and Myrtle has 5. Mr. Mergetroyd drinks as many bottles as his wife. But Mr. Ahmenhotep drinks twice as many as his wife, Mr. Ataturk drinks three times as many as his wife, and Mr. Herkimer drinks four times as many as his wife. Altogether the four couples drink 44 bottles of soda. What is the last name of each of the four ladies?

17. Sam asked his friend Irving, "How many children do you have and how old are they?"

The friend replied "I have three boys. The product of their ages is 72, and the sum of their ages is the street number of my house." Sam examined the street number of the house and declared the problem to be indeterminate.

"Yes, it is indeterminate," said the friend. But I am still hoping that one day my oldest son will quarterback the U.S.C. football team."

What are the boys' ages?

18. Is there a winning strategy for the first player in tic-tac-toe? Can you modify the rules to force such a strategy to exist?

19. Refer to Exercise 18. Show that if the first player fails to play in the center square in his first move, then the second player can force a draw.

20. Explain why jugglers usually juggle 3 or 5 balls (or clubs, or whatever). Here, by "juggling," we mean a system of throwing balls in the air, first with the left hand, then with the right; the cycle repeats. If a ball is thrown by the left hand then it is caught by the right, and vice versa. What is the parity problem involved here?

21. The traveling salesman problem (or family of problems) smells like a game, but it has serious applications in commerce, circuit design, and other branches of human endeavor. Lately some startling applications in complex analysis have been found!

The premise is that a certain salesman must depart the home office and visit k cities. It is known how much it costs to stay in each city and how much it costs to travel from any of the cities to any other, or from the home office to any of the cities, or from any of the cities to the home office. The problem is to find the cheapest route.

In fact the traveling salesman problem has not been completely solved, so we shall not ask you to solve it. Instead, given the setup in the preceding paragraph, determine how many different routes the salesman could travel, in such a way that each city is visited just once and then he returns to the home office.

22. Refer to problem 21 for terminology. Suppose that there are just three cities and that it is much more expensive to travel to or from city C_1 than to or from the other two cities C_2 and C_3. What is the best strategy for the salesman?

23. Refer to problem 21 for terminology. Write a computer program that will input all the data that the salesman has about travel costs and then will calculate the best route.

24. A game is played by two players. The first player writes down some number (a positive integer) from 1 to 10. The second player writes down a number from 1 to 10 and the two numbers are added. Then the first player writes a number from 1 to 10 and this number is added to the running sum. The players continue to alternate.

The player who contributes the number that makes the sum exactly equal to 100 wins. Devise a winning strategy for the first player. Devise a winning strategy for the second player.

25. I recently sent an e-mail to a mischievous friend. His reply was "I couldn't possibly fail to disagree with you less." Write a simple declarative sentence that sums up his meaning.

26. Ten people sit at a round table. The sum of $10 is to be distributed among them so that each person receives the average of what each of his two neighbors receives. In how many different ways can this be achieved?

27. Joe is the captain of a large boat. We write A for his age, C for the number of his children, and ℓ for the length of his boat. We are given that

(a) $A \cdot C \cdot \ell = 32118$;

(b) ℓ equals several feet;

(c) C counts both a non-zero number of sons and a non-zero number of daughters;

(d) $100 > A > C$.

Determine the exact value of A, C, ℓ.

28. In these crypto-arithmetic problems, all created by A. G. Bradbury, identical letters stand for the same digit, different letters stand for different digits, and *'s stand for any digit.

```
                THE
               -----
a)      SHE  |FEARS
                ***
                ---
               ****
               TALK
               ----
                ****
                ****
                ----
```

```
                    RUN
                   ------
b)     RUN |RABBIT
            ****
            ----
              ****
              PUMA
              ----
                ****
                GRAB
                ----
                  **



                    GUM
                   ------
c)     GUM |BUBBLE
            *C**
            ----
              *L**
              *U*
              ----
                **E*
                ****
                ----



d)          YES
            YES
            -----
            ****
            SORT
            **OF
            ------
            SQUARE
```

e)   CAN
            CAN

            ****
            *FOR
            ****

            FROLIC

f)   ERROR
             OR

            ***A**
            ******

            MISTAKE

29. We know that a clock's hands coincide when the time is twelve o'clock. What is the next time that the clock's hands coincide? The time after that?

30. A function f from the real numbers to the real numbers satisfies the equation $f(x+y) = f(x) + f(y)$. If it is known that $f(1) = 1$, then what is $f(1/2)$?

31. Solve this crypto-arithmetic problem of R. J. Lancaster:

NUDE + NOT + RUDE + NOR = CRUDE

32. Solve this crypto-arithmetic problem of Alan Wayne:

AYE + AYE + AYE + AYE = YES + YES + YES

33. Two boats head directly towards each other, one of them traveling 12 miles per hour and the other traveling 17 miles per hour. They begin at a distance of 20 miles from each other. How far apart are they one

minute before they collide? [Do this in your head, and take no more than one minute.]

34. Take any three digit number. Write it on a piece of paper, and then write the three digits again adjacent to the first three. So you end up with a six digit number like 479479.

Divide the six digit number by 7. The answer will come out even.

Divide the answer that you just obtained by 11. The answer will come out even.

Divide the answer that you just obtained by 13. The answer will come out even. In fact the answer will be the three digit number with which you began.

Why does this work?

35. You have a flask of water and a flask of acid. Each flask holds the same amount of liquid, and each has a little room to spare. You pour a small amount of water into the acid, mix it thoroughly, and then pour the same amount of the mixture back in to the water. The acid now contains a certain percentage of water and the water a certain percentage of acid. Which is greater?

36. Suppose, in the last problem, that you continue to pour the same amount of liquid back and forth, mixing thoroughly after each pour. Will it ever happen, after finitely many pours, that each flask will contain the same amount of acid?

37. The great British philosopher and mathematician Bertrand Russell claimed that he ruined himself for the study of logic and mathematics by considering the following question. Take a piece of paper. On the front side, write the statement "The statement on the other side of this sheet is false." On the back side, write the same statement. Now do an analysis of the truth or falsity of these statements.

38. Three men are seated in a row, one behind the other. Thus the last man can see the first two sitting before him. The middle man can see only the first man sitting before him. And the first man can see nobody. Each man closes his eyes, and either a red or a black hat is placed on his head. *It is known that these hats come from a supply of three red and two black.* After the hats are placed on the heads, the two remaining are hidden from sight. The last man is asked if he knows the color of his hat. After he gives his answer, the middle man is asked the

same question. After he gives his answer then the front man gives his answer.

Give a complete analysis of this game.

39. The celebrated Hungarian mathematician Paul Erdös (see [TIE]) likes to say that, when he was a child, scientists said that the earth was two billion years old; and now they say that it is four billion years old. Therefore he (Erdös) must be two billion years old. What is wrong with this reasoning?

40. According to mathematician Casper Goffman [GOF], every mathematician has an *Erdös number*. (Refer to Exercise 39 for information about Paul Erdös.) It is calculated as follows: if you are Paul Erdös then your Erdös number is zero. Continuing inductively, if you have written a research paper with someone whose Erdös number is $(k - 1)$ then your Erdös number is k.

The Erdös number of the author of this book is 1. What does that mean? Determine the Erdös number of a mathematician that you know. What is the least Erdös number of anyone that you know?

41. Imagine a checker- or chess- board that measures four squares by eight squares. Is it possible for a knight (the standard chess piece that makes *L*-shaped moves) to begin on one square, visit each of the other squares exactly once, and then return to its initial square? [*Hint:* Color the board in a useful way.]

42. Refer to Exercise 41. Imagine a chess-board that is seven squares by seven squares. Is it possible for the knight to begin on some square and then take exactly 49 moves to visit every other square and then return to the original square?

43. In a certain native tribe in Africa, members grow up learning to shake their head left to right to indicate "yes" (this is the same head movement that we in America use to indicate "no"). In fact this gesture is characteristic of this one particular tribe; no other native Africans use this gesture to have this meaning.

Suppose that you are walking through the jungle, and you encounter a person who you suspect is a member of this tribe. You ask her whether she indeed belongs to the tribe; and she shakes her head left to right (but she says nothing). What can you conclude? Why? Is there another question that you could ask, that could be answered with a motion of the head only, that would settle the matter once and for all?

44. Joe, Bob, and Curly are actors. One of them plays leading roles, one plays villains, and one plays loonies (but not necessarily in this order). The villain wants the leading man in his current movie, but the leading man is already booked to play in the loonie's current project. This is OK with the villain, because he knows that they are both good actors.

But the villain envies the loonie because the loonie is paid so much more than he is. If Bob makes more than Joe, and Curly has never heard of Bob, then which of these three men plays leading roles, which plays villains, and which plays loonies?

45. Historically, a popular gambling game in Australia is "Two Up." It is played as follows. The player, called the *spinner*, places a bet. Then the spinner flips two coins simultaneously (in fact he/she is provided with a wooden *kip* that enables a fair simultaneous flip). If both coins come up heads, then the flip is called a "heads." If they both come up tails, then the flip is called a "tails." If they come up one heads and one tails then the flip is call "odds." The object of the game is to get heads three times consecutively without spinning tails or five consecutive odds. The player keeps playing until (i) he comes up with tails (then loses), or (ii) he flips odds five times in succession (then loses), or (iii) he flips heads three times in succession (then wins).

If the spinner succeeds, he/she is paid 7.5 to 1 and continues as spinner. If he/she fails by either getting tails or getting five consecutive odds, then he/she loses the bet.

Is this a fair game? If not, can you adjust the odds to make it a fair game?

46. The ancient game of Morra is played thusly: There are two players. At the same instant, each player shows either one, two, or three fingers. Simultaneously, each player calls out what he thinks her opponent will show. If both guess right or both guess, wrong, then the game is a draw. If one player guesses right and one wrong, then the wrong player pays the right player a number of dollars equal to the total number of fingers showing. What is your best strategy when playing this game?

47. In the game of bridge, each of four players is dealt thirteen cards from a standard 52 card deck. A hand of thirteen cards is called a

Yarborough (named in honor of Lord Yarborough, a whist player who became famous for betting against the existence of such hands) if it contains no card with point value exceeding a ten-spot. In any given dealing of the 52 cards to the four players, what is the probability that at least one player will hold a Yarborough?

48. In the old days, a roulette wheel had 36 six slots in which the ball could fall, numbered 1 through 36. The wheel was spun in one direction, and the ball put inside the wheel and spun in the other direction. Eventually the ball would fall, at random, into one of the thirty six numbered slots. Players would bet by placing money or chips on a felt board with spaces for each of the thirty six numbers. If a player's number comes up, what should she be paid in a fair game?

Of the 36 numbers, 18 are colored red and 18 are colored black. Players can bet on either "black" or "red." In a fair game, what should a player be paid if she correctly bets black or red?

The casinos in Las Vegas are out to make money. All of the gambling games in Las Vegas are slanted slightly towards the house. For a while, this was done by adding a 37th slot to the roulette wheel. It was labeled '0' and colored green. But the payoffs were kept the same as for a fair game of 36 numbers as described in the last two paragraphs. To what degree did this tilt the game towards the house?

Not satisfied with the profits, the casinos later added a 38th number to the roulette wheel. This slot is labeled '00' and is colored green. But the payoffs remain the same as described for a fair game of 36 numbers as described in the first two paragraphs. To what degree does this tilt the game towards the house?

49. In its original form, the Pennsylvania State Lottery was played as follows. In exchange for fifty cents, the player obtained a ticket bearing a six digit number. Say that your number is '987654'. At the end of the week, the state drew the winner at random. You win

$50,000	if the winning number is	987654
$2,000	if the winning number is	$X87654$ or $98765X$
$200	if the winning number is	$XX7654$ or $9876XX$
$40	if the winning number is	$XXX654$ or $987XXX$.

Are all of these payoffs equally fair? In any given week, what are your chances of winning at least *some* money?

50. In the United States, national elections are held "on the first Tuesday after the first Monday in November." What is the earliest date in November on which a national election could be held? What is the latest date?

Chapter 5

Recreational Math

5.1 Magic Squares and Related Ideas

The concept of "magic square" has many versions and variants. We begin with one of the most basic.

PROBLEM 5.1.1 *Imagine a* 3×3 *array of squares, as shown in Figure 133. The challenge is to put the integers 1 to 9, one in each square, so that each row and each column adds up to the same number.*

Solution: We first determine what the common sum S must be. If we add up each number in each row then the following is true: since there are three rows, we will have obtained the common sum S three different times. So our grand total is $3S$. And we have counted each square exactly once. These contain the numbers 1 through 9, just as we have prescribed. Thus we have

$$3S = [1 + 2 + 3 + \cdots + 9].$$

Using our formula for sums of consecutive integers, this last equation becomes

$$3S = \frac{9 \cdot 10}{2}.$$

Solving for S, we find that $S = 15$. So we need to place the numbers 1 to 9 into the array so that each row and each column adds to 15.

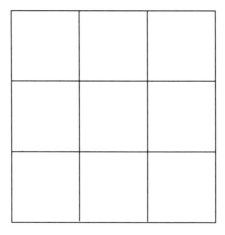

Figure 133

It is often useful to begin with an extreme value, so we put 9 in the center. This puts severe limits on what can go to the left and right of 9, or what can go above and below it. The choices are $1 + 5$ or $2 + 4$ or $3 + 3$. The third of these is of no use to us, since we are only allowed to use 3 once. So we put 4 and 2 to the left and right of 9 and 5 and 1 above and below 9. The situation is now as in Figure 134.

We cannot put 3 in the bottom row, for $1 + 3$ is too small; there is no third number that will make 15. So we put 3 in the upper row; say in the upper left hand corner. This forces the upper right to be 7, which forces the lower right to be 6, which forces the lower left to be 8.

Checking the sums of the three columns and the sums of the three rows, we find that we have constructed our first magic square.   □

The best magic squares not only have all the rows and all the columns summing to the same number, but also the diagonals sum to the same number. Figure 135 shows a 3×3 magic square in which that is true. How might we discover such a magic square? Well, there is always trial and error. Instead of beginning with a 9 in the central square, we could have begun with a different number in the middle; then we could have built the square, as in the last example. There are only nine possible numbers to try in that center square; one could

	5	
4	9	2
	1	

Figure 134

always hope that one of these nine trials will yield success.

When we are dealing with larger squares than 3×3—say 5×5 or 6×6, then such hit-and-miss procedures become rather cumbersome. It is desirable to have some *strategy* for producing these magic squares. We begin by making some observations. Sometimes, when we do not know where we are headed, it is useful to just see what we can learn about the topic at hand.

We start with the magic square that we produced in Figure 135. Suppose that we bump each number "up" (in the vertical direction) one square. This empties the bottom row. But it also pushes the first row off the top; so we rotate it down to the bottom. The result is shown in Figure 136.

Notice that the result is still a magic square, with the same magic number of 15. Of course this is no great surprise, since we have not altered any row (just moved them) and we have simply juggled the members of each column, but preserved each column's contents.

By the same token, we could push everything one unit to the right. This empties the left column, and pushes the right-most column off the right edge. So we just rotate that column off to the left. Try this yourself, and verify that the result is still a magic square with magic number 15.

8	1	6
3	5	7
4	9	2

Figure 135

3	5	7
4	9	2
8	1	6

Figure 136

2	4	9
6	8	1
7	3	5

Figure 137

Emboldened by our success with the last two experiments, we try a diagonal shift of the magic square produced in Figure 136. The completed square is exhibited in Figure 137. Pick up your pencil and follow along. We are going to shift each number in Figure 136 one square to the right and one square up. We label the squares a_{11}, a_{12}, a_{13} for the first row, a_{21}, a_{22}, a_{23} for the second row, and a_{31}, a_{32}, a_{33} for the third row.

Now we take care of the obvious numbers first:

$$4 \rightarrow a_{12}$$
$$9 \rightarrow a_{13}$$
$$8 \rightarrow a_{22}$$
$$1 \rightarrow a_{23}$$

We now think about the other numbers. We have already used the idea of pretending that the upper edge and lower edge are attached, and the left edge and the right edge are attached, to advantage when we were doing simple left-right and up-down shifts. Now we determine whether we may continue to use this notion.

If we shift the number 3 one to the right and one up, then it seems to get shoved off the top of the array; but if we pretend that the upper edge and the lower edge are attached, then 3 lands in a_{32}. Similarly, 5 gets moved to a_{33}, 2 gets moved to a_{11}, and 6 gets moved to a_{21}. This leaves only 7, and there is nowhere for it to go but a_{31}.

Examine the resulting array, as shown in Figure 137. A quick check shows that it is still a magic square! To summarize, we have discovered that left-right shifts, up-down shifts, and diagonal shifts seem to preserve magic squares. Is there some unifying idea behind all this symmetry?

What happens if you take a square of paper and tape the left and right edges together? If you cannot visualize it, then try it; you get a tube, or cylinder. Now, after having taped the left and right edges together, tape the top and bottom edges together (this is a bit difficult with paper, but you can force the situation). What you obtain is the *surface of a donut*, or what mathematicians call a *torus*. The three operations that we have been considering—left-right translation, up-down translation, and diagonal motion—are all very natural in the setting of a torus.

On the torus, if we move each square one unit to the right, then we no longer have to worry about "falling off the edge." For we have already erased the boundaries by identifying the left and right edges of the square. Likewise, if we move each square one unit up, then we no longer have to worry about falling off the edge. For we have already erased the boundaries by identifying the upper and lower edges of the square. Finally, the diagonal shift operation becomes much less mysterious if we view it in the torus setting.

Perhaps the torus is a much more natural setting in which to view the creation of magic squares. Since we can shift at will from left to right, or up to down, or along diagonals, it does not seem to matter where we begin the magic square. All locations seem to be equivalent to all others. Let us snip the torus with scissors and return it to the form of a square (Figure 138).

We now build a 3×3 magic square by beginning in the location a_{12}. Place a 1 there. The rows and columns in the picture have 3 elements each, so 3 seems to be a natural "period" for this problem. Beginning with a_{12}, we lay out $1, 2, 3$ along a diagonal (there is no sense to lay $1, 2, 3$ out along a row or a column, since rows are supposed to sum to 15). Keeping in mind the structure of the torus, this gives us Figure

Figure 138

Figure 139

8	1	6
3	5	7
4	9	2

Figure 140

139.

Now we exploit the natural period. We laid out 1,2,3 along a diagonal that moves up and to the right. Now we look at diagonals that move up and to the left. We lay out numbers on those diagonals using the natural period 3. Beginning with 1 at a_{12}, we next lay a 4 at a_{31} and then a 7 at a_{23}. Next, beginning with 2 at a_{33}, we lay a 5 at a_{22} and an 8 at a_{11}. Finally, beginning with 3 at a_{21}, we next lay a 6 at a_{13} and then a 9 at a_{32}.

What we have done makes sense geometrically, for it fills out the square. It makes sense number theoretically, for it uses up all the integers from 1 to 9. It makes sense from the point of view of parity, for it exploits the natural period 3 of the problem. And guess what? It produced a magic square. See Figure 140. Notice that in fact it is a special magic square—even the diagonals add to fifteen.

PROBLEM 5.1.2 *Use the ideas developed so far to produce a 5 × 5 magic square.*

Solution: Without doing any further analysis, we attempt to imitate the method that was so successful with the 3 × 3 magic square.

We begin as in Figure 141. We have a 5 × 5 tableau, and we have placed a 1 in the square a_{13}—the center of the top row. Now we lay

Figure 141

Figure 142

10	18	1	14	22
17	5	13	21	9
4	12	25	8	16
11	24	7	20	3
23	6	19	2	15

Figure 143

out the numbers 1,2,3,4,5 along a diagonal moving up and to the right. See Figure 142. Next we lay out diagonals that proceed in the opposite direction—moving up and to the left—and with the numbers having period 5. For example, beginning with 1 at a_{13}, we proceed to lay 6 at a_{52} and then 11 at a_{41} and then 16 at a_{35} and finally 21 at a_{24}. We complete the other skew diagonals in a similar fashion. The result is shown in Figure 143.

This is indeed a magic square. The magic number is 65, as we could have predicted in the same fashion that we predicted the magic number of 15 in Problem 5.1.1 (do this as an exercise). □

CHALLENGE PROBLEM 5.1.3 *Use our algorithm to fill in a 3×3 tableau or a 5 × 5 tableau, but do not begin at the top middle. Begin at some other location. Do you still get a magic square? Are you surprised at the result?*

CHALLENGE PROBLEM 5.1.4 *Use the algorithm developed above to tackle a 4 × 4 tableau. Where will you begin? Why does the method fail? [Your answer should be a geometrical one: think about the torus.]*

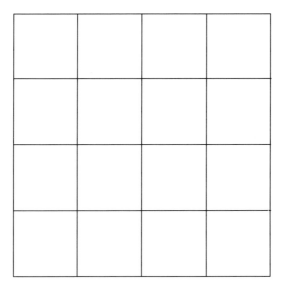

Figure 144

What modification can you make to the method so that it will still work in the 4 × 4 case?

It turns out that magic squares with an even count on each side require an entirely different set of techniques for their construction. In fact the method depends on the parity of the number of squares on a side, even supposing that the number is even. For instance, when the number is a multiple of 4 then one set of techniques applies. When the number equals 6 another set of techniques applies. Since this is not a book on magic squares, we shall forego investing much time in this menagerie of special tricks. We refer the reader to [SIM1] for further details.

We conclude with a few words on magic squares with a multiple of 4 squares on a side. Consider a 4 × 4 tableau as in Figure 144. Now place the numbers 1 through 16 into this tableau in their natural order: 1 through 4 across the first row, 5 through 8 across the second row, and so forth—see Figure 145. *This is not yet a magic square!* For each element in either of the diagonals, replace it with its complementary number. Here, by a complementary number, we mean the number that, added to it, makes 17. For instance, the complementary number to 6 is

1	2	3	4
5	6	7	8
9	10	11	12
13	14	15	16

Figure 145

11 and the complementary number to 13 is 4. We think of 6 and 11 as complementary because 6 is the same "distance" from 1 as 11 is from 16.

Having switched all the elements on the diagonals, we arrive at the array in Figure 146. This is a magic square!

CHALLENGE PROBLEM 5.1.5 *Adapt the method just described for a 4×4 square to an 8×8 square. [Hint: Subdivide the 8×8 square into 4×4 blocks and apply the method for 4×4 squares to each block.]*

CHALLENGE PROBLEM 5.1.6 *Why does the method for 4×4 squares and 8×8 squares work?*

For 180 years it was thought to be impossible to put the numbers 1 - 100 into a 10×10 array to make a magic square. It is now known that it can be done. Can you do it?

5.2   Problems Involving Weighings

We begin with a classic problem involving a collection of objects that appear to be equal but are not.

16	2	3	13
5	11	10	8
9	7	6	12
4	14	15	1

Figure 146

PROBLEM 5.2.1 *Suppose that you have 9 pearls. They all look the same, but 8 of have equal weight and one is different. The odd pearl is either lighter or heavier; you do not know which. The only equipment that you have at hand is a balance scale—see Figure 147. How can you use the scale to find the odd pearl in just three weighings?*

Solution: Notice that weighing one pearl against one is almost a waste of time. If they do not balance then what have you learned? One of them is the odd pearl, but which one?

If instead you weigh one pearl against one and they balance, then you know that neither is the odd pearl; the odd pearl must be one of the other seven. That gives you two pearls that you can use as "controls," but seven more pearls to check.

Yet there are no other moves to be made with a balance scale. What is to be done? We can make more efficient use of this limited number of options by dividing the 9 pearls into three groups of three. Of course 3 is chosen because it is the only number that evenly divides 9 (other than 9 or 1). We may think of each group of 3 as a "super pearl." Label the groups of three with the names G_1, G_2, and G_3.

Now we weigh G_1 against G_2.

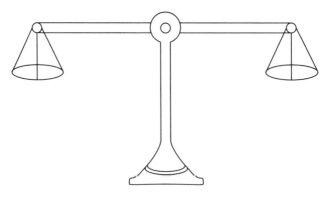

Figure 147

1. If they happen to balance, then all six pearls in G_1 and G_2 are control pearls. The odd pearl is one of the pearls in G_3.

2. If they do not balance, then all the pearls in G_3 are control pearls. The odd pearl is either in G_1 or G_2 but we do not know which.

We first consider Case 1. For Step 2, weigh G_1 against G_3. Of course they will not balance. G_3 will either be lighter or heavier. Make a note of which. Say that, for the sake of specificity, G_3 is heavier. That means that the odd pearl is heavier than the others, and it lies in G_3. Now select any two pearls from G_3 and weigh them against each other. If they balance, then the odd pearl is the third pearl in G_3 and it is heavier. If they do not balance, then the heavier of the two is the odd pearl.

Now consider Case 2. Make a note of whether G_1 or G_2 is heavier. For specificity, say that G_1 is heavier. Now weigh G_1 against G_3. If they balance, then the odd pearl is in G_2 and it is lighter. Pick any two pearls from G_2 and weigh them against each other. If they balance then the odd pearl is the third one from G_2 and it is lighter. If they do not balance then the lighter of the two is the odd pearl.

If instead G_1 and G_3 do not balance, then the only possibility is that G_1 is heavier than G_3 (otherwise there would be three weight categories, which is impossible). So the odd pearl is in G_1, and it is heavier. For the last step, weigh any two pearls from G_1 against each other and proceed as in the earlier cases. □

Notice that, once we realized that our best strategy was to divide into groups of three and create three "super pearls," then our succeeding steps were almost automatic. If we had instead divided into groups of $\{2, 2, 5\}$ or $\{4, 4, 1\}$, then we would not have known what to do after Step 1.

PROBLEM 5.2.2 *Suppose now that you have 12 pearls, all appearing the same but with one having an odd weight. You do not know whether the odd pearl is heavier or lighter. How many weighings are needed to find the odd pearl?*

Solution: The solution that we gave to Problem 5.2.1 seems to be "tight." And it *is*, insofar as use of the ideas that we have considered so far is concerned. Therefore, if we are going to succeed in finding the odd pearl among 12—using only three weighings—then a new idea will be required.

Begin by using the "super pearl" idea. Divide the twelve pearls into three groups of 4. Call them G_1, G_2, G_3. As a first step, weigh G_1 against G_2.

1. If they happen to balance, then all eight pearls in G_1 and G_2 are control pearls. The odd pearl is one of the pearls in G_3.

2. If they do not balance, then all the pearls in G_3 are control pearls. The odd pearl is either in G_1 or G_2 but we do not know which.

We first consider Case 1 (which is relatively easy). Take any three pearls from G_1 and weigh them against any three pearls from G_3. If they balance, then the odd pearl is the remaining pearl from G_3. Weighing that last pearl against one of the pearls from G_1 will tell whether the odd pearl is heavy or light. If they do not balance, then the odd pearl will be among the three selected from G_3 and we will know whether it is lighter or heavier (since the pearls from G_1 are control pearls). Now a third weighing, as usual, will pin down the odd pearl from among those three that we selected from G_3.

For Case 2, we suppose for specificity that G_1 is heavier and G_2 lighter. Give the pearls in G_1 names a, b, c, d and give the pearls in G_2 the names a', b', c', d'. For the second weighing, we weigh $\{a, b, a'\}$ against $\{c, d, b'\}$.

(a) If they balance, then the odd pearl is one of c', d' (the two pearls from G_1 and G_2 that we omitted from this second trial). Of course c', d' come from the light side, so we know that the odd pearl is light. For the third weighing, we weigh c' against d'. The odd pearl is the lighter of the two.

(b) If they do not balance, then say that $\{a, b, a'\}$ is heavier. This must mean that c, d are control pearls, and so is a', or else the balance would be the other way. Thus the odd pearl is either a, b or b'. Finally weigh a against b. If they balance, then the odd pearl is b' and it is light. If they do not balance then the odd pearl is the heavier of the two (since a and b come from G).

(c) The case that $\{c, d, b'\}$ is heavier is handled just as in sub-case (b).

□

CHALLENGE PROBLEM 5.2.3 *Show that with 13 pearls, one odd, it is still the case that three weighings will locate the odd pearl. But you cannot tell whether it is heavy or light.*

CHALLENGE PROBLEM 5.2.4 *Show that with 14 pearls the odd one cannot be determined with just 3 weighings.*

PROBLEM 5.2.5 *You have 80 pearls. One is lighter than all the others. Find the odd pearl in just four weighings on a balance scale.*

Solution: The most obvious thing to do is to divide the 80 pearls into two groups of 40 and weigh them against each other. The lighter of the two groups will contain the odd pearl. Then divide that group of

40 into two groups of 20. Weigh them against each other, and find the lighter group of 20. Keep going.

The trouble with this strategy is that, after four weighings, we have only limited our scope to a group of 5 pearls. What are we doing wrong? We are not making full use of the fact that we know that the odd pearl is light. We instead begin by dividing the pearls into three groups of 27, 27, and 26.

Weigh the 27 against the 27. If they balance, then the odd pearl is among the 26, and it is light. If they do not balance, then the odd pearl is in the lighter of the two groups. You can see that, after one weighing, we have narrowed the pearl to either a group of 26 or a group of 27—because we are taking decisive advantage of knowing that it is light.

In the first instance (that the scale balanced), divide the remaining 26 pearls into groups of 9,9, and 8. Weigh the 9 against the nine. And so forth and so on. You can see that after narrowing to 9 we will then narrow to 3, and then we are home.

If the 27 against 27 do not balance, then we focus on the lighter group of 27. We divide that into three groups of 9 and weigh one group of 9 against another. If they balance then we devolve upon the third group of 9; if they do not balance then we choose the lighter group of 9. Then we narrow down to 3, and so forth.

The problem is solved. □

PROBLEM 5.2.6 *You have 24 marbles, all of which appear to be the same. However a certain number of them are made of glass and a certain number are made of quartz. The glass marbles are heavier. All the glass marbles weigh the same and all the quartz marbles weigh the same. How many weighings, using a balance scale, would be required to determine the number of glass marbles and the number of quartz marbles?*

Solution: One procedure would be to designate one marble as the "test marble" and proceed to weigh each of the other marbles, in succession, against it. Say that the kth marble is the first marble against which the test marble does not balance. If the first several marbles balance with the test marble, but the kth marble (for some k) is heavier, then the kth marble is glass; moreover, the test marble and all the marbles tested up to and including the $(k-1)^{\text{st}}$ marble must be quartz. We could then continue to weigh the $(k+1)^{\text{st}}$ marble against the test marble, and then the $(k+2)^{\text{nd}}$ marble against the test marble, and so forth. Any one that is heavier is glass, and any one that balances is quartz. Thus we would have classified all the marbles after 23 weighings (there is no need, nor is it possible, to weigh the test marble against itself). Note that if the first marble not to balance is lighter then we simply note that that marble must be quartz and that all the preceding marbles (including the test marble) must be glass. The problem concludes as before.

What we have presented so far in this solution exhibits no imagination nor any idea. The issue is whether we can come up with a more efficient algorithm. We begin as before. Pick up two marbles and test them against each other. There are now two possibilities:

1. **The marbles do not balance.** Thus one (the heavier) is glass and one (the lighter) is quartz. Now put those two marbles together on one side of the balance scale. Pick up two more marbles and put them on the other side. If the two new marbles are heavier, then they are both glass. If the two new marbles are lighter, then they are both quartz. If the two new marbles balance, then one is quartz and one is glass. In any of these three events, we can *count* how many glass and how many quartz marbles there are among the two new candidates (note that the problem did not ask us to *identify* the marbles—just to count them!). So we set those two new marbles aside and mark our tally on a piece of paper. Then we put two more marbles on the balance scale and weigh them against our first two. We keep going in this fashion. We see that all the marbles will be weighed and counted after $1 + 22/2 = 12$ weighings. This is a substantial improvement!

2. **The marbles balance.** Then either both are glass or both are quartz. Now, as in the first case, we use those two together as a test pair. Pick up another pair of marbles and weigh them against the first two. If the scale balances, then we have two

more marbles of the same kind (either glass or quartz), but we do not know which just yet. Keep going until you find a pair that does not balance. Say that it is the kth pair. If that k^{th} pair is heavier, then we may conclude that the test pair, and all the pairs up to that point, are quartz. If the kth pair is lighter, then we may conclude that the test pair, and all the pairs up to that point, are glass.

Suppose that the kth pair is heavier (the case when they are lighter is handled in a similar fashion). Now separate the two marbles in this k^{th} pair and weigh these two marbles one against the other. If they balance, then they are both glass. If they do not balance, then one of them is glass and you know which one it is. In any event, pick out the glass marble from the kth pair and one of the quartz marbles from the original test pair. Use these two to form a new test pair, and now proceed as in the first case to test the rest of the pairs of marbles. Altogether, we have used $1 + (k - 1) + 1 + (24 - 2k)/2 = 13$ weighings.

We see that, by grouping the marbles in pairs, we can count the number of glass and the number of quartz marbles in 13 weighings. Could we be even more efficient if we use triples of marbles or quadruples of marbles? The trouble with quadruples, just to take an instance, is that there are too many possibilities—five of them, to be exact. They could all be glass, or three glass and one quartz, or two glass and two quartz, or one glass and three quartz, or all quartz. Thus if, for instance, we had a test quadruple that was two glass and two quartz, and we weighed another quadruple against it, then how might things turn out? If the new quadruple *balanced*, then we could be sure that it contained two glass and two quartz marbles. If the new quadruple were *lighter*, then it could be all quartz, or it could be three quartz and one glass. A similar problem would arise if the new quadruple were heavier. It would take two additional weighings each time to sort out which was the case. And just isolating a test quadruple would take several weighings. Check for yourself that using quadruples would result in no improvement. Likewise, you can check that using triples would be no improvement. Matters become very complicated very rapidly if we go on to try groups of five or six.

It is conceivable that there are more elaborate strategies that would count the glass and the quartz marbles in fewer than 13 weighings. We shall not take the time to do an exhaustive treatment here.   □

PROBLEM 5.2.7 (Bachet) *In this problem we use a balance scale. But we will be equipped with a collection of brass weights having standard denominations. In old fashioned dry goods stores, it was standard for the proprietor to have several standardized brass weights: a 1 oz. weight, two 2 oz. weights, a 5 oz. weight, two 10 oz. weights, a 20 oz. weight, and a 50 oz. weight. It is plain to see that, by combining these, any (integer number of ounces) weight from 1 oz. to 100 oz. could be obtained. For example,* $88 = 50 + 20 + 10 + 5 + 2 + 1.$

With how few weights could one measure all integer weights from 1 oz. to 40 oz.?

Solution: Why rely on base 10? Why not use base 2? This suggests that one could use weights of size 1 oz., 2 oz., 4 oz., 8 oz., 16 oz., 32 oz.—just six weights. Since any number between 1 and 40 inclusive can be written in base 2, it is clear that these weights will do the job. For instance, the number which in decimal language we call 27 can be written in base 2 as 11011. This says to use the weights 16 oz., 8 oz., 2 oz., 1 oz.

Could we get away with fewer weights? Suppose that we had a collection of five weights. How many different magnitudes of weight could we measure using these five? Well, how many different subsets does a set with five elements have? The answer (as we know from Chapter 1) is $2^5 = 32$. Since our goal is to be able to measure the forty different weights ranging from 1 to 40, clearly five weights will not do. The least feasible number is six, and we have found a way to do it with six.   □

ounces	left side of scale	right side of scale
1	1	S
2	3	1 + S
3	3	S
4	1 + 3	S
5	9	1 + 3 + S
6	9	3 + S
7	1 + 9	3 + S
8	9	1 + S
9	9	S
10	1 + 9	S
11	3 + 9	1 + S
12	3 + 9	S
13	1 + 3 + 9	S

Table 1

What if we get sneaky and change the parameters of the problem? Say that we are allowed to put weights on *both sides* of the balance scale. For example, the weights $1, 3, 9$ are sufficient to weigh all weights from 1 to 13 (for elegance, we will leave out the units). Here is how. Suppose we are weighing a sack S. Table 1 is a chart showing how to measure each of the weights from 1 to 13: You should have no trouble seeing that what we are doing in six of these lines is setting up a subtraction problem to achieve the weight that we want.

CHALLENGE PROBLEM 5.2.8 *Show that there is no way to make all the weights from 1 oz. to 13 oz. by using just two weights.*

CHALLENGE PROBLEM 5.2.9 *Using the idea of putting weights on both sides of the balance scale, what is the fewest number of weights that could be used to weigh any integral weight from 1 to 40 ounces? You should verify both that the system that you propose works, and that no smaller number of weights will work.*

CHALLENGE PROBLEM 5.2.10 *Give an algorithm for determining the fewest number of weights that would be required to measure all integral* weights from 1 oz. to N oz., for N a positive integer. You should provide one algorithm for the "one side" method and another for the "both sides" method.

PROBLEM 5.2.11 *Suppose that you have 13 pearls and a balance scale. Assume that whenever you weigh any 6 pearls against 6 other pearls they balance. Explain why it follows that all 13 pearls weigh the same.*

Solution: Suppose that the conclusion is false. So at least one pearl weighs differently. Now order the pearls, left to right, so that the heaviest is on the left and they are decreasing in weight. Call the pearls $P_1, P_2, \ldots, P_{13}$.

Now either $\{P_1, P_2, \ldots, P_6\}$ weighed against $\{P_7, P_8, \ldots, P_{12}\}$ will not balance or else $\{P_2, P_3, \ldots, P_7\}$ weighed against $\{P_8, P_9, \ldots, P_{13}\}$ will not balance (because some pearl will weigh more than its neighbor to the right). That is a contradiction.   □

CHALLENGE PROBLEM 5.2.12 *What is special about the numbers 6 and 13 in the last example? Can you give an example in which the conclusion is false if these numbers are changed?*

EXERCISES for Chapter 5

1. Suppose that we have 27 brass weights weighing $1^2, 2^2, 3^2, \ldots, 27^2$ grams respectively. How may we group them into three groups so that each group has the same weight?

2. You have five brass weights, all with the same appearance and all having different weight values. How can you use a balance scale, and as few weighings as possible, to order the weights from lightest to heaviest?

3. A jeep needs to deliver 100 gallons of gas across a 500 mile desert. The jeep only has range 200 miles based on its 10 gallon gas tank. It can carry three 10 gallon cans of gas. Devise a strategy of driving partway into the desert, leaving gas, going back for more gas, refilling at various strategic points, and ultimately delivering 100 gallons of gas to the other side of the desert. Can you devise an optimal strategy?

4. How would your strategy in Exercise 3 change if there were a gas station at the 350 mile point (that the jeep can use for refueling purposes only—not for refilling his gas cans)?

5. How would your strategy in Exercise 3 change if the jeep has a 20 gallon gas tank, still gets 20 miles per gallon, but can only carry two 10 gallon cans of gas in its cargo area?

6. You are on a game show. The host holds out two envelopes and asks you to choose one (each is known to have some money in it). After you make your choice, you are informed that one envelope has three times as much money as the other, but you don't know which is which. You open your envelope and observe that it has $150 in it. Thus the other envelope either has $50 or $450. You are now offered a chance to switch envelopes. Should you switch? Why or why not? If "three" is replaced by "two" or "one and a half" then does your answer change?

7. You have ten pearls, all with the same appearance. But they have three different weights: eight are the same, one is light, and one is heavy. How many weighings with a balance scale does it require to isolate the two odd pearls and say which is light and which is heavy?

8. The source of this problem is [BAL]. Ten checkers are placed in a row on a table. A legal move consists of lifting a checker, passing it over the next two checkers to its right or to its left, and placing the lifted checker atop the next checker after those two. How can one manage to arrange five stacks, each of two checkers, that are equally spaced?

9. Can you form a magic square of size 3×3 using the first nine *odd* integers?

10. Can you form a magic square of size 3×3 using the first nine *even* integers?

11. Can you form a magic square of size 3×3 using *any* consecutive sequence of 9 positive integers?

12. You've purchased a new balance scale. It has three pans. You can put on three separate batches to weigh at once. If all three weigh the same, the scale shows that; if two balance and the third is heavier or lighter, it shows that; if the three batches all have different weights, it exhibits heaviest, medium heaviest, and lightest. Now you have nine pearls, with one odd, as in Problem 5.2.1. Show that you can find the odd pearl in two weighings.

13. Use the balance scale from Exercise 12. How many weighings will it take to find the odd pearl from among twelve (with one odd, either heavier or lighter). What about fifteen?

14. How do Exercises 12 and 13 change if you know in advance that the odd pearl is heavier? How many pearls can you handle with two weighings? How many can you handle with three weighings?

15. A *Latin square* in an $n \times n$ tableau in which we place n different types of objects: say cherries, nuts, beans, coins, and so on. The goal is to have each row and each column contain just one, but not two, of each of these n distinct objects.

Construct a 2×2 Latin square. How many different 2×2 Latin squares are there?

Construct a 3×3 Latin square. How many different 3×3 Latin squares are there?

It turns out that there are more than 10^{21} distinct 8×8 Latin squares and fewer than 10^{22} of them. These estimates are rather difficult to prove. Can you instead derive a rough upper bound for the number of 8×8 Latin squares?

Latin squares are a subject of current research in mathematics. It turns out, for instance, that they are used in designing bias-free experiments in agricultural research.

16. What is the next element in the sequence

$$9 \, , \, 61 \, , \, 52 \, , \, 63 \, , \, 94 \, , \, 46 \, , \, 18 \quad ?$$

17. The Game of Life (invented by John Horton Conway) is played on a board divided into squares—like a large piece of graph paper. Begin by placing x's on some of the squares. These are the "people" in your population. Two people (squares) are "neighbors" if they share either an edge or a corner. Thus each square has eight neighbors—four to the left and right or above and below, and four diagonal.

The rules of the game are these: (i) if three people are neighbors to the same empty square, then they produce an offspring (another person) in that square, (ii) if some person has four or more neighbors, then it dies of overcrowding, (iii) if some person has one or fewer neighbors, then it dies of loneliness. Given any population configuration, all three rules are applied instantly to produce the next configuration.

Is there any initial population that will produce a population that is periodic—i.e. develops a pattern that, after finitely many steps, keeps repeating (try three squares in a horizontal row)? Is there any initial population that will remain static and never increase or decrease? Is there any initial population that will die out quickly—or immediately? Is there any that will keep reproducing and become ever larger without bound?

18. A (six sided) die is rolled. It is numbered, as usual, from 1 to 6 on the six sides. If a 6 does not come up in the first 30 rolls, then you are paid one million dollars. If, instead, a 6 comes up in the first 30 rolls, then you must pay $100 dollars. Is this a game that you should play or that you should pass up?

19. This problem comes from [BAL]. A man is traveling with a wolf, a goat, and a basket of cabbages. The goat cannot be left alone with the wolf, or else it would be eaten. For a similar reason, the cabbages cannot be left alone with the goat. However the wolf has no interest in the cabbages.

The party needs to cross a river, and the only transportation available is a small boat that will hold the man and just *one* of the wolf, goat, and cabbages. How can the trip be managed? What is the fewest number of passages needed to ferry the entire party across the river?

20. This problem also comes from [BAL]. Three men and three boys need to cross a river. The only boat available will hold just one man or just two boys. Everyone is capable of rowing the boat. How can the trip be achieved, and what is the fewest number of passages needed?

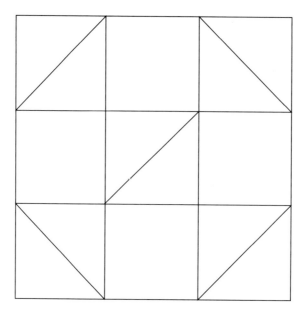

Figure 148

21. In the game of chess, the king may be moved from the square that it occupies to any adjacent square—left or right, up or down, or diagonally. A piece is captured by moving your piece on top of it. What is the maximum number of kings that may be placed on a chessboard so that no king may capture any other?

22. In chess, the queen can move linearly for any number of squares in any direction: up or down, left or right, or diagonally. What is the minimum number of queens that can be placed on the chessboard so that *every* square is under attack. [*Note:* A square that is *occupied* by a queen is not under attack by that queen.]

23. Consider the geometric figure that is shown in Figure 148. Show that it is possible to trace a pencil *along* the figure so that you traverse every segment once and only once without lifting the pencil from the paper. [*Hint:* The *parity* of the vertices is relevant here.]

24. The numbers $1, 2, 3, \ldots$ are written consecutively. What is the $40,000^{\text{th}}$ digit that appears?

25. A merchant has a beaker containing 24 ounces of a precious fluid. At a given transaction, he has available only a 5 ounce, an 11 ounce,

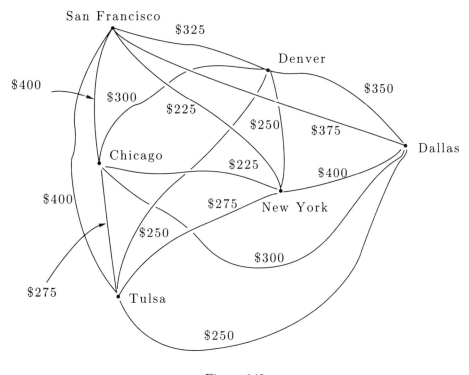

San Francisco

$325

Denver

$400

$300

$225

$250

$375

$350

Chicago

$225

Dallas

$400

$400

$275

New York

$250

$250

$300

$275

Tulsa

$250

Figure 149

and a 13 ounce beaker. How can he divide the fluid into three equal portions?

26. Examine Figure 149. It shows the cost of traveling between various pairs of cities. Assuming that the traveler will start in San Francisco and finish in San Francisco (the location of the home office), what is the cheapest route that will enable the traveler to visit each city (at least) once?

This is a special case of the very important *traveling salesman problem*—a problem whose full solution still has not been found; they were first mentioned in the Exercises at the end of Chapter 4.

27. How many $k \times m$ matrices are there with all entries ± 1 and every row or column having the product of its entries equal to -1?

Chapter 6

Algebra and Analysis

6.1   A Little Algebra

Elementary algebra provides a self-contained venue for exercising problem solving skills. We provide some practice with these techniques in the present section.

PROBLEM 6.1.1 *Show that if n is a positive integer then $n^3 - n$ is always divisible by 3.*

Solution: The number $n^3 - n$ factors as $(n-1)n(n+1)$. These factors are three integers in succession. Therefore one of them is a multiple of 3. As a result, $n^3 - n$ is a multiple of 3.   □

PROBLEM 6.1.2 *Show that if n is a positive integer then $n^5 - n$ is always divisible by 5.*

Solution: If we factor $n^5 - n$, in an attempt to imitate the last problem, then we obtain

$$n^5 - n = n(n^4 - 1) = n(n^2 - 1)(n^2 + 1) = n(n-1)(n+1)(n^2 + 1).$$

Now the picture is not so simple as in the last problem, since the factors do not form a set of five successive integers.

Instead we notice that, if n is an integer ending with one of the digits $0, 1, 4, 5, 6, 9$ then one of $(n-1), n, (n+1)$ is divisible by 5. So the product is divisible by 5. If, instead, n is an integer ending with $2, 3, 7,$ or 8, then n^2 ends with 4 or 9 hence $n^2 + 1$ is divisible by 5. Therefore the product is divisible by 5. Thus, no matter what n is, the number $n^5 - n$ is divisible by 5.   □

CHALLENGE PROBLEM 6.1.3 *Show that if n is a positive integer then $n^7 - n$ is always divisible by 7.*

PROBLEM 6.1.4 *Verify the combinatorial identity*

$$\binom{k}{m} + \binom{k}{m+1} = \binom{k+1}{m+1}.$$

Solution: We write out the left hand side:

$$
\begin{aligned}
\binom{k}{m} + \binom{k}{m+1} &= \frac{k!}{m!(k-m)!} + \frac{k!}{(m+1)!(k-m-1)!} \\
&= \frac{(m+1)k!}{(m+1)!(k-m)!} + \frac{(k-m)k!}{(m+1)!(k-m)!} \\
&= \frac{(k+1)k!}{(m+1)!(k-m)!} \\
&= \frac{(k+1)!}{(m+1)!((k+1)-(m+1))!} \\
&= \binom{k+1}{m+1}.
\end{aligned}
$$

This is the desired result.   □

PROBLEM 6.1.5 *Verify the binomial formula:*

$$
\begin{aligned}
(a+b)^k \ = \ & a^k + \binom{k}{1} a^{k-1} b + \binom{k}{2} a^{k-2} b^2 \\
& + \cdots \binom{k}{k-2} a^2 b^{k-2} + \binom{k}{k-1} a b^{k-1} + b^k.
\end{aligned}
$$

Solution: It is not feasible, for an arbitrary k, to attempt to multiply out the expression $(a + b)^k$. But for small k it is eminently feasible. This suggests that we attempt to use induction.

When $k = 1$ the formula becomes

$$a + b = a + b.$$

This is so simple as to be unenlightening. Just for practice, let us try $k = 2$:

$$(a + b)^2 = a^2 + \binom{2}{1}ab + b^2 = a^2 + 2ab + b^2 = a^2 + \binom{2}{1}a^{2-1}b + b^2.$$

This is familiar and true, and it coincides with the desired formula.

Now we suppose that the formula has been verified for k, and we use that information to verify it for $k + 1$. So we are assuming that

$$(a + b)^k = a^k + \binom{k}{1}a^{k-1}b + \binom{k}{2}a^{k-2}b^2 + \cdots + \binom{k}{k-2}a^2b^{k-2}$$
$$+ \binom{k}{k-1}ab^{k-1} + b^k.$$

We multiply both sides of this equation by $(a + b)$. The result is

$$(a + b)^{k+1} = (a + b)\left[a^k + \binom{k}{1}a^{k-1}b + \binom{k}{2}a^{k-2}b^2 + \cdots \right.$$
$$\left. + \binom{k}{(k-2)}a^2b^{k-2} + \binom{k}{(k-1)}ab^{k-1} + b^k\right].$$

Now we will expand the right hand side. Notice that, except for the terms a^{k+1} and b^{k+1} each term $a^m b^n$ will arise twice in this expansion. Thus we have

$$(a + b)^{k+1}$$
$$= a^{k+1} + \left[1 + \binom{k}{1}\right]a^k b + \left[\binom{k}{1} + \binom{k}{2}\right]a^{k-1}b^2$$
$$+ \left[\binom{k}{2} + \binom{k}{3}\right]a^{k-2}b^3 + \cdots$$

$$+ \left[\binom{k}{k-2} + \binom{k}{k-1} \right] a^2 b^{k-1}$$

$$+ \left[\binom{k}{k-1} + \binom{k}{k} \right] ab^k + b^k.$$

We may use the result from the previous problem about binomial coefficients to write this as

$$(a \mid b)^{k+1} \quad - \quad a^{k+1} + (k+1)a^k b + \binom{k+1}{2} a^{k-1} b^2 + \binom{k+1}{3} a^{k-2} b^3$$

$$+ \cdots + \binom{k+1}{(k-1)} a^2 b^{k-1} + \binom{k+1}{k} ab^k + b^k.$$

This is the desired identity for $(k+1)$. The induction is therefore complete. We have proved the binomial formula. □

PROBLEM 6.1.6 *Which is greater,*

$$\alpha = (1 + 0.000001)^{1,000,000} \qquad or \qquad 2 ?$$

Solution: Before you study the solution to this problem, try fiddling around on a calculator. What problem do you encounter? The same difficulty would arise on most computer systems: you can only keep track of so many decimal places. Now we turn to an analytical solution of the problem.

As a guide to the intuition, we recall that $(1 + 1/k)^k$ tends to the number e, which is $2.718\ldots$. The number α is just this expression with $k = 1,000,000$. So we would anticipate that α is greater than 2.

To bear out this notion, we apply the binomial formula to α:

$$\alpha = (1 + 0.000001)^{1,000,000} = 1^{1,000,000} + 1,000,000 \cdot 1^{999,999} \cdot 0.000001$$

$$+ \text{ other positive terms}$$

$$= 1 + 1 + \text{ positive terms}$$

$$> 2.$$

This confirms our intuition. Indeed, $\alpha > 2$. □

PROBLEM 6.1.7 *Which is greater,*

$$1000^{1000} \qquad or \qquad 1001^{999} \; ?$$

Solution: We again use the binomial theorem:

$$
\begin{aligned}
1001^{999} &= [1000 + 1]^{999} \\
&= 1000^{999} + 999 \cdot 1000^{998} \cdot 1 + \binom{999}{2} \cdot 1000^{997} \cdot 1^2 \\
&\quad + \binom{999}{3} \cdot 1000^{996} \cdot 1^3 + \cdots + \\
&\quad \binom{999}{997} \cdot 1000^2 \cdot 1^{997} + \binom{999}{998} \cdot 1000 \cdot 1^{998} + 1 \\
&< \underbrace{1000^{999} + 1000^{999} + \cdots + 1000^{999}}_{1000 \text{ times}} \\
&= 1000^{1000}.
\end{aligned}
$$

Thus we see that 1000^{1000} is the greater number. $\qquad\square$

The remarkable thing about the last problem is that it virtually defies calculation. Ordinary computer languages, such as FORTRAN—even in double precision mode—cannot handles numbers as large as 1000^{1000}. One could pass to scientific notation— $1000^{1000} = 1 \times 10^{3000}$—but this would not yield the accuracy necessary for the comparison that the problem requests. On the other hand, one could use a computer algebra system such as MATHEMATICA or MAPLE or AXIOM. But it is quite difficult to evaluate a number such as 1001^{999}, with about three thousand digits. Of course, if you are a real hacker, you can always write a filter to compare any given number with any other. But this is a lot of work.

Instead of these more mundane attacks on the problem, we used elementary but important ideas from combinatorial analysis. The solution is therefore simple, straightforward, and easy to understand and to check.

PROBLEM 6.1.8 *Assume that k is a positive integer. Calculate*

$$\frac{1}{1 \cdot 2} + \frac{1}{2 \cdot 3} + + \cdot \frac{1}{(k-1) \cdot k} + \frac{1}{k \cdot (k+1)}.$$

Solution: One approach would be to actually add up the sum for various small values of k, such as $k = 1, 2, 3, 4$, and see whether there is a pattern. We shall try that first. Call the sum S_k.

Now

$$S_1 = \frac{1}{2}$$

$$S_2 = \frac{2}{3}$$

$$S_3 = \frac{3}{4}$$

$$S_4 = \frac{4}{5}$$

Plainly there is a pattern. A pattern such as this suggests a verification by induction.

The statement to be proved is that $S_k = k/(k+1)$ for each k. We have verified S_1. Now we assume that S_j is true. So we are assuming that

$$S_j = \frac{1}{1 \cdot 2} + \frac{1}{2 \cdot 3} + + \cdot \frac{1}{(j-1) \cdot j} + \frac{1}{j \cdot (j+1)} = \frac{j}{j+1}.$$

We add $1/[(j+1)(j+2)]$ to both sides. The result is

$$S_{j+1} = \frac{j}{j+1} + \frac{1}{(j+1)(j+2)} = \frac{j+1}{j+2}.$$

This is precisely the statement that we wished to derive for S_{j+1}. The induction is complete, and we have verified our formula for S_k.

We wish to present a second quick technique for doing this problem. It is a trick, but it is an important trick that you should know: we will learn a method for forcing the sum to "telescope" and hence to collapse.

We write

$$S_k$$

$$= \frac{1}{1 \cdot 2} + \frac{1}{2 \cdot 3} + + \cdot \frac{1}{(k-1) \cdot k}$$

$$+ \frac{1}{k \cdot (k+1)}$$

$$= \left[\frac{1}{1} - \frac{1}{2}\right] + \left[\frac{1}{2} - \frac{1}{3}\right]$$
$$+ \left[\frac{1}{3} - \frac{1}{4}\right]$$
$$+ \cdots + \left[\frac{1}{k} - \frac{1}{k+1}\right].$$

Notice that all the terms, except for the first and last, cancel. Hence

$$S_k = 1 - \frac{1}{k+1} = \frac{k}{k+1}.$$

This is, of course, the same answer that we derived before. But we have now discovered it in an even more elegant fashion. □

CHALLENGE PROBLEM 6.1.9 *Calculate the sum*

$$\frac{1}{1 \cdot 2 \cdot 3} + \frac{1}{2 \cdot 3 \cdot 4} + \frac{1}{3 \cdot 4 \cdot 5} + \cdots + \frac{1}{(k-2)(k-1)k}.$$

Solve this problem twice, using each of the methods presented in the last solution.

PROBLEM 6.1.10 *Calculate the sum*

$$1 \cdot 2 + 2 \cdot 3 + 3 \cdot 4 + \cdots n(n+1).$$

Solution: We can again begin by seeking a pattern. Call the sum T_n. Then:

$$
\begin{aligned}
T_1 &= 2 \\
T_2 &= 8 \\
T_3 &= 20 \\
T_4 &= 40 \\
T_5 &= 70
\end{aligned}
$$

We begin to see the limitations of this method. No pattern is apparent.

We instead attempt to imitate the "forced collapsing" technique that we used in the second half of our last solution. How can we take advantage of the fact that each successive pair of terms has a common factor? We can attempt to write

$$T_n = 2(1+3) + 3(2+4) + 4(3+5) + \cdots + n((n-1)+(n+1)). \qquad (*)$$

Of course this is incorrect algebra. Notice that the term $2 \cdot 3$ occurs twice, as does $3 \cdot 4$ and so forth. The only terms that do not occur twice are the first and last terms. So, while we stress that our attempt in line $(*)$ is WRONG, it gives us an idea.

We learn from our mistake. We write

$$2(1+3) + 3(2+4) + 4(3+5) + \cdots + n((n-1)+(n+1))$$
$$= 2\Big[1 \cdot 2 + 2 \cdot 3 + 3 \cdot 4 \quad + \cdots + n(n+1)\Big]$$
$$-1 \cdot 2 - n(n+1).$$

Notice that we have subtracted off $1 \cdot 2$ and $n \cdot (n+1)$ on the right, because they should not be counted twice. Thus we have

$$2 \cdot 4 + 3 \cdot 6 + 4 \cdot 8 + \cdots + n \cdot 2n = 2T_n - 2 - n(n+1).$$

In other words,

$$2\Big[2^2 + 3^2 + 4^2 + \cdots + n^2\Big] = 2T_n - (n^2 + n + 2). \qquad (**)$$

The sum of squares on the left is one that we have calculated previously. More precisely, we know that

$$1^2 + 2^2 + 3^2 + \cdots + n^2 = \frac{2n^3 + 3n^2 + n}{6},$$

hence

$$2^2 + 3^2 + \cdots + n^2 = \frac{2n^3 + 3n^2 + n - 6}{6}.$$

Putting this information into $(**)$ gives

$$\frac{2n^3 + 3n^2 + n - 6}{3} = 2T_n - (n^2 + n + 2).$$

We may solve for T_n to obtain

$$T_n = \frac{n(n+1)(n+2)}{3}.$$

This completes our solution. $\qquad\qquad\qquad\qquad\qquad\qquad$ □

CHALLENGE PROBLEM 6.1.11 *Calculate the sum*

$$1 \cdot 2 \cdot 3 + 2 \cdot 3 \cdot 4 + 3 \cdot 4 \cdot 5 + \cdots n(n+1)(n+2).$$

Use any method (including building on our last solution).

6.2 Inequalities

Inequalities are a fundamental part of mathematical analysis. They involve a subtle combination of quantitative and qualitative reasoning. In this section we will get some practice with inequalities.

PROBLEM 6.2.1 *If a and b are positive real numbers then show that*

$$ab \le \frac{a^2 + b^2}{2}.$$

Solution: We may rewrite the inequality as

$$2ab \le a^2 + b^2.$$

We recognize, in this display, various factors from the binomial theorem. We rearrange the inequality as

$$0 \le a^2 - 2ab + b^2.$$

Now the right hand side is a perfect square, so we may write our inequality as

$$0 \le (a - b)^2.$$

This is certainly true, for the square of any real number is greater than or equal to zero.

We have used reverse reasoning to reduce the desired inequality to something that is patently true. We check our work by reasoning forward: Certainly $(a-b)^2 \geq 0$ for any real numbers a and b. Therefore

$$a^2 - 2ab + b^2 \geq 0.$$

We may rearrange this as

$$a^2 + b^2 \geq 2ab.$$

Finally, we may divide by 2 and conclude that

$$\frac{a^2 + b^2}{2} \geq ab.$$

This is the desired result.   □

In some of the problems below, we will present a solution using reverse reasoning, but will leave it up to you to reformulate the ideas in forward order as we have just done.

Problem 6.2.1 is a special instance of a general phenomenon known as the fact that "the arithmetic mean majorizes the geometric mean." We now introduce some terminology. If $a_1, a_2, \ldots, a_k$ are positive numbers then their "arithmetic mean" is

$$M = \frac{a_1 + a_2 + \cdots + a_k}{k}.$$

In common parlance, this number M is sometimes called the "average" of $a_1, a_2, \ldots, a_k$. On the other hand, the "geometric mean" of these numbers is

$$G = [a_1 \cdot a_2 \cdot \cdots \cdot a_k]^{1/k}.$$

These are both reasonable methods for averaging k positive numbers —one method based on adding and the other on multiplying. It is reasonable to wish to know the relationship between M and G. We have

PROBLEM 6.2.2 *Show that, for any positive numbers* $a_1, a_2, \ldots, a_k$ *we have*

$$G \leq M.$$

Solution: One method would be to attempt induction on the number of elements that are being averaged. We have already proved this inequality for two elements in the first problem of this section.

Now assume that it has been proved for j elements; that is, assume that we know that

$$[a_1 \cdot a_2 \cdots a_j]^{1/j} \leq \frac{a_1 + a_2 + \cdots + a_j}{j}. \qquad (*)$$

We rename the elements as follows: $a_1 = b_1{}^j$, $a_2 = b_2{}^j$, ..., $a_j = b_j{}^j$. Then our induction hypothesis $(*)$ becomes

$$b_1 \cdot b_2 \cdots b_j \leq \frac{b_1{}^j + b_2{}^j + \cdots + b_j{}^j}{j}$$

or

$$j \cdot [b_1 \cdot b_2 \cdots b_j] \leq b_1{}^j + b_2{}^j + \cdots + b_j{}^j. \qquad (\dagger)$$

In our new notation, we may say that our aim is to prove inductively that

$$(j+1) \cdot [b_1 \cdot b_2 \cdots b_{j+1}] \leq b_1{}^{j+1} + b_2{}^{j+1} + \cdots + b_{j+1}{}^{j+1}. \qquad (\ddagger)$$

Now we study the inequality $(\ddagger)$. Assume, as we may, that the b's don't vanish (if any one does then G is 0 and the desired inequality is obvious). We divide through by $b_{j+1}{}^{j+1}$ and rename $b_1/b_{j+1} = c_1$, $b_2/b_{j+1} = c_2$, ..., $c_j = b_j/b_{j+1}$. Then $(\ddagger)$ becomes

$$(j+1) \cdot [c_1 \cdot c_2 \cdots c_j] \leq c_1{}^{j+1} + c_2{}^{j+1} + \cdots + c_j{}^{j+1} + 1$$

or

$$(j+1) \cdot [c_1 \cdot c_2 \cdots c_j] - 1 \leq c_1{}^{j+1} + c_2{}^{j+1} + \cdots + c_j{}^{j+1} \qquad (**)$$

We need to verify this inequality for any positive numbers $c_1, \ldots, c_j$.

We may apply the induction hypothesis $(\dagger)$ to $c_1{}^{(j+1)/j}, c_2{}^{(j+1)/j}, \ldots, c_j{}^{(j+1)/j}$ and see that

$$j \cdot [c_1{}^{(j+1)/j} \cdot c_2{}^{(j+1)/j} \cdots c_j{}^{(j+1)/j}] \leq c_1{}^{j+1} + c_2{}^{j+1} + \cdots + c_j{}^{j+1}.$$

Putting this information into $(**)$ yields that it suffices for us to prove that

$$(j+1) \cdot [c_1 \cdot c_2 \cdots c_j] - 1 \leq j \cdot [c_1{}^{(j+1)/j} \cdot c_2{}^{(j+1)/j} \cdots c_j{}^{(j+1)/j}].$$

We may simplify this inequality further by setting $m = [c_1 c_2 \cdots c_j]^{1/j}$. Thus we must prove

$$(j + 1)m^j - 1 \le jm^{j+1}$$

for every positive number m and every positive integer j. [Notice how much simpler this is than the original question. Apart from the index j, there is only one unknown m.]

One *could* prove this inequality by induction on j, but such an induction within an induction might become confusing. Instead we do a direct algebraic computation:

$$(j + 1)m^j - 1 - jm^{j+1} = -jm^j(m - 1) + (m^j - 1).$$

But
$$m^j - 1 = (m - 1)(m^{j-1} + m^{j-2} + \cdots + m^2 + m + 1)$$

(just do the long division, for instance—or multiply out the right hand side). Thus our formula becomes

$$
\begin{aligned}
(j + 1)&m^j - 1 - jm^{j+1} \\
&= (m - 1)[-jm^j + m^{j-1} + m^{j-2} \\
&\qquad + \cdots m^2 + m + 1] \\
&= -(m - 1)[(m^j - m^{j-1}) \\
&\qquad + (m^j - m^{j-2}) + \cdots + (m^j - m) + (m^j - 1)] \\
&= -(m - 1)[m^{j-1}(m - 1) + m^{j-2}(m^2 - 1) \\
&\qquad + \cdots + m(m^{j-1} - 1) + (m^j - 1)] \\
&= -(m - 1)[m^{j-1}(m - 1) + m^{j-2}(m - 1)(m + 1) \\
&\qquad + \cdots + m(m - 1)(m^{j-2} + m^{j-3} + \cdots + m + 1) \\
&\qquad + (m - 1)(m^{j-1} + m^{j-2} + \cdots + m + 1)] \\
&= -(m - 1)^2 \cdot \text{(something positive)} \\
&\le 0.
\end{aligned}
$$

This establishes the desired inequality, and completes the induction. □

We now take a look back at this last solution. The most interesting part is the systematic renaming of the variables. This is more than a notational trick. For we are exploiting certain built-in symmetry in the problem. We could have even used a version of these notational changes to handle the simple inequality in Problem 6.2.1. Remember that we were trying to establish

$$2ab \leq a^2 + b^2.$$

Assume that $a \geq b$ and that $b \neq 0$. Suppose that we divide through by b^2 and set $a/b = c$. Then $c \geq 1$ and the problem becomes

$$2c \leq c^2 + 1 \qquad \text{for all} \quad c \geq 1.$$

Suddenly a two variable inequality has become a one variable inequality.

With this simplification, new avenues of approach suggest themselves. For instance, set $f(c) = 2c$ and $g(c) = c^2 + 1$. Notice that $f(1) = g(1)$ and that $f'(c) \equiv 2 \leq 2c = g'(c)$ (we have just used a little calculus). Thus the two functions f, g agree at $c = 1$ and g grows faster than f. It follows that $f(c) \leq g(c)$ for $c \geq 1$ and the last inequality is established.

What is going on behind the scenes in this discussion is that an inequality of expressions involving powers simply *cannot be true* unless the powers on both sides are "in balance." For example, the inequality

$$a^3 + b^3 \leq 3ab + b^2$$

could not possibly be true for all positive a and b. To see this, divide through by b^3 to obtain

$$(a/b)^3 + 1 \leq 3a/b^2 + 1/b.$$

Fix a and let b tend to ∞ through positive values. The inequality becomes $1 \leq 0$, which is patently false. The problem, once again, is that the powers on either side of the alleged inequality are out of balance.

By contrast, the powers in

$$2ab \leq a^2 + b^2$$

are *in balance*. Every power that occurs, that is to say every monomial that appears, is of second order. That is why the change of variable $a/b = c$ is successful and leads to a new proof.

The changes of variables that we performed in our solution of Problem 6.2.2 are just a sophisticated version of the $a/b = c$ substitution. It is a powerful technique that you should make part of your arsenal.

PROBLEM 6.2.3 *Prove that*

$$2 < \frac{1}{\log_2 \pi} + \frac{1}{\log_5 \pi}.$$

Solution: This is a different sort of inequality from the ones that we have considered so far—because it involves transcendental expressions such as the logarithm function.

Certainly we could get out the old pocket calculator or computer and just calculate all the expressions in the inequality. But that is avoiding the challenge. Can we solve the problem just by thinking?

Recall that

$$\log_a b \equiv \frac{\ln b}{\ln a}$$

for positive numbers a and b. Using this fact, we rewrite the desired inequality as

$$2 < \frac{1}{\ln \pi / \ln 2} + \frac{1}{\ln \pi / \ln 5}.$$

Multiply both sides by $\ln \pi$ and simplify to obtain

$$2 \ln \pi \leq \ln 2 + \ln 5$$

or

$$\ln \pi^2 \leq \ln 10.$$

Exponentiating both sides of this inequality gives (since exp is an increasing function)

$$\pi^2 \leq 10.$$

This is certainly true, since we know that $\pi < 3.15$. That establishes the inequality and finishes the problem.   □

CHALLENGE PROBLEM 6.2.4 *Verify that*

$$2 < \frac{1}{\log_2 \pi} + \frac{1}{\log_\pi 2}.$$

PROBLEM 6.2.5 *Show that*

$$|\cos x + \sin x| \le \sqrt{2},$$

with equality only if $\sin 2x = 1$.

Solution: This is another transcendental inequality. Often a good way to understand $|a|$ is to write it as $\sqrt{a^2}$. Using this idea, we have

$$
\begin{aligned}
|\cos x + \sin x| &= \sqrt{(\cos x + \sin x)^2} \\
&= \sqrt{\cos^2 x + \sin^2 x + 2\sin x \cos x} \\
&= \sqrt{1 + 2\sin x \cos x} \\
&= \sqrt{1 + \sin 2x}.
\end{aligned}
$$

Clearly the greatest that $\sin 2x$ can be is 1. That yields

$$|\cos x + \sin x| \le \sqrt{2},$$

which is the required inequality. Since the displayed relations are all equalities, we see that $|\cos x + \sin x|$ can equal $\sqrt{2}$ only if $\sqrt{1 + \sin 2x} = \sqrt{2}$, which is true only if $1 + \sin 2x = 2$ or $\sin 2x = 1$.
    This completes our solution of the problem.   □

CHALLENGE PROBLEM 6.2.6 *Show that*

$$|\cos x - \sin x| \le \sqrt{2},$$

with equality only if $\sin 2x = -1$.

PROBLEM 6.2.7 *Which is greater,* $\sin(\cos x)$ *or* $\cos(\sin x)$?

Solution: Keep in mind that one expression may be greater for one range of x and the other greater for another range of x. Our strategy is to use trigonometric identities to make it simpler to compare the two transcendental expressions.

We begin with

$$\cos\left(\cos x + \frac{\pi}{2}\right) = \cos(\cos x)\cos\frac{\pi}{2} - \sin(\cos x)\sin\frac{\pi}{2} = -\sin(\cos x).$$

This gives us a new way to write one of our two expressions. Thus we have

$$\cos(\sin x) - \sin(\cos x) = \cos(\sin x) + \cos\left(\cos x + \frac{\pi}{2}\right). \qquad (*)$$

Now it is an elementary fact from trigonometry that

$$\cos X + \cos Y = 2\cdot\cos\left(\frac{X+Y}{2}\right)\cdot\cos\left(\frac{X-Y}{2}\right). \qquad (**)$$

[*Hint:* To verify this, write

$$\cos X = \cos\left(\frac{X+Y}{2} + \frac{X-Y}{2}\right)$$

and

$$\cos Y = \cos\left(\frac{X+Y}{2} - \frac{X-Y}{2}\right).$$

Then apply the usual sum/difference formula for cosine and add the results.]

We apply $(**)$ to the right side of $(*)$ to obtain

$$\cos(\sin x) - \sin(\cos x)$$
$$= 2\cdot\cos\left(\frac{\sin x + \cos x + \pi/2}{2}\right)\cdot\cos\left(\frac{\sin x - \cos x - \pi/2}{2}\right)$$
$$= 2\cdot\cos\left(\frac{\sin x + \cos x + \pi/2}{2}\right)\cdot\cos\left(\frac{\cos x - \sin x + \pi/2}{2}\right), \qquad (\dagger)$$

where we have used the evenness of the cosine function in the last equality. Now since, by Problem 6.2.5, $|\sin x + \cos x| \le \sqrt{2}$, and since $\pi \approx 3.141$ and $\sqrt{2} \approx 1.414$, we can be sure that

$$0 < \left|\frac{\sin x + \cos x + \pi/2}{2}\right| \le \frac{1.415 + 1.58}{2} < 1.5 < \frac{\pi}{2}.$$

Likewise, we may use Challenge Problem 6.2.6 to see that

$$0 < \left| \frac{\cos x - \sin x + \pi/2}{2} \right| < \frac{\pi}{2}.$$

[Notice here that $|\sin x + \cos x|$ and $|\cos x - \sin x|$ are too small for the numerators to be 0.] Now $\cos \omega$ is positive when $0 < |\omega| < \pi/2$. Thus we may conclude that the two factors on the right of (†) are positive. Therefore $\cos(\sin x) - \sin(\cos x)$ is always positive, for any value of the argument x.

In conclusion,

$$\sin(\cos x) < \cos(\sin x)$$

for any real number x. □

6.3 Trigonometry and Related Ideas

The ideas of trigonometry date back to the times of ancient Greek mathematics. Originally used in surveying, as well as in understanding rational numbers, trigonometry is now part of the bedrock of mathematics. Since it involves basic ideas such as proportionality, congruence of angles, and similar triangles, it is a rich source of problems.

PROBLEM 6.3.1 *Suppose that α is an angle and that $\tan(\alpha/2)$ is rational. Verify that then $\sin \alpha$ and $\cos \alpha$ are both rational.*

Solution: We know that

$$
\begin{aligned}
1 + \tan^2 \frac{\alpha}{2} &= \frac{\cos^2 \frac{\alpha}{2}}{\cos^2 \frac{\alpha}{2}} + \frac{\sin^2 \frac{\alpha}{2}}{\cos^2 \frac{\alpha}{2}} \\
&= \frac{1}{\cos^2 \frac{\alpha}{2}}.
\end{aligned}
$$

Since $\tan \frac{\alpha}{2}$ is rational we conclude that the left side of this last equation is rational, hence so is the right. It follows that $\cos^2 \frac{\alpha}{2}$ is rational.

Now

$$\begin{aligned}
\cos \alpha &= \cos^2 \frac{\alpha}{2} - \sin^2 \frac{\alpha}{2} \\
&= \cos^2 \frac{\alpha}{2} - [1 - \cos^2 \frac{\alpha}{2}] \\
&= 2\cos^2 \frac{\alpha}{2} - 1.
\end{aligned}$$

Our preceding calculation guarantees that the right side of this last identity is rational, hence so is the left side. We conclude that $\cos \alpha$ is rational. That is half of our task.

Next observe that

$$\begin{aligned}
\tan \alpha &= \frac{\sin \alpha}{\cos \alpha} \\
&= \frac{\sin 2\frac{\alpha}{2}}{\cos 2\frac{\alpha}{2}} \\
&= \frac{2\sin \frac{\alpha}{2} \cos \frac{\alpha}{2}}{\cos^2 \frac{\alpha}{2} - \sin^2 \frac{\alpha}{2}} \\
&= \frac{2\tan \frac{\alpha}{2}}{1 - \tan^2 \frac{\alpha}{2}},
\end{aligned}$$

where in the last equality we have divided both numerator and denominator by $\cos^2(\alpha/2)$. Now we know already that each component of the right hand side of this last identity is rational. We therefore conclude that $\tan \alpha = \sin \alpha / \cos \alpha$ is rational. But since $\cos \alpha$ is rational, we finally see that $\sin \alpha$ is rational. That solves the problem.   □

CHALLENGE PROBLEM 6.3.2 *Formulate and prove a converse to the last problem.*

PROBLEM 6.3.3 *If θ is a positive, acute angle, measured in radians, then show that $\tan \theta > \theta$.*

Solution: Examine Figure 150, which is the standard setup for the trigonometry of the angle θ. The figure makes it plain that $\sin \theta < \theta$. However the question at hand makes it clear that we need an estimate *from above* on θ.

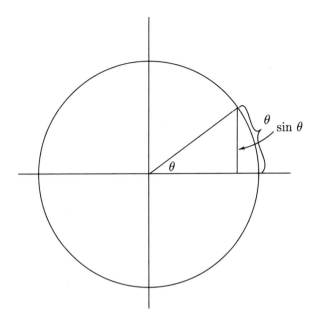

Figure 150

Now look at Figure 151. It is the same as Figure 150, except that some new segments are emphasized. Notice that the base of the triangle with bold sides has length 1. Using similar triangles (compare with the well-known triangle having dotted sides), we see that hypotenuse has length $1/\cos\theta$ and the height is $\sin\theta/\cos\theta$.

Also the height of this triangle is greater than the length of the arc of the circle that is subtended (give a concrete reason for this assertion). But the length of that arc is θ. We conclude that

$$\frac{\sin\theta}{\cos\theta} > \theta.$$

This is what we wished to demonstrate. □

CHALLENGE PROBLEM 6.3.4 (DIFFICULT) *For θ an acute angle measure in radians, explain why*

$$\theta < \frac{\sin\theta + \tan\theta}{2}.$$

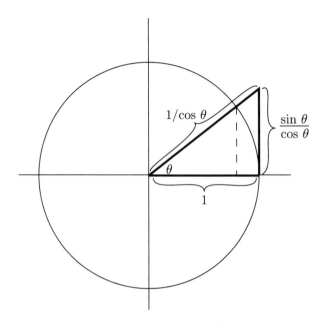

Figure 151

PROBLEM 6.3.5 *Suppose that θ be any angle. Explain why*

$$\cos \frac{\alpha}{2} \, \cos \frac{\alpha}{4} \, \cos \frac{\alpha}{8} = \frac{\sin \alpha}{8 \sin(\alpha/8)}.$$

Solution: It is almost impossible to make any progress in trigonometry without knowledge of the most basic trigonometric identities. In this problem we shall use the fact that $\sin 2\theta = 2 \sin \theta \cos \theta$. With this identity in mind, we are tempted to rewrite the desired equation as

$$\cos \frac{\alpha}{2} \, \cos \frac{\alpha}{4} \left[2 \cos \frac{\alpha}{8} \sin \frac{\alpha}{8} \right] = \frac{\sin \alpha}{4}.$$

But then the left side simplifies and the equation becomes

$$\cos \frac{\alpha}{2} \, \cos \frac{\alpha}{4} \, \sin \frac{\alpha}{4} = \frac{\sin \alpha}{4}.$$

Now we may multiply both sides by 2 and group terms on the left to obtain

$$\cos \frac{\alpha}{2} \left[2 \cos \frac{\alpha}{4} \sin \frac{\alpha}{4} \right] = \frac{\sin \alpha}{2}.$$

This simplifies to

$$\cos\frac{\alpha}{2}\sin\frac{\alpha}{2} = \frac{\sin\alpha}{2}.$$

Again multiplying both sides of the equation by 2, we note that we have reduced the problem to the double angle formula with which we began. Since all steps of this derivation are reversible, we have succeeded in verifying the required identity. □

CHALLENGE PROBLEM 6.3.6 *See whether you can generalize the last identity to one having four terms on the left. Is there an analogous formula having cosines on the right?*

PROBLEM 6.3.7 *How many solutions are there to the equation*

$$\tan x = \tan(x + 10°) \cdot \tan(x + 20°) \cdot \tan(x + 30°) \qquad (*)$$

with $0 < x < 60°$? [Notice here that angles are measured in degrees.]

Solution: Begin by graphing the function on the left side using your graphing calculator or computer algebra software. Graph the function on the right hand side on the same set of axes. What do your graphs suggest?

Now we do a little analysis. We will implement the philosophy enunciated at the start of the book—which is to *try something*. First notice that the function *tangent* is a strictly increasing function when the argument is between $0°$ and $90°$. Therefore the left side of $(*)$ is strictly increasing. Also each factor on the right side is increasing for $0 < x < 60°$, so the entire function on the right side is strictly increasing.

We call the function on the left side of $(*)$ by the name $f(x)$ and that on the right side by the name $g(x)$. Now $f(0) = 0$ and $g(0) > 0$. So the graph of f begins *lower* than the graph of g. However we may use a pocket calculator (be sure to set it on degree mode!) or a book of tables or a computer and calculate that $g(7°) < f(7°)$. In brief, let $h(x) = f(x) - g(x)$. Then $h(0) < 0$ and $h(7°) > 0$. Since h is continuous, it follows that there is a value in between where $h = 0$, that is where

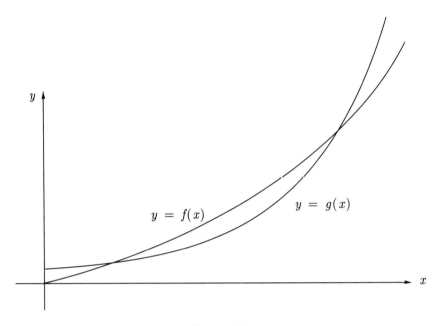

Figure 152

f equals g. We have established that the equation (∗) has at least one solution.

In fact we can do better than that. Because, once again, the graph of g *begins*, at 0, lying above the graph of f. And, when $45° < x < 60°$ then each factor on the right is greater than 1 and greater than the single factor on the left; so the graph of g is eventually above the graph of f again. In between, at $x = 7°$ for instance, the graph of g dips below the graph of f. This can only happen if the graphs cross *at least* twice—see Figure 152. We conclude that the graphs of f and g cross at least twice. [Note that Figure 152 is *not* drawn to scale; it is merely a visual representation of what we have described in words.]

In fact they cross exactly twice. This is rather difficult to see rigorously without the use of calculus. This discussion has served to show how much one can see just by using common sense.

Again, think of your computer algebra software as a friend that you can turn to at times like this. Graph both functions on the same set of axes (be sure that you are in degree mode). Zoom in on the portion of the graph where $0 < x < 10°$. How many points of intersection does the graph show? □

EXERCISES for Chapter 6

1. Prove that if $0 \le a, b, c, d \le 1$ then

$$(1 - a)(1 - b)(1 - c)(1 - d) \ge 1 - a - b - c - d.$$

2. If a, b, c, d are positive real numbers then show that

$$\frac{(a^2 + 1)(b^2 + 1)(c^2 + 1)(d^2 + 1)}{abcd} > 16.$$

3. Suppose that k is a positive integer greater than 1. Prove that

$$\frac{1}{1} + \frac{1}{2} + \frac{1}{3} + \cdots \frac{1}{k}$$

is not an integer.

4. Explain why 7 will evenly divide $2222^{5555} + 5555^{2222}$.

5. Explain why $11^{10} - 1$ is divisible by 100.

6. Assume that N is a positive integer. Show that there is an integral multiple of N whose digits are all 0's and 1's. Show that if 2 does not divide N and 5 does not divide N then there is a multiple of N that has all digits equal to 1.

7. Say that N is a positive integer that is greater than 1000. Which is greater, $99^N + 100^N$ or 101^N?

8. If $a_1, a_2, \ldots, a_k$ are positive real numbers then show that

$$(a_1 + a_2 + \cdots + a_k) \cdot \left(\frac{1}{a_1} + \frac{1}{a_2} + \cdots + \frac{1}{a_k} \right) \ge k^2.$$

9. How many 7's are used in writing out all the positive integers from 1 to 10^8?

10. Find a condition on the positive integer n that will guarantee that $1^n + 2^n + 3^n + 4^n$ is divisible by 5. [*Hint:* One possible answer is "$n = 1$." However we are looking for a "condition" that will be satisfied by infinitely many n. Better still would be to find a condition that is both necessary and sufficient.]

11. Show that the number

$$\gamma_n = \left(\frac{1}{1} + \frac{1}{2} + \cdots + \frac{1}{n} \right) - \ln n$$

satisfies $|\gamma_n| \leq 4$. [*Hint:* Draw a picture.]

12. Solve the equation for real x:

$$|x + 1| - |x| + 3|x - 1| - 2|x - 2| = x + 2.$$

13. Consider the series

$$\frac{1}{1} + \frac{1}{2} + \frac{1}{3} + \cdots.$$

This is the harmonic series, and is known to diverge (refer to your calculus book for the details). Show that if we discard all the terms with a 7 in the denominator then the series converges. Can you estimate the size of the sum?

14. Explain why if $a_1, a_2, \ldots, a_k$ are positive integers such that $a_1 + a_2 + \cdots + a_k \leq n$ then the number

$$\frac{n!}{(a_1)!(a_2)! \cdots (a_k)!}$$

is an integer.

15. Assume that p is a prime number greater than 3. What is the remainder when p^2 is divided by 12? Why is it always the same?

16. Find all integer values x, y, z such that

$$x^2 + y^2 + z^2 = 2xyz.$$

17. What is the first digit of 2^{43}?

18. A 10 year old child puts $100 in the bank. She intends to withdraw the money on her twenty first birthday. Is she better off with an account with 5% percent interest compounded daily or 5.1% interest compounded weekly?

19. Take a and r to be any real numbers. Let $k > 0$ be an integer. Calculate the sum

$$a + a \cdot r + a \cdot r^2 + \cdots + a \cdot r^k.$$

[*Hint:* Use either induction or an algebraic trick.]

20. A woman buys a car for $20,000. She puts $3,500 down. She arranges a loan for 3 years—with 36 equal monthly payments—at 5%

APR (annual percentage rate). What should be the amount of each of her monthly payments? [*Note:* Automobile salespeople and real estate sales people rely on a book of tables to give them these figures. But the figures come from mathematical calculations. Your job is to do the calculations. You may find the result of problem 19 to be useful.]

21. A certain sphere encloses a volume equal to its surface area, and both numbers are a two digit integer times π. What is the volume/area of the sphere?

22. If x, y, z are real numbers such that $x + y + z = 1$ then establish the inequality $xy + yz + xz < 1/2$.

23. Which is larger, $10^{1/10}$ or $2^{1/3}$?

24. Solve the equation

$$8(4^x + 4^{-x}) - 54(2^x + 2^{-x}) + 101 = 0.$$

[*Hint:* Use the substitutions $y = 2^x$ and $z = y + 1/y$.]

25. 37. If $a^2 + b^2 + c^2 + d^2 = ab + bc + cd + da$ then show that $a = b = c = d$. [*Hint:* Complete the squares—the sum of four squares equals zero.]

26. This problem is attributed to Isaac Newton:

> A group of m cows grazes n fields bare in k days. A group of m' cows grazes n' fields bare in k' days. A group of m'' cows grazes n'' fields bare in k'' days.

What relationship is there among the numbers $m, n, k, m', n', k', m'', n''$, and k''?

27. Prove that no positive integer, all of whose digits are 1's, is a perfect square (the only exception being the first positive integer 1).

28. Explain why each of the numbers $49, 4489, 444889, 44448889, \ldots$ is a perfect square.

29. [From a recent Math Olympiad] Construct a set A of positive integers with the property that if S is any infinite set of prime numbers then A contains an element that is a product of at least two distinct elements of S and also the complement of A in the positive integers contains an element that is a product of at least two elements of S. [*Hint:* Map out carefully what this problem says. Do not get fancy; this is a simple problem.]

30. Use the binomial formula to give a new proof that the number of subsets of a set with k elements is 2^k.

31. If α is an irrational number and β is an irrational number then can α^β be rational?

32. Calculate $\cos 36° - \cos 72°$.

33. If θ is an acute angle and $\sin 2\theta = a$ then calculate $\sin \theta + \cos \theta$.

34. If $\sin x + \cos x = 1/5$ and if $0 \le x < \pi$ then what is $\tan x$?

35. Suppose that x is a positive number such that

$$x^{\left(x^{\left(x^{\cdot^{\cdot^{\cdot}}}\right)}\right)} = 2$$

Determine the value of x.

36. Which other positive numbers besides 2 will result in an equation, in Exercise 35, which can be solved for x? [This question was first studied by Gauss.]

37. The hands of a standard two-handed clock will meet at noon. What is the first time thereafter that they meet? What is the second such time? How many such times are there altogether during a twelve hour period?

38. Explain why, if p and q are odd integers, then the equation $x^2 + 2px + 2q$ has no rational roots.

39. Assume that a and b are odd integers and let n be a positive integer. Explain why $a^3 - b^3$ is divisible by 2^n if and only if $a - b$ is divisible by 2^n.

40. The numbers α, β, and γ are the sides of a right triangle, with γ the hypotenuse. If $n > 2$ is an integer then explain why $\gamma^n > \alpha^n + \beta^n$.

41. If n is a positive integer then explain why

$$(n+2)^3 \ne n^3 + (n+1)^3.$$

42. Suppose that j is a positive integer. Explain why

$$\frac{1}{3} + \frac{1}{5} + \cdots + \frac{1}{2j+1}$$

can never be an integer.

43. If n is an integer greater than 1 then explain why 2^n cannot divide $3^n + 1$ evenly.

44. How many five digit positive integers are there such that each digit is a 1 or a 2 or a 3? How many such numbers are there with the property that each of $1, 2, 3$ occurs at least once?

45. If n is a positive integer then show that

$$5^n + 2 \cdot 3^{n-1} + 1$$

is divisible by 8.

46. If $n > 2$ is an integer then explain why

$$(1 \cdot 2 \cdots n)^2 > n^n.$$

47. Assume that a is an integer such that a^2 has the digit 7 in the tens place. What must the ones digit be?

48. Find three distinct natural numbers such that the sum of their reciprocals is an integer.

49. Show that the polynomial $x^4 + 2x^2 + 2x + 2$ is *not* the product of two polynomials of the form $x^2 + ax + b$ and $x^2 + cx + d$, where a, b, c, d are integers.

50. If $a_1, a_2, \ldots, a_n$ are distinct natural numbers, and none of them is divisible by any prime greater than 3, then show that

$$\frac{1}{a_1} + \frac{1}{a_2} + \cdots + \frac{1}{a_n} < 3.$$

51. Assume that $\{a_j\}$ is a non-constant arithmetic sequence. This means that

$$
\begin{aligned}
a_1 &= a \\
a_2 &= a + r \\
a_3 &= a + 2r \\
a_4 &= a + 3r \\
&\cdots
\end{aligned}
$$

for some fixed numbers a, r with $r \neq 0$. Then show that the a_j's cannot all be primes.

52. Explain why, if n is a positive integer, then $n \cdot (n+1) \cdot (n+2) \cdot (n+3)$ cannot be a perfect square.

53. Find the sum of all distinct four digit numbers that contain only the digits $1, 2, 3, 4, 5$, each at most once.

54. Suppose that $a > 0$. Consider the numbers $a, 2a, 3a, \ldots, (n-1)a$ for some fixed positive integer n. Then one of these listed numbers must differ from some integer by at most $1/n$.

55. Say that x, y are integers. Explain why the expression $2x + 3y$ is divisible by 17 exactly when the expression and $9x + 5y$ is divisible by 17.

56. Find all positive integers n such that $2^n + 1$ is divisible by 3.

57. Take n to be a positive integer and assume that n has k distinct prime factors. (Each of these factors could be raised to some power; we say that the number $12 = 2^2 \cdot 3$ has *two* distinct prime factors.) Then show that

$$\log n \geq k \log 2.$$

58. Suppose that

$$a_1 \cdot a_2 + a_2 \cdot a_3 + \cdots + a_n \cdot a_1 = 0,$$

(with each $a_j = \pm 1$). Then show that 4 divides n.

59. If n is a positive integer then show that $(n-1)^2$ will always divide the quantity $n^{n-1} - 1$ evenly.

60. Find the correct analog of Problem 6.3.5 with four terms multiplied together on the left side.

61. Demonstrate that if n is a positive integer exceeding 2 then 360 divides the number $n^2(n^2 - 1)(n^2 - 4)$.

62. If $m > n$ are integers then explain why

$$\left(1 + \frac{1}{m}\right)^m > \left(1 + \frac{1}{n}\right)^n.$$

63. The numbers a and b are positive integers. If the greatest common divisor of a, b is 12 and if their least common multiple is 432 then determine exactly what a and b are.

64. Check that the number

$$\underbrace{11111 \cdots 11}_{91 \text{ times}}$$

is not prime.

65. Check that if m, n, k are positive integers and if $m+n+k$ is divisible by 3 then so is $m^3 + n^3 + k^3$.

66. Check that each odd prime number p is the difference of the squares of two integers; it is possible to arrange this decomposition in just one way for each p.

67. Calculate all triples of positive integers m, n, p such that $m^2 + n^2 = p^2$ (these are called *Pythagorean triples* for obvious reasons). [*Hint:* Write $a = p+n, b = p-n$. The equation reduces to $m^2 = a \cdot b$ with a and b either both odd or both even.]

68. Everyone knows the quadratic formula for solving an equation like $x^2 - 3x - 5 = 0$. Here is an alternate technique, known as the method of *continued fractions*: We write

$$
\begin{aligned}
x &= \frac{3x+5}{x} \\
&= 3 + \frac{5}{x} \\
&= 3 + \frac{5}{3 + \frac{5}{x}} \\
&= 3 + \frac{5}{3 + \frac{5}{3 + \frac{5}{x}}} \\
&= \text{etc.}
\end{aligned}
$$

Carry this procedure out for five iterations, and replace the terminal x by 3. Then calculate the value of x and compare it with the corresponding value of x that comes from the quadratic formula. How many iterations of the continued fraction procedure would be required to attain an accuracy of one decimal place? Of two decimal places?

69. Factor the polynomial $x^8 + x^4 + 1$ into polynomial factors of degree not exceeding 2, with real coefficients.

70. Explain why $\cos^4 \theta$ can be written in the form

$$
\cos^4 \theta = \alpha \cos \theta + \beta \cos 2\theta + \gamma \cos 3\theta + \delta \cos 4\theta + \tau
$$

for suitable constants $\alpha, \beta, \gamma, \delta, \tau$.

71. [Halmos [HAL]] What is the sum of the digits of the number 4444^{4444}?

72. For all positive integers n show that

$$\frac{1 \cdot 3 \cdot 5 \cdots (2n-1)}{2 \cdot 4 \cdot (2n)} < 1/\sqrt{n}.$$

73. If the two legs of a right triangle are squares of integers then show that the hypotenuse cannot be an integer.

74. Find all integer pairs m, n such that $m + n = m \cdot n$.

75. Take n to be a positive integer. Explain why 11 will always divide $n^{11} - n$. Explain why 13 will always divide $n^{13} - n$.

76. Take $p_1, p_2, \ldots$ to be the positive prime integers listed in order. In other words $p_1 = 2, p_2 = 3, p_3 = 5, \ldots$. Explain why the sum

$$\frac{1}{p_1} + \frac{1}{p_2} + \frac{1}{p_3} + \cdots$$

becomes large without bound.

77. Factor $x^{10} + x^5 + 1$ in two ways:

1. As a product of two polynomials with integer coefficients;

2. As a product of five polynomials with real (possibly non-integer) coefficients.

[*Hint:* Think about what degrees the polynomials must be. Can any of them be of first degree? Does the polynomial have any real roots? Why or why not?]

78. Find a polynomial of degree 2, having real coefficients, that divides two of the polynomials

$$x^{3986} + x^{1993} + 1 \qquad x^{3988} + x^{1994} + 1 \qquad x^{3990} + x^{1995} + 1$$

but does not divide the third.

Chapter 7

A Miscellany

7.1 Crossing the River and Similar Exercises

There is a class of problems that dates from the middle ages, and has been attributed to such writers as Alcuin and Tartaglia. It involves a group of people, or animals, that need to cross a river in a small boat subject to a variety of constraints. Here is a simple example:

PROBLEM 7.1.1 *There are two married couples that need to cross a river. A small boat is available that will hold just two people at a time. The males involved are quite jealous. No woman can be left with a man unless her husband is also present. There are no other constraints. How can these four people cross the river? What is the fewest number of trips possible?*

Solution: We denote the people by H_1, H_2 for the husbands and W_1, W_2 for the corresponding wives.

Suppose we begin with H_1 and W_1 crossing the river on the first trip. One person must return. It cannot be W_1, since she would then find herself without a chaperone in the company of H_2. So H_1 returns. We cannot send H_2 and W_2 across the river at this point, for then H_2 would be in the company of W_1 without benefit of H_1's presence. Thus we must send H_1 and H_2 across the river on the second trip. Of course H_1 must then be left on the far shore with W_1; otherwise the rules would be violated. Now H_2 returns to the starting shore, picks up his wife W_2, and the two row across the river.

We have achieved the stated goal with five passages. Clearly an odd number of passages is required. Thus if the goal could be achieved with fewer passages, then the number would have to be three. But each trip, except the last one, only deposits one new person across the river. Thus three passages would only transfer $1 + 2$ people on the far shore, and that would not do the job.   □

CHALLENGE PROBLEM 7.1.2 *In the last problem, can you get all four people across the river in five passages if you begin with some pair of people other than H_1, W_1? [Of course you can do it with H_2, W_2, but can you find a solution that is genuinely different?] If you discard the constraint of doing it in just five passages, then can you begin with some other couple?*

CHALLENGE PROBLEM 7.1.3 *Now suppose that there are three couples, subject to the same rules and constraints. Can you get them across the river in eleven passages?*

CHALLENGE PROBLEM 7.1.4 *How does Problem 7.1.1 change if we suppose that there is an island in the middle of the river?*

CHALLENGE PROBLEM 7.1.5 *It is impossible to do the first problem if there are four couples. However, if there is an island in the river then it becomes possible. Explain.*

PROBLEM 7.1.6 *A general needs to take his troops across the river. He spies two boys with a small boat. He commandeers both the boat and the boys. Unfortunately, the boat will only hold two boys or one soldier. Yet he determines a method for getting his troops across. What could it be?*

Solution: This is more of a problem in logic than in combinatorics. Notice that the number of soldiers is not given, suggesting that the problem is independent of the number of soldiers and therefore (perhaps) elementary.

For the first trip, there is no sense to send one soldier. For all he could do would be to go across and then either (i) stay and leave everyone else stranded or (ii) just row back. So, for the first trip, the two boys go. One boy returns. *Then* one soldier goes across. Then the boy on the far side of the river can take the boat back.

Now matters are just as at the start, except that one soldier has been transferred across the river. So now the two boys cross again. One boy stays on the far shore (with the lone soldier) and the other returns with the boat. Now a second soldier can go across. The boy returns with the boat. Now both boys are on the starting shore with the remaining soldiers.

Clearly this process can be repeated indefinitely to get all the soldiers, and the commander, across. □

PROBLEM 7.1.7 (Halmos) *We leave jealous couples behind for a while and talk about coupling railroad cars. A railroad engine can first couple with, and then either pull or push, either one or two cars. Of course the two cars can be coupled to each other as well.*

At a certain junction, the railroad track is configured as in Figure 153. Note that the portion of track between γ and δ in the figure is a dead end and can hold either just one car or just the engine. However the portion of track to the left of α and the portion of track to the right of β have no restrictions and can hold any number of cars.

How can the engine reverse the positions of the black car and the white car (that is, put the black car on the right track between β and γ and the white car on the left track between α and γ) and return to its original position, facing right? This should be done in at most 10 moves. Here a move *consists either of having the engine go to some point and couple with a car, or having the engine pull a car to some point and uncouple.*

Solution: Call the white car W, the black car B, and the engine E. The moves are these. Draw a sketch to accompany each move so that you can see how the cars are moving.

1. E drives past β, backs into $\beta\delta$, and couples with the white car.

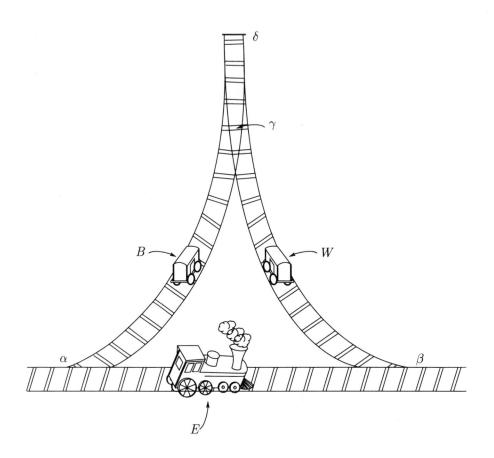

Figure 153

2. E backs the white car into $\gamma\delta$, uncouples, and moves out along $\beta\delta$.

3. E moves past β, backs along $\alpha\beta$, goes forward into $\alpha\gamma$, and couples its front end on the black car.

4. E pushes B forward, couples it on W, and backs out past α.

5. E pushes both cars forward until W is midway between α and β, then uncouples β.

6. E backs past α, then pushes B into $\alpha\gamma$ and up into $\gamma\delta$, where it uncouples B.

7. E backs down $\alpha\gamma$ past α, then moves forward on $\alpha\beta$ and couples with W.

8. E backs on $\alpha\beta$ past α, then goes forward on $\alpha\gamma$, pushing W to the center of $\alpha\gamma$, where it uncouples W.

9. E backs down $\alpha\gamma$, past α, moves forward on $\alpha\beta$ past β, backs into $\beta\gamma$ all the way to B, and couples with B.

10. E pulls B forward, decouples in the middle of $\beta\gamma$, continues forward past β, and then backs down $\alpha\beta$ to the midpoint of $\alpha\beta$.

That completes the journey of the engine, leaving it facing right in its original position. $\square$

CHALLENGE PROBLEM 7.1.8 *In the last problem if we allow the engine to return to its original position facing left (that is, with its orientation reversed), then how can we accomplish the stated goal in 6 moves?*

7.2 Things That Are Impossible

We begin with a sample of the numerous geometric fallacies that are known.

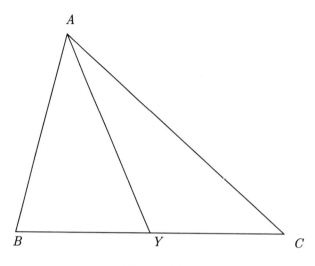

Figure 154

PROBLEM 7.2.1 *We shall now present a "proof" that all triangles are isosceles. We stress that this assertion is false. There is, for instance, a triangle with sides 5, 6, and 7. Such a triangle is clearly not iscosceles. So the "proof" that we are presenting must have an error in it. And the error is a subtle one. The problem is to find the error.*

> **Proof that all triangles are isosceles:** Begin with any triangle $\triangle ABC$. Let AY bisect angle $\angle BAC$ (refer to Figure 154).
>
> There are now two possibilities:
>
> 1. If AY is perpendicular to BC then triangles $\triangle AYB$ and $\triangle AYC$ are congruent. Indeed angles $\angle BAY$ and $\angle CAY$ are equal and angles $\angle BYA$ and $\angle CYA$ are equal. So the two triangles are certainly similar. But they also have a common side. So they are congruent. It follows that $\triangle ABC$ is isosceles.
>
> 2. If AY is not perpendicular to BC then it will intersect the line perpendicular to BC and passing through the midpoint D of BC. Call the point of intersection X.

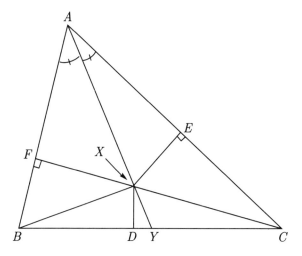

Figure 155

Draw XE perpendicular to AC and XF perpendicular to AB. Refer to Figure 155.

We suppose that X is actually in the interior of $\triangle ABC$, so that E is actually an interior point of AC and F is actually an interior point of AB. Then $\triangle AXF$ and $\triangle AXE$ are congruent: for AX is a common side, $\angle XAF = \angle XAE$, and $\angle XFA = \angle XEA$. Since the triangles are congruent, we may conclude that $AF = AE$. Also the triangles $\triangle BXF$ and $\triangle CXE$ are congruent. To see this, note that XD bisects BC at right angles. So $BX = CX$. Also $XF = XE$ by our preceding congruence. Also, angles $\angle BFX$ and $\angle CEX$ are both right and hence equal. Because of this triangle congruence, we may conclude that $FB = EC$. But then $AF + FB = AE + EC$ or $AB = AC$. Therefore $\triangle ABC$ is an isosceles triangle.

We also must consider the possibility, in Case (2), that X lies *outside* the triangle $\triangle ABC$. An example is shown in Figure 156. Notice that the figure includes the perpendicular XF dropped to the extension of side AB and also

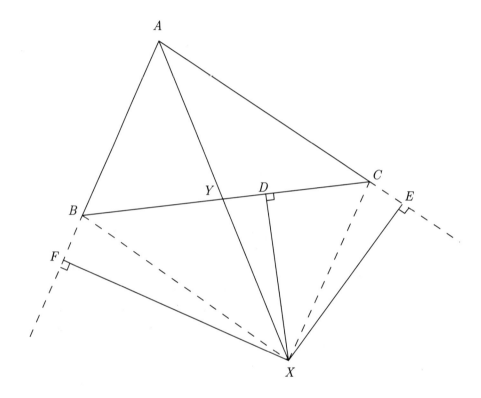

Figure 156

the perpendicular XE dropped to the extension of side AC. Just as before, triangles AXF and AXE are congruent. It follows that $AF = AE$. Also triangles BXF and CXE are congruent. Thus $FB = EC$. Thus $AF - FB = AE - EC$ or $AB = AC$. Once again, we conclude that the triangle $\triangle ABC$ is isosceles.

Solution: The figures already suggest that there must be something wrong with this reasoning. But what is it? The figures are presented only as a guide, to help us picture the concepts. The proof is in the words and ideas, and these seem to cohere.

There is nothing wrong with the instance that the angle bisector at A is perpendicular to the opposite side. That is precisely when the triangle under consideration is isosceles. The error must be in Case (2).

First we consider the possibility that X lies inside the triangle. The remarkable fact is that this case cannot occur! For let θ denote $\angle BAY = \angle CAY$. According to the Law of Cosines,

$$(BY)^2 = (AB)^2 + (AY)^2 - 2 \cdot AB \cdot AY \cdot \cos\theta$$

and

$$(CY)^2 = (AC)^2 + (AY)^2 - 2 \cdot AC \cdot AY \cdot \cos\theta.$$

If $AB > AC$ (for instance) then we can easily see that $BY > CY$ because

$$(AB)^2 + (AY)^2 - 2 \cdot AB \cdot AY \cdot \cos\theta$$
$$= (AY)^2 + AB \cdot (AB - 2 \cdot AY \cdot \cos\theta)$$
$$> (AY)^2 + AC \cdot (AC - 2 \cdot AY \cdot \cos\theta).$$

Thus the true picture is as in Figure 157.

We leave it to you to find the error when X lies outside the triangle.
$\square$

PROBLEM 7.2.2 (Turton) *Find the error in the following "proof" that $\pi/4 = \pi/3$.*

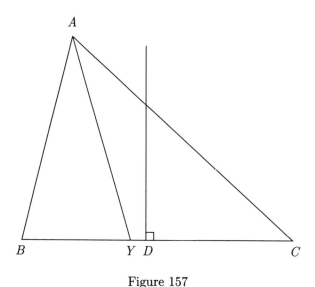

Figure 157

Before we present this fallacious proof, we must emphasize that proofs of false statements are deadly. If A is a false statement then the syllogism $A \Rightarrow B$ is true, no matter what B is (see [KRA1]). Therefore if we can find a "proof" of A then we can prove absolutely anything. A "proof" that $\pi/4 = \pi/3$ is not merely mildly amusing. It cuts at the very fiber of analytical thought.

Solution: Consider an isosceles right triangle $\triangle ABC$ with hypotenuse BC. The triangle XBC is an equilateral triangle with common side length BC (Figure 158). Choose a point H on CX so that $CH = CA$. We write K for the midpoint of BA. Draw the line through H and K so that it intersects the extension of side BC in a point L. Draw segment AL.

We write M for the midpoint of AL. We write N for the midpoint of HL. Suppose that the perpendicular to AL at M and the perpendicular to HL at N intersect at a point O. Note that O is on the side of AL opposite to X. We complete the figure by drawing OC, OA, OH, and OL.

Now triangles $\triangle OML$ and $\triangle OMA$ are congruent in an obvious way: they share a side, $AM = LM$, and they have oppositely situated right angles. Thus $OA = OL$. Similarly, triangles $\triangle ONL$ and $\triangle ONH$

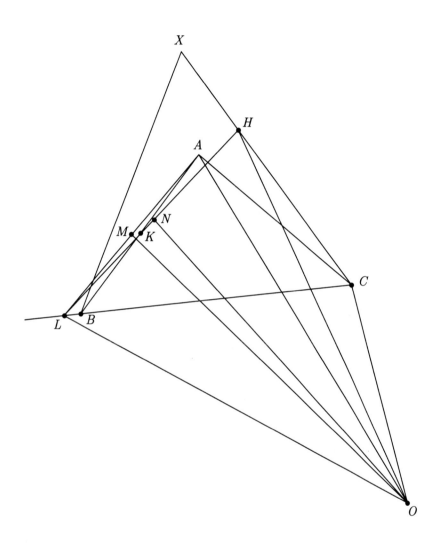

Figure 158

are congruent. So $OA = OH$.

Now compare triangles $\triangle OCA$ and $\triangle OCH$. We know that $OA = OH$, $CA = CH$ (as we constructed), and they share the side OC. So these two triangles are congruent. But this forces $\angle BCA = \angle BCH$. That is, $\pi/4 = \pi/3$.

Since the conclusion of this argument is patently false (it would imply, for instance, that $1 = 0$), there must be an error. Where is it? If there is no error in the formal logic (and apparently there is not), then the mistake must be in the way we are picturing the situation. Curiously, the source [BALL] from which the author derived this argument provides no picture. The most slippery part of the argument is the claim that O is on the side of AL opposite to X. We challenge the reader to find the error in this proof.

PROBLEM 7.2.3 *Explain why the line drawing in Figure 159 cannot be traced with a single, continuous, non-overlapping stroke of the pen.*

Solution: Did we learn anything when studying the Königsberg bridge problem and other impossible situations of that nature?

The line drawing in Figure 159 contains two types of nodes or vertices: those which have an even number of edges emanating and those which have an odd number of edges emanating. If the "trace" is to enter a node and then leave it (with no overlaps allowed) then there must be an even number of edges emanating from that node. If instead there are an odd number of edges emanating then either

(i) the trace will not begin at that node but, at some time, the trace will arrive at that node and never leave (that is, the trace will end at that node)

or

(ii) the trace will begin at that node but not end there.

Notice that the drawing in Figure 159 has *four* nodes from which an odd number of edges emanate. The trace must either begin or end at each one of these. That is clearly impossible.   □

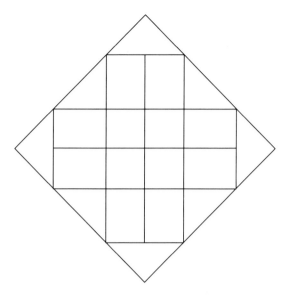

Figure 159

Figure 160

CHALLENGE PROBLEM 7.2.4 *Explain how to delete a single linear segment (this single segment could contain several edges, in the sense of graph theory) and convert Figure 159 to a drawing that can be traced with a single, continuous, non-overlapping stroke of the pen.*

A B C D E F G H I J K L M N
O P Q R S T U V W X Y Z

Figure 161

EXERCISES for Chapter 7

1. Can we use each of the digits 0,1,2,3,4,5,6,7,8,9 just once to create a collection of positive integers that sum to 100?

2. In a distant land, bigamy is common. There are six people who want to cross a river in this land. This group consists of two men, each with two wives. No man can tolerate any of his wives being in the company of another man unless he is present to chaperone. There is a boat that holds two people to be used for crossing the river. Can they do it? In how many crossings?

3. Same as Exercises 2 except the boat will hold three people.

4. Same as Exercise 2 except that there are three men, each with three wives; and the boat will hold three people.

5. Same as Exercises 2 except that there are three men, each with three wives; and there are two boats, each of which will hold two people.

6. Explain why it is impossible to trace the line drawing in Figure 160 with a single, continuous, non-overlapping stroke of the pen.

7. Which characters from the block capital, sans serif roman alphabet can be traced with a single, continuous, non-overlapping stroke of the pen (Figure 161)? Why?

8. Explain why, if two positive real numbers sum to 100, then their product cannot be 3000.

9. It is not possible to completely fill up a closed square of side one with finitely many closed, round discs (circles, together with their interiors), even if we allow their boundaries to touch. Explain why.

10. It is not possible to fill up a closed disc of radius one with finitely many closed squares, even if we allow their boundaries to touch. Explain why.

11. Suppose that T is an equilateral triangle made of cardboard. Explain why it is not possible to take a pair of scissors and cut T into two pieces—with a single cut—that can be recombined to form a square.

12. Two walkers begin at opposite ends of a straight road. At a given moment, they begin walking towards each other. Each travels at a constant speed, but one is faster. They pass each other at a point 720 meters from the right hand end of the road. When each reaches the end of her walk (the end of the road), she rests for ten minutes. Then they start back to their initial positions, walking at the same speed that they walked before. On this second part of the walk, they pass when they are 400 meters from the *left* end of the road. How long is the road?

13. The following sequence has become known as the John H. Conway sequence, after the celebrated Princeton mathematician. Can you determine the next term of the sequence?

$$1, 1, 1, 3, 1, 4, 1, 1, 3, 6, 1, 2, 3, 1, 4, 8, 1, 3, 3, 2, 4, 1, 6,\ ?$$

14. An explorer is only able to carry provisions that will last him for three days. He begins his journey on the frontier of a desert, and wants to journey as far as possible into the desert. Because of a contract with traders, he is allowed to stock up on provisions at most ten times. He is allowed to journey a certain distance into the desert, deposit provisions in an oasis, and return for more provisions. He can walk eight miles per day. How far into the desert will he be able to go?

15. Calculate the area of Nevada. [*Hint:* In order to do this, you will need a good map and perhaps a protractor to measure the angles.]

16. Suppose that you have twelve sticks of wood, each one foot long. In how many different ways can you assemble them to form the skeleton of a cube?

17. Two child's building blocks sit on a table. One is 4 inches on a side and the other is 2 inches on a side. The volume of the larger is $4^3 = 64$ cubic inches and the volume of the smaller is $2^3 = 8$ cubic inches.

We see that the average side length of the cubes is $(2 + 4)/2 = 3$ and the average volume is $(8 + 64)/2 = 36$. But the cube of the average side length is not equal to average volume. What is going on here?

18. Here is a variant of the famous *Prisoner's Dilemma*, which is the basis for much analysis in psychology, sociology, and economics.

You are in a room with 49 other people. You are all blindfolded and do not communicate with each other. The leader stands at the front of the room. The leader declares that you have five minutes to consider your options. If, at the end of five minutes, nobody raises his/her hand then you each must pay $10 and you are free to go. However if anyone raises his/her right hand then those with raised hands will pay $20 and everyone else must pay $100.

Clearly the best option for everyone is to not raise their hands. But if someone else *does* raise his/her hand then you are better off for having raised yours (since you will then only have to pay $20 instead of $100).

What should you do? Is there a clear answer? Is there a best strategy?

19. You are on a game show. The host offers you $600 right now or you can spin a wheel which gives you an 80% chance of winning $800 and a 20% chance of winning nothing. What is your best choice? How could the figure $800 be modified to induce you to change your choice? What if instead the odds on the wheel are changed to 75%?

20. Suppose that we want to count the number of bees in a hive. We pull out 100 of them and mark them with a dye label. Then we return these bees to the hive and allow them to mix with the other bees. After a period of time we take a random sample of 100 bees and note that six of them have the die marker. What can we conclude about the number of bees in the hive?

Can you anticipate any faults that this method of counting the bees might have?

21. Here is a problem that has been popularized by the Hungarian mathematician Paul Erdös (see [MPI]). Say that N is a positive integer. What is the fewest number of people who need to be present in a room so that we can be sure that at least N people know each other or N do not? For instance, if there are just two people in the room then they will either know each other or they will not. So that solves the problem for $N = 2$. Explain why, when $N = 3$, the answer is 6.

This problem becomes very complex very quickly. For instance, the answer is not known when $N = 6$.

22. Complete the following outline to demonstrate that there is no rational number whose square is 2:

a) Suppose that there is a rational fraction $\mu = m/n$ such that $\mu^2 = 2$. We may assume that m, n are positive and have no common factors (that is, the fraction is in lowest terms).

b) Our hypothesis means that

$$\left(\frac{a}{b}\right)^2 = \mu^2 = 2.$$

Conclude that

$$a^2 = 2b^2. \tag{$*$}$$

c) Since 2 divides the right side of the last equation, it also divides the left side. Therefore 2 divides a. Thus $a = 2\alpha$ for some positive integer α.

d) Substituting this last equation for a into $(*)$ gives

$$2\alpha^2 = b^2.$$

e) Conclude that, since 2 divides the left side of this last equation, then it divides the right side. Thus 2 divides b.

f) We have shown that both 2 divides a and 2 divides b. This means that a and b have a common factor. But our hypothesis was that they do not. This contradiction means that the rational number $\mu = a/b$ does not exist.

23. Prove that there is no rational number whose square is 8. [*Hint:* Either use the result of Exercise 22 or imitate the method of solution of Exercise 22.]

24. Assume that k is a positive integer. Prove that if k has a rational square root then in fact it has an integer (whole number) square root.

25. Explain why, between any two rational numbers, there lies an irrational number.

26. Explain why, between any two irrational numbers, there lies a rational number.

27. This exercises involves techniques from several different parts of this book. It is tricky. Use it as a basis for discussion with a friend; determine ways to experiment.

Four points, labeled A, B, C, D, are selected at random from the unit square. They are connected, in order, with line segments: A to

B, B to C, C to D, D to A. What is the probability that this process forms a convex body? [This problem is due to Jade Vinson.]

28. An intrepid explorer walks one mile south, one mile due east, and one mile north. She ends up at the same place that she began. How is this possible? Well, it is possible if the explorer began at the north pole. Find infinitely many other ways in which it is also possible.

29. [This problem and the next are adapted from notes by Mike Fellows and Neal Koblitz.] The following text represents an *encryption* of an English message (in plain English, the message is in secret code):

ESPNTASPCSLDMPPYMCZVPY

The encryption was performed by shifting each letter in the original message a fixed number of letters to the right or to the left. For example, if we perform a +5 shift on the message "**HELLO THERE**," then the resulting encrypted message is

MJQQT YMJWJ

Observe that 'M' is five letters *after* (to the right of) 'H' (that is, the first letter of the encryption is five letters in the alphabet after the first letter of the original message); also 'J' is five letters *after* (to the right of) 'E' (that is, the second letter of the encryption is five letters in the alphabet after the second letter of the original message); and so forth.

Alternatively, if we perform a −3 shift on the message "**BOO HOO**," then the resulting encrypted message is

YLL ELL

Observe that we treat the alphabet as though it runs in a loop: after we reach the end "**X, Y, Z**," then we return immediately to '**A**'. Thus when we shift three to the left from **B**, we count '**A, Z, Y**'.

The encoded message given at the beginning of this problem was produced by a shift method, either positive or negative (such a method is called a *Cæsar cipher*). Determine the original English message. (*Hint:* We have omitted the blank spaces from the message. Also, the most commonly used letter in English is '**E**'. What is the second most commonly used letter? What is the third? Use this idea to guess what letter some of the elements of the encrypted message must correspond to.)

30. Refer to Exercise 29 for some of the basic ideas about encrypted messages.

A *Vigenère cipher* is an encryption method that consists of shifts, but the shifts are modeled on a key word. Here is how the method works. Suppose that our key word is "**FLAT**". The first step is to convert the key word to numbers: **F** is the sixth letter of the alphabet, **L** is the twelfth letter of the alphabet, **A** the first, and **T** the twentieth letter. Thus we convert the key word to the sequence 6-12-1-20.

Now suppose that we are encrypting the message "**SEE THE HOG.**" We shift the first letter to the right by 6 (the first digit from the key word). Therefore **S** is replaced in the encryption by **Y**. We shift the second letter by 12 (the second digit from the key word). Thus **E** is replaced by **Q**. Now notice that the next **E** is *not* replaced by **Q**. We must follow the rules dictated by the key word. We will shift the third letter of our message by 1 (the third digit from the key word). Thus **E** is replaced by **F**. Continuing, we replace **T** by **N**.

Now we have reached the end of the key word (having cycled through four letters of the message) so we now start again: We shift **H** to the right by 6. Thus **H** is replaced by **N**. Then we shift **E** to the right by 12. So **E** is replaced by **Q**. We next shift **H** to the right by 1. Hence **H** is replaced by **I**. We shift **O** to the right by 20. So **O** is replaced by **I**. Finally, we shift **G** to the right by 6. Thus **G** is replaced by **M**.

In summary, the encryption of "**SEE THE HOG**," as determined by Vigenère cypher from the key word **FLAT**, is

YQF NNQ IIM

Now here is an encrypted message for you to decode. Your hint is that the key word has just two letters; moreover, as usual, we have omitted the blank spaces from the code.

CPTOTXTCVPCNNCTWXPU

Chapter 8

Real Life

8.0 Introductory Remarks

The fact is that genuine problems that come up in everyday life can be quite complex. Often they involve specialized ideas and terminology, and many times they do not lend themselves to precise measurement or formulation. Often the solver or analyst must use guesswork and approximation just to formulate a question that can be analyzed. Sometimes a huge amount of data must be processed before one can decide what question to ask. Thus we see that problems of this nature would not lend themselves well to a brief, elementary textbook such as the present one.

What we can do instead in this chapter is to give you just a taste of some problems that lend themselves to analytical thinking but are not already formulated in the language of analytical or mathematical thought. If some of the problems seem overly simple, or fanciful, then take that observation under advisement. The problems are offered to you for practice and experience.

8.1 Everyday Objects

Here we will look at a variety of questions that involve common household items. The main strategy is to try to look at familiar items in a new way. Do not be constrained by common wisdom, or by what is

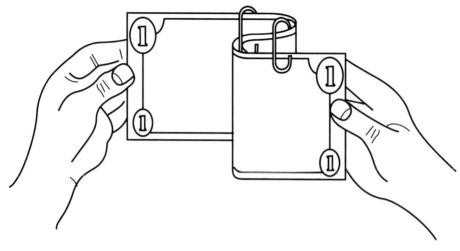

Figure 162

obvious. Resist the temptation to look at a solution and say to yourself "Oh, that's just a trick." It really is not. It is just an original way of looking at things.

PROBLEM 8.1.1 *Examine the configuration of two paper clips and a dollar bill shown in Figure 162. If the two ends of the dollar bill are pulled apart sharply, then the paper clips will spring free of the dollar bill and will be linked. Explain why they become linked.*

   Solution: Pull the ends of the dollar bill apart slowly. Watch what is happening with the two paper clips. You can imitate the operation *without* the aid of the dollar bill (Figure 163). You are pulling each paper clip between two tines of the other paper clip, thus linking them. The final jerk of the paper tosses the front paper clip over the top of the dollar bill to join the other paper clip in back, thus freeing the linked clips.   □

PROBLEM 8.1.2 *Take a standard 3″ × 5″ index card. How can you cut a hole in it that you can walk through?*

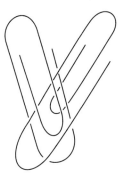

Figure 163

Solution: Figure 164 shows how to cut the card. After you have made this cut, you can gently pull the card apart to form a ring of circumference about four feet—large enough to step through if you are gentle. □

PROBLEM 8.1.3 *Two volumes of Gibbon's* The Rise and Fall of the Roman Empire *sit in order on the shelf. The cover material of these books is 1/8″ inch thick. The 500 pages in each volume are 2″ thick. A small worm bores a hole and crawls from the very first page of Volume 1 to the very last page of Volume 2. How far does the worm crawl?*

Solution: Look at Figure 165. Notice that Volume 1 is on the left and Volume 2 is on the right. Notice that the first page of Volume 1 is just to the left of center and the last page of Volume 2 is just to the right of center. In fact the worm only has to bore from the inside front cover of Volume 1 to the outside of Volume 1 (between the two books) and then bore into the back cover of Volume 2. In other words, the worm only bores through two book covers, and no pages. So the worm travels a total of 1/4″. □

CHALLENGE PROBLEM 8.1.4 *Suppose that you have another edition of Gibbon with 4 volumes. The covers are still 1/8″ thick, but the paper portion in each volume is just 1″ thick. Then how far does the worm have to crawl to get from the very first page of Volume 1 to the very last page of Volume 4?*

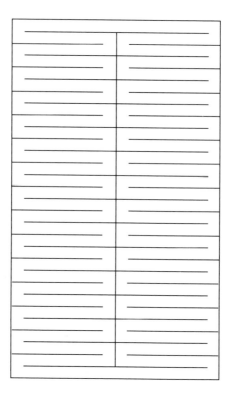

Figure 164

Figure 165

PROBLEM 8.1.5 *You have a piece of paper with a circle of radius between 2″ and 4″ drawn on it. You also have a plastic square of side 10″. You have no ruler and no compass. How can you find the center of the circle?*

Solution: This is in the vein of a ruler and compass construction, except that we have no compass. What we have is the ability to draw a straight line (using the edge of the plastic square) and the ability to draw a right angle.

Place a corner of the square so that it touches the circle from the inside. Thus you have a right angle inscribed inside the circle. We know from geometry that a right angle subtends a semicircle. Thus the two points where the square crosses the circle are at opposite ends of a diameter (we are purposely not supplying a figure here so that *you* will supply the figure). Using the edge of the square, draw that diameter.

Now use the method of the last paragraph to draw a second diameter. The point of intersection of the two diameters is the center of the circle. □

CHALLENGE PROBLEM 8.1.6 *Can you do the last problem if you discard the square and replace it with a large plastic equilateral triangle?*

PROBLEM 8.1.7 *A room has a floor that measures 8′ × 10′. The ceiling is 7′ high. A spider perches on one of the 8′ × 7′ walls, just 6″ from the ceiling and midway between the two adjoining walls. A fly is on the opposite wall, just 6″ from the floor and midway between the two adjoining walls. See Figure 166.*

The spider decides to quietly sneak up on the fly, walking along walls, floor, and ceiling. What is his shortest possible path?

Solution: Disassemble the room as shown in Figure 167. The shortest path from the spider to the fly is a linear one as shown. [*Note:* There are other ways to open up and flatten out the room, and they will give rise to other linear paths from the spider to the fly. Try those and convince yourself that the one in Figure 167 is the shortest. □

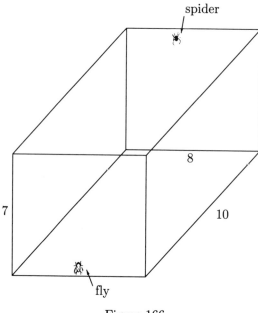

Figure 166

The last solution illustrates an important principle: *You do not have to analyze a problem as given. Bend it so that you can understand it.*

CHALLENGE PROBLEM 8.1.8 *Redo the last problem if the spider and the fly are at opposite corners of the room (i.e. one is at the corner of the ceiling and the other is at the opposite corner of the floor).*

PROBLEM 8.1.9 *Say that a bottle has a round or square, flat, bottom and it has straight sides. The bottle is partly full (about half) of liquid. See Figure 168. It is tapered at the top (as bottles usually are) and has a screw-on cap. How can you accurately determine the volume of the bottle if you are equipped with only a ruler?*

Solution: The enemy is the tapered part of the bottle, which would be difficult to measure even if we had very sophisticated tools. The unusual resource that we have available—which it is unclear how to use—is the liquid in the bottle. How can we use the latter to address the former?

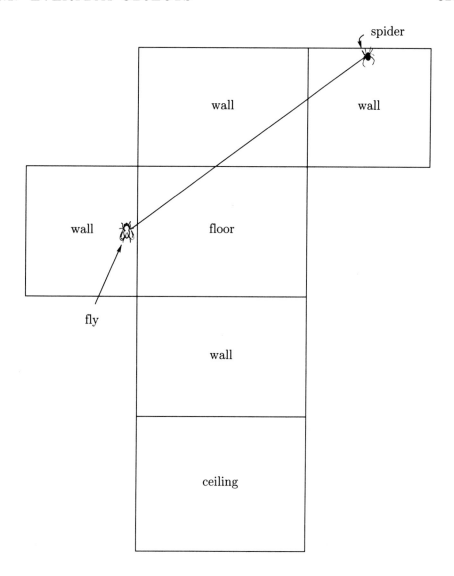

Figure 167

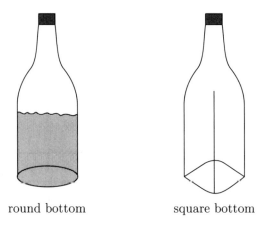

round bottom   square bottom

Figure 168

First, use the ruler to measure the base. Calculate the area. Call that A. Now measure the height h of the water. Then the volume of the water in the bottle is $V = A \cdot h$.

Now turn the bottle upside down (be sure that the cap is on!). Look at Figure 169. We see that the water fills up the (difficult to measure) neck, and that the part not filled by water is cylindrical. Now measure the height h' of the air column inside the bottle and above the water. The volume of that air column is $V' = A \cdot h'$.

The total volume inside the bottle is then just $\mathcal{V} = V + V'$.   □

PROBLEM 8.1.10 *A new car is equipped with three fuel saving devices. Device A, by itself, saves 25% on fuel; device B, by itself, saves 45% on fuel; and device C, by itself, saves 30% on fuel.*

Now suppose that the three devices are used together, and that they act independently. Will the combination save $25 + 45 + 30 = 100$ *percent on fuel? Probably not. What is the correct answer?*

Solution: Before we solve this problem, you might find it helpful to refer to Exercise 26 of Chapter 6.

Of course 100% cannot be the correct answer, just because of the basic physical principle that energy cannot be created from nothing.

Figure 169

A correct analysis is as follows. Device A results in using only .75 of the fuel that the machine would use without any devices. Device B applied on top of device A results in .55 of that fuel being used to achieve the same mileage. And device C on top of those two results in .70 of that fuel being used to achieve the same mileage.

All told, equipped with devices A, B, and C, we need only use .75 × .55 × .70 as much fuel to achieve the same mileage as the car without any fuel saving devices. That is, we need only use .28875 as much fuel. Thus, in total, we are saving .71125, or 71.125% on fuel consumption. □

PROBLEM 8.1.11 *A martini is made by mixing k parts gin with 1 part vermouth. Gin is usually 40% alcohol while vermouth is 20% alcohol. A martini is said to be "dry" if it contains relatively little vermouth. For instance, if $k = 15$ then the martini is said to be dry. If instead $k = 5$ then the martini is said to be "sweet."*

Some people refuse to drink dry martinis, as they claim it makes them drunk very quickly. Others prefer dry martinis because they taste better. Shed some light on this discussion by calculating the amount of alcohol in a dry martini vs. a sweet martini as described in the last paragraph.

Solution: We first consider the sweet martini. It is made up of 6 parts—five of them gin and one of them vermouth. Each part consisting of gin is 40% alcohol—this gives a total of $.4 \cdot 5 = 2$ parts alcohol. The one part that is vermouth is 20% alcohol—this gives a total of $.2 \cdot 1 = .2$ parts alcohol. Altogether we have 2.2 out of 6 parts alcohol. Thus the percentage of alcohol in a "sweet martini" is 2.2/6 or 36.67% alcohol.

The dry martini has 16 parts—fifteen of them gin and one of them vermouth. Each part consisting of gin is 40% alcohol—this gives a total of $.4 \cdot 15 = 6$ parts alcohol. The one part that is vermouth is 20% alcohol—this gives a total of $.2 \cdot 1 = .2$ parts alcohol. Altogether we have 6.2 out of 16 parts alcohol. Thus the percentage of alcohol in a "dry martini" is 6.2/16 or 38.75% alcohol.

We see that the difference in alcoholic content between the sweet and the dry martini is about 2.09%—not very much. Aficionados, however, will claim that there is a great difference in taste.   □

PROBLEM 8.1.12 *The continuity method is one of the most powerful in mathematics. We encountered it earlier in Section 2.3. It shows that certain types of problem have a solution, without necessarily constructing that solution.*

We shall concentrate here on what are known as "ham sandwich problems." While ostensibly a bit frivolous, these are in fact a prototype for a number of important problems in topology and geometry.

The first question is this: suppose that we are given a two dimensional quantity of ham in the plane—in any configuration you like. The ham could be shaped like a star, or a square, or just a blob with no particular shape at all—see Figure 170. Is there a vertical slice (parallel to the y-axis in the figure) that cuts the area of the ham exactly in two?

Solution: The basic idea is to introduce a continuous function and then to take advantage of the properties of continuous functions. We assume that our ham has total area 1, and lies in a bounded part of the plane (that is to say, like most ham that we encounter in real life, the ham in this problem does not wander in dribs and drabs out to infinity).

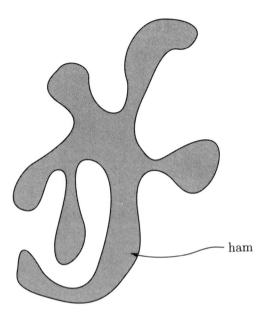

Figure 170

For each value x in the horizontal axis, let $f(x)$ be the area of the ham to the *left* of the vertical line erected at x (Figure 171). Notice that if x is sufficiently negative (say $x = -\alpha$), then the vertical line is all the way to the left of the ham, so that $f(x) = 0$ (that is, there is no ham to the left of the vertical line at x). Refer to Figure 172. On the other hand, if x is sufficiently positive (say $x = \beta$), then *all of the ham* is to the left of the vertical line at x. Thus $f(x) = 1$. See Figure 173.

Now the function f is continuous—this means that if we move the value x just a little bit then the value $f(x)$ changes just a little bit. You should think about why this is so (although, to make the matter completely rigorous, the advanced subject of "measure theory" would be required).

Recall that a continuous function (with domain an interval) is one whose graph can be drawn without lifting the pencil from the paper. In other words, the graph has no breaks or jumps in it. Now our graph passes through the point $(-\alpha, 0)$ and also through the point $(\beta, 1)$. Because the graph has no breaks, it must cross the line $y = 1/2$ at least once—see Figure 174. We denote the point of intersection in the figure

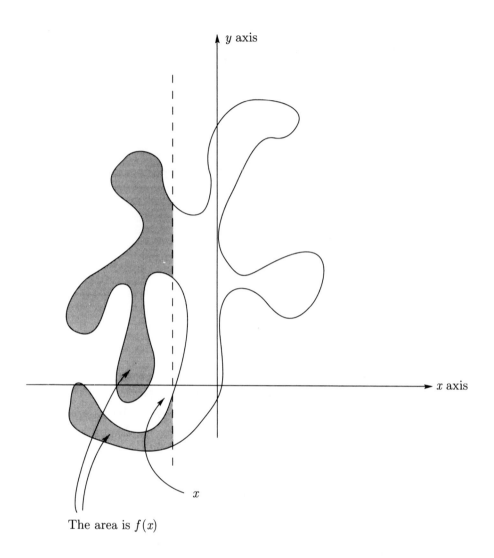

The area is $f(x)$

Figure 171

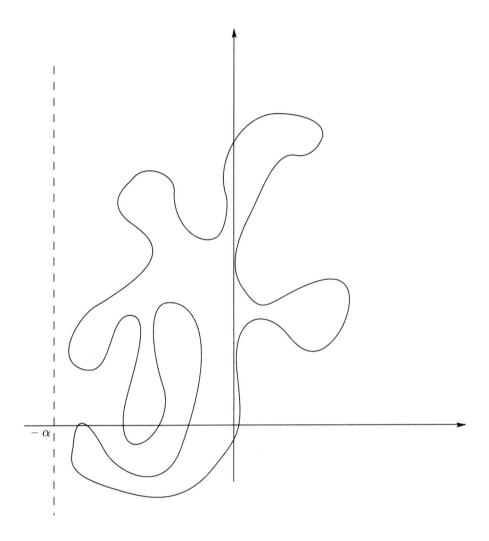

Figure 172

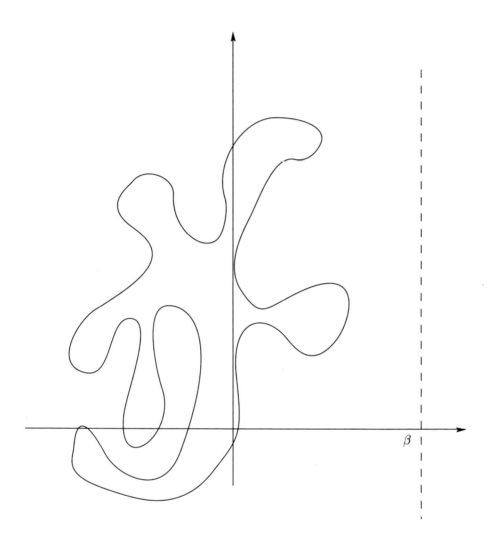

Figure 173

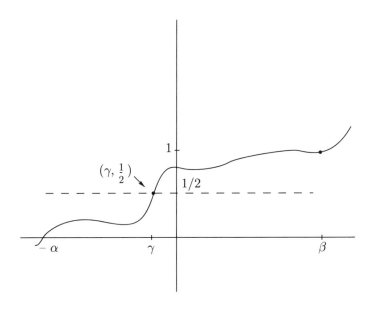

Figure 174

by $(\gamma, 1/2)$.

When $x = \gamma$ then $f(x) = 1/2$. This means that precisely half of the ham, measured by area, is to the left of the vertical line at $x = \gamma$. But that means that precisely half of the ham is also to the right of that same vertical line. This is shown in Figure 175. We have solved the problem, although we have *not* found a way to actually produce the vertical line that does the job. □

Is there anything special about vertical lines in our solution of the last problem? The answer is "no." If instead we were interested in lines that make an angle of $\pi/6$ with the horizontal (Figure 176), then we could simply rotate coordinates (Figure 177), solve the problem, just as before, in the rotated coordinates, and then rotate back again. In conclusion, given any direction angle θ_0, we can find a line having that direction and cutting the given quantity of ham in half.

PROBLEM 8.1.13 *Now we will elaborate on the last problem. Suppose that we are given a quantity of ham, in any configuration whatever,*

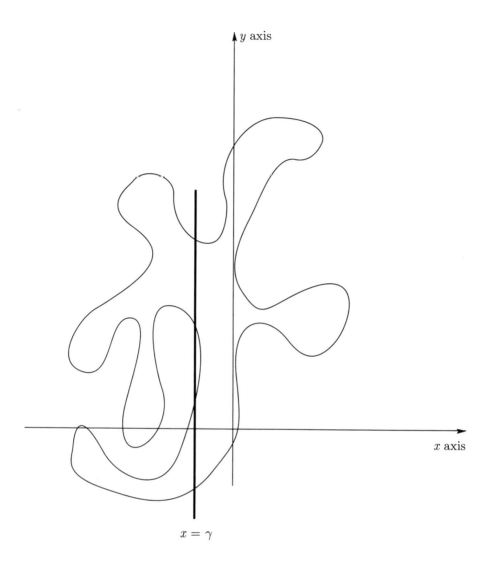

Figure 175

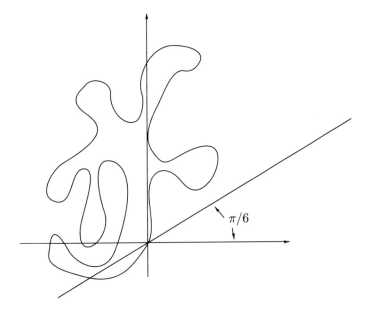

Figure 176

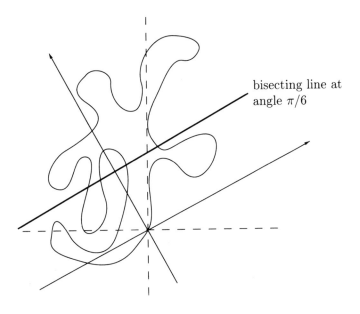

bisecting line at
angle $\pi/6$

Figure 177

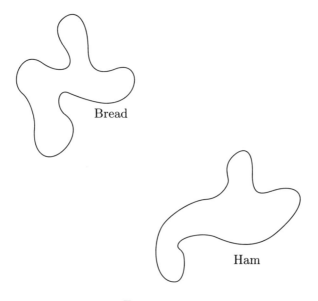

Figure 178

and also a quantity of bread. For simplicity, both of these quantities are in the Euclidean plane—see Figure 178.

Is it possible to find a single straight linear cut that bisects both the ham and the bread (measured as usual by area)?

Solution: We build on what we learned in the last problem. For specificity we work with the particular configuration of ham and bread that is shown in Figure 178. We suppose that the ham still has area 1 and the bread has some area b (there is nothing special about these numbers, as you will see in a moment). You can easily adapt the argument to any other configuration that you like.

Again we will introduce a certain continuous function. To each angle θ between 0 and π radians we assign the line ℓ_θ with direction angle θ that bisects the ham—refer to Figure 179. We already noted, in the remarks preceding this problem, that such a line ℓ_θ will exist. We let $g(\theta)$ denote the area of the quantity of bread that is above and to the left of the line ℓ_θ.

Notice (Figure 180) that $g(\pi/4) = b$; that is to say, all of the bread is above and to the left of the line with direction angle $\pi/4$ that bisects

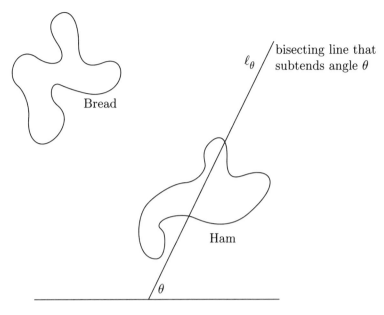

bisecting line that
subtends angle θ

ℓ_θ

Bread

Ham

θ

Figure 179

the ham. Also notice that $g(11\pi/12) = 0$. This says that there is no bread above and to the left of the line with direction angle $11\pi/12$ (Figure 181).

Reasoning as in the last example, the function g is continuous. It takes the value b at $\theta = \pi/4$ and the value 0 at $\theta = 11\pi/12$. Figure 182 shows the graph of a continuous function g that has these properties. Since the graph of a continuous function is an unbroken curve, the graph must cross the horizontal line at height $b/2$ at some point (Figure 182). Let the corresponding value for θ be η. Thus $g(\eta) = b/2$.

This means that the line ℓ_η—which we have constructed so that it bisects the ham—also bisects the bread. We have found the line that we seek. □

It turns out that if we add one more level of complexity to the problem—by throwing in a quantity of *cheese*, then it is not possible to find a single line in the plane that simultaneously bisects the ham, the bread, and the cheese. This is not a fact about weird shapes; you may assume that each of the bread, the ham, and the cheese is a perfect

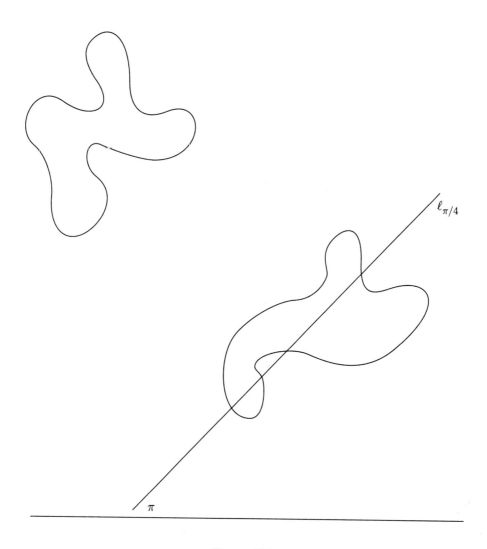

Figure 180

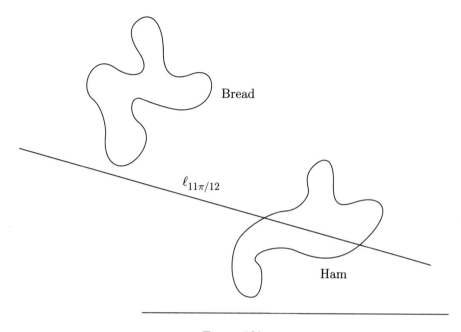

Figure 181

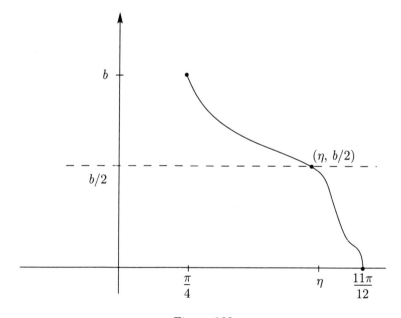

Figure 182

unit disc if you like. It still cannot be done. We leave it as a challenge to you to give an example.

The problems we are discussing are really problems of dimension. If you have ham, bread, and cheese in *three dimensional space*, then it *is* possible to find a single *planar* cut that will bisect all three quantities (measured by volume). The technical details involved in seeing this fact are rather advanced, so we omit them for now. But we encourage you to do some experiments to convince yourself that the assertion is true.

8.2   Some Case Studies

In this section we actually take some topics from the scientific and other academic literature. The purpose is to let you see problem solving "in action"—in real life situations. You are encouraged to think over, and to discuss in your class, what problem solving techniques are being applied, or might be applicable, in each example.

PROBLEM 8.2.1 (Different Voting Schemes) *The theory of voting is well developed. The goal of this theory is to have a voting system that most closely reflects the will of the voters. It is a theorem of Arrow [ARR] that essentially any voting system may be manipulated. This means that the voters can cast their votes, not necessarily for their favorite candidate, in such a way as to eliminate certain members of the opposition and increase their favorite's chances of success. As a consequence of Arrow's theorem, there is not now, nor will there ever be, a perfect voting system.*

In this "problem," we shall compare and contrast three systems of voting: (i) the plurality method, (ii) the Borda method, and (iii) the Hare method. The exercises at the end of the chapter will give you further practice in thinking about these ideas.

Imagine that a certain election has three candidates: A, B, C. Now we describe the three voting systems as they would apply to these candidates.

Method (i) is the simplest, and perhaps the most flawed: the candidate with the greatest number of votes wins. In method (ii), each voter ranks the candidates first, second, and third. The "average rank" of each candidate is calculated, and the candidate with the greatest average wins. In method (iii), each voter ranks the candidates first, second, and third. If no candidate gets a clear majority of firsts, then the candidate with the fewest firsts is eliminated. Each of that candidate's votes is given to the candidate whom each voter ranked second.

In order to make these three methods clear, and to highlight their differences, we work a concrete example.

Solution: Imagine an election involving three candidates: A, B, C. There are 33 voters. So that we may treat all voting methods at once, we suppose that every voter votes, and that every voter gives a linear ranking to the three candidates. The results are tabulated as follows:

Ranking	No. of Voters
ABC	10
ACB	4
BAC	2
BCA	7
CAB	3
CBA	7

We see (from the first line of the table) that ten voters ranked A first, B second, and C third. From the second line, we see that four voters ranked A first, C second, and B third. And so forth.

We first consider voting method (i). Fourteen voters prefer A (from lines one and two of the table), nine voters prefer B (from lines three and four), and ten voters prefer C (from lines five and six). The candidate with the greatest number of votes is A. Thus A wins the election by the plurality method.

Now consider the Borda method. This requires a little more work. We assign a candidate 3 points for each voter who ranks him first, 2 points for each voter who ranks him second, and 1 point for each voter who ranks him third. The first row of the table accounts for ten of the voters. According to this information, A receives $10 \times 3 = 30$ points, B receives $10 \times 2 = 20$ points, and C receives $10 \times 1 = 10$ points.

Continuing in this fashion down the rows, we find that

total number of points for A
$$= (10 \times 3) + (4 \times 3) + (2 \times 2) + (7 \times 1) + (3 \times 2) + (7 \times 1) = 66.$$

total number of points for B
$$= (10 \times 2) + (4 \times 1) + (2 \times 3) + (7 \times 3) + (3 \times 1) + (7 \times 2) = 68.$$

total number of points for C
$$= (10 \times 1) + (4 \times 2) + (2 \times 1) + (7 \times 2) + (3 \times 3) + (7 \times 3) = 64.$$

Plainly A's average rank is $66/33$, B's average rank is $68/33$, and C's average rank is $64/33$. With this voting method, B wins.

Now we examine the third, or the Hare, method. Plainly no candidate has a majority of first place votes. We eliminate B, because B has the fewest first place votes. Two of B's first place votes rank A second, so we give those two votes to A. Seven of B's first place votes rank C second, so we give those seven votes to B. Thus A ends up with $14 + 2 = 16$ votes, and C ends up with $10 + 7 = 17$ votes. As a result, C wins the election using voting method (iii).

In summary, we have shown three valid methods of vote analysis that give three different results using the same set of voting data. In the exercises, we will ask you to explore ways in which these voting methods can be manipulated. □

PROBLEM 8.2.2 *There have been sociological and other studies that have noted that most convicted criminals come from larger than average families. These studies suggest, at least implicitly, that it therefore behooves us to understand better what influences a large family has on children that might cause them to be attracted to criminal activities.*

An important principle of statistics is that all statistical results can be influenced by point of view, by sampling methods, and by statistical technique. In this problem we will present an analysis that suggests that most people (not just most criminals) come from larger than average families.

Solution: For specificity, we assume that we are dealing with a population of twenty families. Further suppose that in nineteen of these families there is one child and in one of these families there are two children. We now address the question raised in the last paragraph for *this particular* collection of families. In order to avoid irrelevant data, we concentrate only on the children.

There are a grand total of $19 \cdot 1 + 1 \cdot 2 = 21$ children. And there are twenty families. So the average number of children per family is $21/20$. But now we calculate the *average size of family from which a child comes*. Note here that we are changing point of view: for the first statistic the point of view was "per family;" now the point of view is "per child". This is a very important statistical device.

There are a total of 21 children. Nineteen of those children come from a one-child family. Two of those children come from two-child families. Thus the average family size, from the *child*'s point of view, is

$$\frac{19 \cdot 1 + 2 \cdot 2}{21} = \frac{23}{21}.$$

Observe that

$$\frac{23}{21} > \frac{21}{20}.$$

This says precisely that, on average, most children come from larger than average families. □

CHALLENGE PROBLEM 8.2.3 *Can you set up a different analysis for the last problem that would suggest that, on average, most children come from smaller than average families?*

PROBLEM 8.2.4 *Many paradoxes and puzzles arise from a misunderstanding of "conditional probability." Conditional probability considers the probability of event A, given event B. The notion is best understood by way of an example.*

Suppose that you submit to a certain test for a specific cancer. The doctor tells you that the test is 95% percent accurate. The test results are positive (here positive, in standard medical jargon, means that the test indicates that you have the disease). If you did not really analyze the situation, you might conclude that you have cancer with 95% certainty. This turns out not to be correct. In fact your chances of having cancer are much less. Before we explain why, it is worth pointing out that an understanding of these matters is of more than casual interest. These days, many employers submit employees, and job applicants, to urinalysis in an attempt to detect substance abuse. If the given test is only 95% accurate, and if you test positive, then it is important for you to know (and for your attorney to know) just what this means. On the other hand, most medical and life insurance companies will not provide insurance unless the applicant submits to a test for the HIV virus. The same comments apply: every test is accurate only a certain percentage of the time. It is important for a person who tests positive to understand, and for the person or company administering the test to understand, just what a positive reading signifies.

Solution: We will deal with very specific data. Suppose that the test being administered is known to be 95% accurate. Just what does this mean? It means that 95% of all tests are correct. This means that 95% of all positive tests are correct and 95% of all negative tests are correct. The understanding of these two simple facts is the key to our analysis.

Again, for specificity, we suppose that the test is administered to every member of a population of 20,000. And suppose that 1% of the population actually has the malady that is being tested for. This is the setup.

So our hypothesis is that 1% of 20,000, or 200 people, actually have the malady. Because the test is 95% accurate, just 95% of these 200 people will test positive and 5% will test negative. Therefore 190 of this group will test positive and 10 will test negative.

By the same token, 19,800 members of our population do not have the disease. Of those, 95% will test negative and 5% will test positive. Thus 18,810 people will test negative and 990 will test positive.

Taking the last two paragraphs into account, we find that $190 + 990 = 1180$ people will test positive and $10 + 18,810 = 18,820$ people will test negative. The probability that you have the disease, given that you test positive, is

$$\frac{\text{number of people having the disease who test positive}}{\text{number of people who test positive}} = \frac{190}{1180} \approx 0.161$$

By comparison, the probability that you test positive, given that you have the disease, is

$$\frac{\text{number of people testing positive who have the disease}}{\text{number of people who have the disease}} = \frac{190}{200} = 0.95$$

We see that the two results are very different. If you go in for the test cold, having no idea whether you have the disease or not, and if you test positive, then you have a 16.1% chance of actually having the disease. Instead, if you *know* that you have the disease, then there is 95% chance that you will test positive.

We have learned, in this problem, a specific instance of *Bayes's Theorem* on conditional probability. □

8.3 Statistics

A large part of modern analytical thinking involves statistics. Statistics are used to study data in the medical profession, to study data from political and opinion polls, to study results of psychology exams, to determine the accuracy of DNA fingerprinting, and so forth. With statistics, we attempt to draw conclusions about a population using information about only a piece of the population. In this section we illustrate both correct and spurious uses of statistics.

PROBLEM 8.3.1 *It is claimed that the average child has no time to go to school. For the child spends 8 hours per day, or one third of his/her time sleeping. Based on a 365 day year, that's 121.67 days sleeping.*

Also the child spends three hours per day eating. That's a total of 45 days in the year spent eating.

Also the child spends 90 days taking summer vacation.

Also the child spends 21 days on Christmas and Easter holiday.

Finally, the child has each Saturday and Sunday off. That's a total of 104 days.

In short, we have (rounding to whole days) accounted for

$$122 + 45 + 90 + 21 + 104 = 382$$

days of the year taken up by ordinary child-like activities. This is already more than the 365 days that are known to comprise a year. We conclude that there is certainly no time for the child to attend school.

What is wrong with this reasoning?

Solution: We shall only say a word about what is wrong with this analysis. During the 90 days that the child has summer vacation, the child is also eating and sleeping. Thus those hours have been counted twice. Likewise, the child eats and sleeps on weekends.

Taking into account these redundancies, you should now do a correct analysis and determine how many hours remain during which the child might attend school. □

CHALLENGE PROBLEM 8.3.2 *During the Spanish-American War, a brief conflict that occurred in 1898, the death rate in the Navy was 9 per thousand. At the same time, the death rate in New York City was 16 per thousand.*

These are valid statistics. What conclusion can you draw from these numbers? Is it safer to join the Navy and go to war than to be a retiring civilian in New York City? Is the crime rate in New York City so high that you are better off on the battlefield than taking a walk down the street? Give several different analyses of this problem.

PROBLEM 8.3.3 *A certain small business shows the following data at the end of a certain fiscal year. There are 4 owners and 120 employees. Each owner receives $100,000 per year in annual salary. Each employee is paid $12,000 per year in annual wages. There is a total of $240,000 profit, to be divided among the owners. Set up two different statistical models which could be used to generate a report on the finances of this company.*

Solution: The most simple-minded report (and perhaps the most truthful) is this

1. Each employee receives $12,000—that is all.

2. Each owner receives $100,000 in salary and $60,000 in profits for a total of $160,000.

The trouble with this statistical analysis is that it reveals each owner to be remunerated at a rate that is about 13.333 times the rate at which each employee is remunerated. Moreover each owner receives profits equal to 500% of the wages of a typical employee. These numbers makes for bad public relations, from the point of view of management.

Of course there are a great many ways to do bookkeeping, and these may be used (just like any statistics) to the advantage of those doing the bookkeeping. Suppose that we say that $160,000 of the profits will be used as salary bonuses for the owners. Thus each owner will receive $100,000 in regular salary, $40,000 in salary bonus (for a total of $140,000 salary for each owner), and $20,000 in profits. Look how advantageously this may be reported:

$$\text{average salary} = \frac{120 \cdot 12,000 + 4 \cdot 140,000}{120 + 4} = \$16,129.03.$$

And the profit per owner is now $20,000. This sounds much more benign: the average salary is about $4/3$ of what each worker makes—but that is reasonable because the owners will (and should) make more than the workers. And each owner receives $20,000 in profit. But that makes a total of $80,000 in profits; compare that with $2 million dollars paid in salaries. We see that a very small total profit is being made as compared to the total amount of salaries paid.

Clearly this is a company that is primarily interested in the welfare of its employees, and only just a little in the wealth of its owners. □

PROBLEM 8.3.4 *This problem is old and famous. Its statement appears to be frivolous: "What is the probability that the next breath of air that you take will contain a molecule that was expelled by Julius Cæsar when he exclaimed 'Et tu, Brute?' "*

There are two points to this problem: one is that you can actually set up a mathematical model and arrive at an answer; the second is that the likelihood of your sharing a breath with Cæsar is surprisingly high. The problem is originally credited to James Jeans [JEA], and has been discussed at length in [LIT], [PAUL1], and [REN]. Our treatment is derived from those sources.

Solution: First, we cannot know everything. We must make certain assumptions. One is that the last breath that Julius Cæsar exhaled is uniformly distributed throughout the atmosphere. A second is that all the molecules that were in that breath are still *present* in the atmosphere—they haven't dispersed to parts unknown in the universe, and they haven't decomposed and recombined with other elements (for instance, in a process of oxidation). Finally, we shall assume that molecules of air are evenly distributed in the atmosphere (this is not strictly true, as the atmosphere becomes more rarefied the further we go from the surface of the earth—however near the surface of the earth, where we actually live, the hypothesis is approximately true).

We also need some information, that we will borrow from the sources already indicated. First, one may use *The Handbook of Physics and Chemistry* to find the mass of our atmosphere, the magnitude of Avogadro's number, and the gram molecular weight of the atmosphere. The result is that the atmosphere contains 10^{44} molecules.

The gram molecular weight of any gas at standard temperature fills 22.4 liters and contains 6×10^{23} molecules. Experimentation shows that an average breath contains 0.4 liters of air. Thus the number of molecules in an average breath is

$$0.4 \cdot \frac{1}{22.4} \cdot [6 \cdot 10^{23}].$$

This amounts to 1.0714×10^{22} molecules.

Thus the situation is quite simple: your next breath has 1.0714×10^{22} molecules, Cæsar's last breath had 1.0714×10^{22} molecules, and these molecules are mixing around in a universe of 10^{44} molecules. What is the probability that the two breaths will overlap (i.e. have at least one molecule in common)?

First we discuss the matter intuitively. Round off the number of molecules per breath to 10^{22}. Since the atmosphere has 10^{44} molecules, that makes 10^{22} total breaths in the atmosphere, each having 10^{22} molecules. If Cæsar's last breath of 10^{22} molecules is equally and randomly distributed in the atmosphere, then there is likely one molecule of that last breath in each of the other breaths (for there is one of Cæsar's molecules for each of the breaths in the atmosphere). So it seems nearly certain that your next breath will contain one of Cæsar's molecules.

The trick is to make this precise. And the process of making the calculation precise introduces us to a major problem with scientific computing. According to the preceding simplified figures, the atmosphere contains $10^{44} - 10^{22}$ molecules that are not Cæsar's. Pick a molecule of your next breath. The probability that that is a non-Cæsarian molecule is

$$\frac{10^{44} - 10^{22}}{10^{44}} = 1 - 10^{-22}. \tag{*}$$

This probability applies to each molecule in your next breath. So the probability that *every* molecule in your next breath is non-Cæsarian is the product of the number in line (*) with itself 10^{22} times (once for each molecule in your next breath). Thus

The Probability that your next breath is entirely non-Cæsarian

$$= \left(1 - 10^{-22}\right)^{10^{22}}. \tag{**}$$

Now here is the rub: if you punch in the number $1 - 10^{-22}$ on your calculator, you will just get 1—because your calculator is probably only accurate to 10 digits at most. The number in (**) is most assuredly *not* one. But how can we get our hands on it? Most out-of-the-box computer languages (such as FORTRAN) are accurate to eight digits—sixteen digits in double precision. How can we proceed?

Calculators and computers are no substitute for theoretical mathematics, and theoretical mathematics is virtually the only tool that can save us now (you might, however, try the computer algebra package MATHEMATICA if it is available to you). It is known (check a book of tables such as [CRC]) that the expression $(1-1/k)^k$ tends to $1/e$, where e is Euler's number $e \approx 2.718 \ldots$ as $k \to \infty$. It is further known that $(1 - 1/k)^k$ approximates $1/e$ to an accuracy of k decimal places. Our number $(1 - 10^{-22})^{10^{22}}$ fits this model exactly with $k = 10^{22}$. We conclude that the probability of our next breath *not* containing a molecule of Cæsar's last breath is

$$\left(1 - 10^{-22}\right)^{10^{22}} \approx \frac{1}{e} \approx \frac{1}{2.718} = 0.368.$$

In other words, the odds are at least 63% that your next breath *will* contain a molecule of Julius Cæsar's last breath.   □

CHALLENGE PROBLEM 8.3.5 *Suppose that you were unfamiliar with Euler's number e. Can you find another way to estimate* $(1 - 10^{-22})^{10^{22}}$? *[Hint: Logarithms might help.]*

EXERCISES for Chapter 8

1. A railroad track is exactly one mile long. It sits on a piece of ground that is flat. One day, under intense heat from the sun, the track expands one foot in length. Its ends remain fixed to the ground, so the track bows up to form a circular arc of length 5281 feet (remember that a mile is 5280 feet). At the center of the arc, how high is the track above the ground? [*Hint:* Using just hand calculations, you will be able to do this problem up to a point. Then you will need to enlist the aid of calculating or computing equipment, or perhaps very accurate drafting equipment or a CAD. An alternate technique would be to use Newton's method. Discuss this problem with others.] This problem comes from [HAL].

2. Pick up the business page of the newspaper. Write down the first hundred integer numbers that you see cited in articles. For instance, if an article says that the DOW Jones average increased 27 points to 3542 then write down 27 and 3542. Now sort the numbers you have found according to which begin with 1, which begin with 2, and so forth. A naive analysis of the situation would suggest that about one ninth of the numbers begin with 1, about one ninth begin with 2, and so (note that numbers do not usually begin with 0, so 0 is out of consideration). However, in all likelihood, the percentage of your numbers that begins with 1 is greater than $11.11111\ldots$. Can you do an analysis to explain why this is the case? Here are some hints:

For each of the numbers N from 1 to 100, calculate the number $i(N)$ of integers from 1 to N that begins with a 1. Then determine the ratio $i(N)/N$. Notice that this ratio always is at least $1/9$. Now do the same for numbers N from 101 to 1000. Again, the ratio $i(N)/N$ always is at least $1/9$. Can you establish a pattern?

Now, for each positive integer K, average the set of numbers $\{i(1)/1, i(2)/2, \ldots, i(K)/K\}$. This average tends to a limit as $K \to \infty$. What is it? Can you bound it from below? Can you determine it precisely?

3. Go to the library and determine the shape and dimensions of Mt. Fuji. Devise an analysis to determine how long it would take to haul Mt. Fuji to a location 100 miles away using trucks. [*Hint:* Your analysis must be credible. You may not assume that a truck can haul a cubic

mile of earth, for example. You may not assume that you have a million trucks at your disposal.] A fairly detailed discussion of this problem may be found in [PAUL1] and in [RENZ].

4. What is the probability that, with the next breath you take, you will inhale a molecule of air that was exhaled by the great race horse Sea Biscuit the instant before he died? Set up an analysis to give an answer to this question. You will need to know how many liters of air in an average sized breath of a race horse. Of course you can also use some of the ideas in Problem 8.3.4.

5. An economy has two commodities: bread and milk. Last year bread cost fifty cents per loaf and milk one dollar per quart. This year bread costs one dollar per loaf and milk costs fifty cents per quart. Set up an analysis to show that the cost of living has gone up. Set up an analysis to show that the cost of living has gone down. Set up an analysis to show that the cost of living has not changed.

6. A survey indicates a high correlation between college students who smoke and college students with low grades. One might conclude, therefore, that there is a connection between smoking and low grades. Or that not smoking will lead to higher grades.

Suggest three reasons why this conclusion could be in error.

7. Each morning I purchase an item for 99 cents and in the afternoon I sell it for one dollar. I do this each day for one year.

Do an analysis showing that I'm making 1% profit on total sales.

Now do an analysis showing that I'm making 365% on money invested.

8. A ballpoint pen manufacturer used to advertise that his disposable 19 cent pen would write (that is, draw a line) of length one mile. Is this impressive? How many average pages of writing would that be?

9. How fast does hair grow in miles per hour?

10. You borrow $100 from the bank for one year at 6% simple interest. How much do you actually end up paying for the use of the money? [*Hint:* Assume that you pay exactly one twelfth of the principal back each month. The monthly interest payment is *not* constant.]

11. A test for venereal disease is known to be 98% accurate. This means that if a person has VD and takes the test then 98% of the time a positive reading results; and if a person does not have VD and takes the test then 98% of the time a negative reading results.

Now imagine that this test is administered to Irving and that the test results are positive. What is the probability that he actually has VD? For concreteness, assume that it is known that, in a typical population, 0.5% of the people have VD. Also assume that the population sample has 100,000 people.

Now suppose that Irving is tested twice, and that both times the test is negative. What is the probability that Irving has VD?

12. Some studies indicate that lie detector tests (and, for that matter, PAP smears) are about 75% accurate. Devise an analysis, similar to that in Exercise 11, to determine what exactly it means if you flunk a lie detector test, or if you get a positive indication from a PAP smear.

13. A student at Princeton University has a girl friend in New York City and another in Philadelphia. He visits them by catching the train at Princeton Junction. Trains to New York and Philadelphia come equally often—at twenty minute intervals. The student goes out to Princeton Junction when the mood strikes him and just takes the first train that comes along—whether it is going to Philadelphia or to New York. He finds, over a period of two years, that he visits the girl in New York nine times as often as the girl in Philadelphia. How could this be?

14. Sam can type a certain manuscript in 10 hours. George can do it in 5 hours. How long will it take for the two of them to do it together?

15. This problem is sometimes known as "Kant's clock." Immanual Kant (1724-1804) was a celebrated philosopher and mathematician of eighteenth century Germany. He was born and raised in Königsberg, and was reputed never to have left the town. Each day he went for a walk at the same time. He always took the same route. His pace was reputed to be so regular that his walks always had the same duration.

One day Kant's clock stopped. He had no other clock or watch in the house. At a certain time, he then walked to a friend's house. He remained for a while to chat. Then he left and went straight home by the same route. When he arrived home, he was able to set his clock with the correct time. How did he do it? [*Hint:* This is *not* a trick question; it is a question of logic.]

16. Suppose that there are 250 million people in the United States. Suppose that each person has 1500 acquaintances. If two people meet at random on a train, then what is the probability that they have a mutual

acquaintance? [*Hint:* You may assume that everyone's acquaintances are randomly distributed throughout the U.S.]

Now change the question: if two people, A and B, meet at random, then what is the probability that there exist people α and β such that A knows α, B knows β, and α knows β?

17. Set up a statistical model to answer the following question: what is the likelihood that two people in New York City have the same number of hairs on their head? [*Hint:* You will need to determine the number of people in New York City, the number of hairs on an average head, and proceed from there.]

18. You plan to flip a coin continuously until a "head" appears. If this does not happen until the 15th flip, then you win one million dollars. If the head comes up before the 15th flip, then you pay \$10.

Would it be wise for you to play this game? What are your chances of winning? What are your chances of losing? How do these compare with the payoff?

19. On Friday evening the weatherperson predicts 50% chance of rain on Saturday and 50% chance of rain on Sunday. What is the probability that it will rain at some time this weekend? [*Hint:* You must think carefully about what it means to say that there is a 50% chance of rain. It is *incorrect* to conclude that there is 100% chance of rain this weekend.]

20. How fast does the height of a newborn baby increase in kilometers per minute? [*Hint:* You will have to go to the library and find out how fast babies grow with respect to *some* units. Then you can begin to answer the question.]

21. If you were to take all the human blood from all the living people in the United States and pour it into Busch Stadium in St. Louis, how deep would it be? [*Hint:* How many people are in the United States? How many pints of blood in each person? How many cubic feet per pint? What is the area inside Busch Stadium?]

22. If you were to take all the hairs on your head and lay them end to end, how far would they reach?

23. An efficiency expert is doing a study of a certain fast food restaurant. She observes that a particularly clumsy waiter drops 30% of all the hamburgers that he serves. What is the probability that he will drop exactly four of the next ten?

24. A certain game has a spinner with the letters A, B, C, D, E, F on it. The spinner is spun 100 times and the letters that come up are recorded in a sequence across the page. What is the probability that one of the words *BAD, CAD, DAD, FAD, BED, DAB,* or *FED* will appear?

25. How many people need to be in a (large) building before we can be sure that two of them have the same number of hairs on their heads? How many before the probability is greater than .5 that two of them have the same number of hairs on their heads?

26. One of the most famous and often used Wall Street con games goes as follows. On Monday our con man writes 1000 letters to 1000 different people, predicting that on Thursday the stock of United XOLYTL Company will go up. He also writes 1000 letters to 1000 other people predicting that on Thursday the stock of United XOLYTL Company will go down.

Say that Thursday comes and goes and the stock of United XOLYTL has gone down. The con man forgets the first group of 1000 and concentrates on the second. He now divides this group into two subgroups of 500. To one subgroup he sends a letter predicting that, on the following Thursday, the stock of Aardvark International will go up; to the other subgroup he sends a letter predicting that, on the following Thursday, the Aardvark stock will go down.

The following Thursday comes and goes and Aardvark International has gone up. The con man discards the second subgroup of 500 and concentrates on the first. He divides this subgroup of 500 into two new subgroups of 250. To the first of these, he sends out 250 letters predicting that, on the following Thursday, Blink, Inc. stock will go up. And he sends another 250 letters (to the second group) predicting that Blink, Inc. stock will go down.

That third Thursday comes and goes. Now the con man has a group of 250 people singled out who believe that this man can predict activities in the stock market! After all, he has sent each of these 250 people three correct predictions (and no incorrect predictions). He now sends a letter to each of those 250 people claiming that he is now ready to make a marvelous prediction—that will make them a great deal of money—but this time they will have to pay for his advice. Considering postage and other expenses, how much will he have to charge in order to make a profit of $100,000?

27. The most famous con game of all is the "Ponzi scheme," named after Charles Ponzi (1877-1949). A typical Ponzi scheme works like this. Say that a very desirable computer costs $10,000. You approach your "mark" (i.e. your victim) and tell him that you can obtain this computer for him/her for a mere $5,000. The only catch is that they must give you the money up front, and they must be willing to wait two months for delivery.

So far so good. What the mark doesn't know is (i) that you are paying the full price of $10,000 for each computer but (ii) that you are taking orders at triple the rate at which you are making deliveries.

Thus, in the first month, let us say that you take ten orders but deliver no computers. In the second month you take twenty more orders but only deliver computers to your ten customers from the first month. We see that by the end of the second month you have taken in $30 \times$ $5,000$ but have only delivered ten computers at $10,000 each. You have made a profit of $50,000.

Clearly, if the con artist is to make money, he must at some point disappear, leaving a (large) number of orders unfilled. Your assignment is to design a Ponzi scheme so that, at the end of one year, the con man can make away with an even one million dollars.

28. A certain insurance company specializes in sports injuries. Based on its actuarial tables, it anticipates that in any given year, if it insures 50,000 people, then the following will occur: (a) two of these people will have a valid claim of $20,000, (b) twenty of these people will have a valid claim of $10,000, (c) two hundred of these people will have a valid claim of $1,000, and (d) one thousand people will have a valid claim of $250. Calculate the average number of dollars paid out by the company per policy, and determine what premium the company should charge so that it is assured of clearing one million dollars per year.

29. Two fishermen, Forrest and Bubba, are very competitive. They never go fishing together. In 1987 Forrest averages more fish per trip than Bubba. And in 1988 Forrest averages more fish per trip than Bubba. But in 1987 and 1988 taken together, Bubba averages more fish per trip than Forrest. How is this possible?

30. Here is a problem involving "cooked dice" that is due to Bradley Efron (see [PAUL1, p. 100]. Die α has 4's on four faces and 0's on the

other two. Die β has 3's on all six faces. Die γ has 2's on four faces and 6's on the other two. Die δ has three faces with 5 and three faces with 1.

A dice game is played by having each player rolling one of these special dice. The player with the highest number wins. Show that if α plays β then α wins 2/3 of the time. If β plays γ then β wins 2/3 of the time. If γ plays δ then γ wins 2/3 of the time. Since α beats β and β beats γ and γ beats δ (two thirds of the time) then one might conclude that α will beat δ. But show that, in fact, δ beats α a *total of* 2/3 of the time.

31. Arrow's theorem says, in effect, that any voting system can be manipulated. Explain, for each of the three voting systems treated in the text, how voters can skew the outcome of a vote by (possibly) voting for a candidate that would not ordinarily be their first preference. More precisely, how can voters cast their votes for a less favored candidate in early rounds of voting in order to eliminate challengers who might be a real threat to their preferred candidate?

Do not simply philosophize about this problem: come up with concrete sets of data, just as we did in the text.

32. Read an article—in an encyclopedia, for example—about the Electoral College of the United States. Learn how it operates. Come up with examples that show how the popular vote can determine one outcome while the Electoral College will determine another.

33. You are walking through a steady rain. Are you better off running at a steady rate or walking at a steady rate? That is, which method of locomotion will result in less rain falling on you? [*Hint:* Your answer will depend on whether the rain is coming down vertically or at an angle.]

34. It begins snowing some time before noon. The snow falls steadily, when measured by the rate of change of depth. At exactly noon, a snow plow begins working at a steady rate (in terms of cubic feet of snow removed per hour). The plow clears two blocks during the first hour of work, and one block during the second hour.

At what time did it begin snowing?

35. Mary was reading an advertisement for automobile tires. Tires guaranteed to last 20,000 miles were $45 apiece. Tires guaranteed to last 30,000 miles were $60 apiece. Tires guaranteed to last 40,000 miles

were \$75 apiece. Mary noticed that the company, if it chose, could be manufacturing just one kind of tire that would last n miles and then selling it at three different prices. Assuming that all three types of tires sell in equal numbers, which value of n would maximize the company's profits?

36. Imagine a sandwich made from a piece of wheat bread, a piece of white bread, and a piece of cheese. As is usually the case with these matters, each piece of bread and the piece of cheese is of an irregular shape. Is it true that there is a single, straight, planar knife cut that bisects the wheat bread, bisects the white bread, and bisects the cheese? (Here we say that the cheese is bisected if each piece has the same volume; the same for each piece of bread.) [*Hint:* Try the problem first for one piece of bread and one piece of cheese.]

37. In [PAUL1], a statistical model is set up to support this contention: if you have unprotected sex on a first date, with someone that you meet in a bar, then you are more likely to be killed in your car driving home than by AIDS contracted in the sexual encounter.

Try to separate the emotional overtones of this claim from the statistical assertion itself. Set up your own statistical model. Do you agree with Paulos's conclusions? Renz [REN] is vehement in contradicting Paulos. After doing your own analysis, read Renz's comments and evaluate the merit of his remarks.

38. In a gambling casino, the game of "blackjack" is played as follows. As a player, you do not play against the other players. You only play against the dealer, who works for the house. The dealer deals cards to you from an ordinary deck of 52. Each card numbered 2 through 10 counts a number of points corresponding to its face value; so a $3\heartsuit$ counts 3 points, a $7\clubsuit$ counts 7 points, and so forth. The Jack, Queen, and King are each worth 10 points. The ace is worth either one point or eleven points; it is your choice.

The game begins with each player placing a bet and being dealt two cards; usually the first card for each player is face down and the second card for each player is face up (a variant is that only the dealer's second card is face up). In turn, the dealer deals additional cards to each player until she is told to stop. As you are dealt cards, you sum the total number of points in your hand. You want to get as close to 21 as possible, without going over. If you go over then you lose your bet.

After the dealer has dealt cards to you, then she deals cards to herself. She, too, stops at a certain point so as not to exceed 21. Whichever of you or the dealer has the highest score (not to exceed 21) wins. If you win, the dealer pays you an amount of money equal to your bet. If you tie, then the game is a draw, and your bet is returned to you.

The "blackjack" rule is this: If, at the very outset, you are dealt an ace plus either a ten, Jack, Queen, or King, then you have "blackjack" or a "natural." That is obviously 21, and beats 21 formed in other ways. Instead of just winning an amount equal to your bet, you win 1.5 times your bet. (This is true unless the dealer also has blackjack, in which case the game is a "push," and you only win an amount equal to your bet.)

Now, as previously noted, the dealer works for the house. She plays by a strict rule: if she has sixteen or fewer points in her hand, then she takes another card (she is "hit"); if she has seventeen or more points, then she does not take another card (she "stands"). There are no exceptions to this rule. Typically, players (playing for themselves) decide whether or not to take another card based on a variety of emotional and intuitive considerations—card counting, lucky numbers, "systems," and so forth. But the house rule for the dealer is very simple. Explain where the house rule comes from, and why sixteen is the right choice for the cutoff.

39. In most city streets, every block has one or more round holes in the center. These are placed so that city workers can access sewer lines, gas lines, and so forth. The steel covers to these holes are called "manhole covers." The hole, and the cover, are always round.

Why is a manhole cover always round? Is there another shape that will work as well?

40. You are driving west on Interstate 70. Coming to St. Louis, you intend to turn north on Lindbergh Boulevard. Lindbergh is a major artery, so you know that there will be separate turnoffs for Lindbergh north and Lindbergh south. Which turnoff will come first? Why?

41. [Feynman] A common type of lawn sprinkler appears as in Figure 183. Notice that it has two arms, and it rotates about the pedestal. When water enters the sprinkler through the hose, it squirts in a fine

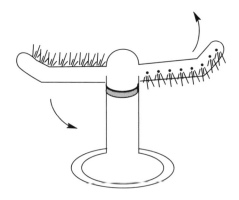

Figure 183

stream from holes in the arms. By Newton's second law, the arms then spin around.

Now imagine that such a sprinkler, attached to a hose, is placed at the bottom of a swimming pool full of water. Then water is *sucked out* of the pool, through the hose, at a steady rate. At the instant this process begins, in which direction does the sprinkler rotate?

42. Imagine a sealed can on one end of a balance scale. The can is filled with water, except that there is a small balloon full of air inside the can. The balloon is attached to the bottom of the can by a string. A weight is placed on the other side of the balance scale so that the system is in equilibrium—see Figure 184.

At a given instant, the string attached to the balloon breaks. [Since air is considerably lighter than water, the balloon would rise if it were in a can that was in a system at rest.] In that first instant, will the end of the scale with the can move up or down?

43. In many large parking lots, cars are parked diagonally—refer to Figure 185. What is the reason for this? Consider a configuration in which cars are parked at a 30° angle. How many more cars will this fit than if the cars are parked in a "rectangular" fashion (Figure 186)? What angle will fit the most cars? Will extreme angles cause problems with entering or exiting the parking space? Set up a detailed model for this problem and discuss it with others.

44. The Pitofsky family of Scarsdale, New York seems to have more than the usual number of male children. In fact, in 1959, the forty-

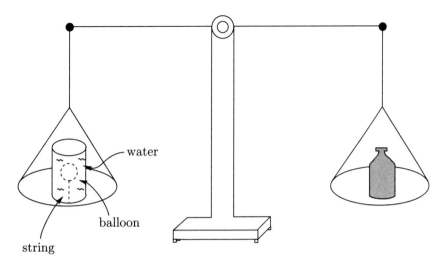

Figure 184

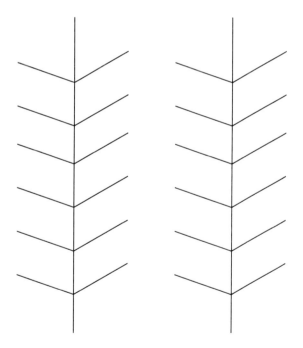

Figure 185

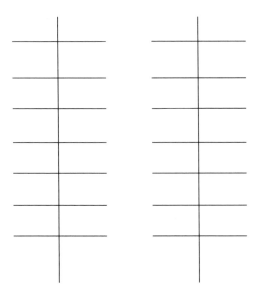

Figure 186

seventh consecutive boy was born to the Pitofsky line. These births span seven generations of Pitofsky's. Assuming equal likelihood of male and female children, what is the probability of this event? The source of this problem is [HUF2].

45. "If enough monkeys pound on enough typewriters for enough years, one of them will eventually pound out *Hamlet*." Assuming, for the sake of argument, that *Hamlet* is 100,000 words long, and that the average length of a word is five characters, how many monkeys and or how many years would it take to make the probability of this event greater than .5?

46. Perform the following experiment. Lightly hold a penny on its edge on a flat table by using the tip of the index finger of one hand. Flick the penny sharply with the other hand, so that it spins rapidly. When the penny falls flat to the table, make a note of whether it comes up heads or tails. Perform this experiment fifty times. With what frequency does 'heads' occur?

Now balance a penny on its edge on the table, so that it stands by itself, and has no spin or other motion. Slam the flat of your hand down on another part of the table so that the penny falls. Record whether it comes up heads or tails. With what frequency does 'heads' occur?

Your answers will be strikingly different. Explain why.

47. In some cities, cars guilty of a certain number of unpaid parking violations are slapped with a "Denver boot." This is a device that is attached to the right rear wheel of the car and prevents the vehicle from being driven until the fines are paid. This problem asks you to design a Denver boot. It should have the following properties:

1. It can easily be applied, on the street side of the car, by a single traffic officer *without lifting the car.*

2. It does not obstruct traffic.

3. It cannot be removed by the owner of the car.

4. It makes the car undriveable.

Your solution to this problem should consist of a drawing, a description of the device, and instructions for its use.

48. George goes into a 7-11 convenience store. He selects some licorice, some jerky, some potato chips, and a soda and proceeds to the counter. Being good at math, he adds up the total cost and takes a $10 bill from his wallet to pay. George lives in a state with no sales tax on food.

The cash register is broken, and the clerk uses a hand calculator to tally the bill. However the clerk is dishonest and George notices that, after each item is punched in, the clerk hits the 'multiply' key rather than the 'add' key. Thus George is extremely surprised that the clerk ends up with the same answer that he himself got with addition: $7.11. What are the prices of the individual items?

49. Joe pledges to love Samantha until "Niagara Falls erodes the cliffs beneath them and blends into Lake Erie." Set up a theoretical model to determine how long Joe will love Samantha.

50. Joe and Sam have a physics test on Wednesday. But they are partying in the next town on Tuesday night, and they do not make it back to the test on time. They throw themselves on the Professor's mercy—claiming that they had a flat tire—and he agrees to give them another test. He gives Joe and Sam each the same test, but puts them in separate rooms.

The new exam has just two questions. The one on the front, worth 5 points, is an elementary problem about falling bodies. The one on the back, worth 95 points, asks which tire had the flat. The boys have not consulted on this particular item. What is the probability (assuming that the car has four tires) that the boys will give the same answer?

51. A perfectly insulated room has temperature 72°. The source of climate control is turned off. But a refrigerator is put into the room and plugged in. The adjustment inside the refrigerator is turned to "maximum cold" and the door to the refrigerator *is left open. Only the refrigerator affects the temperature in the room.* After one hour, is the room hotter or colder than the original 72°?

52. Three women rent a hotel room to share for the night. The room clerk charges them $75 for the room. Later, the clerk realizes that he has made a mistake and that the charge should have been $70. He gives the bellhop $5 to return to the women. Realizing that 3 does not divide $5 evenly, the bellhop gives each of the women $1 and pockets the remaining $2.

On the way back to his post, the bellhop reviews the situation: each woman paid $24 = $25 - $1. And he has $2. That makes $(3 \times \$24) + \$2 = \$74$. What happened to the missing $1?

Bibliography

[MPI]   D. Albers and J. Alexanderson, *Mathematical People: Profiles and Interviews*, Birkhauser, Cambridge, 1985.

[BAL]   W. W. Rouse Ball and H. S. M. Coxeter, *Mathematical Recreations and Essays*, 13th ed., Dover, New York, 1987.

[BER]   E. R. Berlekamp, *et al*, *Winning Ways for Your Mathematical Plays*, Academic Press, New York, 1982.

[CRC]   S. Krantz, K. Rosen, and D. Zwillinger, eds., *Standard Mathematical Tables*, 30th ed., CRC Press, Boca Raton, 1996.

[BHS]   G. Blom, L. Holst, D. Sandell, *Problems and Snapshots from the World of Probability*, Springer Verlag, Berlin, 1994.

[CUN]   F. Cunningham, The Kakeya problem for simply connected and star-shaped sets, *Am. Math. Monthly* 78(1971), 114-129.

[DOR]   H. Dörrie, *100 Great Problems of Elementary Mathematics: Their History and Solution*, Dover Publishing, New York, 1965.

[ERD]   P. Erdös, On the fundamental problem of mathematics, *Am. Math. Monthly* 79(1972), 149-150.

[GAR]   M. Gardner, ed., *Mathematical Puzzles of Sam Loyd*, Dover, New York, 1959.

[GOF]   C. Goffman, And what is your Erdös number?, *Am. Math. Monthly* 76(1969), 791.

[HAL]   P. Halmos, *Problems for Mathematicians Young and Old*, The Mathematical Association of America, Washington, D. C., 1991.

[HUF1]   D. Huff, *How to Lie with Statistics*, 34th Edition, W. W. Norton & Co., New York, 1954.

[HUF2]   D. Huff, *How to Take a Chance*, W. W. Norton & Co., New York, 1959.

[JEA]   J. Jeans, *An Introduction to the Kinetic Theory of Gases*, Cambridge University Press, Cambridge, 1942.

[KLW]   V. Klee and S. Wagon, *Old and New Unsolved Problems in Plane Geometry and Number Theory*, Mathematical Association of America, Washington, D.C., 1991.

[KRA1]   S. Krantz, *The Elements of Advanced Mathematics*, CRC Press, Boca Raton, 1995.

[KRA2]   S. Krantz, *Real Analysis and Foundations*, CRC Press, Boca Raton, 1992.

[LAK]   Lakatos, *Proofs and Refutations*, Cambridge University Press, Cambridge, 1976.

[LAR]   L. Larsen, *Problem Solving through Problems*, Springer Verlag, Berlin, 1983.

[LIT]   J. E. Littlewood, *A Mathematician's Miscellany*, Methuen, London, 1953.

[GUI]   P. Matthews, *The Guinness Book of World's Records*, Bantam Books, New York, 1994.

[MOO]   David S. Moore, *Statistics: Concepts and Controversies*, W. H. Freeman and Co., San Francisco, 1979.

[MON]   O. Morgenstern and J. von Neumann, *The Theory of Games and Economic Behavior*, Princeton University Press, Princeton, 1946.

[PAUL1] J. A. Paulos, *Innumeracy*, Hill and Wang, New York, 1988.

[PAUL2] J. A. Paulos, *Beyond Innumeracy*, Vintage, New York, 1992.

[POL1] G. Polya, *How to Solve It*, Princeton University Press, Princeton, 1988.

[POL2] G. Polya, *Mathematics and Plausible Reasoning*, in two volumes, Princeton University Press, Princeton, 1954.

[POK] G. Polya and J. Kilpatrick, *The Stanford Mathematics Problem Book*, Teachers College Press, New York, 1974.

[REN] P. Renz, Thoughts on *Innumeracy*: Mathematics Versus the World, *Am. Math. Monthly* 1993, 732-742.

[RIN] G. Ringel, *Map Color Theorem*, Springer Verlag, 1974.

[SCHO] A. Schoenfeld, *Mathematical Problem Solving*, Academic Press, New York 1985.

[SH] J. R. Shoenfeld, *Mathematical Logic*, Addison-Wesley, Reading, 1967.

[SIM1] W. Simon *Mathematical Magic*, Charles Scribner's Sons, New York, 1964.

[SIM2] W. Simon, *Mathematical Magic*, Dover Books, New York, 1993.

[STR] S. Straszewicz, *Mathematical Problems and Puzzles from the Polish Mathematical Olympiads*, Pergamon Press, Oxford, 1965.

[SUP] P. Suppes, *Axiomatic Set Theory*, Dover Publications, New York, 1972.

[TIE] J. Tierney, Paul Erdös is in town. His brain is open, *Science 84* 5(1984), 40-47.

Index

Solutions to
Odd-Numbered Problems

Preface

This manual contains the solutions to most of the odd-numbered exercises in the book **Techniques of Problem Solving** by Steven G. Krantz, hereinafter referred to as "the text."

It is essential that this manual be used only as a reference, and never as a way to learn how to solve the exercises. It is strongly encouraged never to look up the solution of any exercise before attempting to solve it. The 'attempt time' will always be as rewarding to the student—or maybe more—as solving the exercise itself.

Notation and references as well as the results used to solve the problems are taken directly from the text

We would like to express our gratitude to Nicola Arcozzi, Steven Krantz and Vladimir Maşek for their valuable comments on several of the exercises.

Luis Fernández and Haedeh Gooransarab.

St. Louis, May 15th 1996.

Chapter 1

Basic Concepts

1.1. Let us use induction. We will prove something that at first seems stronger: $\left(\sqrt{2}-1\right)^{k} = \sqrt{N_k} - \sqrt{N_k - 1}$ for N_k a positive integer satisfying $\sqrt{2}\sqrt{N_k}\sqrt{N_k - 1} \in \mathbb{Z}$. We added this last condition because it helps in the induction argument.

The statement is true for $k = 1$: picking $N_1 = 2$, we have

$$\left(\sqrt{2}-1\right) = \sqrt{2} - \sqrt{2-1},$$

and

$$\sqrt{2}\sqrt{1}\sqrt{2} = 2 \in \mathbb{Z}.$$

Suppose that the statement is true for $k = n$. Our goal is to find a number N_{n+1} such that

$$\left(\sqrt{2}-1\right)^{n+1} = \sqrt{N_{n+1}} - \sqrt{N_{n+1} - 1}$$

and

$$\sqrt{2}\sqrt{N_{n+1}}\sqrt{N_{n+1} - 1} \in \mathbb{Z}.$$

From the induction hypothesis we have:

$$
\begin{aligned}
\left(\sqrt{2}-1\right)^{n+1} &= \left(\sqrt{2}-1\right)^{n}\left(\sqrt{2}-1\right) \\
&= \left(\sqrt{N_n} - \sqrt{N_n - 1}\right)\left(\sqrt{2}-1\right) \\
&= \left(\sqrt{N_n}\sqrt{2} + \sqrt{N_n - 1}\right) - \left(\sqrt{2}\sqrt{N_n - 1} + \sqrt{N_n}\right)
\end{aligned}
$$

Now observe that:

$$\left(\sqrt{N_n}\sqrt{2}+\sqrt{N_n-1}\right)^2 = 2N_n + (N_n-1) + 2\sqrt{2}\sqrt{N_n}\sqrt{N_n-1}$$
$$= 3N_n - 1 + 2\sqrt{2}\sqrt{N_n}\sqrt{N_n-1}$$
$$\in \mathbf{Z}.$$

Let K be the number $3N_n - 1 + 2\sqrt{2}\sqrt{N_n}\sqrt{N_n-1}$.

$$\left(\sqrt{2}\sqrt{N_n-1}+\sqrt{N_n}\right)^2 = 2\left(N_n-1\right) + N_n + 2\sqrt{2}\sqrt{N_n}\sqrt{N_n-1}$$
$$= 3N_n - 2 + 2\sqrt{2}\sqrt{N_n}\sqrt{N_n-1}$$
$$= K - 1 \in \mathbf{Z}$$

Therefore we have:

$$\sqrt{K}-\sqrt{K-1} = \left(\sqrt{2}\sqrt{N_n}+\sqrt{N_n-1}\right) - \left(\sqrt{2}\sqrt{N_n-1}+\sqrt{N_n}\right)$$
$$= \left(\sqrt{2}-1\right)^{n+1},$$

and

$$\sqrt{K}\sqrt{K-1}\sqrt{2}$$
$$= \left(\sqrt{N_n}\sqrt{2}+\sqrt{N_n-1}\right)\left(\sqrt{2}\sqrt{N_n-1}+\sqrt{N_n}\right)\sqrt{2}$$
$$= 3\sqrt{N_n}\sqrt{N_n-1}\sqrt{2} + 2N_n + 2\left(N_n-1\right)$$
$$\in \mathbf{Z},$$

since $\sqrt{2}\sqrt{N_n}\sqrt{N_n-1} \in \mathbf{Z}$ by the induction hypothesis. So K has all the properties we want for N_{n+1}. Therefore, if we take $N_{n+1} = K$, we are done.

1.3. Let us first find a formula for the sum of the first k squares of integers. We will follow the same scheme as in PROBLEM 1.1.2 in the text. First observe that

$$\ell^3 - (\ell-1)^3 = (\ell^3 - \ell^3 + 3\ell^2 - 3\ell + 1) = 3\ell^2 - 3\ell + 1.$$

Adding now from $\ell = 1$ to k we obtain a 'telescopic sum' on the left hand side in which most of the terms will cancel:

$$(k^3 - (k-1)^3) + ((k-1)^3 - (k-2)^3) + \cdots + (2^3 - 1) + (1 - 0)$$
$$= (3k^2 - 3k + 1) + (3(k-1)^2 - 3(k-1) + 1) + \cdots + (3 - 3 + 1).$$

Simplifying, reordering, and applying the formula for the sum of the first k integers, we obtain:

$$
\begin{aligned}
k^3 &= 3(k^2 + (k-1)^2 + \cdots + 1) \\
&\quad -3(k + (k-1) + \cdots + 1) + (1 + 1 + \cdots + 1) \\
&= 3(k^2 + (k-1)^2 + \cdots + 1) - 3\frac{k(k+1)}{2} + k \\
&= 3(k^2 + (k-1)^2 + \cdots + 1) - \frac{3k^2 + k}{2}.
\end{aligned}
$$

Finally, solving for $(k^2 + (k-1)^2 + \cdots + 1)$, we find:

$$(k^2 + (k-1)^2 + \cdots + 1) = \frac{2k^3 + 3k^2 + k}{6}.$$

For the sum of the cubes, we repeat this scheme again: we first observe that

$$\ell^4 - (\ell-1)^4 = 1 \cdot (\ell^4 - \ell^4 + 4\ell^3 - 6\ell^2 + 4\ell - 1) = 4\ell^3 - 6\ell^2 + 4\ell - 1.$$

Adding now from $\ell = 1$ to k we obtain a 'telescopic sum' on the left hand side in which most of the terms will cancel:

$$[(k^4 - (k-1)^4] + [((k-1)^4 - (k-2)^4] + \cdots + [((2^4 - 1) + (1 - 0)]$$
$$= [(4k^3 - 6k^2 + 4k - 1] + [(4(k-1)^3 - 6(k-1)^2] + [(4(k-1) - 1]$$
$$+ \cdots + (4 \cdot 1^3 - 6 \cdot 1^2 + 4 \cdot 1 - 1).$$

Simplifying and reordering the last expression, we find:

$$k^4 = 4(1 + 2^3 + \cdots + k^3) - 6(1 + 2^2 + \cdots + k^2) + 4(1 + 2 + \cdots + k) - (k).$$

Solving for $(1 + 2^3 + \cdots + k^3)$, we find:

$$1^3 + 2^3 \cdots + k^3 = \frac{k^4 + 6(1 + 2^2 + \cdots + k^2) - 4(1 + 2 + \cdots + k) + (k)}{2}$$

$$= \frac{1}{2}\left\{ k^4 + 6\frac{2k^3 + 3k^2 + k}{6} - 4\frac{k^2 + k}{2} + k \right\}$$

$$= \frac{k^2(k+1)^2}{4} \quad, \text{ after simplifying.}$$

1.5. Write the equation as

$$n(m - 1) = m.$$

This means that $m - 1$ divides m. But this can only happen if $m = 2$ or if $m = 0$.

If $m = 2$, the equation above reads

$$n(2 - 1) = 2,$$

which implies $n = 2$.

If $m = 0$, the equation above reads

$$n(0 - 1) = 0,$$

which implies $n = 0$.

Thus, the only solutions are $m = n = 0$ and $m = n = 2$.

1.7. Proceed as follows:

$$
\begin{aligned}
2^{300} \cdot 5^{600} \cdot 4^{400} &= 2^{300} \cdot 5^{600} \cdot 2^{800} \\
&= 2^{600} \cdot 5^{600} \cdot 2^{500} \\
&= 10^{600} \cdot 2^{500}.
\end{aligned}
$$

Therefore, the number $2^{300} \cdot 5^{600} \cdot 4^{400}$ ends in 600 zeros.

1.9. Between 1 and 100, we have:

9	numbers with 1 digit	=	9 digits
90	numbers with 2 digits	=	180 digits
1	number with 3 digits	=	3 digits
	TOTAL		192 digits

1.11. Suppose that we have a number N with k digits, which we write as $N = a_k a_{k-1} \ldots a_1 a_0$. We can also write N as:

$$
\begin{aligned}
N &= a_k 10^k + a_{k-1} 10^{k-1} + \cdots + a_1 10 + a_0 \\
&= a_k(\underbrace{99 \cdots 9}_{k \text{ digits}} + 1) + a_{k-1}(\underbrace{99 \cdots 9}_{k-1 \text{ digits}} + 1) + \cdots + a_1(9 + 1) + a_0 \\
&= [a_k \underbrace{99 \cdots 9}_{k \text{ digits}} + a_{k-1} \underbrace{99 \cdots 9}_{k-1 \text{ digits}} + \cdots + 9] + [a_k + a_{k-1} + \cdots + a_0]
\end{aligned}
$$

Since both N and the first term are divisible by 9, the second term, namely $a_k + a_{k-1} + \cdots + a_0$, must also be divisible by 9. Also, the number $a_k + a_{k-1} + \cdots + a_0$ has fewer digits than the original number N that we started with. When we add the digits of a number divisible by 9 we obtain a number with fewer digits than the original that is also divisible by 9. If we continue this process, at some point we will obtain a number with only one digit that is divisible by nine. This number has to be 9.

1.13. Let us proceed using the same strategy as in Exercise 6. Suppose that we write out all the numbers that we are multiplying to form $n!$, i.e. $1 \cdot 2 \cdot 3 \cdots n$. Put k dots, arranged vertically, over each number of the string that is divisible by p^k until we exhaust all numbers in the string. It is clear that the number of factors of p in $n!$ equals the number of dots, so let us count the dots.

When we count how many numbers are divisible by p it is as if we were counting the bottom dots. If we now count how many numbers are divisible by p^2, we are counting the dots 'at the second level'. Proceeding this way, we will eventually reach some k such that no numbers in the string are divisible by p^k (when $p^k > n$), i.e. we have exhausted all the 'levels'.

Therefore, the number of factors of p that occur in $n!$ equals the number of numbers between 1 and n that are divisible by p plus the number of numbers between 1 and n that are divisible by p^2, etc. Now, how many numbers are divisible by p^k, some k, between 1 and n? We will have that $1 \cdot p^k$, $2 \cdot p^k$, ..., $l \cdot p^k$ are the ones that are divisible by p^k, up to the greatest l such that $l \cdot p^k$ is less than or equal to n. This implies that between 1 and

n there are exactly

$$\left[\frac{n}{p^k}\right]$$

numbers divisible by p^k, where $[x]$ denotes the greatest integer lesser than x.

This is because

$$p^k \cdot \left[\frac{n}{p^k}\right] < n,$$

and

$$p^k \cdot \left(\left[\frac{n}{p^k}\right] + 1\right) > n,$$

so that $\left[\dfrac{n}{p^k}\right]$ is the greatest l such that $l \cdot p^k$ is less than or equal to n. Thus, the final formula is

$$\sum_{k=1}^{\infty} \left[\frac{n}{p^k}\right].$$

(Note that we can safely sum to ∞ since $\left[\dfrac{n}{p^k}\right]$ equals 0 for all k sufficiently large.)

1.15. The total number of games played, if each team plays every other exactly once, is $14+13+12+\cdots+2+1 = 105$. To see this, count first the games that the best team played (14), then the games that the second best team played, excluding the game with the best team—that we have already counted—(13), etc. Each game generates a total of 4 points, shared between the two teams in that game. Thus the total number of points is $4 \cdot 105 = 420$.

Now, if every team ends up with a different total score and the team with lowest total scored 21, it must be that the team with second lowest total scored at least 22, the one with third lowest total scored at least 23, up to the best team which scored at least

35 points. Adding up the total scores we must have that the total number of points has to be greater than or equal to

$$21 + 22 + 23 + \cdots + 34 + 35 = 420.$$

Since this is exactly the total number of points, it must be that the team with second lowest total scored exactly 22, the one with third lowest total scored exactly 23, and the best team scored exactly 35 points (note that if any team had scored more, then the sum of the final scores of all the teams would exceed 420, which is impossible).

The maximum number of points that a team could have received is

$$3 \text{ points} \times 14 \text{ games} = 42 \text{ points}.$$

Thus the best team lost only 7 points. Note that, for each loss, 2 points are subtracted (a win is 3 but a loss is 1). If the best team had not had any draws, then the total number of points lost would be even, never 7. Therefore one of the games of the best team was surely a draw.

1.17. The correct number is $2 - 2k$.

1.19. One can color the plane in the following way. The hexagons are regular and have diameter 1. Each letter stands for a color. We color the inside and the left half of the boundary of each hexagon, including the top vertex and excluding the bottom one, with the color corresponding to the letter. Notice that the distance between two hexagons of the same color is always greater than one.

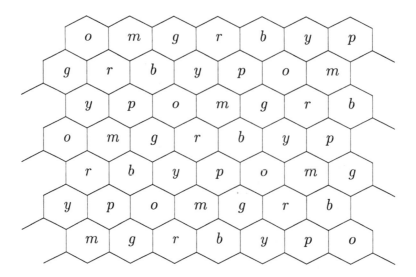

1.21. If the mayor announces how many husbands were unfaithful, everything will be clear right away: all the wives that know about fewer unfaithful husbands than the number given by the mayor will immediately know that they have been cheated.

1.23. Note that

$$\left[\frac{1}{2!} + \frac{2}{3!} + \cdots + \frac{n}{(n+1)!}\right] + \left[\frac{1}{2!} + \frac{1}{3!} + \cdots + \frac{1}{(n+1)!}\right]$$
$$= \left[\frac{2}{2!} + \frac{3}{3!} + \cdots + \frac{n+1}{(n+1)!}\right]$$
$$= \left[\frac{1}{1!} + \frac{1}{2!} + \cdots + \frac{1}{n!}\right].$$

Therefore we have:

$$\left[\frac{1}{2!} + \frac{2}{3!} + \cdots + \frac{n}{(n+1)!}\right]$$
$$= \left[\frac{1}{1!} + \frac{1}{2!} + \cdots + \frac{1}{n!}\right] - \left[\frac{1}{2!} + \frac{1}{3!} + \cdots + \frac{1}{(n+1)!}\right]$$
$$= 1 - \frac{1}{(n+1)!}$$

1.25. For the first strategy, the probability of winning is:

$$\frac{\text{number of winning cases}}{\text{number of possible cases}} = \frac{a}{a+b}.$$

To find the probability of winning with the second strategy, we have to take into account the fact that the probability of drawing a white ball in the second draw depends on which ball was thrown away in the first draw. We have:

Pr{drawing a white ball at the end}

$= $ **Pr**{white at the end | assuming 1ˢᵗ white} · **Pr**{1ˢᵗ white}

$+$**Pr**{white at the end | assuming 1ˢᵗ black} · **Pr**{1ˢᵗ black}

$$= \frac{a-1}{a+b-2} \cdot \frac{a}{a+b} + \frac{a}{a+b-2} \cdot \frac{b}{a+b}$$

$$= \frac{a^2 - a + ab}{(a+b)(a+b-2)}$$

$$= \frac{a(a+b-2) + a}{(a+b)(a+b-2)}$$

$$= \frac{a}{a+b} + \frac{a}{(a+b)(a+b-2)}.$$

It is similar to the Monty Hall problem: player B eliminates one of the black balls, just like Monty Hall would eliminate one of the doors in the game.

1.27. In all the cases asked it is possible to tile the floor—and actually not too hard. If two adjacent corners are missing, then tile the entire floor placing the tiles parallel to the side that has the missing corners. If the omitted squares are adjacent to each other, then place the tiles parallel to these two adjacent squares; then filling up the rest will be straightforward.

Chapter 2

A Deeper Look at Geometry

2.1. a) For example, the complete graph on four vertices in the sphere requires 4 colors.

b) The complete graph on seven vertices in the torus requires 7 colors, as is shown in the figure below. We picture the torus as a rectangle in which we identify the top edge with the bottom edge and the left edge with the right edge. The letters a, a', b, b' in the figure indicate this identification.

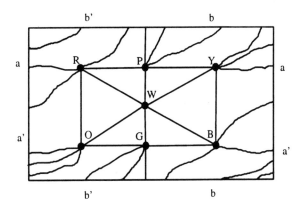

c) The chromatic number of a torus with two holes is 8.

2.3. View the triangle lying on one of its sides, as in the figure:

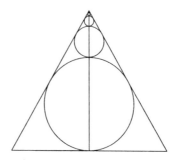

If we draw a vertical segment from the base of the triangle to the top vertex, then the length of this segment will be exactly the sum of the diameters of all the circles in the figure. Since the altitude of the triangle is 3, we have that the sum of the lengths of the diameters of all the triangles is 3, which implies that the sum of their radii is 1.5. Now, since we are doing this process in every vertex of the triangle, the sum of the radii of all the circles involved is $3 \cdot 1.5 - 2 = 2.5$. Notice that we are subtracting 2 because, otherwise, the radius of the circle in the center (which has length 1) would be counted thrice. Thus, the answer is 2.5.

2.5. View the triangle as lying on its longest side, denoted by a, and let b and c be the left and right sides respectively, as in the figure below:

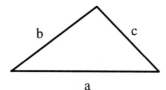

We are assuming that $a = n$. If $b = k$, for k an integer between 1 and n (both inclusive), then c can be $(n-k+1), (n-k+2), \ldots, n$ (note that we must have $a < b + c$, otherwise the figure cannot be a triangle). Thus, if $b = k$, we have k choices for c. This gives a total of

$$1 + 2 + 3 + \cdots + n = \frac{n(n+1)}{2} \quad \text{triangles.}$$

Note, though, that the isosceles triangles for which two of the sides have length n are congruent, so they have been counted twice (namely, for $a = b = n$, $c = k < n$ and for $a = c = n$, $b = k < n$). Since there are $n - 1$ such triangles, the final answer is

$$\frac{n(n+1)}{2} - (n-1) = \frac{n^2 - n + 2}{2} \quad \text{non-congruent triangles.}$$

2.7. To find the proportion of the plane covered in the square packing, just divide the area of the inscribed circle (of diameter 1) by the area of the square of side 1 in which the circle is inscribed. This gives $\pi/4$.

In the case of the hexagon, divide the area of the inscribed circle (of radius $\sqrt{3}/2$) by the area of a hexagon of side 1 in which the circle is inscribed. This gives $\pi/(2\sqrt{3})$.

Note that the second packing is more efficient.

2.9. Adjoining two congruent triangles along a corresponding side, we obtain parallelograms. The plane can always be tiled by parallelograms of any shape (see Figure 3 in the text), so the answer is affirmative.

2.11. False: an equilateral triangle of side d has diameter d, but it cannot be inscribed in a circle of diameter d, since the distance from the center of the triangle to each vertex is $d/\sqrt{3}$, which is greater than the radius of the circle.

2.13. Convexity can be defined as follows: a set is convex if, for any two points p, q in the set, all the points of the form

$$p \cdot t + q \cdot (1-t), \quad 0 \le t \le 1$$

also lie in the set.

Let $p, q \in X + Y$, and let $0 \le t \le 1$. We want to show that $p \cdot t + q \cdot (1-t) \in X + Y$. By definition of $X + Y$, we can write $p = p_X + p_Y$ and $q = q_X + q_Y$, with $p_X, q_X \in X$ and $p_Y, q_Y \in Y$. Since X is convex, the point $p_X \cdot t + q_X \cdot (1-t)$ lies in X, and since Y is convex, the point $p_Y \cdot t + q_Y \cdot (1-t)$ lies in Y. Thus, we have

$$
\begin{aligned}
p \cdot t & + q \cdot (1-t) \\
&= (p_X + p_Y) \cdot t + (q_X + q_Y) \cdot (1-t) \\
&= (p_X \cdot t + q_X \cdot (1-t)) + (p_Y \cdot t + q_Y \cdot (1-t)) \in X + Y
\end{aligned}
$$

Therefore, $X + Y$ is convex.

The only thing that can be said about the diameter is that it is at least $d\sqrt{2}$ and at most $2d$. To show this, use the triangle inequality. These bounds are sharp: taking for example two discs of diameter 1, the sum will be a disc of diameter 2. On the other hand, taking two perpendicular segments of length d, their sum will be a square of side d, which has diameter $d\sqrt{2}$.

Concerning the width, nothing can be said. For example, taking X as a horizontal infinite stripe of diameter d and Y as a vertical infinite stripe of diameter d, $X + Y$ will be the whole plane, which has infinite diameter.

2.15. The area gets multiplied by $2^2 = 4$. To show this think first of the fact that, when we multiply by 2, the sides of any square in the plane doubles, and so its area quadruples. Since squares are the building blocks to measure area (i.e. to find the area of a set we tile it as best as we can with very small squares and then we add the areas of the squares), the area of any set gets multiplied by 4.

Note that the original position of the set does not play any role. When we multiply by 2, if the set is originally far from 0 it will be now twice as far, but its shape will be the original one rescaled by 2.

2.17. For subsets of the line, a set is convex if and only if it contains all the points between two given points, i.e. if it is connected. The sum of two connected sets (here, connected means that it has no 'holes') is clearly connected.

The diameter and the width are the same quantity for subsets of the line. For subsets of the line, the diameter of the sum of two sets is the sum of the diameters of the sets.

2.19. Denote the bigger angle by α and the smaller by β. Then we have $\sin\alpha = 1/\sqrt{5}$, $\cos\alpha = 2/\sqrt{5}$, $\sin\beta = 1/\sqrt{10}$ and $\cos\beta = 3/\sqrt{10}$. This implies

$$\begin{aligned}
\sin(\alpha + \beta) &= \sin\alpha\cos\beta + \sin\beta\cos\alpha \\
&= \frac{1}{\sqrt{5}}\frac{3}{\sqrt{10}} + \frac{2}{\sqrt{5}}\frac{1}{\sqrt{10}} \\
&= \frac{3}{5\sqrt{2}} + \frac{2}{5\sqrt{2}} \\
&= \frac{1}{\sqrt{2}} \\
&= \sin 45°.
\end{aligned}$$

Therefore, $\alpha + \beta = 45°$.

2.21. We can assume that the vertices of the triangle lie in the boundary of the polygon. The perimeter of the polygon is the sum of the lengths of the sectors of the polygon joining each pair of vertices of the triangle. Each of these lengths is no less than the length of the corresponding side of the triangle. Therefore the sum of the lengths of the sectors of the polygon joining each pair of vertices of the triangle is greater than or equal to the sum of the lengths of the corresponding sides of the triangle, which is exactly the perimeter of the triangle.

2.23. Let the vertices of the triangle be denoted by A, B, C. Let us find the set of points N such that $\angle NAB = \angle NBC$. Given an angle θ, let N_θ be a point such that $\angle N_\theta AB = \angle N_\theta BC = \theta$. To find this point, draw a line through A at an angle θ from the segment AB and draw a line through B at an angle θ from the segment BC. These lines are not parallel (if they were, it is easy to see that the angle $\angle ABC$ would be $180°$). The point N_θ is the point of intersection of both lines (note that since N_θ is in the first line,

$N_\theta AB = \theta$ and since N_θ is in the second line, $N_\theta BC = \theta$). This is illustrated in the figure below.

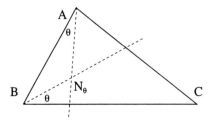

As we change θ, N_θ will describe a convex arc, as in the figure below:

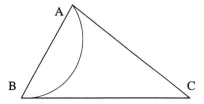

Similarly, the set of points M such that $\angle MBC = \angle MCA$ is a concave arc, as in the following figure:

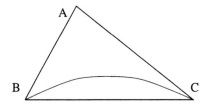

The first arc is tangent to BC, whereas the second is transversal. Since the first arc ends at A and the second ends at C , the arcs must intersect, as in the figure:

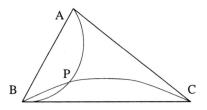

Let us denote the point of intersection by P. Since P is in the first arc, $\angle PAB = \angle PBC$, and since P is in the second arc, $\angle PBC = \angle PCA$. Thus, $\angle PAB = \angle PBC = \angle PCA$, as desired.

2.25. It can be solved using analytic geometry: fix two coordinate axes and write everything explicitly. A nicer way is the following: denote the sides by p, q, r, and let a, b, c be the distances from P to the sides p, q, r respectively. Suppose that the triangle is laying on its side r. Let h be the altitude of the triangle.

Draw a line through P parallel to the side p. We obtain a smaller triangle $T1$, whose altitude is $h - a$. Then draw a line through P parallel to q. We obtain an even smaller triangle $T2$ inside $T1$ whose altitude is the altitude of $T1$ minus b, i.e. $h - a - b$. On the other hand, the top vertex of $T2$ is P, and the base lies on r. Therefore the altitude of $T2$ is equal to the distance from P to r, which is equal to c. Thus we have $h - a - b = c$, which is what we wanted to prove.

2.27. Assume that m is the hypotenuse. Then we must have $m^2 = \ell^2 + 100$, or $m^2 - \ell^2 = 100$. This can be written as $(m+\ell)(m-\ell) = 100$. Denote $m + \ell$ by a and $m - \ell$ by b. Then a and b divide 100 and their product is 100. Also, we have $m = (a + b)/2$ and $\ell = (a - b)/2$, so for m and ℓ to be integers we must have that a and b have the same parity, that is, they are either both odd or both even. Inspecting all the divisors of 100 we find that the only possibilities are $a = b = 10$ and $a = 50$, $b = 2$. This corresponds to $m = 10$, $\ell = 0$, which is the degenerate case, and $m = 26$, $\ell = 24$.

2.29. Assume that one of the axes of symmetry is horizontal. Denote the other axis by ℓ, and denote the angle between the axes by α. If we apply the symmetry along the horizontal axis first, the other axis will move to form an angle $-\alpha$ with the horizontal. This means that the line m that forms an angle $-\alpha$ with the horizontal is also an axis of symmetry. Since there are only two axes of symmetry, it must be that $\ell = m$, which implies $\alpha = 90°$.

2.31. Since the problem can be solved without knowing the radius, r, of the hole, the solution must be independent of r. We have to do a calculation, and we know that the final answer is independent of the value of r. So we might as well choose $r = 0$ (any other r would work, but it would make the computation much harder). In this case, the volume of the portion that remains is the volume of the original ball, and since the length of the hole is 6 inches, the diameter of this ball must be 6 inches. This implies that its volume is 36π. Thus, the volume of the portion that remains is 36π.

2.33. Let $P = (p_1, p_2)$. Let $X = (x, 0)$ be the point of intersection of the line with the x-axis, and let $Y = (0, y)$ be the point of intersection of the line with the y-axis. Finally, denote the point $(p_1, 0)$ by R and the point $(0, p_2)$ by S. All this is depicted in the following figure:

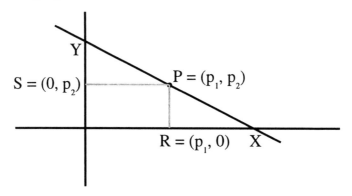

By similarity of the triangles $\triangle YSP$ and $\triangle RXP$, we have

$$\frac{(y - p_2)}{p_2} = \frac{p_1}{(x - p_1)}.$$

This implies

$$y = \frac{p_2 x}{(x - p_1)}.$$

Denote the area of the triangle by $A(x)$. Then we have $A(x) = (xy)/2$. Thus

$$A(x) = \frac{p_2}{2} \cdot \frac{x^2}{(x - p_1)}.$$

We want to find the value of x that gives the triangle with least area. Note that, from the inequality

$$0 \leq (x - 2p_1)^2 = x^2 - 4p_1 \cdot (x - p_1),$$

we obtain

$$4p_1 \leq \frac{x^2}{(x - p_1)},$$

which implies

$$A(x) \leq 2p_1 p_2.$$

But $A(2p_1) = 2p_1 p_2$. Thus, the minimum area is attained when $x = 2p_1$ and $y = 2p_2$.

2.39. Here is a way to cut a torus in 12 pieces with three planar cuts.

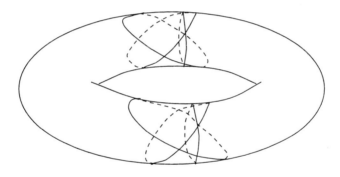

We do not know if this is the maximum number of pieces that one can get with three cuts.

2.41. The length of each of the approximations is exactly 2 (note that, in the nth approximation, we are going up n steps of length $1/n$ each and we are going left n steps of length $1/n$ each, so the total is 2). This suggests that the length of the diagonal is 2, but we know from the Pythagorean theorem that the length is $\sqrt{1^2 + 1^2} = \sqrt{2}$. This seems to be a contradiction. But it is not: the length of the limit of a sequence of sets need not be the limit of the lengths of the sets.

Note that two curves can be very close together but have completely different lengths. For example, look at the following picture. The saw-like grey curve is much longer, yet they are very close.

Chapter 3

Problems Involving Counting

3.1. Let the players be A and B. If player A receives one card, then there are n choices, namely all the ways to choose the card that player A will receive.

If player A receives 2 cards, then we have to count all possible ways to choose 2 cards out of a deck with n cards, i.e. $\binom{n}{2}$.

Continuing in this fashion, we have that if player A receives k cards, then the number of possible ways will be $\binom{n}{k}$.

Therefore, the total number of ways to deal the cards will be

$$\sum_{k=1}^{n-1} \binom{n}{k} = 2(2^{n-1} - 1).$$

This last equality can be proved as follows:

From the text we know that

$$\sum_{k=0}^{n} \binom{n}{k} = 2^n.$$

Therefore we have

$$
\begin{aligned}
\sum_{k=1}^{n-1} \binom{n}{k} &= \sum_{k=0}^{n} \binom{n}{k} - \binom{n}{0} - \binom{n}{n} \\
&= 2^n - 1 - 1 \\
&= 2(2^{n-1} - 1),
\end{aligned}
$$

as desired.

393

3.3. Let us study the parity of the first four numbers of each row. Let o stand for 'odd' and e stand for 'even'. The first four numbers of the third row are $\{1, e, o, e\}$. The first four numbers of the subsequent rows will be as follows:

$$
\begin{array}{ll}
3^{\text{rd}} \text{ row:} & \{1, e, o, e, \ldots\} \\
4^{\text{th}} \text{ row:} & \{1, o, e, o, \ldots\} \\
5^{\text{th}} \text{ row:} & \{1, e, e, e, \ldots\} \\
6^{\text{th}} \text{ row:} & \{1, o, o, e, \ldots\} \\
7^{\text{th}} \text{ row:} & \{1, e, o, e, \ldots\}
\end{array}
$$

$$\vdots \qquad\qquad \vdots$$

After the 7th row, the pattern repeats. Since every row in the pattern above has an even number among the four first numbers and the pattern repeats, we must have that every row has at least one even number among its first four elements.

3.5. The strategy we will use is the following: assuming that the couple has n children, find the probability that they have two sons (s) and one daughter (d). Then find n so that this probability is greater than one-half.

Given that the couple has n children,

$$
\begin{aligned}
\mathbf{Pr}\{2 \text{ s}, 1 \text{ d}\} &= 1 - (\mathbf{Pr}\{\text{less than 2 s}\} + \mathbf{Pr}\{\text{less than 1 d}\}) \\
&= 1 - (\mathbf{Pr}\{0 \text{ b}\} + \mathbf{Pr}\{1 \text{ b}\} + \mathbf{Pr}\{0 \text{ d}\}) \\
&= 1 - \left(\frac{1}{2^n} + \frac{n}{2^n} + \frac{1}{2^n} \right).
\end{aligned}
$$

We want to find the least n such that

$$
1 - \left(\frac{1}{2^n} + \frac{n}{2^n} + \frac{1}{2^n} \right) > \frac{1}{2},
$$

or, reordering,

$$
2^{n-1} > n + 2.
$$

By simple inspection we find that $n = 4$.

3.7. This problem is quite hard, and requires some more advanced notions of probability. We are receiving one card out of a deck of 52 for each purchase of a pack of baseball cards. Let us do a more general case and assume that for each purchase we receive one card out of a deck of n cards, which we will number from 1 to n. Let X_n be the number of purchases made when we complete the whole deck of n cards. We want to find

$$E[X] = 1 \cdot \mathbf{Pr}\{X = 1\} + 2 \cdot \mathbf{Pr}\{X = 2\} + \cdots + m \cdot \mathbf{Pr}\{X = m\} + \cdots.$$

Let us first find the probability that $X_n \geq k$. For $k \leq n$, this probability is always 1. In general, it is quite complicated, but it can be found as follows:

$$\mathbf{Pr}\{X_n \geq k\} = \mathbf{Pr}\{\text{some card is missing after } k - 1 \text{ purchases}\}.$$

Now, the probability that some card is missing is the probability of the union of the events

$$A_i^k = \{\text{card } i \text{ is missing after } k - 1 \text{ purchases}\}, \ 1 \leq i \leq n.$$

The probability of the union of n events can be found using the following formula. The proof of this formula is not hard using induction, and is left as an exercise for the reader. It is best to work out a few easy cases (say $n = 1, 2, 3$) to see that the formula makes sense (see also Exercise 19 in this chapter).

$$\mathbf{Pr}\{A_1^k \cup A_2^k \cup A_3^k \cup \cdots \cup A_n^k\}$$
$$= \sum_{\ell=1}^{n} \mathbf{Pr}\{A_i^k\} - \sum_{i<j} \mathbf{Pr}\{A_i^k \cap A_j^k\} + \sum_{i_1<i_2<i_3} \mathbf{Pr}\{A_{i_1}^k \cap A_{i_2}^k \cap A_{i_3}^k\}$$
$$+ \cdots + (-1)^{d+1} \sum_{i_1<i_2<\cdots<i_d} \mathbf{Pr}\{A_{i_1}^k \cap A_{i_2}^k \cap \cdots \cap A_{i_d}^k\}$$
$$+ \cdots + (-1)^{n+1} \mathbf{Pr}\{A_1^k \cap A_2^k \cap A_3^k \cap \cdots \cap A_n^k\}.$$

Now, $\mathbf{Pr}\{A_i\}$ is the same for every i (the probability that card 1 is missing is the same as the probability that any other card is missing). The probability that card i is missing after $k - 1$ purchases is

$$\left(\frac{n-1}{n}\right)^{k-1}.$$

The probability that two cards are missing (i.e. $\mathbf{Pr}\{A_i^k \cap A_j^k\}$) is also independent of i and j, and equals

$$\left(\frac{n-2}{n}\right)^{k-1}.$$

In general, the probability that d cards are missing, (in other words, $\mathbf{Pr}\{A_{i_1}^k \cap A_{i_2}^k \cap \cdots \cap A_{i_d}^k\}$), is also independent of $i_1, \ldots i_d$, and equals

$$\left(\frac{n-d}{n}\right)^{k-1}.$$

Thus, applying the formula above we obtain

$$\mathbf{Pr}\{X_n \geq k\}$$
$$= \sum_{\ell=1}^{n} \left(\frac{n-1}{n}\right)^{k-1} - \sum_{i<j} \left(\frac{n-2}{n}\right)^{k-1} + \sum_{i_1<i_2<i_3} \left(\frac{n-3}{n}\right)^{k-1}$$
$$+ \cdots + (-1)^{d+1} \sum_{i_1<i_2<\cdots<i_d} \left(\frac{n-d}{n}\right)^{k-1}$$
$$+ \cdots + (-1)^{n+1} \left(\frac{n-n}{n}\right)^{k-1}.$$

The summation in the third line of the equation above has $\binom{n}{d}$ terms. Using this fact and skipping the last term (which is 0), we can rewrite the last expression as

$$\mathbf{Pr}\{X_n \geq k\}$$
$$= \binom{n}{1}\left(\frac{n-1}{n}\right)^{k-1} - \binom{n}{2}\left(\frac{n-2}{n}\right)^{k-1} + \binom{n}{3}\left(\frac{n-3}{n}\right)^{k-1}$$
$$+ \cdots + (-1)^{d+1}\binom{n}{d}\left(\frac{n-d}{n}\right)^{k-1}$$
$$+ \cdots + (-1)^n \binom{n}{n-1}\left(\frac{1}{n}\right)^{k-1}.$$

This can be rewritten in a more compact form as

$$\mathbf{Pr}\{X_n \geq k\} = \sum_{d=1}^{n-1}(-1)^{d+1}\binom{n}{d}\left(\frac{n-d}{n}\right)^{k-1}.$$

Once we have found $\mathbf{Pr}\{X_n \geq k\}$, we could find $\mathbf{Pr}\{X_n = k\}$ and use the formula for $E[X_n]$ above. Instead we will use the following: We have

$$E[X_n] = \sum_{k=1}^{\infty} i \cdot \mathbf{Pr}\{X_n = k\}.$$

Since multiplying by i is the same as adding i times, we can rewrite the last expression as

$$E[X_n] = \sum_{i=k}^{\infty} \sum_{j=1}^{k} \mathbf{Pr}\{X_n = k\}.$$

Reversing the order of summation we obtain

$$E[X_n] = \sum_{j=k}^{\infty} \sum_{k=j}^{\infty} \mathbf{Pr}\{X_n = k\}.$$

But we also have

$$\sum_{k=j}^{\infty} \mathbf{Pr}\{X_n = k\} = \mathbf{Pr}\{X_n \geq j\}.$$

Thus, we obtain the formula

$$E[X_n] = \sum_{j=1}^{\infty} \mathbf{Pr}\{X_n \geq j\}.$$

Therefore, in our case we have (recall that $\mathbf{Pr}\{X \geq k\} = 1$ for $k \leq n$)

$$E[X_n] = \sum_{j=1}^{n} 1 + \sum_{j=n+1}^{\infty} \sum_{d=1}^{n-1} (-1)^{d+1} \binom{n}{d} \left(\frac{n-d}{n}\right)^{j-1}.$$

Simplify the first sum and reverse the order of summation in the second:

$$E[X_n] = n + \sum_{d=1}^{n-1} (-1)^{d+1} \binom{n}{d} \sum_{j=n+1}^{\infty} \left(\frac{n-d}{n}\right)^{j-1}.$$

Using the formula for a geometric series, we get

$$E[X_n] = n + \sum_{d=1}^{n-1} (-1)^{d+1} \binom{n}{d} \frac{n}{d} \left(\frac{n-d}{n} \right)^n .$$

This is actually the final solution. The only thing that remains is to substitute $n = 52$. Calculating this sum by hand is very tedious. Fortunately, we can use a computer to do the job. For $n = 52$ and using Mathematica we obtained $E[X_{52}] = 235.978$.

3.9. If all the points lie in the same half disc, then there is an angle formed by the rays through two of the points that contains the third point, and the measure of this angle is less than or equal to 180°. If we replace the middle point with its antipodal point then the points do not lie in the same half disc any more.

In other words, substituting the middle point with its antipodal gives a function from the set {configurations lying in the same half disc} to the set {configurations not lying in the same half disc}. This function is 3 to 1: each configuration of points not lying in the same half disk has three preimages under our function, as in the picture below:

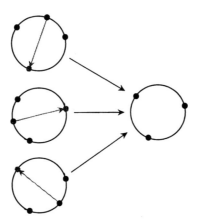

Thus, the sets {configurations lying in the same half disc} and {configurations not lying in the same half disc} are in 3 to 1 correspondence. Thus, the probability that the points do not lie in the same half disk is 1/4.

3.11. Although this problem seems similar to the previous two, it is actually much easier. We are assuming that the square has been divided beforehand, either diagonally, horizontally or in any other way. Then the probability that each of the points lies in a given half square is 1/2. Therefore, the probability that all three points lie in a given half square is

$$\frac{1}{2} \cdot \frac{1}{2} \cdot \frac{1}{2} = \frac{1}{8}.$$

Since there are two half squares, the probability that all three points lie in the same half square is $2 \cdot 1/8 = 1/4$.

3.13. In the previous exercise we only took into account the fact that there was an ordering, not the values of the numbers involved. In this exercise, even though we do not know what the numbers are or how they are sequenced, we do know that there is an ordering, and that is the only thing that matters. Therefore the answer is the same as in the previous exercise.

3.15. *Step 1:* Fill the 8 quart container. Then fill up the 5 quart container using the contents of the 8 quart container. Then 3 quarts remain in the 8 quart container.

Step 2: Empty the 5 quart container and pour the 3 quarts from the 8 quart container into it. Then fill up the 8 quart container again and top-off the 5 quart container using the contents of the 8 quart container. Since the 5 quart container already had 3 quarts of water, 6 quarts still remain in the 8 quart container.

Step 3: Empty the 5 quart container and fill it up using the contents of the 8 quart container again. Since we had 6 quarts in the 8 quart container, only 1 quart remains in the 8 quart container, as desired.

3.17. Proceed as follows:

From 1 to 9	there are	$9 \cdot 1 = 9$ digits.
From 10 to 99	there are	$90 \cdot 2 = 180$ digits.
From 100 to 750	there are	$651 \cdot 3 = 1,953$ digits.
	TOTAL	2,141 digits.

It will require 2,141 digits.

3.19. An easy way to do this kind of problems is by means of a Venn diagram. There is also a formula—which is not hard to prove after looking at a Venn diagram—that reads as follows: If A, B, C are finite sets,

$$|A \cup B \cup C| = |A| + |B| + |C| - |A \cap B| - |B \cap C| - |C \cap A| + |A \cap B \cap C|,$$

where $|\cdot|$ means 'number of elements'. In our case, let A, B and C stand for 'Algebra', 'Biology' and 'Chemistry' respectively. We have

$$\#\{\text{Students who failed any exam}\} = 12 + 5 + 8 - 2 - 6 - 3 + 1 = 15.$$

We can see this in the following Venn diagram:

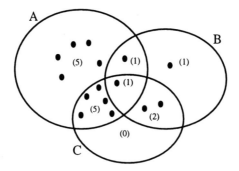

3.21. It is actually true that most people come from larger than average families. This can be proved as follows: let f_i be the number of families with i children, and let c_i be the number of children that come from families of size i. We must have $c_i = if_i$. The average family size is the sum of the number of families times their size divided by the total number of families, i.e.

$$\text{Av}_f = \frac{\displaystyle\sum_{i=1}^{K} if_i}{\displaystyle\sum_{i=1}^{K} f_i},$$

where K the maximum number of children found in any family.

On the other hand, if we pick a person, how big will her family be, on average? This is a different question. We have to add the number of people times the size of each person's family, and then divide by the total number of people, i.e.

$$Av_p = \frac{\sum_{i=1}^{K} ic_i}{\sum_{i=1}^{K} c_i} = \frac{\sum_{i=1}^{K} i^2 f_i}{\sum_{i=1}^{K} if_i}.$$

We will show that $Av_f \leq Av_c$, thus showing that if we pick a person in the street then, on average, she will come from a larger than average family.

We need to show that

$$\frac{\sum_{i=1}^{K} if_i}{\sum_{i=1}^{K} f_i} \leq \frac{\sum_{i=1}^{K} i^2 f_i}{\sum_{i=1}^{K} if_i}$$

or, equivalently,

$$\left(\sum_{i=1}^{K} if_i\right)\left(\sum_{i=1}^{K} if_i\right) \leq \left(\sum_{i=1}^{K} i^2 f_i\right)\left(\sum_{i=1}^{K} f_i\right).$$

Multiplying this out,

$$\sum_{i=1}^{K} ij f_i f_j \leq \sum_{i=1}^{K} i^2 f_i f_j.$$

We can split the sums to obtain

$$\sum_{1 \leq i \leq j \leq K} ij f_i f_j + \sum_{1 \leq j < i \leq K} ij f_i f_j \leq \sum_{1 \leq i \leq j \leq K} i^2 f_i f_j + \sum_{1 \leq j < i \leq K} i^2 f_i f_j.$$

Interchanging i and j in the last summation of both sides (this is just a change of variables), we get

$$\sum_{1 \leq i \leq j \leq K} ij f_i f_j + \sum_{1 \leq i < j \leq K} ji f_j f_i \leq \sum_{1 \leq i \leq j \leq K} i^2 f_i f_j + \sum_{1 \leq i < j \leq K} j^2 f_j f_i.$$

Rearranging, we have

$$\sum_{1\leq i<j\leq K} ij\, f_i f_j + \sum_{1\leq i<j\leq K} j\, i f_j f_i + \sum_{1\leq i\leq K} i^2 f_i^2$$

$$\leq \sum_{1\leq i<j\leq K} i^2 f_i f_j + \sum_{1\leq i<j\leq K} j^2 f_j f_i + \sum_{1\leq i\leq K} i^2 f_i^2.$$

We can subtract $\sum_{1\leq i\leq K} i^2 f_i^2$ from both sides to obtain

$$\sum_{1\leq i<j\leq K} ij\, f_i f_j + \sum_{1\leq i<j\leq K} j\, i f_j f_i \leq \sum_{1\leq i<j\leq K} i^2 f_i f_j + \sum_{1\leq i<j\leq K} j^2 f_j f_i.$$

Now, both terms in the left hand side are equal, and in the right hand side we can factor $f_j f_i$. We obtain

$$\sum_{1\leq i<j\leq K} 2ij\, f_i f_j \leq \sum_{1\leq i<j\leq K} (i^2 + j^2) f_i f_j.$$

Finally, note that since $0 \leq (i - j)^2 = i^2 + j^2 - 2ij$, we have $2ij \leq i^2 + j^2$. Thus, the coefficients of $f_i f_j$ in the left hand side are always less than or equal to the corresponding coefficients in the right hand side. Thus, the inequality is true, proving that most people come from larger than average families.

3.23. In how many ways can we distribute l grapes into k glasses, subject to the given rules? Well, by definition, exactly $\binom{k}{l}$. Thus, if we count the number of subsets with 0 elements, plus the number of subsets with 1 element, plus the number of subsets with 2 elements, ..., plus the number of subsets with k elements, we have the sum

$$\binom{k}{0} + \binom{k}{1} + \binom{k}{2} + \cdots + \binom{k}{k}.$$

By the binomial theorem, this equals 2^k.

3.25. The probability that the other side is also red is the probability that we chose the card with both sides red at the beginning. The probability that we chose the card with both sides red at the beginning given that one of the sides of our card is red is 2/3: there are 2 favorable cases (each of the red faces of the all-red card) and 3 possible cases (the 3 faces we have not seen yet). Thus the probability that the other side is also red is 2/3.

3.27. The number 30^4 can be decomposed as $2^4 3^4 5^4$. Any divisor of 30^4 can be decomposed uniquely as $2^a 3^b 5^c$, with a, b, c nonnegative integers not exceeding 4. Thus the number of divisors is exactly the number of ordered triples (a, b, c), where a, b and c are integers between 0 and 4 inclusive. This number is exactly $5 \cdot 5 \cdot 5 = 125$.

3.29. We just have to count the number of digits used:

From 1 to 9	there are	$9 \cdot 1 = 9$ digits.
From 10 to 99	there are	$90 \cdot 2 = 180$ digits.
From 100 to 599	there are	$500 \cdot 3 = 1,500$ digits.
From 600 to 659	there are	$60 \cdot 3 = 180$ digits.
From 660 to 666	there are	$7 \cdot 3 = 21$ digits.
	TOTAL	1,890 digits.

Therefore, the book has 666 pages.

3.31. The general pattern is

$$1^2 - 2^2 + 3^2 - 4^2 + \cdots + (-1)^{n+1} n^2 = (-1)^{n+1} \cdot (1 + 2 + 3 + \cdots + n).$$

For n even, the left hand side can be written as

$$(1^2 - 2^2) + (3^2 - 4^2) + \cdots + ((n-1)^2 - n^2)$$
$$= (1-2)(1+2) + (3-4)(3+4) + \cdots$$
$$+ ((n-1) - n)((n-1) + n)$$
$$= -(1+2) - (3+4) - \cdots - ((n-1) + n)$$
$$= -(1 + 2 + 3 + \cdots + n), \quad \text{which is the desired formula.}$$

For n odd, the left hand side can be written as

$$(1^2 - 2^2) + (3^2 - 4^2) + \cdots + ((n-2)^2 - (n-1)^2) + n^2$$
$$= (1-2)(1+2) + (3-4)(3+4) + \cdots$$
$$+ ((n-2) - (n-1))((n-2) + (n-1)) + n^2$$

$$= \ -(1+2) - (3+4) - \cdots - ((n-2) + (n-1)) + n^2$$
$$= \ -(1+2+3+\cdots+(n-1)) + 2(1+2+3+\cdots n) - n$$
$$= \ 1+2+3+\cdots n, \qquad \text{which is the desired formula.}$$

Note that we have used the fact that, using the formula stated in the solution to the previous exercise, we have

$$2\,(1+2+3+\cdots n) - n \ = \ 2 \cdot \frac{(n+1)\,n}{2} - n$$
$$= \ n^2 + n - n$$
$$= \ n^2.$$

3.33. The pattern is

$$(n^2-n+1)+(n^2-n+3)+(n^2-n+5)+\cdots+(n^2-n+(2n-1)) = n^3.$$

Note that the left hand side has n summands. Thus it can be written as

$$n \cdot n^2 - n \cdot n + (1 + 3 + 5 + \cdots + 2n - 1).$$

Now, $1 + 3 + 5 + \cdots + 2n - 1$ equals

$$1 + 3 + 5 + \cdots + 2n - 1$$
$$= \ (2 \cdot 1 - 1) + (2 \cdot 2 - 1) + (2 \cdot 3 - 1) + \cdots + (2 \cdot n - 1)$$
$$= \ 2\,(1+2+3+\cdots+n) - \underbrace{(1+1+1+\cdots+1)}_{n\text{-summands}}$$
$$= \ 2 \cdot \frac{n^2+n}{2} - n$$
$$= \ n^2.$$

Thus we have that the expression above equals:

$$n \cdot n^2 - n \cdot n + (1 + 3 + 5 + \cdots + 2n - 1) = n^3 + n^2 - n^2 = n^3,$$

which is the desired result.

3.35. The probability that he got TOLEDO correct can be found as follows: the probability that T is correct is 1/20, since there are 10 letters and 2 positions for each letter. The probability that O is correct when T is correct is 4/9, since 9 letters remain, 4 are O's, and the position of the O does not matter. The probability that L is correct when T and O are correct is 1/16 (8 letters remain and L has 2 positions). Continuing this way we find:

$$\mathbf{Pr}\{\text{TOLEDO correct}\} = \frac{1}{20} \cdot \frac{4}{9} \cdot \frac{1}{16} \cdot \frac{1}{14} \cdot \frac{1}{12} \cdot \frac{3}{5}$$

$$= \frac{1}{201600}$$

$$\approx 4.96032 \cdot 10^{-6}$$

Proceeding in the same manner, we find that

$$\mathbf{Pr}\{\text{OHIO correct}\} = \frac{4}{10} \cdot \frac{1}{9} \cdot \frac{1}{8} \cdot \frac{3}{7}$$

$$= \frac{1}{420}$$

$$\approx 2.38095 \cdot 10^{-3}$$

The probability that he got both words correct is the probability that he got TOLEDO correct times the probability that he got OHIO correct given that he got TOLEDO correct. Proceeding as before we find

$$\mathbf{Pr}\{\text{both correct}\} = \frac{1}{201600} \cdot \frac{2}{4} \cdot \frac{1}{3} \cdot \frac{1}{2}$$

$$= \frac{1}{2419200}$$

$$\approx 4.1336 \cdot 10^{-7}$$

3.37. First note that, for the two teams that played the first game, the number of losses equals the number of games—out of the 11—that they did not play. This is because they will sit out in a game if and only if they lost the previous one, and one of them won the last one against New York. For the New York team, this rule also holds, with the exception of the first game, in which New York sat out without having lost the previous game; but this is compensated by the fact that they lost the last game (i.e. we can think, as an abstraction, that they did not play the first game because they lost the last one). Therefore, for every team, the number of lost games equals the number of games they missed.

On the other hand, for each team we have

$$\#\{\text{games won}\} + \#\{\text{games lost}\} + \#\{\text{games missed}\}$$
$$= \#\{\text{total number of games}\}$$
$$= 11$$

Therefore we must have that, for each team

$$\#\{\text{games won}\} + 2 \cdot \#\{\text{games lost}\} = 11.$$

This means that each team won an odd number of games.

Let w_1, w_2, w_3 denote the number of games won by each team. Since, by hypothesis, they all won a different number of games, it must be that the w_i's are all different numbers. Thus the w_i's must be odd numbers, all different and must add up to 11 (since every game had a winner). By inspection, we see that the only possibility is 1,3,7. Also, by the last equation, we also know that the team that won 7 games lost 2, the team that won 3 games lost 4 and the team that won 1 game lost 5.

Note that this does not specify which team won 1,3 or 7 games. In fact, there are valid configurations in which the New York team won 1,3 or 7 games respectively, so this information cannot be inferred from the data given in the exercise.

3.39. The probability of getting a 12 when rolling two dice twenty-four times is

$$1 - \mathbf{Pr}\{\text{not getting a 12 in twenty-four rolls}\}$$
$$= 1 - \left(\frac{35}{36}\right)^{24}$$

$$= 1 - \left(\frac{5}{6}\right)^4 \cdot \left(\frac{7}{6}\right)^{24} \cdot \left(\frac{5}{6}\right)^{20}$$

$$= 1 - 0.508596$$

$$= 0.491404$$

$$< 0.5.$$

Chevalier de Méré was betting even money even though the game was slightly unfavorable for him. In fact, the payoff was only 98.2808 francs for every 100 francs he bet.

3.41. For each toss, the number of possible outcomes is $2^5 = 32$. The number of outcomes that settle the game can be counted as follows: If the game is settled, that means that one person got a tail when all the others had heads or vice versa. Therefore, each person wins in 2 out of the 32 possible outcomes. Thus, the number of outcomes that settle the game is $2 \cdot 5 = 10$. Thus, the probability of having the game settled in the first toss is $5/16$. The probability of having it settled in the second toss is the probability that nobody won in the first toss times the probability that someone won in the second toss. This is, we have

$$\mathbf{Pr}\{\text{game settled in second toss}\} = \left(1 - \frac{5}{16}\right) \cdot \frac{5}{16} = \frac{55}{256}.$$

3.43. Let us follow the scheme given in PROBLEM 3.3.3. Let

$$F(x) = a_0 + a_1 x^1 + a_2 x^2 + a_3 x^3 + a_4 x^4 \cdots.$$

Notice that

$$3xF(x) = 3a_0 x + 3a_1 x^2 + 3a_2 x^3 + 3a_3 x^4 + 3a_4 x^5 \cdots,$$

and

$$x^2 F(x) = a_0 x^2 + a_1 x^3 + a_2 x^4 + a_3 x^5 + a_4 x^6 \cdots.$$

Grouping like powers of x, we obtain

$$F(x) - 3xF(x) + x^2 F(x)$$
$$= a_0 + (a_1 - 3a_0)x + (a_2 - 3a_1 + a_0)x^2$$
$$\quad + (a_3 - 3a_2 + a_1)x^3 + (a_4 - 3a_3 + a_2)x^4 + \cdots.$$

Now, since $a_j - a_{j-1} + a_{j-2} = 0$ for all $j \geq 2$, the expression above simplifies to

$$F(x) - 3xF(x) + x^2 F(x) = a_0 + (a_1 - 3a_0)x.$$

Since $a_0 = 2$ and $a_1 = 1$, we have

$$F(x)(1 - 3x + x^2) = 2 - 5x,$$

or

$$F(x) = \frac{2 - 5x}{1 - 3x + x^2}.$$

Manipulating the last expression, we find

$$F(x) = \left(1 - \frac{2}{\sqrt{5}}\right)\left[\frac{1}{1 - \frac{2}{3 - \sqrt{5}}x}\right] + \left(1 + \frac{2}{\sqrt{5}}\right)\left[\frac{1}{1 - \frac{2}{3 + \sqrt{5}}x}\right].$$

This can be written as

$$F(x) = \left(1 - \frac{2}{\sqrt{5}}\right)\sum_{j=0}^{\infty}\left(\frac{2}{3 - \sqrt{5}}x\right)^j + \left(1 + \frac{2}{\sqrt{5}}\right)\sum_{j=0}^{\infty}\left(\frac{2}{3 + \sqrt{5}}x\right)^j.$$

Therefore, the coefficient of x^j in the last expression is

$$\left(1 - \frac{2}{\sqrt{5}}\right)\left(\frac{2}{3 - \sqrt{5}}\right)^j + \left(1 + \frac{2}{\sqrt{5}}\right)\left(\frac{2}{3 + \sqrt{5}}\right)^j.$$

Since, on the other hand,

$$F(x) = \sum_{j=1}^{\infty} a_j x^j,$$

we must have

$$a_j = \left(1 - \frac{2}{\sqrt{5}}\right)\left(\frac{2}{3 - \sqrt{5}}\right)^j + \left(1 + \frac{2}{\sqrt{5}}\right)\left(\frac{2}{3 + \sqrt{5}}\right)^j.$$

3.45. Proceed as in the two previous exercises. The solution is

$$a_j = 1 - 2^j.$$

3.47. Proceeding as in the previous exercise, the desired probability is

$$\frac{\binom{12}{1}\binom{40}{k-1}}{\binom{52}{k}}.$$

Note that, when $k > 40$, this probability is 1 (by the pigeonhole principle, for example).

3.49. We will assume that each cow has probability $1/500$ of having the disease, *independent of the fact that other cows may or may not have the disease.* Thus, the probability that some cow has the disease in a randomly selected group of 100 is $1/5$.

For 100 cows, the expected number is

$$1 \cdot \mathbf{Pr}\{\text{all clean in } 100\} + 101 \cdot \mathbf{Pr}\{\text{some infected in } 100\}$$
$$= 1 \cdot \frac{4}{5} + 101 \cdot \frac{1}{5}$$
$$= \frac{105}{5}$$
$$= 21.$$

Thus, the expected number of tests for a total population of 5,000 cattle is $50 \cdot 21 = 1,050$.

3.53. We will find the probability that the other has a pair or better (i.e. a pair, two-pairs, three of a kind, full house or poker) both when you have a pair and when all your cards are different.

Suppose that all your cards are different. Note that it does not matter which cards you have, as soon as they are all different, so we can assume that your cards are 1,2,3,4,5 of hearts (here, 1 stands for an ace). We want to find the probability that the other has a pair or better. Note that

$$\mathbf{Pr}\{\text{pair or better}\} = 1 - \mathbf{Pr}\{\text{all 5 cards different}\},$$

so let us instead find the probability that all her cards are different. The number of possible hands that she can have is $\binom{47}{5}$. To find how many of these hands contain no pair, we have to consider several cases:

If all her cards are in the set $\{1, 2, 3, 4, 5\}$, then there are 3^5 different hands with no pair (since there are 3 choices for 1, 3 for 2, etc).

If exactly four of her cards are in the set $\{1, 2, 3, 4, 5\}$, there are $\binom{5}{4} 3^4 \binom{8}{1} 4^1$ different hands with no pair. This is because there are $\binom{5}{4}$ ways of choosing 4 numbers among $\{1, 2, 3, 4, 5\}$ and 3 suits per number, and $\binom{7}{1}$ ways of choosing 1 number among $\{6, 7, 8, 9, 10, J, Q, K\}$ and 4 suits per number.

If exactly three of her cards are in the set $\{1, 2, 3, 4, 5\}$, there are $\binom{5}{3} 3^3 \binom{8}{2} 4^2$ different hands with no pair. The explanation is the same as above.

If exactly two of her cards are in the set $\{1, 2, 3, 4, 5\}$, there are $\binom{5}{2} 3^2 \binom{8}{3} 4^3$ different hands with no pair.

If exactly one of her cards is in the set $\{1, 2, 3, 4, 5\}$, there are $\binom{5}{1} 3^1 \binom{8}{4} 4^4$ different hands with no pair.

Finally, if none of her cards are in the set $\{1, 2, 3, 4, 5\}$, there are $\binom{8}{5} 4^5$ different hands with no pair.

Thus, the probability that she has a pair or better when all your cards are different is

$$1 - \frac{1}{\binom{47}{5}} \left(3^5 + \binom{5}{4} 3^4 \binom{8}{1} 4^1 + \binom{5}{3} 3^3 \binom{8}{2} 4^2 + \binom{5}{2} 3^2 \binom{8}{3} 4^3 \right.$$

$$\left. + \binom{5}{1} 3^1 \binom{8}{4} 4^4 + \binom{8}{5} 4^5 \right).$$

Now let us find the probability that all her cards are different when you have a pair. As before, we can assume that your cards are, for example, 1 of spades and 1,2,3 and 4 of hearts. There are again several cases. In each case, the number of hands is found using the same ideas as before.

If she has a 1 and exactly 3 cards in the set $\{2, 3, 4\}$, there are $2 \cdot 3^3 \cdot \binom{14}{1} 4^1$ hands with no pair (we have 2 choices of 1, 3 choices for each card in $\{2, 3, 4\}$, $\binom{14}{1} 4^1$ choices of number in $\{5, 6, 7, 8, 9, 10, J, Q, K\}$ and 4 choices of suit in this set.

If she has a 1 and exactly 2 cards in the set $\{2, 3, 4\}$, there are $2 \cdot \binom{3}{2} 3^2 \cdot \binom{14}{2} 4^2$ hands with no pair. The explanation of this is as above.

If she has a 1 and exactly 1 card in the set $\{2, 3, 4\}$, there are $2 \cdot \binom{3}{1} 3^1 \cdot \binom{14}{3} 4^3$ hands with no pair.

If she has a 1 and no cards in the set $\{2, 3, 4\}$, there are $2 \cdot \binom{14}{4} 4^4$ hands with no pair.

Now, if she has no aces, we proceed similarly:

No aces and exactly 3 cards in the set $\{2, 3, 4\}$: $\binom{3}{3} 3^3 \cdot \binom{14}{2} 4^2$ hands.

No aces and exactly 2 cards in the set $\{2, 3, 4\}$: $\binom{3}{2} 3^2 \cdot \binom{14}{3} 4^3$ hands.

No aces and exactly 1 card in the set $\{2, 3, 4\}$: $\binom{3}{1} 3^1 \cdot \binom{14}{4} 4^4$ hands.

No aces and no cards in the set $\{2, 3, 4\}$: $\binom{14}{5} 4^5$ hands.

This gives that the probability that she has a pair or better when you have a pair is

$$1 - \frac{1}{\binom{47}{52}} \left(2 \cdot 3^3 \cdot \binom{9}{1} 4^1 + 2 \cdot \binom{3}{2} 3^2 \cdot \binom{9}{2} 4^2 + 2 \cdot \binom{3}{1} 3^1 \cdot \binom{9}{3} 4^3 \right.$$
$$+ 2 \cdot \binom{9}{4} 4^4 + \binom{3}{3} 3^3 \cdot \binom{9}{2} 4^2 + \binom{3}{2} 3^2 \cdot \binom{9}{3} 4^3$$
$$\left. + \binom{3}{1} 3^1 \cdot \binom{9}{4} 4^4 + \binom{9}{5} 4^5 \right).$$

Calculating these quantities, we find that the probability that the other has a pair or better when you have no pair is approximately 0.489636, and the probability that the other has a pair or better when you have a pair is approximately 0.495182. Thus, the second one is slightly higher.

Chapter 4

Problems of Logic

4.1.   a) We start with E. The addition of E and O has yielded O. Hence, either $E = 0$, and nothing has been carried from the previous column, or $E = 9$, and there has to be a carry from the addition of N and R. Let us assume that the first case, $E = 0$, is true. This forces A to be 5 (How else can we get zero from $A + A$ in the fourth column?). Now we have

$$
\begin{array}{c}
\;\;1 \\
\;\;\text{D O N 5 L D} \\
+\;\;\text{G 0 R 5 L D} \\
\hline
\;\;\text{R O B 0 R T}
\end{array}
$$

Since we cannot have carrying from $N + R$, and $5 + 5 = 10$ forces a carry it follows that $N + R$ must be at most 8. In particular, since zero has been used and hence N has to be at least 1, we have that R is 7 or less. On the other hand, $D + G = R$, so R has to be at least 3. Now R cannot be 3, because then one of the pair D or G has to be 1 (and the other 2), and at the same time since $L + L$ produces 3 in the fifth column, L has to be 1 too.

If $R = 4$, then L has to be 2, and since $D + G = R = 4$, then one of the pair, D or G has to be 1 and the other 3. So by now all numbers from 0 to 5 are taken. This makes N at least 6 which means $N + R$ is at least 10, and we will have

to have a carry from this column. But that contradicts the
$0 + O = O$ in the next column. So R cannot be 4.

Since 5 is already taken, this leaves us with 6 and 7 for R.
Let us try $R = 6$. This forces L to be 3, and also means
that $D + D$ in the first column cannot produce a carry, so
D is 4 or less. At the same time, N cannot be more than
2, otherwise $N + R + 1$ forces an unwanted carry. It follows
that D is not 1, because then $T = 2$, and the next choice
for N would be too large. We cannot allow $D = 2$ either,
because then G and T both have to be 4. So if $R = 6$, D
has to be 4. Let us see what we have

$$
\begin{array}{r}
1 \\
\text{D O N 5 3 4} \\
+ \text{G 0 R 5 3 4} \\
\hline
\text{R O B 0 6 T}
\end{array}
$$

Next, we have $T = 8$ and $G = 2$. Now N has to be 1; but
this cannot be, because then B would have to be 8, and 8
has already been taken.

The last choice for R is 7. Assuming this, N can only be 1.
Furthermore, $L = 3$ and there has to be a carry from $D + D$,
so that $L + L$ yields 7. Our display reads

$$
\begin{array}{r}
1 \quad 1 \\
\text{D O 1 5 3 D} \\
+ \text{G 0 7 5 3 D} \\
\hline
\text{7 O B 0 7 T}
\end{array}
$$

Now D is greater than 5, since otherwise we will not have a
carry from $D + D$. At the same time, since $D + G = R = 7$,
D is less than 7. That leaves us with only 6 for D. But if
$D = 6$ then G must be 1, and 1 is already taken.

We have run out of options for R, so we cannot proceed.
The only thing we can do at the moment is to go back and
change $E = 0$ to $E = 9$. This makes $A = 4$, and forces a

carry from $L + L$. We have

```
    1 1   1
    D O N 4 L D
  + G 9 R 4 L D
  ─────────────
    R O B 9 R T
```

Since $1 + D + G = R$, and none of D or G could be zero, R is at least 4. Now R cannot be 4, because $A = 4$. So R must be 5 or greater. Let us assume that $R = 5$. Then L would have to be 7, and we would have to have a carry from $D + D$. This makes D greater than 5 which cannot be, because $1 + D + G = R = 5$. Likewise, if $R = 7$ (or any other odd number), then D has to be greater than 5. But this time $1 + D + G = R$, forcing D to be 5. Then G has to be 1, and L has to be 8. And we have

```
    1 1   1
    5 O N 4 8 5
  + 1 9 7 4 8 5
  ─────────────
    7 O B 9 7 T
```

Clearly T must be zero. The only numbers left are 2, 3 and 6. With a little experimenting, we see that $N = 6$, $B = 3$ and $O = 2$. So the puzzle is solved as

```
    5 2 6 4 8 5
  + 1 9 7 4 8 5
  ─────────────
    7 2 3 9 7 0
```

We leave it to the reader to check that $R = 6$ or 8 do not yield any additional solutions.

c) The T in $TWELVE$ arises from carrying and since

$$SEVEN + EIGHT < 1000000 + 1000000 = 2000000,$$

T must be 1. Furthermore, notice that in the third column from the left, $E + I$ yields E. Hence I is either zero or 9. Let us first assume that $I = 0$.

In the last column (counting from the left), $N + T = N + 1$ yields E. Since E cannot be zero, we cannot have a carry from the right, and we must have $N + 1 = E$. We have

$$\begin{array}{c}
\text{S \ E V E N} \\
+ \ \text{E \ 0 \ G \ H \ 1} \\
\hline
\text{1 \ W E L \ V E}
\end{array}$$

We see that E has occurred five times in the above addition. Hence, knowing E would give a lot of information. So it is worthwhile to try different values for E.

Since $N + 1 = E$, and N is at least 2, we start with $E = 3$. Then

$$\begin{array}{c}
\text{S \ 3 V 3 \ 2} \\
+ \ \text{3 \ \ 0 G H \ 1} \\
\hline
\text{1 \ W 3 L \ V 3}
\end{array}$$

Now S has to be 7, 8 or 9, so that $S+3$ in the second column forces a carry. This implies that $W = 0, 1$ or 2. But all of these numbers are already taken. This means that we have to try another number for E. If $E = 4$, we have

$$\begin{array}{c}
\text{S \ 4 V 4 \ 3} \\
+ \ \text{4 \ \ 0 G H \ 1} \\
\hline
\text{1 \ W 4 L \ V 4}
\end{array}$$

Obviously S has to be at least 6 to force a carrying operation. On the other hand, S cannot be 6, 7 or 9 (otherwise $W = 0, 1$ or 3, and all these are already taken). This forces S to be 8 and W to be 2. Now, since all the numbers from 0 to 4 have been taken, $V + G$ has to be at least 11. But we cannot have a carry from this column. So, assuming $E = 4$ leads to contradiction.

The next natural choice is $E = 5$. Substituting this we get

$$\begin{array}{c}
\text{S \ 5 V 5 \ 4} \\
+ \ \text{5 \ \ 0 G H \ 1} \\
\hline
\text{1 \ W 5 L \ V 5}
\end{array}$$

The possible values for S are 7 and 8. If $S = 7$, then $W = 2$. Since $V + G$ cannot produce a carry, one of V or G has to be less than 5. The same is true for V and H (why?). Since there is only one such number left, namely 3, $V = 3$. Then $H = 8$, and G has to be 6. But we are in trouble here, because $3 + 6$ with a carry yields 0 and a carry. We have a contradiction so we proceed to the next choice for S.

If $S = 8$, we get $W = 3$. Similar reasoning as in the previous paragraph implies that $V = 2$, $H = 7$ and $G = 6$. Then $L = 9$, and the puzzle is solved as

$$
\begin{array}{r}
8\ 5\ 2\ 5\ 4 \\
+\ 5\ 0\ 6\ 7\ 1 \\
\hline
1\ 3\ 5\ 9\ 2\ 5
\end{array}
$$

Going back to the beginning of the solution, we see that we have not explored the possibility that $I = 9$. As a matter of fact, this gives us another solution as follows:

$$
\begin{array}{r}
6\ 3\ 7\ 3\ 2 \\
+3\ 9\ 8\ 4\ 1 \\
\hline
1\ 0\ 3\ 5\ 7\ 3
\end{array}
$$

We leave the details to the reader.

e) This puzzle has many solutions. Among them are

$$
\begin{array}{r}
3\ 4\ 2 \\
+\ 1\ 3\ 5\ 0 \\
\hline
1\ 6\ 9\ 2
\end{array}
$$

and
$$
\begin{array}{r}
4\ 6\ 2 \\
+\ 8\ 4\ 5\ 0 \\
\hline
8\ 9\ 1\ 2
\end{array}
$$

g) There are many solutions, such as

$$
\begin{array}{r}
1\ 7\ 3 \\
+\ 2\ 9\ 5 \\
\hline
4\ 6\ 8
\end{array}
$$

and

$$
\begin{array}{r}
2\ 8\ 9 \\
+\ 4\ 6\ 1 \\
\hline
7\ 5\ 0
\end{array}
$$

i) By trial and error one gets these as possible solutions to the puzzle

$$
\begin{aligned}
63 \times 154 &= 9702 \\
54 \times 168 &= 9072 \\
59 \times 136 &= 8024 \\
26 \times 345 &= 8970
\end{aligned}
$$

4.3. In the Gregorian Calendar, there are 52 weeks and 1 day in a normal year. Leap years have 1 extra day, February 29th. Hence, if year x starts on a Saturday, year $x + 1$ will start on a Sunday if x is a normal year; otherwise it will start on Monday.

Recall that all years which are divisible by 4 are leap years, except the years which are divisible by 100, in which case they are leap years only if they are divisible by 400. So year 2100 is not a leap year, whereas year 2000 is.

On the other hand, a period of 400 years has exactly 20871 weeks (refer to Exercise 12). Thus years x and $x + 400$ start with the same day of the week, no matter which year x is. This implies that to know the relative frequencies by which New Year's Day falls in different days of the week, it is enough to know these frequencies only in a period of 400 years.

It would be a terribly boring and tedious job if we were to sit down and write 400 consecutive years and their corresponding New Year's Days. Fortunately, there are steps that we can take to make the job easier.

First it is obvious that each period of 400 years has one and only one year which is divisible by 400. If it were not for this year, we could divide the interval of 400 years into 4 subintervals of 100 years, and then find how many times each particular day becomes New Year's Day in the first 100 year. Then since all the other 3 subintervals would have had the same pattern, except that each starts on a different day, by renaming the days of the week we could find the number of times each day becomes New Year's Day in the other subintervals. Finally by adding the figures we could answer the question.

We can do this if we choose the period so that the "troubling" year is at the end of one of the subintervals, preferably at the end of the interval itself. For example, the interval from 2001 to 2400 will do.

Before starting to count, let us refer to each day of the week by numbers $1, 2, \ldots, 7$, assuming that the year 2001 starts with day 1. We will give the appropriate names at the end.

To make counting even easier, we notice that in each interval of 28 years which does not include the years which are divisible by 100, New Year's Day fall on each day of the week exactly 4 times. We leave it to the reader to either prove this or convince himself/herself by counting. Thus by the year 2084 each day will have been New year's day exactly for $12 = 3 \times 4$ times. We only have to include the last sixteen years which we do simply by counting. Knowing that the years 2001 and 2085 start on the same day we have

$$1, 2, 3, 4, 6, 7, 1, 2, 4, 5, 6, 7, 2, 3, 4, 5$$

as New Year's Days for the last 16 years. Notice that the next period of one-hundred years will start with day 6.

We summarize all the results in the following table.

n	1	2	3	4	5	6	7
$A_1(n)$	14	15	14	15	14	14	14

Here $A_i(n)$ denotes the number of times New Year's Day falls on day n during the ith subinterval.

As we mentioned before, the next hundred years starts with day 6. Hence, by relabeling the above table, we get

n	6	7	1	2	3	4	5
$A_2(n)$	14	15	14	15	14	14	14

Similarly we get the following tables.

n	4	5	6	7	1	2	3
$A_3(n)$	14	15	14	15	14	14	14

n	2	3	4	5	6	7	1
$A_4(n)$	14	15	14	15	14	14	14

Adding the corresponding figures for each day we get Table 4.1, in which $A(n)$ refers to the number of times day n will be New Year's Day in the period 2001 to 2400. Now it only remains to give appropriate name to each of the numbers. This can be done easily by checking a calendar to see that the year 2001 starts on a Monday, so in Table 4.1 Saturday is day 6, and Sunday is day 7. Thus, New Year's Day falls more often on Sunday than on Saturday.

n	1	2	3	4	5	6	7
$A(n)$	56	58	57	57	57	56	58

Table 4.1

4.5. In her first move, the first player should place the center of the poker chip at the center of the table. After that, each time the second player makes a move, the first player should place her chip in exactly the symmetric position with respect to the center of the table. This way each time that the first player completes her move, the position of the poker chips on the table are symmetric with respect to the center. Hence, if the second player has a move, the first player will also have a move. So she has to be the player who puts the last chip.

4.7. Theodore's first and last statements are either both false or both true. Since each student has said exactly one false statement, both of these must be true. So Theodore is not the culprit.

Now we examine David's statements. In his third statement, he claims that Theodore has stolen the purse. We know that this is false. So we know that his other two statements are true, including the statement claiming that he, David, was not acquainted with Margaret before the beginning of this school year. From this we conclude that Margaret is lying when she says that David has known her for many years. So she is telling the truth in her other two statements, including when she says that Judy has taken the purse.

4.9. It follows from the first statement that Nod and Schmotzky have different mothers, so they cannot be the same person. Naturally, Nod's first name is not Schmotzky. On the other hand, Blinken and Schmotzky are different people by the fourth statement. So Schmotzky's last name must be Winken. He also must be 12 years old, because he began first grade when he was 7, and now he is beginning sixth grade.

From the last statement, we cannot conclude that Blinken and Plotzky are different people. And the assumption that Plotzky's last name is Blinken is consistent with all the other statements. However, with this assumption we do not have enough information to find Blotzky Nod's age. So this problem is solvable only if Plotzky and Blinken are different people. Then the three boy scouts are as follows: Schmotzky Winken 12, Blotzky Nod 13 and Plotzky Blinken 13.

4.11. The question is how many times we can switch the minute and the hour hands and still get a valid time. For example, if the clock shows 1 o'clock, after switching the hands, the hour hand will be exactly on 12, and the minute hand will be on 1, which is not a valid time because the hour hand would have to be a little past the top when the minute hand is past the top.

Now suppose h is the time. It also coincides with the position of the hour hand in the clock (we make the convention that 12:00

is the hour zero.) Also let L denote the position of the minute hand. Then

$$h = k + \frac{L}{12},$$

where $k = 0, 1, \ldots, 11$. If we switch the hands, and the clock still shows a valid time, then the following must be true too.

$$L = k' + \frac{h}{12},$$

where $k' = 0, 1, \ldots, 11$. Eliminating L between the above two equations we get

$$h = \frac{144k + 12k'}{143}.$$

This gives 12×12 combinations. We have to take into the account that the beginning of the cycle, corresponding to $k = k' = 0$, and the end of the cycle, corresponding to $k = k' = 11$, are actually both the same time, which is 12 o'clock. Hence as time passes the clock would show 143 valid times.

We suggest to the dubious reader to make a table of h values for all the 144 combinations of k and k', to see that the only repeated values are for $k = k' = 0$ and $k = k' = 11$. We believe that after computing the first two rows and the first two columns he or she will be convinced.

4.13. It is possible to cover the whole board in 64 moves. To find a way to do so, we make an ordinary chess board of 64 cells. We move the knight on the board till there are no more moves. We label the remaining squares by $a, b, c, \ldots$. Then we try to add them to the route. We illustrate this through one example. Suppose that we have the following route.

42	21	54	9	40	19	52	7
55	10	41	20	53	8	39	18
22	43	24	63	30	59	6	51
11	56	31	60	27	62	17	38
32	23	44	25	58	29	50	5
45	12	57	28	61	26	37	16
a	33	2	47	14	35	4	49
1	46	13	34	3	48	15	36

We have covered everything except square a. Notice that a commands the square 57, and 63 commands the square 56. So if we change the sequence to $1, \ldots 56, 63, \ldots 57$, we can add a to the end of the route. After renumbering we have

42	21	54	9	40	19	52	7
55	10	41	20	53	8	39	18
22	43	24	57	30	61	6	51
11	56	31	60	27	58	17	38
32	23	44	25	62	29	50	5
45	12	63	28	59	26	37	16
64	33	2	47	14	35	4	49
1	46	13	34	3	48	15	36

Sometimes one might need to change the sequence a few times before one can add any new cell to the route. As an exercise, the reader can try to make the above path re-entrant (i.e. the knight finishes in the same square that it started.). For further reading on the subject see "Mathematical Recreations and Essays" by W. W. Rouse Ball.

4.15. Simple counting shows that there are 49 ways of forming 50 cents using quarters, dimes, nickels, and pennies. Here we do the counting methodically.

Let $N_i(k)$, $i = 1, 5, 10, 25$, denote the number of ways that one can make k cents, using coins of value less than or equal to i. Here we want to find $N_{25}(50)$. Obviously, $N_1(k) = 1$, and $N_5(5k) = k + 1$.

In order to calculate $N_{25}(50)$, we break it into to three subproblems. First, we may not use any quarters, in which case there are $N_{10}(50)$ ways of forming 50 cents. Or we may use one quarter and make the other 25 cents using dimes, nickels and pennies. So the number in this case is $N_{10}(25)$. Finally one may use two quarters, and of course there is only one way of forming 50 cents using two quarters. Now everything is covered. Hence,

$$N_{25}(50) = N_{10}(50) + N_{10}(25) + 1 \tag{4.1}$$

Now we have to calculate $N_{10}(50)$ and $N_{10}(25)$. Similarly, to make 50 cents using dimes, nickels, and pennies, we may use no dimes, one dime, two dimes, etc. So

$$
\begin{aligned}
N_{10}(50) &= N_5(50) + N_5(40) + \cdots + N_5 + 1 \\
&= 11 + 9 + 7 + 5 + 3 + 1 \\
&= 36
\end{aligned}
$$

and,

$$
\begin{aligned}
N_{10}(25) &= N_5(25) + N_5(15) + N_5(5) \\
&= 6 + 4 + 2 \\
&= 12.
\end{aligned}
$$

Substituting these into (4.1) we get

$$N_{25}(50) = 36 + 12 + 1 = 49.$$

In this way we can calculate $N_{25}(k)$ for any number of dollars. For example,

$$N_{25}(100) = N_{10}(100) + N_{10}(75) + N_{10}(50) + N_{10}(25) + 1$$

In the above, we already know the last three terms. So we only have to find the first two, which is done similarly. Next we can find $N_{25}(125)$ and etc.

It is possible to calculate a formula for $N_{25}(50k)$. In fact

$$N_{25}(50k) = \frac{100k^3 + 135k^2 + 53k + 6}{6}.$$

Since the process of calculating the above formula is rather tedious, we skip it. But it is worthwhile to mention that once we have the formula, we can actually prove it by induction. First we check the formula for $k = 1$ (since we have just found $N_{25}(50)$ it is easy to check that the formula is correct in this case). Then we prove that if it is valid for k, then it must be valid for $k + 1$ as well. In this manner we cover all the integers. [The relation $N_{25}(50(k+1)) = N_{10}(50(k+1)) + N_{10}(50k+25) + N_{25}(50k)$ will be helpful in the induction step.]

4.17. The following table is useful.

$$
\begin{array}{rcll}
72 & = & 1 \cdot 1 \cdot 72 & 1 + 1 + 72 = 74 \\
72 & = & 1 \cdot 2 \cdot 36 & 1 + 2 + 36 = 39 \\
72 & = & 1 \cdot 3 \cdot 24 & 1 + 3 + 24 = 28 \\
72 & = & 1 \cdot 4 \cdot 18 & 1 + 4 + 18 = 23 \\
72 & = & 1 \cdot 6 \cdot 12 & 1 + 6 + 12 = 19 \\
72 & = & 1 \cdot 8 \cdot 9 & 1 + 8 + 9 = 18 \\
72 & = & 2 \cdot 2 \cdot 18 & 2 + 2 + 18 = 22 \\
72 & = & 2 \cdot 3 \cdot 12 & 2 + 3 + 12 = 17 \\
72 & = & 2 \cdot 4 \cdot 9 & 2 + 4 + 9 = 15 \\
72 & = & 2 \cdot 6 \cdot 6 & 2 + 6 + 6 = 14 \\
72 & = & 3 \cdot 3 \cdot 8 & 3 + 3 + 8 = 14 \\
72 & = & 3 \cdot 4 \cdot 6 & 3 + 4 + 6 = 13 \\
\end{array}
$$

We know that Sam knows the product of the boys' ages, which is 72. He also knows the sum of their ages, which we do not know. However, we know that the problem is indeterminate. In the above table, we have written 72 as product of three integers in all possible ways. We have also included the sum of the integers in each row. Now 14 is the only number which appears more than once. Had the street number been any of the other numbers, Sam would have had enough information to find the boys' ages. So the street number is 14, and then his friend has three boys at ages either 2, 6, 6 or 3, 3, 8. Then he says that he hopes that one day his oldest son will be quarterback in the U.S.C. football team. So he has one oldest son, and it follows that his boys have ages $3, 3$ and 8.

4.19. This problem is done similarly to the previous exercise.

4.25. "I completely disagree with you."

4.27. First 32118 factors to $2 \cdot 3 \cdot 53 \cdot 101$. From the third statement we get that $C \geq 2$. Since $C < A < 100$, the only choice for A is 53. On the other hand we can have several legitimate choices for C and l, which we list below.

$$C = 2, \quad l = 303;$$
$$C = 3, \quad l = 202;$$
$$C = 6, \quad l = 101.$$

4.29. Right after 12 o'clock, the hands start moving. But since the minute hand goes faster, the hands will not coincide before the minute hand makes a complete cycle. Now the hour hand is at 1. They continue moving, now with the minute hand chasing the other hand from behind. After some time, before the minute hand makes another cycle, they must coincide again. At this moment the minute hand has made one complete cycle and a fraction of cycle, say λ. Meanwhile, the hour hand has only covered the fraction λ of one complete cycle. Since the minute hand moves 12 times faster,

$$1 + \lambda = 12\lambda$$

From the above we get $\lambda = \frac{1}{11}$ of a cycle. It takes one hour for the minute hand to complete one cycle, so after 1 hour and $\frac{60}{11}$ minutes the hands coincide again.

4.31. Notice that $CRUDE = C \times 10000 + RUDE$. So we can cancel $RUDE$ from both sides of the equation and get

$$NUDE + NOT + NOR = C \times 10000.$$

On the other hand, the left hand side of the above equation is less than 12000. This forces C to be 1. Now we have

$$NUDE + NOT + NOR = 10000.$$

If N is 7 or less, then

$$
\begin{aligned}
NUDE + NOT + NOR \quad &< \quad 8000 + 800 + 800 \\
&= \quad 9600 \\
&< \quad 10000.
\end{aligned}
$$

Therefore, N must be 8 or greater. On the other hand, $N = 9$ is too large since

$$
\begin{aligned}
NUDE + NOT + NOR \quad &> \quad 9000 + 900 + 900 \\
&= \quad 10800 \\
&> \quad 10000.
\end{aligned}
$$

Hence $N = 8$.

Bearing this in mind, there are many solutions; among them are

$$
\begin{aligned}
8350 + 824 + 826 \quad &= \quad 10000; \\
8251 + 873 + 876 \quad &= \quad 10000; \\
8213 + 890 + 897 \quad &= \quad 10000.
\end{aligned}
$$

4.33. Each hour the boats get $12 + 17 = 29$ miles closer. So each minute they get $29/60$ of a mile closer. So one minute before they collided they were $29/60$ of a mile apart.

4.35. For simplicity we assume that we have one unit of each liquid. We also assume that flask A contains water and flask B contains acid. After transferring liquids back and forth according to the problem, both flasks still hold one unit of mixed liquid each. Let r be the amount of water in flask B. Then flask B holds $1 - r$ units of acid. Since we started with one unit of acid, the rest of it, $1 - (1 - r) = r$, should be in flask A. So we have the same amount of acid in A that we have water in B.

4.37. We cannot cut the cube into 27 sub-cubes with fewer than six cuts. Suppose that we have cut the cube into 27 sub-cubes of equal size some way or another. Imagine that they are still in their original position as part of the larger cube. One of these sub-cubes is completely in the center of the larger cube while the rest of them have at least one face which is part of one of the faces of the original cube. All the faces of the inner cube have to be cut. It has six faces so we need at least six planar cuts.

4.39. The assumption that at both times scientists were expressing the truth is wrong, and we can conclude anything from a wrong assumption.

4.41. Let us color the chess board in the following way.

If, in fact, the knight could visit all the squares exactly once and come back to the original square, it should not matter from which

square it starts. If such a loop exists starting from one square, it will exist if we start from any other square.

Suppose that the knight starts from the lower left corner of the chess board. This square is colored white. The knight has only two squares to which it can move, so if we are able to complete a loop, we have to come back to the original square via one of these two. We also need one of them to get out of the corner square. Notice that both of these squares are colored white. So the first move and the last move are to and from a white square. In the mean time, we have to visit all the black squares exactly once. But notice that the only time the knight can go to a black square from a white square or vice versa is in the two middle rows. Otherwise the knight cannot change color. Since the first and last moves are from white squares, the first black square and the last black square that the knight visits both have to be in the two middle rows.

There are 8 black squares in the lowest and highest rows. Each time that the knight is in one of these squares, the next move will be to a black square in the middle two rows (these are the only moves available). So in order to visit all the black squares in the top and bottom rows, we need a total of nine black squares in the middle two rows: one to start with, and one after each visit to one of the 8 squares in the top and bottom rows. But we only have 8 black squares in the middle two rows. Hence, the answer to the question is no.

But it is possible to cover all the squares exactly once. We leave it to the reader to find a solution. Only remember that in this case the starting position is important.

4.43. One can ask her if she is a woman. If she answers with left to right motion of head, we know she is from that particular tribe. Any other motion of head tell us that she is not from that tribe.

4.47. We need some notation before we start to solve the problem. Let A, B, C and D denote the four players of the game and let

$$P(X) = \mathbf{Pr}\{X \text{ gets a Yarborough hand}\},$$

$$P(X,Y) = \mathbf{Pr}\{X \text{ and } Y \text{ get Yarborough hands}\}.$$

Also, let P denote the probability that at least one player gets a Yarborough hand. It would seems reasonable that

$$P = P(A) + P(B) + P(C) + P(D),$$

but this equation needs some corrections. If we examine the right hand side of the above equality, we see that $P(A,B)$ has been included twice, both in $P(A)$ and in $P(B)$. The same is true for $P(B,C)$ and so on. To correct this, we have to subtract all the combinations of $P(X,Y)$ once. Now we have

$$P = P(A) + P(B) + P(C) + P(D) - P(A,B) - \cdots - P(C,D).$$

Since no more than two players can get Yarborough hands at the same time, no other terms are needed and the above equation is correct. Notice that all $P(X)$'s are equal. Similarly all different combinations of $P(X,Y)$ are equal. Thus we can write

$$P = 4P(A) - 6P(A,B). \tag{4.2}$$

There are $\binom{36}{13}$ possible Yarborough hands out of $\binom{52}{13}$ possible hands so

$$P(A) = \frac{\binom{36}{13}}{\binom{52}{13}}.$$

If A has a Yarborough hand then there are $\binom{23}{13}$ Yarborough hands out of the $\binom{39}{13}$ left for B. So

$$P(A,B) = \frac{\binom{36}{13}\binom{23}{13}}{\binom{52}{13}\binom{39}{13}}.$$

Substituting these into (4.2), we get

$$P = 4\frac{\binom{36}{13}}{\binom{52}{13}} - 6\frac{\binom{36}{13}\binom{23}{13}}{\binom{52}{13}\binom{39}{13}} \approx 0.0145528.$$

4.49. Let us answer the last question first. To win $40 or more, the winning number should at least have the first three digits or the last three digits in common with 987654. There are 1000 integers of the form $XXX654$ and 1000 integers of the form $987XXX$. Since 987654 is counted twice, and it is the only number which is counted twice, there are $1000 + 1000 - 1 = 1999$ integers of either form. So the chances that the winning number be one of these are 1999 out of 1000000.

In the same way we can calculate the odds of winning $200 or more, $2000 or more and so on. The result is in the following table.

Odds of winning	$50,000	or more are	1 in 900,000
Odds of winning	$2,000	or more are	19 in 900,000
Odds of winning	$200	or more are	199 in 900,000
Odds of winning	$40	or more are	1999 in 900,000

We get another table which shows the odds of winning exactly each prize. For example to calculate the odds of winning $40 , we have to exclude the cases for which we would win $200 or more. Hence for $1899 - 189$ cases out of 900000 we win exactly $40. The rest of the table is calculated the same way.

Odds of winning	50,000	are	1 in 900,000
Odds of winning	2,000	are	18 in 900,000
Odds of winning	200	are	180 in 900,000
Odds of winning	40	are	1800 in 900,000

If we compare the first two rows of the above table, we see that the odds of winning are 18 times better in the second row but the payoff is 25 times less, whereas it should have been 18 times less if both payoffs were equally fair. The payoffs in the second and the third row are equally fair.

Notice that none of the payoffs is fair according to the odds.

Chapter 5

Recreational Math

5.1. Adding all the squares from 1 to 27 we obtain $6930 = 3 \cdot 2310$. Thus, the weight of each subset must be 2310. One possible solution, obtained using a computer, is

$$
\begin{aligned}
2310 &= 1^2 + 2^2 + 3^2 + 4^2 + 5^2 + 6^2 + 7^2 + 8^2 \\
&\quad 9^2 + 10^2 + 11^2 + 13^2 + 14^2 + 15^2 + 18^2 + 19^2 + 23^2 \\
2 > 310 &= 12^2 + 17^2 + 24^2 + 25^2 + 26^2 \\
2310 &= 16^2 + 20^2 + 21^2 + 22^2 + 27^2.
\end{aligned}
$$

5.3. A possible strategy is to carry as many gallons as needed in five 100-mile steps. Note that the jeep can go from the starting point to the first step and back without refueling. Thus, for each step, the jeep needs 4 cans of gas in order to deliver 3 (the extra can is used as fuel for the jeep). Deliver first a certain amount of gas to the first step. Note that once all the gas has been delivered to this first step, the tank of the jeep is still half full. Fill it up (so now we have one container with only 5 gallons of gas) and repeat the same process to get to step 2, and so on. One can count carefully how many gallons are needed so that exactly 100 are delivered at the last step: we will have 430 at the start (assuming that the jeep's tank is empty at first; if it is full, we need only 420), 320 at the first step, 235 at the second, 180 at the third, 135 at the fourth and 100 at the last step.

5.9. Take any conventional 3×3-magic square, multiply all its entries by 2 and subtract 1 from all of them. You obtain a magic square whose entries are the first nine odd integers.

5.11. Let $a + 1, a + 2, \ldots, a + 9$ be any sequence of nine consecutive integers. Take any conventional 3×3-magic square, and add a to all its entries. You obtain a magic square whose entries are $a + 1, a + 2, \ldots, a + 9$, as desired.

5.13. With twelve, put four pearls in each tray. One of them will not balance, so the odd pearl is among the four in this tray. Now weigh three of these four pearls, and keep the fourth in your hand. If one tray does not balance, it contains the odd one. If the trays balance, then the odd one is the one you have in your hand.

With fifteen, put also four pearls in each tray. If it balances, the odd pearl is among the remaining three, which can be weighted to find the odd one. If it does not balance, just proceed as with twelve.

5.15. The only 2×2 Latin squares are

$$\begin{matrix} a & b \\ b & a \end{matrix} \qquad \text{and} \qquad \begin{matrix} b & a \\ a & b \end{matrix},$$

where a and b are arbitrary objects.

There are twelve 3×3 Latin squares, namely all the squares generated by all the permutations of $\{a, b, c\}$ in

$$\begin{matrix} a & b & c \\ c & a & b \\ b & c & a \end{matrix} \qquad \text{and} \qquad \begin{matrix} a & b & c \\ b & c & a \\ c & a & b \end{matrix}.$$

Note that given, without loss of generality, that the first row is a, b, c, then in the second row we have only two choices for a, and the positions of b and c are forced once a is located. So only two cases are possible up to permutations of $\{a, b, c\}$.

To find an upper bound to the number of 8×8 Latin squares, we can do the following. There are 8! arrangements of the first row (all the permutations of the 8 objects). Given one such arrangement, there are 7! arrangements of the first column (the permutations of 7 objects, since the object that occupies the top left corner is already fixed). Then there are 7! ways to arrange the second row, once we have an arrangement of the first row and column, and then there are 6! arrangements of the second row. Continuing in this fashion we find that an upper bound to the number of 8×8 Latin squares is

$$8! \, 7! \, 7! \, 6! \, 6! \, 5! \, 5! \, 4! \, 4! \, 3! \, 3! \, 2! \, 2! = 63,415,300,800,997,490,688 \cdot 10^7$$

This bound is actually very rough. The actual number of 8×8 Latin squares is $108,776,032,459,082,956,800$, a much smaller number, but this fact is very hard to prove.

One can easily derive a lower bound. Let us count the possibilities per row. Denote the objects by a, b, c, d, e, f, g, h. For the first row, we clearly have 8! arrangements (all the ways to permute 8 elements). Let us see in how many ways we can arrange the second row for each given first row. The object a can be placed in 7 positions in the second row (all but the one that it occupied in the first row). For each position that a takes, the object b can be placed at least in 6 positions (all but the one that it occupied in the first row and the one that is already taken by a). Note that, if a in the second row is placed in the same column as b in the first row, then we can put b in 7 different positions in the second column, so 6 is just a lower bound. For each position that a and b take, the object c can be placed in at least 5 positions (all but the one that it occupied in the first row and the ones that are already taken by a and b). As before, there are cases where c can actually take 6 different positions. Following in this fashion, we see that, for each arrangement of the first row, there are at least 7! arrangements of the second row. We can reason in the same manner for rows 3 to 8, and obtain at least 6! arrangements of the third row for each arrangement of the first and second row, at least 5! arrangements of the fourth row for each arrangement of the first, second and third row, etc. Thus, at least we have

$$8! 7! 6! 5! 4! 3! 2! = 5,056,584,744,960,000$$

different 8×8 Latin squares.

For more on Latin Squares, see [BAL, p. 189 ff.].

5.17. A configuration that produces a periodic population is

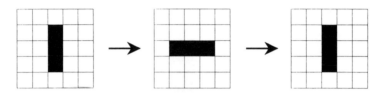

Unless we have infinitely many people, a static configuration is impossible. If there are only one or two squares, they die. If there are more, one can easily check that if one person has three neighbors, an offspring is always produced. Thus, for the configuration to remain static, each person must have at most two neighbors. On the other hand, the following configurations also produce offsprings:

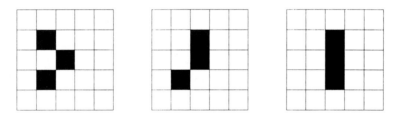

Thus, the only possibility is if all the squares are arranged in a diagonal line:

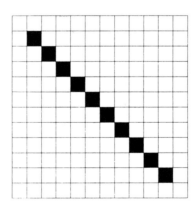

But then the ones at the ends will die of loneliness (of course, unless the line has no ends, for which we need infinitely many people).

A configuration that dies immediately is

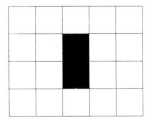

There are configurations that grow without bound. One such configuration was found in 1970 by B.W Gosper. It is called the 'Glider Gun'. It looks as follows:

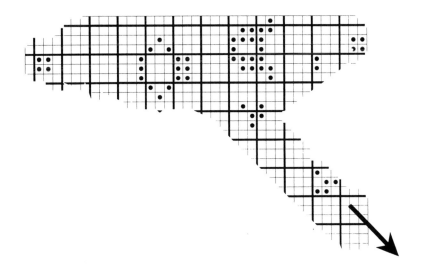

The reader can check that every 30 generations, a new 'glide' is shot from the gun (top of the figure) in the southeast direction. For more on 'The Game of Life' and other games, we refer the interested reader to the book *Winning Ways,* by Elwyn R. Berlekamp, John H. Conway and Richard K. Guy.

5.19. Take the goat to the other side, come back, pick up the wolf, take it to the other side and bring the goat back to its original position. Then pick up the cabbages, take them to the other side and leave them with the wolf. Finally, come back and pick up the goat. Bring the goat to the other side, and you are done.

5.21. We can put a maximum of 16 kings. Note that we cannot put more than 4 kings per row. If we have 4 kings in a row the next row must be empty, and if we have 3 kings, the next one can only have 1 king. Therefore we cannot put more than 16 kings. A possible configuration with 16 kings is the following:

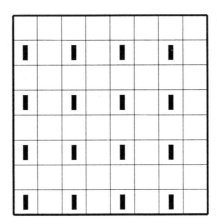

5.23. Note that all the vertices have an even number of edges except for two of the central ones, which have five. Thus we have to start at one of these vertices with five edges and finish at the other one. A possible route is shown below; the numbers denote the sequence of paths.

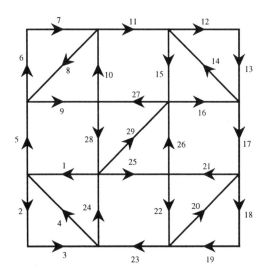

5.25. *Step 1:* Fill the 5 oz. and the 11 oz. containers with the liquid. Note that exactly $24 - (5 + 11) = 8$ oz. remain in the original container.

Step 2: Pour all the contents of the 5 oz. container in the 13 oz. container, and refill the rest with the contents of the 11 oz. container. Note that exactly $11 - (13 - 5) = 3$ oz. remain in the 11 oz. container.

Step 3: Fill the 5 oz. container with the contents of the 13 oz. container, and then empty the 5 oz. container in the 11 oz. container. Now we have 8 oz. of liquid in the original container, 8 oz. of liquid in the 11 oz. container and 8 oz. of liquid in the 13 oz. container .

5.27. Let us denote the elements of the matrix by a_{ij}, $1 \le i \le k$, $1 \le j \le m$. Let r_i be the product of all the entries in row i, and c_j the product of all the entries in column j. That is,

$$r_i = a_{i1} \cdot a_{i2} \cdots a_{im} \quad \text{and} \quad c_j = a_{1j} \cdot a_{2j} \cdots a_{kj}.$$

Note that

$$c_1 \cdot c_2 \cdots c_m \cdot r_1 \cdot r_2 \cdots r_k$$
$$= (a_{11} \cdot a_{21} \cdots a_{k1}) \cdot (a_{12} \cdot a_{22} \cdots a_{k2}) \cdots (a_{1m} \cdot a_{2m} \cdots a_{km})$$

$$\cdot (a_{11} \cdot a_{12} \cdots a_{1m}) \cdot (a_{21} \cdot a_{22} \cdots a_{2m}) \cdots (a_{k1} \cdot a_{k2} \cdots a_{km})$$

$$= \prod_{i=1}^{k} \prod_{j=1}^{m} a_{ij}^2$$

$$= 1$$

Therefore, if we want c_j and r_i to be -1 for all i, j, we must have that $k + m$ is an even number. Thus, for $k + m$ odd, there are no $k \times m$ matrices of this type.

When $k + m$ is even we can do the following. First note that, for each row, we have 2^m possibilities (since for each entry we have 2 possibilities and we have m entries). This is without taking into consideration that we want the product of its entries (r_i) to be -1. For how many of these do we have $r_i = -1$? Well, for exactly half of them (this may take a minute of thought, but note that for each combination in which $r_i = 1$, we have another for which $r_i = -1$—just multiply all the entries by -1. Thus the combinations with $r_i = 1$ are in one-to-one correspondence with those for which $r_i = -1$). Therefore, we have $2^m/2 = 2^{m-1}$ possibilities for each row.

We can now write the first $k - 1$ rows arbitrarily, and we have $(2^{m-1})^{k-1}$ overall possibilities. Now note that in the last row there are no choices since we need to make sure that $c_j = -1$ in each column. So far we have $c_j = -1$ for $j = 1, 2, \ldots m$ and $r_i = -1$ for $i = 1, 2, \ldots k - 1$. It only remains to check that $r_k = -1$. By the formula above, and using the fact that if $k + m$ is even then $k + m - 1$ is odd, we have

$$c_1 \cdot c_2 \cdots c_k \cdot r_1 \cdot r_2 \cdots r_m = (-1)^{k+m-1} \cdot r_k$$
$$= -r_k$$
$$= 1.$$

Therefore we must also have $r_k = -1$. Thus, the total number of $k \times m$ matrices of this type is

$$2^{(k-1)(m-1)} \qquad \text{for } k + m \text{ even}$$

$$0 \qquad \text{for } k + m \text{ odd.}$$

Chapter 6

Algebra and Analysis

6.1. We can proceed as follows:

$$(1-a)(1-b)(1-c)(1-d)$$
$$= 1 - a - b - c - d + ab + ac + ad + bc + bd + cd$$
$$- abc - abd - acd - bcd + abcd$$
$$= 1 - a - b - c - d + ab(1-c) + bc(1-d)$$
$$+ cd(1-a) + ad(1-b) + ac + bd + abcd$$
$$\geq 1 - a - b - c - d,$$

since $0 \leq a, b, c, d \leq 1$ implies

$$ab(1-c) + bc(1-d) + cd(1-a) + ad(1-b) + ac + bd + abcd \geq 0.$$

6.3. Let
$$M = 1 + \frac{1}{2} + \frac{1}{3} + \cdots + \frac{1}{n},$$

with $n > 1$. Let k be the greatest integer such that $2^k \leq n$. Note that $k \geq 1$. By the definition of k, we must have

$$2^k \leq n < 2^{k+1}.$$

Now note that none of the numbers $2^k, 2^k + 1, 2^k + 2, \ldots, n$ is divisible by 2^k (if one of these numbers is divisible by 2^k, then it must be of the form $\ell \cdot 2^k$, with $\ell \geq 2$. But then we would have

441

$2 \cdot 2^k \leq n$, contrary to the choice of k). Thus, only one of the denominators in the right hand side of

$$M = 1 + \frac{1}{2} + \frac{1}{3} + \cdots + \frac{1}{n}$$

is divisible by 2^k. Now, let D be the least common multiple of $1, 2, 3, \ldots n$. Note that D is divisible by 2^k, but not divisible by 2^{k+1}. Then, writing the expression above with a common denominator, we have

$$
\begin{aligned}
M &= 1 + \frac{1}{2} + \frac{1}{3} + \cdots + \frac{1}{n} \\
&= \frac{D + D/2 + D/3 + \cdots + D/2^k + \cdots + D/n}{D}.
\end{aligned}
$$

Finally, note that every summand in the numerator of the last expression is even except for $D/2^k$, which is odd. Thus, the numerator must be odd (since the sum of even numbers is even and the sum of an even number plus an odd number is odd), whereas the denominator is even (since D is divisible by 2^k). But an odd number divided by an even number is never an integer. So M cannot be an integer.

6.5. We can use the binomial theorem as follows:

$$
\begin{aligned}
11^{10} &- 1 \\
&= (10 + 1)^{10} - 1 \\
&= \left[\binom{10}{0} 10^{10} + \binom{10}{1} 10^9 + \cdots + \binom{10}{8} \cdot 100 \right. \\
&\qquad\qquad\qquad\qquad\qquad \left. + \binom{10}{9} \cdot 10 + 1 \right] - 1 \\
&= \left[\binom{10}{0} 10^{10} + \binom{10}{1} 10^9 + \cdots + \binom{10}{8} \cdot 100 + 10 \cdot 10 \right] \\
&= 100 \left[\binom{10}{0} 10^8 + \binom{10}{1} 10^7 + \cdots + \binom{10}{8} + 1 \right].
\end{aligned}
$$

6.7. It is easy to check with a pocket calculator that

$$\left(\frac{99}{101}\right)^{50} + \left(\frac{100}{101}\right)^{50} < 1 = \left(\frac{101}{101}\right)^{50}.$$

Therefore, since

$$\left(\frac{99}{101}\right)^{N} \le \left(\frac{99}{101}\right)^{50}$$

and

$$\left(\frac{100}{101}\right)^{N} \le \left(\frac{100}{101}\right)^{50}$$

for any $N \ge 50$, we must have

$$\left(\frac{99}{101}\right)^{N} + \left(\frac{100}{101}\right)^{N} < 1 = \left(\frac{101}{101}\right)^{N}$$

or, multiplying by 101^N,

$$99^N + 100^N < 101^N,$$

in particular, for all $N \ge 1000$.

6.9. We can count them as follows: We have:

1 for every 10 numbers, in the units slot . . . . 10^7
10 for every 100 numbers, in the tens slot . . . . 10^7

$$\vdots$$

10^6 for every 10^7 numbers, in the millions slot . . . . 10^7

TOTAL . . . . $7 \cdot 10^7$

6.11. $\ln n$ is just the area under the curve $y = 1/x$ and between $x = 1$ and $x = n$. The sum

$$1 + \frac{1}{2} + \frac{1}{3} + \cdots + \frac{1}{n}$$

is the area of the rectangles under the curve in the figure below.

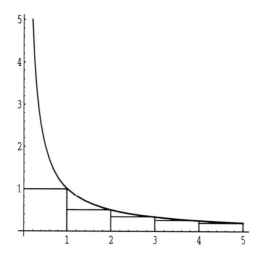

An approximation to

$$1 + \frac{1}{2} + \frac{1}{3} + \cdots + \frac{1}{n} - \ln n$$

is 1 minus the sum of the areas of the regions between each rectangle and the curve. This region is almost a triangle. The kth triangle (i.e. the one over the rectangle of height $1/k+1$) has area

$$\frac{1}{2}\left(\frac{1}{k} - \frac{1}{k+1}\right).$$

Adding up from 1 to n we obtain a telescopic sum that equals

$$\frac{1}{2}\left(1 - \frac{1}{n+1}\right).$$

Therefore, the value of

$$1 + \frac{1}{2} + \frac{1}{3} + \cdots + \frac{1}{n} - \ln n$$

is approximately

$$1 - \left[\frac{1}{2}\left(1 - \frac{1}{n+1}\right)\right] = \frac{1}{2} + \frac{1}{2(n+1)},$$

which is definitely less than 4.

A more geometric way to estimate the sum of the areas of the regions between each rectangle and the curve is sliding all these regions horizontally to the first square (the one that has $(0,0)$ as a vertex). Then they will all be disjoint regions contained in a square of area 1, so the sum of their areas must be less than 1.

6.13. Let S_n be the partial sum up to n in the harmonic series. Then, as we saw in Exercise 11, $S_n \approx \ln n$. The idea is that the sum of the numbers in S_n that have a 7 in the denominator is roughly of size $\ln (n/10)$. Thus, S_n minus the numbers in S_n that have a 7 in the denominator is approximately of size

$$\ln n - \ln (n/10) = \ln \left(\frac{n}{n/10} \right) = \ln 10 < \infty.$$

We leave the details to the interested reader.

6.15. Note that $p^2 - 1 = (p+1)(p-1)$. Since p is prime, it is not divisible by 3, so either $(p+1)$ or $(p-1)$ is divisible by 3. In particular, $(p+1)(p-1)$ is divisible by 3. Notice that p is not divisible by 2 either, so both $(p+1)$ and $(p-1)$ are divisible by 2. In particular, $(p+1)(p-1)$ is divisible by 4. Thus, 12 divides $p^2 - 1$. In other words, the remainder when we divide p^2 by 12 is always 1.

6.17. The solution is 8. One way to solve it is to write 2^{43} as $(1,000 + 24)^4 \cdot 8$ and then multiply.

6.19. One way to proceed is as follows:

$$\begin{aligned} S_k &= a + a \cdot r + a \cdot r^2 + \cdots + a \cdot r^k \\ r \cdot S_k &= a \cdot r + a \cdot r^2 + \cdots + a \cdot r^k + a \cdot r^{k+1}. \end{aligned}$$

Subtracting the above equations, we obtain

$$S_k - r \cdot S_k = a - a \cdot r^{k+1}.$$

Solving for S_k we finally obtain

$$S_k = \frac{a(1 - r^{k+1})}{1 - r}.$$

6.21. The area of a sphere of radius r is $4\pi r^2$, and the volume is $4/3\pi r^3$. Thus we have the equation

$$4\pi r = \frac{4}{3}\pi r^3.$$

Solving for r we obtain $r = 3$, which implies that the volume/area of the sphere is 36π.

6.23. After raising both $10^{1/10}$ and $2^{1/3}$ to the 30th power, we obtain 10^3 and 2^{10}, so it is equivalent to compare these last numbers. Now, $2^{10} = 1,028 > 10^3$, so $2^{1/3}$ is greater than $10^{1/10}$.

6.25. Multiply both sides of the equation by 2. We have

$$\begin{aligned}
0 &= 2a^2 + 2b^2 + 2c^2 + 2d^2 - 2ab - 2bc - 2cd - 2da \\
&= (a^2 - 2ab + b^2) + (b^2 - 2bc + c^2) + (c^2 - 2cd + d^2) \\
&\qquad\qquad\qquad\qquad\qquad\qquad\qquad + (d^2 - 2da + a^2) \\
&= (a - b)^2 + (b - c)^2 + (c - d)^2 + (d - a)^2
\end{aligned}$$

Thus, since the last expression is zero only when the summands are zero, we must have $a = b = c = d$.

6.27. Let a and b be, in order, the last two digits of some number n. Then $n = 100T + 10a + b$, where T is an integer. Then we have

$$n^2 = 100L + 2ab10 + b^2,$$

where L is some integer. Thus, the last two digits of n^2 are the last two digits of $2ab10 + b^2$. If we assume that all the digits of n^2 are 1's, then we must have that the last two digits of $2ab10 + b^2$ are 1's. This implies that $b = 1$ or $b = 9$. If $b = 1$, then the second digit will be the last digit of $2a$, which is even, so it cannot be 1. If $b = 9$, then the second digit will be the last digit of $2a+8$ (8 comes from what we carry over to the second digit when we multiply $9 \cdot 9$), which is also even, so it cannot be 1. Thus no perfect square has 1's as the last two digits of its decimal expression.

6.29. Take A to be the set of products of all pairs of distinct primes, this is

$$A = \{p \cdot q, \text{where } p \text{ and } q \text{ are distinct primes}\}.$$

Then, if S is any set of primes, then A will contain all products of pairs of elements of S, and the complement of A will contain all the products of triples of elements of S. (Note that the exercise says 'at least two elements of S'.)

6.31. Yes it can. Let us assume the contrary. We know that $\sqrt{2}$ is irrational. By our assumption, we must have that

$$\sqrt{2}^{\sqrt{2}}$$

is irrational. But then

$$\left(\sqrt{2}^{\sqrt{2}}\right)^{\sqrt{2}} = (\sqrt{2})^{\sqrt{2} \cdot \sqrt{2}}$$
$$= (\sqrt{2})^2$$
$$= 2$$

must be irrational, which is false, so we arrive at a contradiction.

6.33. We have $\sin 2\theta = 2 \sin \theta \cos \theta = a$. Note that

$$(\sin \theta + \cos \theta)^2 = \sin^2 \theta + \cos^2 \theta + 2 \sin \theta \cos \theta$$
$$= 1 + a.$$

Thus, since θ is acute, $\sin \theta + \cos \theta \geq 0$, and

$$\sin \theta + \cos \theta = \sqrt{1 + a}.$$

6.35. Since we are assuming that

$$2 = x^{\left(x^{\left(x^{\cdot^{\cdot^{\cdot}}}\right)}\right)},$$

we have that

$$x^2 = x^{x^{\left(x^{\left(x^{\cdot^{\cdot^{\cdot}}}\right)}\right)}}$$
$$= 2$$

This gives $x = \sqrt{2}$.

6.37. Let L denote the position of the long hand measured in minutes with $0 \le L < 60$, and let l denote the position of the short hand measured in hours with $0 \le l < 12$, (i.e. at three o'clock, $L=0$ and $l = 3$). Then we must have that l and L satisfy the equation

$$k + \frac{L}{60} = l,$$

where $k = 0, 1, 2, \ldots, 11$. The hands meet when $5l = L$. Thus we have that, in this case, l satisfies

$$k + \frac{l}{12} = l.$$

Thus the hands will meet at $l = \dfrac{12k}{11}$ hours and $L = \dfrac{60k}{11}$ minutes, with $k = 0, 1, 2, \ldots, 11$. Now, since for $k = 11$ we obtain $l = 12$ and $L = 60$ (which actually corresponds to $l = 0$, $L = 0$, which is the case $k = 0$), we have that the hands meet 11 times in a 12 hour period.

6.39. Note that $a^3 - b^3 = (a - b)(a^2 + ab + b^2)$. Since a and b are odd, $(a^2 + ab + b^2)$ is odd, and therefore is not divisible by 2^n for any $n \ge 1$. Thus 2^n divides $a^3 - b^3$ if and only if it divides $a - b$.

6.41. Assume the contrary. If n is even then the left hand side is even and the right hand side is odd, so n must be odd. If n is odd then, writing the equation as $(n + 2)^3 - n^3 = (n + 1)^3$ we must have, after expanding,

$$8 + 12n + 6n^2 = (n + 1)^3.$$

The right hand side is divisible by 8. The left hand side is not, since that would imply that $6n + 3n^2$ is divisible by 4, which would imply n even. Therefore the equality cannot hold.

6.43. For n even we have that, for some integer k,

$$3^n + 1 = (4 - 1)^n + 1 = 4k + (-1)^n + 1 = 4k + 2,$$

which cannot be divisible by 4, and therefore cannot be divisible by 2^n for $n > 1$.

For n odd, writing $n = 2\ell + 1$, we have that, for some integer k',

$$3^n + 1 = 3 \cdot (8+1)^\ell + 1 = 8k' + 3 \cdot 1^\ell + 1 = 8k' + 4,$$

which cannot be divisible by 8, and therefore cannot be divisible by 2^n (note that we are assuming that $n > 1$ and n odd, so $n \geq 3$).

6.45. Since $5 = 8 - 3$ we can write

$$
\begin{aligned}
5^n + 2 \cdot 3^{n-1} + 1 &= (8-3)^n + 2 \cdot 3^{n-1} + 1 \\
&= 8 \cdot k + (-3)^n + 2 \cdot 3^{n-1} + 1.
\end{aligned}
$$

For n even, $n = 2\ell$,

$$
\begin{aligned}
8 \cdot k + (-3)^n + 2 \cdot 3^{n-1} + 1 &= 8 \cdot k + 5 \cdot 3^{n-1} + 1 \\
&= 8 \cdot k + (8-3) \cdot 3^{n-1} + 1 \\
&= 8 \cdot k' - 3^n + 1 \\
&= 8 \cdot k' - (8+1)^\ell + 1 \\
&= 8 \cdot k'' - 1^\ell + 1 \\
&= 8 \cdot k''',
\end{aligned}
$$

where k, k', k'', k''' are integers.
For n odd, $n = 2j + 1$,

$$
\begin{aligned}
8 \cdot m + (-3)^n + 2 \cdot 3^{n-1} + 1 &= 8 \cdot m - 3 \cdot 3^{n-1} + 2 \cdot 3^{n-1} + 1 \\
&= 8 \cdot m - 3^{n-1} + 1 \\
&= 8 \cdot m - 3^{2j} + 1 \\
&= 8 \cdot m - (8+1)^j + 1 \\
&= 8 \cdot m' - 1^j + 1 \\
&= 8 \cdot m''
\end{aligned}
$$

where m, m', m'' are integers.

6.47. Without loss of generality we can assume that a has only two digits, i.e. $a = 10 \cdot b + c$, with $0 \leq b, c \leq 9$. Then $a^2 = 100b^2 + 10(2bc) + c^2$. So we have the conditions:

the ones digit of $2bc$ + the tens digit of $c^2 = 7$.

First this implies that the tens digit of c^2 is odd, which restricts our choices to $c = 4$ or 6. If $c = 4$, then we must have that the ones digit of $2bc$ is 6, or, substituting $c = 4$, that the ones digit of $8b$ is 6, which implies $b = 2, 7$ or 9. If $c = 6$, then we must have that the ones digit of $2bc$ is 4 or, substituting $c = 6$, that the ones digit of $12b$ is 4, which implies $b = 2$ or 7. Thus, the possible values of a are 24, 74, 94, 26, 76, and the ones digits must be 4 or 6.

6.49. Expanding the left hand side of the equation $(x^2 + ax + b)(x^2 + cx + d) = x^4 + 2x^2 + 2x + 2$ we obtain the relations

$$
\begin{aligned}
a + c &= 2 \\
b + ac + d &= 2 \\
ad + bc &= 2 \\
bd &= 2
\end{aligned}
$$

From the last equation we can assume $|b| = 2$, $|d| = 1$. From the first equation we have that a and c have the same parity (i.e. they are both odd or both even). If they are both even, then the left hand side of the second equation is odd, whereas the right hand side is even. Thus they must both be odd. But then the left hand side of the third equation is odd, whereas the right hand side is even. Therefore a, b, c, d cannot all be integers.

6.51. Assume $r \neq -1$ (this case is trivial). If $|a| > 1$, then $a \neq 1$ divides $a_{a+1} = a + ar$. If $a = -1, 0$ or 1, then $a + 3r \neq 1$ divides $a_{a+3r+3} = a + ar + 3r^2 + 3r = (a + 3r)(1 + r)$.

6.53. There are $\binom{5}{4} \cdot 4! = 5 \cdot 24$ numbers of this kind (we have $\binom{5}{4}$ ways to choose the 4 digits and 4! permutations of each choice). Write the numbers in a column as follows:

$$
\begin{aligned}
&1234 \\
&1235 \\
&1243 \\
&2543 \\
&\vdots
\end{aligned}
$$

Then observe that each of $1, 2, 3, 4, 5$ appears $1/5$ of the time in the units slot, $1/5$ of the time in the tens slot, $1/5$ of the time in the hundreds slot, etc. Thus, the sum of all these numbers is

$$24 \cdot 1111 + 24 \cdot 2222 + 24 \cdot 3333 + 24 \cdot 4444 + 24 \cdot 5555 = 399,960.$$

6.55. $17x + 17y - (9x + 5y) = 8x + 12y = 4(2x + 3y)$. Thus $2x + 3y$ is divisible by 17 if and only if $9x + 5y$ is divisible by 17.

6.57. The least value n can have is $p_1 \cdot p_2 \cdots p_k$, where p_i are consecutive primes in increasing order with $p_1 = 2$. Thus $p_i \geq 2$, which implies $n \geq 2^k$, which is equivalent to $\log n \geq k \log 2$.

6.59. The number $n^{n-1} - 1$ can be written as $((n-1)+1)^{n-1} - 1$. Using the binomial theorem, we obtain

$$
\begin{aligned}
n^{n-1} - 1 &= ((n-1)+1)^{n-1} - 1 \\
&= \binom{n-1}{0}(n-1)^{n-1} + \binom{n-1}{1}(n-1)^{n-2} + \cdots \\
&\quad + \binom{n-1}{n-3}(n-1)^1 + \binom{n-1}{n-2} + 1 - 1 \\
&= \binom{n-1}{0}(n-1)^{n-1} + \binom{n-1}{1}(n-1)^{n-2} + \cdots \\
&\quad + \binom{n-1}{n-3}(n-1)^2 + (n-1)(n-1),
\end{aligned}
$$

where we have used the fact that $\binom{n-1}{n-2} = n - 1$. Finally, note that every term of the last sum is divisible by $(n-1)^2$. Thus, $(n-1)^2$ divides $n^{n-1} - 1$.

6.61. Note that $n^2(n^2 - 1)(n^2 - 4) = (n-2)(n-1)n^2(n+1)(n+2)$ (five consecutive integers). One of these numbers is divisible by 4, another one by 2, two of them by 3 and one of them by 5. Thus, the product is divisible by $4 \cdot 2 \cdot 3 \cdot 3 \cdot 5 = 360$.

6.63. We can write $a = 12r$ and $b = 12s$, with r and s relatively prime. Then $12rs = 432$, or $rs = 36 = 2 \cdot 2 \cdot 3 \cdot 3 \cdot$. Since r and s do not have common factors, we must have $r = 9$, $s = 4$ (or vice versa). Thus $a = 108$, $b = 48$ (or vice versa).

6.65. Expanding $(m + n + k)^3$, we have

$$
\begin{aligned}
(m + n + k)^3 &= k^3 + 3k^2m + 3km^2 + m^3 + 3k^2n + 6kmn \\
&\quad + 3m^2n + 3kn^2 + 3mn^2 + n^3 \\
&= m^3 + n^3 + k^3 + 3K,
\end{aligned}
$$

where K is some integer. Thus $(m + n + k)^3$ is divisible by 3 if and only if $m^3 + n^3 + k^3$ is.

6.67. Write $m^2 = p^2 - n^2 = (p+n)(p-n)$. Call $a - (p+n)$, $b = (p-n)$. Note that for each value of a and b we can find p and n by just solving the equation that defines a and b. This actually gives

$$
p = \frac{a + b}{2}
$$
$$
n = \frac{a - b}{2}
$$

Since p and n are integers, our only condition on a and b is that they be either both odd or both even (so that both $a+b$ and $a-b$ are divisible by 2).

Thus, for each m, and for any two integers a, b with same parity satisfying

$$
m^2 = a \cdot b,
$$

we can find two integers p, n in a unique way so that the equation

$$
m^2 + n^2 = p^2
$$

is satisfied. This classifies all the Pythagorean triples.

6.69. The factorization with real coefficients is

$$
x^8 + x^4 + 1 = (1 - x + x^2)(1 + x + x^2)(x^2 - x\sqrt{3} + 1)(x^2 + x\sqrt{3} + 1).
$$

6.71. We have to find the sum of the sum of the sum of the digits of 4444^{4444}. We will use the fact that, if a number can be written as

$9c + r$, then the sum of its digits can be written as $9c' + r$ (same r). First note that $4444 = 9 \cdot 494 - 2$. Thus

$$4444^{4444} = (9 \cdot 494 - 2)^{4444} = 9 \cdot \ell + 2^{4444},$$

where ℓ is an integer. Now, since $2^3 = 8 = 9 - 1$, and $4444 = 3 \cdot 1481 + 1$, we have

$$
\begin{aligned}
2^{4444} &= 2^{3 \cdot 1481 + 1} \\
&= 8^{1481} \cdot 2 \\
&= (9 - 1)^{1481} \cdot 2 \\
&= (9 \cdot k - 1) \cdot 2 \\
&= 9 \cdot k' - 2,
\end{aligned}
$$

where k, k' are integers. Therefore, the number 4444^{4444} can be written as

$$9 \cdot \ell + 9 \cdot k' - 2 = 9 \cdot (\ell + k') - 9 + 7 = 9 \cdot k'' + 7,$$

where k'' is an integer.

Thus, we must have that the sum of the sum of the sum of the digits of 4444^{4444} is also of the form $9c + 7$. The number 4444^{4444} is less than 10000^{4444}, which has 4445 digits. Thus, the sum of the digits of 4444^{4444} is less than or equal to $9 \cdot 4445 = 40005$. Now, 40005 has 5 digits, so the sum of its digits is at most $5 \cdot 9 = 45$. Finally, the sum of the digits of a number that is less than 45 is always a one-digit number. Therefore, we have that the sum of the sum of the sum of the digits of 4444^{4444} is a one-digit number of the form $9c + 7$. The only possibility is that this number is 7 itself. Thus, the sum of the sum of the sum of the digits of 4444^{4444} is 7.

6.75. We will show that $n^{11} - n$ is divisible by 11, the case $n^{13} - n$ being similar. First, since every number n can be written as $11 \cdot m + q$, $0 \le q < 11$, we have, using the binomial theorem,

$$
\begin{aligned}
n^{11} - n &= (11 \cdot m + q)^{11} - (11 \cdot m + q) \\
&= 11 \cdot A + q^{11} - q.
\end{aligned}
$$

Thus $n^{11} - n$ is divisible by 11 if and only if $q^{11} - q$ is divisible by 11 for $0 \leq q < 11$. This is easy to check by hand.

In general, it is true that $n^k - n$ is divisible by k for any integers n and k. This is called 'Fermat's Little Theorem' (not to be confused with 'Fermat's Last Theorem'). The proof of this result is not too difficult using modular arithmetic.

Chapter 7

A Miscellany

7.1. Here is one example

$$4 + 5 + 9 + 13 + \frac{72}{8} + 60.$$

We cannot do this without using fractions. We explain the reason in the following way:

$$0 + 1 + 2 + \cdots + 9 = 45.$$

Notice that 45 is divisible by 9. We know that any number is divisible by 9 if and only if the sum of its digits is divisible by 9. In fact, any positive integer, divided by 9, has the same remainder as the remainder of the sum of it is digits divided by 9. This means that if we subtract the sum of the digits of a positive integer from the number itself, the result is going to be divisible by 9. For example, $28 - (2+8) = 18$, $49 - (4+9) = 36$, and so on. Suppose N is the sum of a collection of positive integers in which all the digits $0, 1, \ldots, 9$ have been used and they have been used just once. Then $N - (0 + 1 + \cdots + 9) = N - 45$ should be divisible by 9. So N cannot be 100 because $100 - 45 = 55$, and 55 is not divisible by 9.

7.3. Let us use the same conventions as in the previous exercise. It is obvious that the solution for the previous problem still works for this one, but it does not use the entire capacity of the boat. One possible solution which uses the entire capacity of the boat is as follows:

(a) A, M and m go to side 2.

(b) A takes the boat back to side 1.

(c) A, a and b go to side 2.

(d) A takes the boat to side 1 (if you think that A is doing all the work you can replace her with any of the other women).

(e) Finally A and B go to side 2.

7.5. We refer to people as in the previous exercise and assume that they want to transfer from side 1 to side 2. Also, let us call the boats T_1 and T_2.

(a) a_1 and b_1 in T_1, and a_2 and b_2 in T_2 go to side 2.

(b) a_1 in T_1 and a_2 in T_2 take the boats back to side 1.

(c) a_1 and c_1 in T_1, and a_2 and c_2 in T_2 go to side 2.

(d) b_1 and b_2 take the boats T_1 and T_2 back to side 1.

(e) m_1 and b_1 in T_1 and, m_2 and b_2 in T_2 go to side 2.

(f) Now in side 1, there are only four people, the third man with his three wives, and the boat is on side 2. Since the first two men cannot send any of their wives to side 1, otherwise their wives would be without chaperone in the other side of the river with m_3, they have to take the boats back to side 1 themselves.

(g) In T_1, m_3 and one of his wives go to side 2, and in T_2, m_1 and m_2 go to side 2.

(h) Now any two women in side 2 can take the boats to side 1 and bring the two remaining women to side 2.

7.7. The solution is: B, C, D, G, I, J, L, M, N, O, P, Q, R, S, U, V, W, Z. For further explanation see **PROBLEM** 7.2.3.

7.9. Obviously if we allow the interiors of the circles to intersect the sides of the square then the problem is solvable even by using only one circle. So the assumption is that the interior of a circle does not intersect the sides of the square. At most the boundary of a circle can touch one or two of the sides. Obviously if we are to fill the square by finitely many circles, some of them must touch the sides. A line and a circle touch at exactly one point. With finitely many circles we can at most cover finitely many points on the sides of the square; since a square has infinitely many points on its sides, all but finitely many points on the sides of the square will be outside all the circles.

7.11. If an equilateral triangle has side 1, then it has area $\sqrt{3}/4$. Thus if it could be turned into a square then that square would have side $\sqrt[4]{3}/2$. Also it would have diagonal $\sqrt[4]{3} \cdot \sqrt{2}/2$. Note that both this side length and this diagonal length are less than 1. So, if the triangle could be cut with a single cut so that the two pieces can form a square, then all three sides of the triangle (having length 1) would have to be cut (to achieve the desired shortness). This is clearly impossible with a single cut.

7.13. We start with 1. We count what we see: ONE 1 or "1" 1. We add these to the sequence, and we get

$$1, 1, 1.$$

We count again. Now we see "THREE" 1's. We add 3, 1 to the sequence, to obtain
$$1, 1, 1, 3, 1.$$

Now we see "FOUR" 1's and "ONE" 3. By adding these to the sequence we get
$$1, 1, 1, 3, 1, 4, 1, 1, 3.$$

Now there are "SIX" 1's, "TWO" 3's and "ONE" 4. The sequence now grows to

$$1, 1, 1, 3, 1, 4, 1, 1, 3, 6, 1, 2, 3, 1, 4.$$

Continuing this way we get

$$1, 1, 1, 3, 4, 1, 1, 3, 6, 1, 2, 3, 1, 4, 8, 1, 3, 3, 2, 4, 1, 6, 1, 2.$$

So "?" stands for 1.

7.17. In general, $(a^3+b^3)/2$ is not equal to $((a+b)/2)^3$ because $Y \to Y^3$ is not a linear function.

7.19. Suppose 1000 people decide to spin the wheel. According to the odds approximately 800 are going to win \$800. Hence, 200 of them will win nothing. So, on average, each person wins 640 dollars. So on average, people get more money by spinning the wheel. So it seems that it is wiser to spin the wheel.

7.23. Suppose there is such a rational number. Let us refer to it by r. So the assumption is that $r^2 = 8$. If r is a rational number then so is $r/2$. But

$$\left(\frac{r}{2}\right)^2 = \frac{r^2}{4} = \frac{8}{4} = 2.$$

So we just found a rational number whose square is 2. But this contradicts Exercise 7.22, in which we have shown that there is no such rational number. Hence, we conclude that the assumption that $\sqrt{8}$ is rational is incorrect.

7.25. Let r and s be two different rational numbers, r being the smaller one. Then $a = (s - r)/\sqrt{2}$ is an irrational number, because otherwise $\sqrt{2} = (s - r)/a$ implies that $\sqrt{2}$ is a rational number which contradicts Exercise 7.22. On the other hand, a is positive and is less than $s - r$. So $r + a$ is greater than r and less than s. At the same time, $r + a$ is an irrational number, otherwise $a = r + a - r$ would be rational, but we just showed that this is not the case.

Chapter 8

Real Life

8.1. Let R be the radius of the circular arc in the problem, and let ϕ be the angle that it spans in radians. Then we must have

$$2R \sin \frac{\phi}{2} = 5280$$

and

$$R\phi = 5281.$$

We want to find

$$h = R - R \cos \frac{\phi}{2}.$$

Using the first equation we have

$$h = R - \sqrt{R^2 - (2640)^2}.$$

Thus, everything reduces to finding R. This is no easy task, but it can be done. The first two equations give

$$R \sin \frac{2640.5}{R} = 2640.$$

One can find an approximate numerical solution using a computer package. Another possibility is to use a computer to plot, for example, the graph of $R \sin 2640.5/R - 2640$, and then patiently finding the interval in which the function is approximately 0. Using this method and the computer package Mathematica, we found $R \approx 78335.08051$. This gives $h \approx 44.4985$ feet, which is much larger than one would expect.

459

8.5. The idea is that figures change depending on what year we take as a base for the price of the commodities. See also the nice exposition in the book *How to Lie with Statistics*, by Darrell Huff.

The cost of living has gone up: Take last year as the base year. This means that, to find a percentage of how much prices have changed, we take the price of the commodities last year to be 100. That means that the price of bread is 200% higher now than it was last year, and the price of milk had a drop of 50%. The average of 200 and 50 is 125. Therefore, the cost of living has gone up 25%.

The cost of living has gone down: Take this year as the base year. Assume that the price of the commodities this year is 100. Last year, milk used to cost 200% as much as it does now, and bread was selling for 50% as much. The average is 125. Thus, the cost of living was 25% higher last year.

The cost of living did not change: Take last year as the base year, but use geometric average instead of arithmetic. The price of milk now is 50% of last year's, and the price of bread is 200%. The geometric average is $\sqrt{50 \cdot 200} = 100$. Thus, the prices are 100% of last year's prices; in other words, the cost of living has not changed.

8.7. Same reference as in the previous exercise, page 82. It is clear that one is making 1% on total sales (1 cent for each item, one dollar per item). Also, the money invested is 99 cents and the total profit is 365 cents, approximately 365% on money invested.

8.9. According to the Encyclopædia Britannica, hair grows at a speed of 0.5 inches per month. There are $24 \cdot 30 = 720$ hours in a month, and $12 \cdot 5280 = 63360$ inches in a mile. Therefore, hair grows at a rate of

$$\frac{0.5 \cdot 720}{63360} = 0.315657 \cdot 10^{-4} \text{ miles per hour.}$$

8.11. In this problem we use Bayes' formula (see Chapter 3 for details):

Pr{Irving has VD | test +}

$$= \frac{\mathbf{Pr}\{\text{test} + | \text{ has VD }\} \cdot \mathbf{Pr}\{\text{ has VD}\}}{\mathbf{Pr}\{+| \text{ VD }\} \cdot \mathbf{Pr}\{\text{VD}\} + \mathbf{Pr}\{+| \text{ no VD }\} \cdot \mathbf{Pr}\{\text{ no VD}\}}$$

$$= \frac{0.98 \cdot 0.005}{0.98 \cdot 0.005 + 0.02 \cdot 0.995}$$

$$= 0.197581,$$

which is remarkably low. See also the discussion of this problem in [PAUL1, p. 89]

The probability that Irving has VD when one test is negative is

$$\mathbf{Pr}\{\text{Irving has VD} \mid \text{test} -\}$$

$$= \frac{\mathbf{Pr}\{\text{test} - | \text{ has VD }\} \cdot \mathbf{Pr}\{\text{ has VD}\}}{\mathbf{Pr}\{-| \text{ VD }\} \cdot \mathbf{Pr}\{\text{VD}\} + \mathbf{Pr}\{-| \text{ no VD }\} \cdot \mathbf{Pr}\{\text{ no VD}\}}$$

$$= \frac{0.02 \cdot 0.005}{0.02 \cdot 0.005 + 0.98 \cdot 0.995}$$

$$= 0.000102543.$$

Now, since different tests are uncorrelated, the probability of Irving having VD after two negative tests is the square of the probability of Irving having VD after one negative test, i.e. it is the square of 0.000102543.

Thus, the probability that Irving has VD after two negative tests is approximately 10^{-8}.

8.13. The important point in this exercise is that he takes *the first train* that comes along. This means that if the train to New York always arrives 2 minutes before the train to Philadelphia, he will very rarely take this last train. In fact, unless he arrives in this two-minute interval, he will always end up in New York. There are 3 trains per hour, i.e. 3 two-minute intervals of this kind per hour. Hence the probability that he takes the train to Philadelphia is $2 \cdot 3/60 = 1/10$. In other words, he visits his girlfriend in New York nine times as often as his girlfriend in Philadelphia.

8.15. He counted the paces to his friend's house. Then, while he was with his friend, he timed the walk by counting up to the same number at approximately the same rhythm as his paces. He noted the time when he left his friend's house and added the time length of the walk when he set up his clock.

8.17. The maximum number of hairs in the human scalp is about 500,000. Since there are about 10 million people in New York, by the pigeonhole principle two people must have the same number of hairs. See [PAUL1, p. 42] for a more detailed discussion.

8.19. The probability that it does not rain is $(1/2) \cdot (1/2) = 1/4$. Therefore the probability that it does rain is $1 - 1/4 = 3/4$, or 75%.

8.21. According to the Encyclopædia Britannica, there are approximately 60 mililitres of blood per kilogram in the human body. Take the average weight of a person to be 50 kilograms (note that children are included). There are 250 million people in the U.S., which will give $60 \cdot 50 \cdot 250 \cdot 10^6 = 75 \cdot 10^{10}$ mililitres, or 750 cubic meters. Now you have to find the radius r in meters of the base circle of Busch Stadium, and then solve for h in the equation

$$\pi r^2 h = 750.$$

8.23. The probability that he drops a hamburger is 0.3. We assume that the events are independent, i.e. for each hamburger the probability is 0.3 no matter what happened with the other hamburgers. Thus the probability that he drops four of the next ten is

$$0.3^4 \cdot 0.7^6 \cdot \binom{10}{4} \approx 0.200121.$$

8.25. Since the maximum number of hairs in the human scalp is about 500,000, each person can have from 0 to 500,000 hairs, so there are 500,001 possibilities. Thus, we need at least 500,002 people to be absolutely sure that two of them have the same number of hairs.

The problem of finding how many people we need in order to find two scalps with the same number of hairs is similar to the birthday problem in the text. We will assume that the distribution of number of hairs in the population is uniform and ranges between

0 and $500,000$, and that the number of hairs of two different people are uncorrelated variables. We have

$$\mathbf{Pr}\{\text{at least two of } N \text{ people have same no. of hairs}\}$$
$$= 1 - \mathbf{Pr}\{N \text{ people have different number of hairs}\}$$
$$= 1 - \frac{500,001 \cdot 500,000 \cdots (500,001 - N + 1)}{500,001^N}$$

With the help of a computer, we found that this value is greater than $1/2$ for $N \geq 833$ and less than $1/2$ for $N < 833$. Thus, we need 833 people in order to have probability at least $1/2$ of finding two people with the same number of hairs.

8.29. The average of both years does not equal the sum of the averages of each year. For example, if Forrest got 4 fish in 1 trip in 1987 and 3 fish in 1 trip in 1988, and if Bubba got 31 fish in 8 trips in 1987 and 5 fish in 2 trips in 1988, then we have

$$\frac{4}{1} > \frac{31}{8}$$
$$\frac{3}{1} > \frac{5}{2} \tag{8.1}$$

But the average for the two years for Forrest is

$$\frac{4+3}{1+1} = \frac{7}{2} = 3.5,$$

and for Bubba,

$$\frac{31+5}{8+2} = \frac{36}{10} = 3.6.$$

We see that Bubba's average over the two years is greater.

See also [PAUL1, p.44] for this and other related problems.

8.33. If the rain is falling vertically, then clearly the best strategy is not to move, since in this way we expose less surface area to the rain. If the rain is falling at an angle then the best strategy is to move in the direction of the rain and at the same horizontal speed as the rain. The idea is that if we move with the rain, exactly at the same speed and the same direction, it is essentially as if the rain were falling vertically and we were standing still.

8.35. Assuming that the cost of manufacturing a tire is proportional to its durability, if they made tires that last less than 20,000 miles, then they would be giving out a lot of money in replacements of tires. Similarly, if they were making tires that lasted longer than 40,000 miles, then the prices are too low. The number that maximizes profit in these cases is the average; in our case, they should make tires that last 30,000 miles. Note that, in average, only half the people that purchased 30,000 mile-guaranteed tires will return them.

8.37. See [PAUL1, p.28] and [REN] for a discussion of these matters.

8.39. The reason they are round is so that they do not fall through the hold and injure the worker below. Clearly a miniscule perturbation of round will still do the job, but make it more difficult to replace the cover properly into its place when the job is done (these covers are very heavy).

8.45. The probability of a monkey typing Hamlet, assuming that the typewriter has 35 keys and that Hamlet has 500,000 characters is 1/35 to the power 500,000. Let us call this probability p. If we have a very long chain of characters of length K, Hamlet could appear in the first 500,000 characters, or in characters 2 to 500,001, or in characters 3 to 500,002, etc. Thus, Hamlet could start in the first, second, third, up to the $K - 500,000 + 1$ character. Thus we have $K - 499,999$ ways of obtaining Hamlet in the string of characters. This implies that the probability of finding Hamlet in this string is $p \cdot (K - 499,999)$. Since we want this last probability to be 0.5, we must have

$$K = 499,999 + \frac{1}{2 \cdot p} = 499,999 + \frac{1}{2 \cdot 35^{500,000}} \geq 10^{727272}.$$

Assuming that in a year the monkeys may type, say, a billion characters per year (this is more than 400,000 pages, since each page has about 2,400 characters), the monkeys would take more than 10^{727263} years to type Hamlet by chance. The age of the universe is estimated to be much, much less than this figure. See [PAUL1, p.75] for an interesting and humorous discussion of this and other related problems. We also recommend to the reader the short story *'The Library of Babel'*, by Jorge Luis Borges, in which ideas similar to the one posed in this problem are discussed in a literary and poetic manner.